# *Marbury v. Madison* and Judicial Review

# *Marbury v. Madison* and Judicial Review

ROBERT LOWRY CLINTON

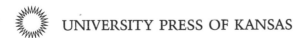 UNIVERSITY PRESS OF KANSAS

For Wallace Mendelson

© 1989 by the University Press of Kansas
All rights reserved

Published by the University Press of Kansas (Lawrence, Kansas 66045),
which was organized by the Kansas Board of Regents and is operated and
funded by Emporia State University, Fort Hays State University, Kansas State
University, Pittsburg State University, the University of Kansas, and Wichita
State University

Library of Congress Cataloging-in-Publication Data

Clinton, Robert Lowry.
    Marbury v. Madison and judicial review / Robert Lowry Clinton
    p.    cm.
    Bibliography:  p.
    Includes index.
    ISBN 0-7006-0411-1 (alk. paper)
    1. Judicial review—United States—History.   2. Separation of
powers—United States—History.   3. Marbury, William, 1761 or
2–1835—Trials, litigation, etc.   4. Madison, James, 1751–1836—Trials,
litigation, etc.
KF4575.C554      1989
347.73′12—dc20
[347.30712]                                                    89-34651
                                                                  CIP

British Library Cataloguing in Publication Data is available.

Printed in the United States of America
10  9  8  7  6  5  4  3  2  1

The paper used in this publication meets the minimum requirements of the
American National Standard for Permanence of Paper for Printed Library
Materials Z39.48-1984.

# Contents

# Preface

Like many others who end up writing books, I once had no intention of writing exactly this one. The project that culminated in the present, perhaps somewhat immodest, volume began as a considerably more modest effort to determine the significance of the Marshall Court in the Progressive reinterpretation of American constitutional history. Certainly I did not think of writing a book on the subject of judicial review. I rather doubted whether any more such books ought to be written at all, in a field where so much ink seemingly has been spilled to so little avail.

As it turned out, there was simply no escaping the fact that the most important legal aspect of the Progressive reinterpretation was rooted in an intense conflict between reformers and conservatives in the late nineteenth century over judicial review and its seminal precedent, *Marbury v. Madison* (1803). Until recently, I shared with most others in the fields of American government and constitutional law the belief that Chief Justice Marshall's opinion in *Marbury* enunciated and established the currently prevailing doctrine of judicial review. This doctrine holds that the courts are entitled to overturn any act of Congress they find to be unconstitutional, as long as a relevant case is brought before them. Moreover, such a finding by the Supreme Court of the United States is final, not subject to further action by any other agency of government, except in conformity with the Court's decision.

In completing the research for this study, I was persuaded that the foregoing version of *Marbury* is essentially mythological and that the conception of the judicial function that it is held to support is ahistorical. Evidence gathered from continental European, English, and colonial American sources, as well as from the words of the Founders and the debates over ratification of the Constitution, suggests a much narrower idea of judicial review: that federal courts are entitled to invalidate acts of Congress and the president with finality only when to let such acts stand would violate constitutional restrictions on judicial power. A close reading of *Marbury* itself supports no more than this narrow view. Subsequent decisions of the Supreme Court lend additional support. *Marbury* was not cited by the Court as a precedent for judicial review until the late nineteenth century, and only infrequently before the 1950s. Furthermore, *Marbury* was not mentioned in support of the idea that the Court's determinations of constitutional questions is final until 1958, more than a century and a half after the case was decided.

The modern doctrine of judicial review may be traced to a handful of late nineteenth century legal scholars and publicists who were involved in a bitter controversy over the role of courts in the United States. This debate culminated in the well-known Progressive reinterpretation of American constitutional history in the early twentieth century, a reinterpretation that included a novel version of *Marbury v. Madison*. This new version of the case, together with the broad doctrine of judicial power with which Americans are now so familiar, has been handed down to subsequent generations in a manner not unlike that of Plato's "noble lie." The judicial mythology embedded there has served to authorize small groups of judges to preempt other organs of government in deciding fundamental constitutional questions.

This work is not a comprehensive history of judicial review in America. Such a project could hardly be accomplished in a single volume, even a very large one, and would have to include a survey of federal court decisions invalidating state laws, as well as the important subject of judicial review of coordinate agencies of government by state courts. The study is perhaps best described as a history of the history of Supreme Court review of federal law: how the relation between the Supreme Court and coordinate agencies of national government, especially Congress, has been conceived during various periods in American history. Its primary focus is the separation of powers.

More importantly, and more simply, it is the story of the making of a myth. In a society obsessed with legalism, it is crucial to realize the ease with which legal precedents become "little constitutions," encrusted with an aura of other-worldliness usually associated with constitutions proper. Failure to recognize this tendency stifles the "sober second thought" without which rational analysis is impossible. In this vein, I hope that this book will advance our understanding of the legal process in a previously overlooked area.

Much credit for whatever is worthwhile in this study is due to Professor Wallace Mendelson of the University of Texas at Austin. To itemize his various influences upon it, and upon me, would require a level of verbosity greatly offensive to his sensibilities. Since several passages in the book no doubt already approach that level, I shall rest content to point out his most remarkable contribution: his example of what it means to be a scholar and the knowledge that to be a scholar is a very good thing.

I should like also to express my deepest appreciation to Professor Martin Shapiro of the University of California Law School (Berkeley), whose interesting comments on the manuscript raised unanticipated questions of such importance that I shall probably have to write another book to address them fully and fairly. Professor Christopher Wolfe of Marquette University gave the manuscript a thorough reading and provided an exhaustive commentary on both its strengths and its shortcomings. Professor G. Edward White, of the University of Virginia Law School, provided a helpful critique of an earlier version of this work. Each of the following individuals read and commented upon portions of the work at varying stages of development: Professor Charles F. Cnudde of Florida State University; Professor Thomas Schwartz of the University of California at Los Angeles; Professors John Higley, David Prindle, Bruce Buchanan, and Carl Leiden of the University of Texas at Austin. To these persons I wish to extend my heartiest appreciation.

To Professor Ryan J. Barilleaux of Miami University (Ohio), who has played the various roles of friend, advisor, colleague, and critic, I extend my heartfelt thanks. Professor Paul Kens of Southwest Texas State University has provided many afternoons of engaging conversation on the subject of this study and other topics as well. Professors Liane Kosaki, of Washington University (St. Louis), and Priscilla Machado, of the University of Vermont, have been helpful and supportive colleagues. Professor Michael Greenberg of Dickinson College has been a stalwart friend and colleague and, together with his wife, Beth Ryshavi, has helped to break the tension of this project with many an evening of good old-fashioned card-playing.

I owe also a debt of gratitude to several of my colleagues in the Department of Political Science at Southern Illinois University. Al Melone read an earlier version of the work and, though disagreeing with much that he read, proved a worthy adversary in many an afternoon of stimulating debate. John Foster, departmental chairperson, and John S. Jackson, Dean of the College of Liberal Arts, have provided moral and other support for this project, and they deserve much credit for the stable work environment I presently enjoy. Uday Desai, a worthy example of the scholarly life, has imparted breadth and perspective to my endeavors and even loaned a research assistant or two when they were most needed. Jack Jacobini gave helpful advice on the jurisprudential aspects of the project and invaluable moral support as well. Richard Dale suffered through portions of the work and provided helpful mentoring in other areas. William Garner read and commented on an earlier version of the history of *Marbury* in article form. William Turley rendered much-needed advice on aspects of the publication process. Matthew Franck furnished helpful commentary from the perspective of political theory on the ideas expressed in several chapters. Ron Mason has been an intellectually stimulating friend and colleague from the beginning of my days here. Randall Nelson—friend, colleague, and neighbor, who has committed to memory more constitutional law cases than anyone I know—has given generously of his storehouse of knowledge on the subject and thereby enhanced my work. Brian Chapman, Assefaw Bariagaber, and Seshan Subramaniam contributed valuable research assistance at different periods of the study. To Sandy Mason, Cathy Croquer, Aline Wilson, Carla Fuller, and Karen Swearingen, each of whom performed the thankless chores of typing, editing, and putting up with my temperamental eccentricities, I owe a debt of gratitude I can surely never repay.

Finally, I am indebted to the members of my family. Dr. Robert L. Clinton and Wanda Lowry Clinton, my father and mother, in addition to their other many contributions, worked tirelessly in the typing of early drafts and some later ones, too. David R. Clinton and Ronald D. Clinton, my brothers, have been supportive in ways only siblings who also are best friends can be. Lois Ann Pugh has put to rest all the myths about mothers-in-law, in her role as an interested and helpful friend throughout this project. Margaret-Anne, my wife, has provided love, emotional support, intellectual stimulation, and a lot of editing throughout. She and our daughter, Winter, have endured far more than words can express during the preparation of this book. They are the ones who deserve primary credit for its ultimate completion. It goes without saying that none of the persons named above share any of the blame for what follows.

I would like to thank the editors of the following journals for their permission to use here materials that appeared earlier in different form in their journals: *Constitutional Commentary, Journal of Law and Politics, Saint Louis University Public Law Review,* and *University of Arkansas–Little Rock Law Journal.*

# Part One · Judicial Power in the Early American Republic

Since the main project of this study is to elaborate the development of a judicial by mythology that is based largely upon a single decision of the United States Supreme Court, it is crucial that this decision be thoroughly understood. Were *Marbury v. Madison* just another law case, unencrusted by myth, it would be unnecessary to explore its background extensively. But since *Marbury* has been the receptacle for so many ideas that are wholly modern in their origin, some "unlearning" is essential before we can understand the case itself.

In Chapter 1 the discussion ranges widely over the topic of judicial power in America and places the study in the context of present-day controversies on the subject. I refer to recent exercises of judicial review by the Supreme Court, along with recent challenges to some of the Court's more controversial constitutional doctrines, and the limitations of most contemporary analyses of the Court's modes of constitutional interpretation. Most importantly, I articulate the main thesis of the study from a theoretical standpoint. My claim is that there existed before, during, and after the decision of *Marbury*, a generally agreed-upon notion of the reach of judicial power in constitutional matters: that federal courts are entitled to invalidate acts of coordinate branches of government only when to allow such acts to stand would violate constitutional restrictions on judicial power, not on legislative or executive power. This notion is reflected in a preponderance of the evidence bearing on the relevant periods.

The philosophical underpinnings of this conception are elaborated and discussed, along with their relation to the ideas of Blackstone, Marshall, and Jefferson. I argue that the American understanding of the judicial function during the eighteenth century was thoroughly Blackstonian, most pointedly embodied in that author's famous Tenth Rule of Statutory Construction. This principle holds that legislation may be overruled by common-law courts only when its application would necessarily result in absurdity, repugnancy, or impossibility of performance—in other words, when a statute is internally defective or self-contradictory. When this theory is applied under a written constitution that circumscribes legislative power by explicit directives, a court must regard each statute properly before it as an embodiment of relevant constitutional authorizations or prohibitions. A statute in manifest contradiction with a relevant constitutional provision cannot be performed, since such a law is essentially self-contradictory, in conflict with the ground of its own existence. Constitutional adjudication is therefore simply a special case of statutory construction. This implies that courts possess no legitimate authority to revise or repeal statutes on grounds of policy and that no coordinate legislative body is bound to prevent enforcement of laws declared invalid by a court. This understanding, I submit, is the one most compatible with Articles III and VI of the Constitution, the decision in *Marbury v. Madison*, and the cases in which state and federal courts invalidated legislation in the early American Republic.

In Chapter 2 I begin the historical survey by examining some important laws, institutions, and court decisions—primarily Roman, Italian, French, and English—that legal historians have considered precedent for (or against) various notions of judicial power in the United States, especially ideas about judicial review. Some of these were certainly familiar to learned Americans of the Founding Era, and I make relevant connections wherever appropriate. An exhaustive treatment of these materials would range far beyond the scope of this work. My purpose is merely to show the existence of traditions regarding the exercise of judicial power on the Continent and in Great Britain at the time of the American Founding, that some of these were noted by important commentators of that day, and that they are consistent with the views respecting judicial power outlined in Chapter 1. Finally, I argue that a rather clear-cut framework of attitudes regarding the power of courts vis-à-vis other agencies of government was inherited by colonial Americans from across the Atlantic—an inheritance crucial to the development of peculiarly American institutions.

In Chapter 3 I examine factors bearing on the evolution of ideas about judicial power and judicial review in the colonial, revolutionary, and Confederation periods. An effort is made to connect the main doctrinal threads discussed in the preceding chapters with the distinctive American experience. In other words, it is not enough to notice the inherited legal framework. It must also be shown that the framework was ripe for application because a set of shared experiences made its institutionalization appear desirable.

The survey of the historical background of *Marbury v. Madison* is completed in Chapter 4. The debates in the Constitutional Convention bearing most directly on the judicial power to invalidate laws are examined, as are the key constitutional provisions that resulted from these debates. Careful scrutiny of Articles III and VI provides strong support for the theory of judicial function outlined in the first chapter. I also examine the ratification debates, with special focus on the crucial Publius-Brutus controversy in New York. Finally, the debates in Congress during the 1790s and important decisions of the state and lower federal courts of that decade are used to shed light on the understanding of the nature and scope of judicial authority in the Founding Era.

# 1 · A Historical and Theoretical Perspective

A parade of ghostly dignitaries has recently emerged out of the foggy depths of the American past. The identities are known, but the features are unclear. Easy familiarity with such names as Washington, Hamilton, Henry, Jefferson, and Marshall conceals the uneasy relations among the ideals for which they are most often invoked. The names are larger than life, the ideals symbolic of the primordial struggles from which our nation was born. Public order, property rights, individual liberty, self-government, the rule of law—all these and more have had exalted status in the bicentennial celebration of the Constitution. And well they should, for as the Romans once knew (then forgot and remembered again too late), popular history has its place in the life of a healthy republic.

But popular history is not History. A procession of heroes and villains can only reflect, and thereby conceal, underlying sequences of complex human activity like those Henry Adams once hoped could be made to appear "rigorously consequent."[1] Nor do the raw ideas that give substance to heroism and villainy reveal much more than the heroes and villains themselves. As Plato warned long ago, great truths often embody noble lies; and the acknowledged truths of American constitutional history are no exceptions.

Alongside the Constitution itself, and perhaps overshadowing it in the present century, stands the arcane field of constitutional law. Consisting of an imposing and ever-expanding array of judicial decisions, mostly of the United States Supreme Court, this field has emerged as a volatile battleground upon which divergent conceptions of values dear to Americans are championed. The engine that powers this perpetual conflict is the institution of judicial review—the Court's authority to invalidate

4

laws—without which there would doubtless be no constitutional law in the usual sense.[2]

In the United States, research on constitutional development has been influenced by a number of presuppositions about the historical foundations of judicial power. Perhaps the most important of these foundations is the 1803 decision of the Supreme Court in the case of *Marbury v. Madison*, which is generally thought by both proponents and opponents of judicial power to have established the American doctrine of judicial power to overturn national laws.[3] The standard view of *Marbury* is that the Marshall Court went out of its way to invalidate a statutory provision in order to avoid a direct political conflict with the executive branch and in order to assert an authority over the legislative branch that could not be directly challenged in the circumstances of the case, yet could nonetheless be regarded as a legal basis for future assertions of a similar authority.

The modern view is stated best by Chief Justice Marshall's most distinguished biographer, Albert J. Beveridge, who said that

> [*Marbury*], for perfectly calculated audacity, has few parallels in judicial history. In order to assert that in the Judiciary rested the exclusive power to declare any statute unconstitutional, and to announce that the Supreme Court was the ultimate arbiter as to what is and what is not law under the Constitution, Marshall determined to annul Section 13 of the Ellsworth Judiciary Act of 1789. Marshall resolved to go still further. He would announce from the Supreme Bench rules of procedure which the Executive branch of the Government must observe.[4]

Echoing Beveridge some four decades later, Alexander M. Bickel said that "if any social process can be said to have been 'done' at a given time and by a given act, it is Marshall's achievement. The time was 1803; the act was the decision in the case of *Marbury v. Madison.*"[5]

Underlying these statements is the idea that the *Marbury* opinion was justified neither by the Constitution nor by legal precedent. The implication is that Chief Justice Marshall was an "activist," a judicial "policymaker," whose establishment of the doctrine of judicial review was an innovation. Donald O. Dewey goes so far as to charge that the decision was unabashedly "political," an example of early Federalist politics par excellence.[6]

The prevailing orthodoxy that regards *Marbury* as the prime exemplar of aggressive judicial behavior is apparent not only from sources in constitutional law, but from those in the field of American government as well. One text declares that "when the courts make decisions so as to set policy, we have what is known as an 'activist' court. Yet, in fact, a majority of the United States Supreme Court has been nothing else since Chief Justice Marshall, in *Madison v. Marbury* (1803), proclaimed the Court's right to be the final interpreter of the Constitution."[7] Another claims that "Marshall went out of his way to declare Section 13 unconstitutional."[8] Yet another, alluding to the legendary Marshall-Jefferson conflict, says that "John Marshall's unwillingness to do battle with Jefferson was, in fact, the reason he contrived a way out by using judicial review in *Marbury v. Madison*."[9] Fashionably stated, Marshall is said to have "read" judicial review "into" the Constitution, thereby establishing a policy of "judicial supremacy" and creating a forum for the propagation of conservative political ideology.[10]

Several generations of political scientists, lawyers, and historians have been nurtured by such views, which have legitimized American ideas about the appropriate extent of judicial power throughout most of the present century. Wallace Mendelson has recently observed that "not a few admirers of the Warren Court undertook to justify Warrenism on the basis of a comparable aggressiveness they claimed to find in Chief Justice Marshall."[11] Yet both proponents and opponents of assertive federal courts have made extensive use of *Marbury*'s allegedly innovative character. Proponents have urged the "statesmanship" of the Great Chief Justice in his disposition of the case. Opponents have pointed out that statesmanship is a "political" function that judges have no business performing.

Most authorities appear to concede the idea so eloquently embodied in Robert G. McCloskey's portrayal of the case: "a masterwork of indirection, a brilliant example of Marshall's ability to sidestep danger while seeming to court it, to advance in one direction while his opponents are looking in another."[12] According to the prevailing theory, Marshall's handling of the case was motivated primarily by political, not legal, concerns; and the institution of judicial review is thereby tainted with something like original sin.

In the past few years, a number of works have strongly suggested that the orthodox tradition should be subjected to serious reexamination. P. Allan Dionisopoulos and Paul Peterson have recently argued that judicial review was an accepted part of the American institutional structure well before 1803; Marshall and his Court would have had no reason to resort to subterfuge to "establish" an already established institution.[13] Christopher Wolfe has asserted that Marshall's jurisprudence was faithful to constitutional principle and that *Marbury* constitutes a poor basis for modern judicial review.[14] Hadley Arkes has attacked the popular notion that *Marbury* established the Supreme Court as the sole interpreter of the Constitution.[15] Finally, Wallace Mendelson has assailed the idea that judicial review is a device that Marshall "in an artful opinion foisted upon the nation, and then used extravagantly for his own purposes; namely to promote nationalism at the expense of local self-government, and property at the expense of human or personal rights."[16]

Semantics are important here. "Judicial review," as a term used to describe the constitutional power of a court to overturn statutes, regulations, and other governmental activities, apparently was an invention of law writers in the early twentieth century. Edward S. Corwin may have been the first to coin the phrase, in the title of an article in the 1910 *Michigan Law Review.*[17] This suggests a significant divergence from the views of our ancestors on the relation of courts to other agencies of government; for the phrase, when used in the constitutional sense, connotes something like the sweeping, general, supervisory function which many have come to expect courts to perform in modern times. That the phrase was apparently unknown to Marshall's contemporaries may tell us much.

It is difficult to imagine people in the early years of the American Republic subscribing to the assessment of judicial power provided in 1967 by Archibald Cox—that judicial review "calls upon the Court to go over the very social, political, and economic questions committed to the Congress and State legislatures."[18] Such a calling empowers the Supreme Court to travel far beyond those particular controversies mentioned in Article III and to exercise supervisory authority over questions of public policy. It invokes the famous remark of Bishop Hoadly, so often recalled by Americans of bygone eras, that whoever "hath an absolute authority to interpret any written or spoken laws, it is he who is truly the lawgiver, to all intents and purposes, and not the person who first spoke or wrote them."[19]

Christopher Wolfe's recent volume on the history of judicial review in America sharply differentiates "traditional" and "modern" forms of judicial review, characterizing the former as "constitutional interpretation" and the latter as "judge-made law."[20] Though I shall presently argue for a slightly different form of traditional judicial review, I do believe that his work is a major contribution to the ongoing debate over the role of the Supreme Court in the American constitutional order. If Professor Wolfe's book is taken as seriously as it deserves to be, it may help to fashion the terms of this debate for many years to come.

## Judicial Review

Disputes about the proper role of the Supreme Court in the American constitutional system and the appropriate method of discovering the law in constitutional cases have recently been waged on two major fronts. In the political arena, the problem of judicial review has stimulated an unprecedented public debate between an associate justice of the Supreme Court and the attorney general of the United States. Justice William J. Brennan argued that the Constitution must be read in a contemporary light, providing solutions for the social, economic, and political problems of America in the 1980s.[21] Attorney General Edwin Meese contended that constitutional provisions should be strictly construed according to the intentions of their makers two hundred years ago.[22]

The controversy then entered a second, more interesting, phase. The attorney general suggested that public officials need not always defer to the Supreme Court but may be guided by their own views of the Constitution's meaning in some instances.[23] Accordingly, though a Supreme Court decision "binds the parties in a case . . . such a decision does not establish a 'supreme law of the land' that is binding on all persons and parts of the government, henceforth and forever more."[24] In response, Eugene C. Thomas, then president of the American Bar Association, said that "Supreme Court decisions are the law of the land just as acts of Congress are the law of the land."[25] Anthony Lewis assailed the attorney general for "making a calculated assault on the idea of law in this country: on the role of judges as the balance wheel in the American system."[26] Benno Schmidt, Jr., added that the attorney general was on a "disastrous" course, speaking as "a man of power, not a man of law."[27] Recent Senate confirmation hearings for Chief Justice William Rehnquist, Associate Justice Antonin Scalia, and Judge Robert Bork indicate that the debate has yet to reach a satisfactory conclusion.

The problem is hardly a new one. Scholars, judges, and politicians have argued for decades about "judicial restraint" and "judicial activism" and, for decades before that, about "strict construction" and "liberal construction." The argument is probably as old as the Republic itself, though variations in nuance are apparent from generation to generation. However, there are some novelties in the present controversy. Even Abraham Lincoln, arguing against the Court's infamous *Dred Scott* decision more than a century ago, stopped short of suggesting that persons public or private might disregard decisions of the Court.[28] And surely it is unusual for a sitting justice of the Court to venture so far as to articulate a *public* defense of judicial activism.[29]

Doubtless the Brennan outburst was triggered by Reagan Administration efforts to persuade the Court to overturn previous decisions in such areas as reproductive rights, race discrimination, and school prayer.[30] The government's effort itself has been enlivened by the belief of Meese and others that the decisions in question were themselves a result of an earlier Court's willingness to overturn ancient understandings of the Constitution.[31] Indeed, following the trail back further, a Court full of Roosevelt appointees once overturned some important decisions of the Nine Old Men,[32] decisions which themselves had overturned a century's worth of precedents in such fields as commerce, taxation, and economic regulation.[33]

Antedating this political controversy by a decade or so, the academic front has carried on a more refined debate in books and scholarly journals on "interpretivism" in American constitutional law. Three of the more important works, which represent a broad spectrum of views on the subject, are books by Raoul Berger,[34] John Hart Ely,[35] and an article by Thomas Grey.[36]

Berger's main thesis is that the federal courts have usurped legislative functions in several areas, most notably desegregation and reapportionment.[37] These judicial excesses have been caused by wholesale judicial misinterpretation of the Fourteenth Amendment, and similar mistakes may be avoided only by adopting a mode of constitutional interpretation that determines the meaning of a specific constitutional provision by reference to the specific intention of its drafters.[38] This approach has since been labeled "clause-bound interpretivism."[39]

At the other end of the spectrum, Grey has argued that the exercise of judicial review should not be encumbered by any theories of constitutional interpretation that depend on the determination of "intent." Intent cannot be reliably discerned, and even if it could be, the courts should be free to expound "basic national ideals of individual liberty and fair treatment, even when the content of these ideals is not expressed as a matter of positive law in the written Constitution."[40] Not surprisingly, this theory has been labeled "non-interpretivism."[41]

Ely has tried to sketch out a middle ground between Berger and Grey, suggesting that the exercise of judicial review by federal courts may have been excessive in some areas (e.g., birth control, abortion) and justifiable in others (e.g., voting rights, reapportionment).[42] This distinction is based on Ely's theory of constitutional interpretation, which plausibly may be called "non-clause-bound interpretivism."[43] The theory holds that judicial interpretations of constitutional provisions need not be grounded in the specific intention of their drafters *with respect to each particular clause*, but should be grounded in the "general themes of the entire constitutional document and not from some source entirely beyond its four corners."[44]

Though numerous refinements of these categories have been articulated, lengthy discussion of them would be far beyond the scope of this study.[45] The crucial point is that most of the work in the field of constitutional interpretation during the past decade has been done within a framework generated by such categories, and the categories themselves tend to obscure matters of great importance. The primary reason for this is that such notions as "intent," "overall purposes," or "basic national ideals" are abstractions; to frame arguments on the proper scope of judicial review in accordance with them begs important historical and empirical questions which should be answered before theoretical consistency can be attempted, let alone achieved. Approaching the problem from a purely theoretical standpoint at the outset simply divorces constitutional law from constitutional history and drives the former field into a kind of Ptolemaic oblivion, where there is nothing to do but evolve fresh philosophical rationalizations for judicial policy-making in specific areas.

For example, even if one accepts Berger's thesis that the intentions of the framers of the Fourteenth Amendment are knowable, intentions respecting other provisions intimately connected with that amendment may not be equally clear. Indeed, some of the misinterpretations which Berger so carefully documents are contemporaneous with a major transformation in the outlook of legal scholars toward *Marbury v. Madison* and judicial review (see Chapter II). Yet Berger apparently fails to notice this development, even though judicial review is a necessary precondition of the misinterpretations he deplores. Perhaps that is why Berger, in a work sincerely devoted to a restrictive conception of judicial review, nonetheless advocates his own brand of judicial policy-making—that the Founders of 1787 intended the Supreme Court to assume primary responsibility for the separation of powers by policing "the boundaries drawn in the Constitution."[46] If the present study proves anything at all, it should be that the Founders could not possibly have envisioned such a role for the Court. One cannot, however, rely solely on their "vision" to establish this conclusion. *Marbury* and other evidence are important as well.

On the other hand, Grey's theory demands acceptance of the idea that all those concerned both know and agree on"basic national ideals"—a notion that is clearly refuted by two centuries of our national experience. Ely's theory fares little better; if the positions of Berger and Grey are based on flawed categories, then attempts to reconcile them are not likely to be successful.

In short, abstract theorizing about the "right" way to interpret constitutional provisions fails because it ignores the cardinal feature of all Anglo-American legal systems: the articulation of legal doctrine by creation, dissemination, and dissolution of *precedent*. It is this foundation which imparts continuity, stability, and predictability to the legal experience and on which we rely for the maintenance of constitutional controls on the excesses of politics.

These observations on precedent bring into focus the difficulty of solving problems in constitutional interpretation by using the intentions of the Framers. Beneath the surface of the intent question rests a deeper problem involving the doctrine of *stare decisis*.[47] Intentionality and precedent are intertwined in American law, as Judge Bork's confirmation hearings pointedly illustrated.[48] Together the two concepts comprise an important part of the law's doctrinal method for relating past to present, thereby advancing the continuity so prized in common-law-based systems.[49] Hence, they are incorporated into our legal fabric as complementary, not conflicting, values.

The effect of *stare decisis* normally attaches to the most recent authoritative declaration of the law under which important rights have vested.[50] But suppose that such a declaration later is discovered to be incompatible with a more "original" understanding? Then there is a collision between the rule of precedent and the principle that a law is to be construed so as to effect the will of the lawgiver.[51] In an ordinary case, the difficulty might be resolved through the interplay of traditional rules of statutory construction.[52] But in constitutional law, the problem is exacerbated, because constitutional theory lacks any widely-accepted principle that would resolve the conflict in particular instances. Thus arguments about original intent frequently boil down to the relative importance of original intentions versus the role of precedent.

That issue was illustrated in the political arena during the confirmation hearings for Justices Rehnquist and Scalia. Senator Arlen Specter

(R.-Pa.), apparently fearing that Congress might regulate the appellate jurisdiction of the Supreme Court in certain cases involving individual liberty, asked both nominees whether their avowed commitment to the philosophy of judicial restraint would lead them to overrule what the senator thought to be the fundamental principle of judicial review in the American system, articulated in *Marbury v. Madison*: that the Supreme Court is the final arbiter of constitutional questions generally.[53] The query is a relevant one, since *Marbury* is concededly the seminal precedent for judicial power to invalidate federal laws, and precedent is widely regarded to be an independent basis for judicial decision.

On the academic side, Professor Daniel O. Conkle has appropriately characterized the central point at issue as "the legitimacy of the Supreme Court's recognition of non-originalist constitutional rights."[54] The major objection of those who do not regard such rights as legitimate is the supposed "finality" of the Court's constitutional pronouncements.[55] Conkle argues that the doctrine of judicial finality is not controversial in the context of originalist judicial review, because the Court's function there is merely "to determine the intentions of the constitutional framers and to ensure that those intentions are protected 'permanently' against majoritarian transgression."[56] He then suggests that the notion of judicial finality in originalist review is grounded in Chief Justice Marshall's opinion for the Court in *Marbury v. Madison*, where "the Supreme Court first claimed for itself the power of judicial review."[57]

Senator Specter's query and Professor Conkle's suggestion rouse an interesting feature of the contemporary debate on judicial review, especially when that debate is couched in terms of original intent. Both originalists and nonoriginalists appear to have accepted the premise that *Marbury* is the foundation of judicial review in the United States, yet the Marshall Court's disposition of that famous case is considered a model of judicial innovativeness.[58] It is difficult to understand why nonoriginalists, presumably those who favor the idea of judicial updating of the Constitution to accommodate *contemporary* aspirations, should find it necessary to rely so heavily upon a precedent almost as *old* as the Constitution itself. On the other hand, why should originalists, who would restrict judicial decision making to the determination of intent two hundred years *past*, accept the authority of a precedent *presently* thought of as contrary to their view? It seems that both sides want to have their cake and eat it too. Oliver Wendell Holmes once said that "a page of history is worth a volume of logic."[59] If that is true, then the area of common agreement between the proponents and opponents of originalism should be examined carefully. For if the conventional understanding of *Marbury* is mistaken, then the terms of debate are flawed and the argument needs to be redirected.

It is therefore hoped that the present study will enhance understanding of the American doctrine of judicial review, as it is elaborated in the various transformations of its major precedent. The assumption is that, in common-law-based systems, historical treatment of a legal doctrine largely involves its unfolding as precedent; and, that *stare decisis*, rather than political philosophy, social policy, or subjective notions of original intent, is the primary form of justification for a judicial decision. The history of *Marbury v. Madison* is, from this perspective, a history of judicial review in the United States.

There are at least three additional ways that I hope this study will make a contribution to knowledge. First, it may be the first attempt to trace the history of an important court decision through all its subsequent transformations as a legal precedent. Second, since interpretations of *Marbury*, both on and off the bench, will be examined, the all-important relation between the federal judiciary and one of its main constituencies, the academy, will be elaborated. Finally, existing research on *Marbury v. Madison* is shockingly inadequate, in view of the importance of the case in American constitutional history. Only one full-length book has been written on the case, that by Donald O. Dewey, published in 1970.[60] Unfortunately, Dewey's book is devoted entirely to the political squabble between President Jefferson and Chief Justice Marshall which has obscured so many other important aspects of the case. Furthermore, Dewey's work relies heavily on two earlier articles which are themselves questionable respecting many legal aspects of the case.[61]

The historiography of *Marbury* is important for several reasons. First, judicial review has been thought by many to constitute a self-developed power, not specifically granted in the Constitution, but rather fashioned by the Supreme Court itself in Marbury's case and elaborated later in subsequent cases.[62] So conceived, the power of review is analogous to the power of Congress to create executive departments pursuant to the necessary and proper clause,[63] or even to the president's power to deploy troops in order to protect national security interests.[64] Such powers have resulted from initiatives of those departments themselves, rather than from explicit constitutional directives.[65] Acceptance of this analogy probably accounts in part for the controversial nature of judicial review throughout modern American history and for the tendency of such advocates as Senator Specter to return to *Marbury*, rather than to the Constitution, for doctrinal support.

Second, *Marbury* has been the subject of intense controversy at various junctures in American constitutional development. When Progressive reformers attacked the courts in the late nineteenth and early twentieth centuries, one of the focal points was *Marbury*. Opponents of the courts regarded *Marbury* as a "usurpation" of legislative authority and judicial review as an unwarranted power.[66] Supporters of the courts hailed the decision as having established a principle that, in its effect if not in its purpose, was as important a "charter of American liberty" as the Declaration of Independence and the Constitution itself.[67] Neither of these viewpoints represents a reasonable interpretation of what the Court actually said (and did) in *Marbury*, but they do indicate the symbolic power of precedent in our constitutional system.

Finally, the view of *Marbury* that is explicit in Senator Specter's "loyalty oath," implicit in Professor Conkle's analysis, and appears to command at least a qualified assent from every quarter, is a highly questionable interpretation of the actual decision. Careful scrutiny of the Marshall opinion, when placed in the context of the litigation, reveals no explicit declaration of the Court's authority to issue final proclamations on constitutional issues generally, so as to bind coordinate departments to the judicial declaration. The statement from the *Marbury* opinion which is usually cited to support such a reading is that where the Court asserts its duty to "say what the law is."[68] But the obvious qualification which immediately follows that statement has been overlooked: that this duty is exercised only "of necessity," whenever those "who apply the rule to particular cases" *must* determine which of two "conflicting rules governs the case."[69] The conclusion is that, in *some* cases, "the constitution must be looked into by the judges."[70] That there is no denial of the legislature's (or the executive's) power to do likewise is made clear a few paragraphs later: "it is apparent, that the framers of the constitution contemplated that instrument, as a rule for the government of courts, *as well as of the legislature.*"[71]

The assertion that the Constitution is a rule for the government of courts and legislatures alike and that judges may "look into it," at least whenever the performance of judicial functions is at issue (as they were in the *Marbury* situation), is very different from saying that the Court is the final, infallible interpreter of the document as it applies to the powers of *coordinate* branches of government. Yet the Supreme Court, in 1958, pronounced the following in *Cooper v. Aaron*: "This decision [*Marbury*] declared the basic principle that the federal judiciary is supreme in the exposition of the law of the Constitution, and that principle has ever since been respected by the Court and the country as a permanent and indispensable feature of our constitutional system."[72] Surely, if such a principle has *ever since* been respected by the Court, we should have no trouble discovering abundant evidence of that respect in its post-1803 opinions and in the commentaries about judicial decisions. If not, then perhaps Senator Specter should have asked whether justices Rehnquist and Scalia would overrule, not *Marbury*, but rather *Cooper v. Aaron*. I suggest that the difference matters, for the degree of respect accorded a time-honored precedent should be a function of the length of time it has been honored. I further suggest that the view of *Marbury* embodied in the *Cooper* dictum is ahistorical—an observation strongly supported by the subsequent treatment of *Marbury* by the Supreme Court itself from 1803 to the present. Before proceeding any further, we should take a closer look at the case itself.

### Marbury, *Blackstone, and the Constitution*

The facts in Marbury's case are well known.[73] A lame-duck Federalist Congress had, on February 13 and 27, 1801, passed acts, one of the effects of which was to create some new positions within the federal judiciary.[74] Four of the new appointees under the act of February 27 failed to receive their commissions due to nondelivery, and on December 17, 1801, they sued for a writ of mandamus compelling delivery in an original action before the United States Supreme Court.[75] Before the case came to trial, Congress, now dominated by Republican majorities, passed an act on March 3, 1802, that repealed the act of February 13.[76]

On April 23, Congress passed another measure which eliminated the June and December terms of the Court.[77] The latter measure was probably an attempt by Congress to prevent the Court from ruling upon the constitutionality of the repeal act before it took effect, and one of its incidental results was to postpone the Court's hearing of Marbury's case until its February term in 1803.[78]

Chief Justice Marshall's opinion for the Court was rendered on February 24, 1803.[79] The first section deals with the related questions of Marbury's right to receive his commission and the appropriate legal remedy to enforce the right, if such exists.[80] The Court's rulings on these points are straightforward: (1) that Marbury had been duly appointed, that delivery of the commission was merely incidental to the appointment, and that therefore the secretary of state did not have the privilege of later withholding it;[81] (2) that it is the duty of a government of laws to supply remedies for violated rights;[82] and (3) that the writ of mandamus is an appropriate legal remedy for resolution of a dilemma such as Marbury's.[83]

The second section of the opinion deals with the power of the Court to issue the requested writ; that is, whether it may take jurisdiction of the case for such a purpose.[84] The Court's answer is negative, on the ground that the act on which Marbury relied is one that unwarrantably enlarges the original jurisdiction of the Supreme Court, a jurisdiction clearly spelled out in Article III of the Constitution.[85] In short, Marbury is entitled to his commission, has applied for an appropriate legal remedy, but is in the wrong court.

The second section of the *Marbury* opinion contains the famous argument which justifies the Court's refusal to enforce Section 13 of the Judiciary Act of 1789.[86] The relevant portion actually contains two subarguments. The first supports the conclusion that "an act of the legislature, repugnant to the constitution, is void."[87] The second supports an altogether different conclusion that "courts, as well as other departments, are bound by that instrument."[88] Marshall clearly distinguishes between a law *being* null due to incompatibility with the Constitution, and a court having the *power* to nullify such a law. He does not, as has so often been suggested, attempt to derive his second conclusion *by implication* from premises that will support only the first conclusion.[89] It is, of course, the second conclusion which pertains directly to the power of judicial review.

The nullity of unconstitutional laws is drawn primarily from the original right of the people "to establish, for their future government, such principles as, in their opinion, shall most conduce to their own happiness."[90] As steps in this argument, Marshall invokes certain principles: (1) that the government of the United States is a government of strictly "defined and limited" powers; (2) that the Constitution is a law of "superior obligation"; and (3) that the nullity of invalid laws is a theory "essentially attached to a written constitution."[91] Though none of these ideas are specified in the argument for judicial review, they are nonetheless necessary to the Court's ultimate result. For if an unconstitutional law is not invalid in the first place, then any court must enforce such a law in every case, regardless of its nature.

Obviously, Marshall's first conclusion follows from a straightforward argument. The Constitution is a "law of superior obligation" *if* the people do in fact have a right to establish binding rules for their future government, *and* the set of such rules is the Constitution. Likewise, if the law of superior obligation is a written one that defines and limits legislative power (i.e., one whose legislative authority is purely *delegated*), then *all* legislative acts against it are *ipso facto* void (i.e., void by the mere fact that their passage has occurred prior to their authorization by explicit constitutional delegation). Finally, if all legislative acts are *ipso facto* void prior to delegation of authority, then the proposition that all legislative acts in violation of the Constitution are void is a mere truism. Perhaps that is why Marshall plausibly can say that "the question, whether an act, repugnant to the constitution, can become the law of the land, is a question . . . not of an intricacy proportioned to its interest."[92]

The argument which leads to Marshall's second conclusion (that courts, as well as other departments, are bound by the Constitution) begins with the rhetorical question left unanswered at the close of the first argument: "If an act of the legislature, repugnant to the constitution, is void, does it, notwithstanding its invalidity, bind the courts, and oblige them to give it effect?"[93] The answer commences with the famous statement quoted before, that the Court has an obligation to "say what the law is," even in situations where conflicting constitutional and statutory provisions are simultaneously applicable to a particular controversy which the Court must decide.[94] If an act in violation of the Constitution is *not law* (Marshall's first conclusion) and the Court's duty is to apply *law* in particular cases, then the application of an unconstitutional statute would violate the judge's oath to support the Constitution. Since the judicial power extends to cases "arising under" the Constitution and laws, and only those laws made "in pursuance" of the Constitution have constitutional status, courts therefore may prefer constitutional over incompatible statutory provisions when operating within their acknowledged authority to resolve particular disputes. They are not bound to "close their eyes on the constitution, and see only the law."[95]

Whatever one may think about the Marshall Court's handling of other aspects of Marbury's case,[96] or the admittedly oversimplified logic of the argument analyzed above, it is difficult to find any evidence that establishes final authority in the Supreme Court on constitutional questions. The only notion of finality which may be drawn from the opinion is that the statutory provision invalidated in the case pertains to the Court's performance of its own functions. In other words, the Court's pronouncement on Section 13 is final and binding on the other departments because the section is a jurisdictional provision which only the Court can exercise.

On the basis of this view, the most that may be claimed for judicial review in *Marbury* is that the decision entitles the Court to disregard legislation in resolving particular controversies *only where such legislation bears directly upon the performance of judicial functions.*[97] Moreover, since the Court believed that the provision invalidated in *Marbury* was one that unwarrantably *enlarged* its original jurisdiction, an even *narrower* reading is appropriate: that the Court is entitled to disregard laws *only when such laws violate constitutional restrictions on judicial power.*

Arguably, these understandings were shared by those at the Philadelphia Convention in 1787. After some debate over Article III, the Founders apparently extended the federal judicial power to cases "arising under the Constitution, Laws, and Treaties of the United States" only after it had been "generally supposed that the jurisdiction given was constructively limited to cases of a Judiciary nature."[98] According to Benjamin F. Wright, "There is room to differ as to Madison's meaning of 'judiciary nature' here, but at least it would appear to represent a theory of judicial review which did not recognize the courts as the exclusive or final interpreters of all parts of the Constitution."[99] This understanding is also consistent with cases decided by state courts prior to 1787 (see Chapter 3) and with cases decided by federal courts in the 1790s (see Chapter 4).

Finally, this understanding of *Marbury* is consistent with the American common-law tradition inherited from English courts prior to the Revolutionary War. During that period, a prominent group of English jurists were deciding cases which involved apparent contradictions between statutory law and more "fundamental" principles. In the process, they developed rules of statutory construction which were later summarized in the *Commentaries* of William Blackstone, the most influential law book of the Founding era.[100] These rules of interpretation, when read in the light of early American experience, suggest a conception of the judicial function which I believe is embodied in both the Federal Constitution and *Marbury v. Madison.*

In fact, Americans of the Founding Era seem to have understood and agreed with the conception of the judicial function so fully that it was taken for granted. This consensus was based in part on what Professor Wolfe has observed: that "there were in use generally accepted rules for interpreting laws and legal documents, that were readily applicable to constitutional interpretation."[101] The rules to which he refers are those found at the end of the second section of Blackstone's introduction to his *Commentaries*, which are designed to assist courts in ascertaining the legislative will.[102] According to Wolfe, these rules amount to using five basic signs to explore the intention of the lawgiver: "the words, the context, the subject-matter, the effects and consequences, or the spirit and reason of the law."[103]

I have no difficulty accepting Professor Wolfe's assertion that these rules were so widely accepted at the time of the Founding that few, if any, ventured to question them. As such, they are regarded appropriately as the cornerstone of the prevailing doctrine of constitutional interpretation in that period. However, it should also be noted that the rules assist only in determining "intent," broadly conceived, with respect to specific constitutional or statutory provisions, taken one at a time. They do not tell us what to do whenever constitutional and statutory provisions, *read together*, appear to collide. In other words, they do not tell us anything about the *scope* of judicial power. Yet Blackstone raised this issue and resolved it, for his own purposes, in a subsequent section of his great work.

The relevant passage, found at the end of the third section of Blackstone's introduction, contains ten rules of statutory construction.[104] Included in the list are rules respecting remedial statutes, penal statutes, "statutes against frauds," saving clauses, and repealing laws. The Tenth Rule reads:

> Lastly, acts of parliament that are impossible to be performed are of no validity; and if there arise out of them collaterally any absurd consequences, manifestly contradictory to common reason, they are, with regard to those collateral consequences, void. I lay down the rule with these restrictions; though I know it is generally laid down more largely, that acts of parliament contrary to reason are void. But if the parliament will positively enact a thing to be done which is unreasonable, I know of no power that can control it: and the examples usually alleged in support of this sense of the rule do none of them prove, that where the main object of a statute is unreasonable the judges are at liberty to reject it; for that were to set the judicial power above that of the legislature, which would be subversive of all government. But where some collateral matter arises out of the general words, and happens to be unreasonable; there the judges are in decency to conclude that this consequence was not foreseen by parliament, and therefore they are at liberty to expound the statute by equity, and only *quoad hoc* disregard it. Thus if an act of parliament gives a man power to try all causes, that arise

within his manor of Dale; yet, if a cause should arise in which he himself is party, the act is construed not to extend to that; because it is unreasonable that any man should determine his own quarrel. But, if we could conceive it possible for the parliament to enact, that he should try as well his own causes as those of other persons, there is no court that has power to defeat the intent of the legislature, when couched in such evident and express words, as leave no doubt whether it was the intent of the legislature or no.[105]

The passage may be read as having laid down a theory of legislative supremacy. And so it does. But it says more in its articulation of the conditions under which judges are entitled to disregard laws. The appropriate grounds are impossibility of performance and collateral absurdity, both of which point to situations where the laws in question may be regarded as *self*-contradictory. Yet in the context of Blackstone's example, the internal contradiction of the rule has a particular form; for the principle offended by the situation in the manor of Dale is *not* explicitly contained within the special act empowering the Lord of Dale to try all of his causes, but rather is a kind of constitutional principle that is assumed to be part of the act.

Blackstone's Tenth Rule is the culmination of a line of cases through which English judges attempted to restrict the application of statutes according to fundamental principles. These decisions were familiar to Americans of the Founding Era and were cited at important junctures, as will be shown later. When added to the rules of interpretation discussed previously and adapted to American conditions, the Tenth Rule generates a theory of the judicial function which treats constitutional interpretation as a special case of statutory construction. Such a theory is completely consistent with the language and purposes of the Constitution, with the words and context of the decision in *Marbury v. Madison*, with important state court decisions both before and after the Philadelphia Convention, and with federal court decisions both before and after *Marbury*.

## Constitutional Review
## in the Early American Republic

The central ingredient in the attitudes which informed the conception of judicial power in the early American Republic was a perceived necessity of placing legislative authority under some kind of formal constraint. Politically, the concern is manifest in the proliferation of written constitutions which carefully delegated legislative power and explicitly limited such power. The best known of these early documents is the famous Massachusetts Constitution of 1780. According to Merrill Peterson, this document "was the first to embody the full-blown theory of constituent sovereignty. It had been framed in a special convention and ratified by the people in town meetings. In this and in its provision for an elective chief magistrate, a broadly representative legislature, and an independent judiciary, it avoided some of the paramount errors of the early constitutions."[106] Although the Massachusetts document contained the most comprehensive attempt to limit legislative authority by an explicit separation provision, several other states had attempted legislative restriction through institutional checks.[107]

Legally, the drive to limit legislative power is evident in the widespread adoption by courts of a rule that voids acts of a delegated authority that exceed its mandate. The modern version of this rule has been ascribed generally to Vattel;[108] its origins, however, are much earlier[109]

It has long been held that the principle of legislative limitation derives from natural law;[110] and that, since belief in natural law was widespread among early Americans, legislative limitation was accepted on that basis.[111] However, that is only part of the story. There have been numerous attempts, from the dawn of Western civilization, to restrict legislative bodies in accordance with some set of generally accepted rules.[112] Most of these endeavors were failures, presumably because they often involved legislatures attempting to limit their successors, in derogation of the long-standing rule of *lex posterior derogat priori*.[113] Blackstone's Ninth Rule of Statutory Construction is a version of the same principle: "Acts of parliament derogatory from the power of subsequent parliaments bind not."[114] In his discussion of the Ninth Rule, Blackstone refers to Cicero's letters to Atticus, noting that the great Roman lawyer "treats with a proper contempt these restraining clauses which endeavor to tie up the hands of succeeding legislatures."[115]

The tradition of unsuccessful attempts to limit legislative power in the absence of a written constitution, a tradition inherited by Americans of the colonial and postcolonial periods, was joined in the early Republic with another concerning the proper role of courts. According to that tradition, the judicial function was constrained to judgments affecting only the rights and duties of parties litigating their claims immediately before a court.[116] Implications of the court's rules, beyond the decision of the particular case at hand, arose only incidentally as a consequence of the application of the English doctrine of *stare decisis* by subsequent courts in the decision of analogous cases. The doctrine of precedent in fact *implies* that the main function of any court is the narrow one of ruling only upon the particular case before it. If a court's decision automatically extended beyond the case at hand, then it would make no sense to invoke the principle of "deciding similar cases similarly" in *justification* of a future judgment.

The Americans also inherited principles of statutory construction, carefully developed over a period of two centuries by English judges and articulated by Blackstone in 1769.[117] The most crucial of these, for present purposes, held that a court has power to refuse application of relevant statutes in particular cases only when such laws are "absurd, repugnant, or impossible to be performed."[118] In other words, the only appropriate justification for a court's declaration that a law is void for the case at hand is the existence of some *internal* defect in the law that makes it impossible to apply without contradiction. Such instances would include conflicting statutory provisions within the law, or conflict between a statutory and constitutional provision when the former's very existence is predicated upon the latter's authority.

Of course, since the foregoing rule was developed within the environment of an unwritten constitution, its primary function was to provide courts with a rationale for refusing to impute absurdities to parliament, as is evident in Blackstone's qualification—that whenever such an absurdity is "unmistakably" legislated by parliament, no court has power to prevent its enforcement.[119] But this function does not hold in the context of a written constitution, one of the main purposes of which is to place definite limits on legislative power. In such an environment, so long as the judiciary is independent, application of Blackstone's Tenth Rule means that every statute passed pursuant to a delegated authority in the constitution (or that contravenes an explicit limitation) is assumed to have embodied in it the provision containing the delegation (or limitation).

If the constitutional provision is not presupposed by the statute, then the collision is *external*— between the law and a principle from without. Under that interpretation, whenever a court fails to apply a clearly relevant statute in the decision of a case, it does so on a *revisionary* basis, since the procedure involves the setting of one law (constitutional) beside another (statutory), and revising or repealing the latter in accordance with the requirements of the former. This approach is not one of *statutory* construction, but something entirely different.

I submit that the difference between these two ways of thinking about what a court is doing when it invalidates a law on constitutional grounds matters greatly. An approach that "sets the law beside the constitution" for constitutional decision making is one of the intellectual hallmarks of modern judicial review and leads inexorably to judicial activism (see Chapter 12). Such an approach should not be used to characterize the exercise of judicial review by American courts during any period prior to the end of the Civil War. Most, if not all, of the cases in the colonial, revolutionary, Founding, and Marshall eras (and most in the Taney era as well), in which courts refused application of legislation, are best explained in accordance with the "statutory construction" approach. It follows that any imputation of an activist orientation to the early American judiciary should be suspect.

Despite the narrow conception of judicial power in "constitutional" cases held by early Americans, and widely respected by early American courts, there is generally a powerful compulsion to enforce constitutional restrictions on the potentially arbitrary legislative will. Where lies the ultimate authority to prevent enforcement of an invalid statute? It is my view that the answer to this question was clearly given by the Founders, that it is the key to understanding the proper functioning of the separation of powers which they contrived, and that it was the controlling doctrine of American constitutional law for at least a hundred years thereafter.

The answer is suggested by joining Blackstone's Tenth Rule with the Founders' understanding of Article III's "arising under" jurisdiction. The Tenth Rule requires that courts apply relevant statutory provisions unless they are "absurd," or "impossible to be performed."[120] The Founders' understanding of Article III restricts the jurisdiction over cases arising under the Constitution, laws, and treaties to those "of a Judiciary nature."[121] The class of controversies that are *both* "of a Judiciary nature" *and* involve statutes "impossible to be performed" are those in which the applicable statutes are incompatible with the performance of legitimate judicial functions.

Conjoining Blackstone's Tenth Rule with Article III qualifies the principle of legislative limitation itself, by partitioning constitutionally invalid laws into two categories. One group includes those instances in which judicial review is appropriate, because final authority for nonapplication of an unconstitutional law rests in the courts by virtue of the nature of the judicial function. The most obvious example is an act which operates "unconstitutionally" on a court's performance of its own duties.

In the other category, constitutional judicial review is inappropriate, because the performance of judicial duty in those instances is unaffected by the constitutional infirmity of the law.

So interpreted, *Marbury v. Madison* falls within the first category. If relevant constitutional provisions (part of the "law of the land") are implied in every act of valid legislation, as the "pursuance" provision of Article VI suggests,[122] then the following obtains: whenever a judge is asked to apply an act of legislation which clearly contradicts a relevant constitutional provision, and the act involves the court's exercise of its own functions (as in *Marbury*), then that act is *ipso facto* "impossible to be performed." This must be so because such an act contains two parts: (1) the act itself, and (2) the relevant constitutional provisions implied in the act. Since the performance of the act depends *entirely* upon the Court's decision whether to apply the act or not (a case of *purely* judiciary nature), the court cannot apply the act at all without falling into contradiction with itself.

The judicial function here refers merely to the application of existing law in deciding cases immediately before a court. Since the performance of this function is a *duty* of courts (not simply a right), any legislative act which impairs the ability of a court to perform the function properly must violate the separation of powers—one of the central doctrines of the American constitutional system. So long as it is truly independent, the judiciary has the final authority to apply or not apply a statute in such instances. On the other hand, when courts claim more than such narrow, self-protective authority, they jeopardize the system by which disputes are peacefully resolved, since no court has the physical power to reach outside its own domain to compel obedience when it refuses to apply an invalid law. That the Founders were acutely aware of this natural limitation on judiciaries will be shown in Chapter 4.

This categorization suggests an important facet of constitutional decision making. As it was understood by those who structured the American system in 1787 and by those judges, including Marshall, who gave the boundaries of the system more explicit definition, the process is better described as "departmental," "concurrent," or "coordinate" review than "judicial" review. The functional distinction between policy and legality, the origins of which have been attributed by George Haskins to the Marshall Court,[123] is really the heart of the separation concept embodied in the Constitution. It is this connection between Marshall and the Founders which refutes the prevalent charges of activism in the opinions of the Great Chief Justice—charges which Professor Wolfe has rightly termed "amazing."[124]

When the Framers undertook to place formal limitations on the legislative power, they left little room for doubt as to what they had done. First, they provided for executive review of policy by instituting the veto power.[125] Second, they provided for legislative review through the override capacity.[126] Third, they provided for limited judicial review in cases of a judiciary nature.[127]

This kind of coordinate review bears little resemblance to the famous Jeffersonian idea which sometimes carries a similar label.[128] His central point seems to be that all the agencies of national government possess a similar capacity to pass judgment on constitutional questions, no matter what the question involved. Jefferson wrote to Judge Roane in 1819 that each of the three branches of government "is truly independent of the others, and has an equal right to decide for itself what is the meaning of the Constitution in the cases submitted to its action."[129] This view seems at best a prescription for constitutional anarchy in government and at worst a formula for executive tyranny.[130] Carried to the limit, it would justify executive refusal to enforce specific court decisions or ministerial duties assigned by Congress. Such a failure of the president to execute faithfully the law would be constitutionally self-contradictory. That Jefferson was prepared to carry the doctrine so far is apparent from his remarks on the Sedition Act:

> nothing in the Constitution has given [the judges] a right to decide for the Executive, more than to the Executive to decide for them. Both magistracies are equally independent in the sphere of action assigned to them. The judges, believing the [Sedition] law constitutional, had a right to pass a sentence of fine and imprisonment; because the power was placed in their hands by the Constitution. But the Executive, believing the law to be unconstitutional, were [sic] bound to remit the execution of it; because that power has been confided to them [sic] by the Constitution.[131]

For purposes of this study, I will use the designation "arbitrary review" to identify the Jeffersonian variant of coordinate review. "Arbitrary" in this theory denotes that chance must inevitably determine the outcome of any contest over who has the power to give a final authoritative interpretation of the Constitution. In effect, "arbitrary coordinate review" amounts to a strict (perhaps absolute) separation of powers without principled functional limits.

The "Marshallian" variant will be designated "functional review."

Under this theory, the decision as to where power to make a final authoritative determination of constitutionality lies depends upon the type of case involved; and specifying the type of case in turn depends upon functional relations which stem from the system of balanced government established in the Constitution.

In view of the amount of ink that has been spilled over the question whether the Framers intended judicial or coordinate review—coordinate review having been defined generally as arbitrary review[132]—it is surprising to discover that there is little evidence of such a strict separation doctrine prior to the year 1800. As Professor Mendelson has pointed out, Jefferson himself at first subscribed to the theory of purely judicial review and evidently changed his mind in an attempt to justify executive refusal to enforce court decisions arising from application of the Alien and Sedition Acts.[133] Furthermore, examination of debate in Congress during the 1790s reveals that most prominent Republicans of that time supported an even broader doctrine of judicial review than did their Federalist counterparts.

Perhaps the strongest advocate of coordinate review during the period prior to the decision of *Marbury* was James Madison. Madison articulated the doctrine in his remarks in the First Congress on the president's power of removal. Many scholars mistakenly have equated Madison's view with that of Jefferson. Jefferson's statements on coordinate review were made largely to justify executive refusal to enforce particular judicial applications of congressional acts. As I have suggested, such a view approaches arbitrariness in its failure to account for functional distinctions inherent in the separation of powers, and it could place the president in conflict with the constitutional mandate to execute the laws faithfully.

Madison, on opposite ground, is arguing in support of the idea that the removal power is vested solely in the president, *by virtue of the executive functions implied in the constitutional division of authority.* Against the argument that the Senate should be joined with the executive in the removal authority, Madison says

> if the officer when once appointed, is not to depend upon the president for his official existence, but upon a distinct body (for where there are two negatives required either can prevent the removal), I confess I do not see how the president can take care that the laws be faithfully executed. . . . But what an aspect will this give to the executive? Instead of keeping the departments of government distinct, you make an executive out of one branch of the legislature;

you make the executive a two-headed monster . . . you destroy the great principle of responsibility, and perhaps have the creature divided in its will, defeating the very purposes for which an unity in the executive was instituted.[134]

Such words might well have been uttered by Marshall himself, who later asserted in *Marbury v. Madison* a strong defense of executive integrity—when it functions in its *political* capacity. Because Madison and Jefferson were on the same side politically in the *Marbury* dispute (and others as well) does not mean that they advanced the same constitutional doctrines. Throughout the entirety of Madison's contribution to the removal controversy, he displayed an impressive, sharp sense of the intricacies of functional differentiation in the separation of powers. Few have discovered a similar sensitivity in Jefferson, although his other accomplishments were substantial and numerous.

Later in the removal debate, Madison responded to the charge that the legislature had no right to interpret the Constitution:

I acknowledge, in the ordinary course of government, that the exposition of the laws and constitution devolves upon the judicial. But, I beg to know, upon what principle it can be contended, that any one department draws from the constitution greater powers than another, in marking out the limits of the powers of the several departments. The constitution is the charter of the people to the government; it specifies certain great powers as absolutely granted, and marks out the departments to exercise them. If the constitutional boundary of either be brought into question, I do not see that any one of these independent departments has more right than another to declare their sentiments on that point. . . . There is not one government on the face of the earth, so far as I recollect, there is not one in the United States, in which provision is made for a particular authority to determine the limits of the constitutional division of power between the branches of the government. In all systems there are points which must be adjusted by the departments themselves, to which no one of them is competent. If it cannot be determined in this way, there is no resource left but the will of the community, to be collected in some mode to be provided by the constitution, or one dictated by the necessity of the case.[135]

Professor Wolfe suggests that Madison's "mode to be provided by the constitution" is formal amendment and that the modes "dictated by the necessity of the case" may be elections, impeachments, or even revolutions.[136] Perhaps so; but I fail to see why, in context, "necessity of the case" might not refer merely to the three branches of government working out the functional differentiations inherent in the separation of powers. After all, it was Madison who just two years previously had recorded approvingly the Philadelphia Convention's restriction of the "arising under" jurisdiction of federal courts to cases "of a Judiciary nature." Also, in the passage just quoted, Madison only denies the power of the courts to issue final constitutional pronouncements in those cases which involve interpretations of the constitutional powers of coordinate agencies of government. Cases *not* of a judiciary nature that also arise under the Constitution are preeminently those that require determination of the constitutional authority of the legislative or executive branch. Thus appropriate cases must be those which do *not* require such a decision. Is it not likely, then, that the 1787 cases of a judiciary nature are exactly those 1789 cases in which, "in the ordinary course of government," the exposition of the "constitution devolves upon the judicial"? If so, then coordinate review is the appropriate reading of Article III.

In sum, by the time of the Philadelphia Convention, Americans had become familiar with a set of ideas involving the principle of legislative limitation and the nature of judicial power. When read into the American environment of the 1780s, these ideas led the Founders straight to a theory of constitutional review that is best described as functional coordinate review—the controlling doctrine of American constitutional law throughout much of the nineteenth century. John Marshall and his Court adhered conspicuously to the Framers' model.

The theory of judicial function, developed during the colonial and revolutionary periods and adopted at Philadelphia, was essentially the English theory of Blackstone's *Commentaries*, adapted to American conditions. It may be summarized as follows. The basic function of courts is to settle disputes between *individuals*. Courts accomplish this task by rendering *judgments*, which determine the respective rights and duties of parties to a particular dispute before the court. In rendering judgments, a court must rule in accordance with, or apply, *existing* statutory law, not create new law. If relevant statutory provisions are contradictory, then one or the other of those provisions is "impossible to be performed" and therefore must be disregarded in the decision of the case. Whenever statutory provisions are drafted "in pursuance" of delegated constitutional authority, and where that authority is restricted by explicit constitutional limitations, then an otherwise applicable statutory provision may be defective because (1) it clearly exceeds the boundaries of the delegated authority or (2) it explicitly contravenes the limitations. Since all laws in such a system are assumed to be drafted in pursuance of delegated legislative authority and within explicit constitutional limitations, if either (1) or (2) is true, then there must be an internal contradiction within the law that renders it "impossible to be performed" in the particular controversy before the court (i.e., it is "repugnant"). The courts, duty-bound to resolve disputes by rendering judgments, must then exercise discretion as to which pole of the law's contradiction to apply. Otherwise, they cannot decide the case and so have not performed their primary function.

Clearly, the modern idea of judicial review—conceived as a *general* power of courts to invalidate legislation or administrative regulations—cannot fairly be drawn from this early-American theory, for it only countenances a power to decide *particular* disputes. The only variant of judicial review that can be squared with the theory is that of a *derivative* discretion in courts to disregard specific enactments whenever they cannot be rendered consistent with constitutional provisions which they presuppose. The relevant statutory provision is then "impossible to be performed," in the Blackstonian sense, but the impossibility extends only to the particular circumstances of the litigation immediately before the Court—not to hypothetical circumstances which may give rise to similar cases in the future. Therefore, a law which a court refuses to apply in a particular instance nevertheless remains an enforceable statute, until another court sees fit to dispense with it in another particular case, and so on.

In this context, the meaning of the phrase "cases of a judiciary nature," and its relation to the theory of coordinate review, become even more clear. It is only in cases which involve constitutional provisions directly addressed to the courts that the Supreme Court's refusal to apply a relevant law is *necessarily* final. In cases involving constitutional provisions addressed to other branches of government (e.g., the Article I, Section 8 "necessary and proper" clause), the Court may surely refuse to apply the law, but it may *not* do so with finality in the strict sense. Even though the Court's decision may bind the parties in a particular case, Congress may nonetheless choose to disregard the Court's *constitutional* ruling and provide for executive enforcement of the statute. Congress may even go so far as to utilize its power to regulate the Court's appellate jurisdiction so as to discourage or prevent future appeals on the question of the law's constitutional validity. In such instances, it is the judgment of

Congress—not that of the Court—which will be final. On the other hand, if the case involves such a constitutional provision as that in the Sixth Amendment right to confront one's accusers in a federal criminal trial, then the Court's decision on the constitutional question *will* necessarily be final, since carrying on *any* federal criminal trial requires a court, and federal trial courts are bound by rulings of the Supreme Court.

The theory of constitutional review advanced in this study thus concerns not only what the *Court* is entitled to do in constitutional cases, but also what *other* branches of government are entitled to do in the face of judicial decisions regarded by them as incompatible with the Constitution; or, conversely, what the Court is entitled to do with finality. Finality is an essential aspect of all cases which are of a "purely judiciary" nature, for such cases are susceptible, *by their very nature*, to a final judicial determination. Clearly, if a specific decision could be overturned by another agency of government without recourse, then the case could not have been "judiciary" in that important respect. What is here meant is that susceptibility which obtains when a court is asked to apply a statute which involves the court's exercise of its own functions and which, at the same time, clearly contravenes an applicable constitutional provision. The act, which presupposes the relevant constitutional provision, is therefore "impossible to be performed," in the Blackstonian sense, because, in order to "perform" it, the court must disregard either the statutory or the constitutional provision—*both* of which are parts of the act in question. The point is, in such a situation, the outcome depends entirely upon the court's *discretion* as to which horn of the dilemma to uphold, for it cannot uphold both sides of a contradiction in the decision of a particular case. In the language of *Marbury v. Madison*, if "both the law and the constitution apply to a particular case, so that the court must either decide that case conformably to law, disregarding the constitution; or conformably to the constitution, disregarding the law: the courts must determine which of these conflicting rules governs the case. *This is of the very essence of judicial duty.*"[137]

# 2 · The Blackstonian Inheritance

In the present chapter, a historical basis for the American inheritance of the Blackstonian system will be articulated. I shall examine some important laws, institutions, and court decisions which legal historians have regarded as European precedents for or against various notions of judicial power in the United States. Much of this material was familiar to learned Americans of the Founding Era. My purpose is to show broadly the existence of, and familiarity with, traditions regarding the exercise of judicial power on the continent and in Great Britain prior to the publication of Blackstone's *Commentaries* in 1769. The compatibility of these traditions with the theory of judicial function outlined previously will be assessed by the subsequent commentary that appeared when judicial review emerged as an issue of major importance in the United States.

## Roman Antecedents

Although our main interest is in the development of judicial nonapplication of unconstitutional statutes in Anglo-American law, earlier instances of such nonapplication are found in the Roman law of "rescripts." Brinton Coxe, who wrote the first full-length book devoted entirely to the subject of judicial review, noted that rescripts were acts of imperial legislation which were often ambiguous as to their range of application.[1] It was a function of the jurisconsults to resolve such ambiguities in cases properly before them. According to Justinian, the judges were admonished to "permit no rescript, no pragmatic sanction, and no imperial annotation to be alleged before them, which seems to be adverse to general law or to public utility: but that they have no doubt that general imperial constitutions are to be observed in every way."[2]

The public-utility criterion is given an operational definition in another of Justinian's passages: "rescripts which are obtained from us *contra jus* (contrary to right) shall be rejected by all judges unless perchance there be something therein which injures not another and profits him who seeks it or gives pardons for crime to the suppliants."[3] In other words, if the judges discovered that a *specific* act of legislation by the emperor was in collision with a more *general* act—one held to embody a larger measure of public utility or private right—then they were to reject the specific act in favor of the "general constitution."

The exact nature of this discretionary power of judicial interpretation was apparently never quite clear to the Roman judges, and it was ultimately abandoned. H. F. Jolowicz remarks that

Justinian enacted definitely that imperial judgements given in the presence of the parties were to be valid as precedents for similar cases, and also confused the matter further by insisting on a general imperial power of interpretation. If this means anything, it would seem that rescripts too could be quoted as precedents, so that there is a return to the rule that they are valid as such provided they are not contrary to law, and the judge is left with the impossible task of deciding whether the emperor has merely interpreted the existing law, *or travelled beyond it.*[4]

Two additional aspects of Roman law are relevant here. The first involved the power of the Roman Senate to judge that challenged laws of the Roman Assembly were null, a power that more closely approaches the twentieth-century conception of judicial review. One of the earliest instances of a legal argument made before a judicial body asserting the unconstitutionality of legislation was that of Cicero, when he argued that an enactment by which he had been banished—even though subsequently abrogated—was nevertheless a nullity from the beginning, due to its alleged conflict with *jus legum* (the "law of laws").[5] Cicero cited as precedent a declaration of invalidity by the senate in 91 B.C. involving an act passed by the assembly dealing with three unrelated matters.[6] The senate voided the act because it collided with the *lex Caecilia Didia*, an earlier enactment (98 B.C.) which forbade provisions dealing with unrelated subjects to be included in the same bill.[7]

Since there were no written constitutions of the American type in the

Roman Republic, we must assume that when Cicero referred to *lex Caecilia Didia* as part of the law of laws, he meant one among several attempts of Roman legislatures to bind successors through promulgation of "constitutional" rules.[8] Most of these measures were probably unsuccessful, if "success" is defined in terms of each specific attempt producing subsequent acknowledged restrictions upon legislative power. However, Jolowicz remarks that "though it was sometimes argued by Romans themselves that an act of the people must necessarily be valid even if it was contrary to some previously enacted constitutional principle, because of the implied repeal, the general view seems to have been that the Assembly was not entirely free to enact absolutely whatever it liked."[9]

Jolowicz makes his observation not as a "precedent-seeker"[10] looking for a Roman foundation of judicial review, but as a devotee of John Austin, who claims elsewhere that since "there is no difference between fundamental constitutional laws and others, such limitations cannot strictly bind future assemblies."[11] Jolowicz then cites Austin as authority for the proposition that prohibitions against bills of attainder are not properly laws at all, because "their only force can be that of recommendations by a sovereign body of one moment to its successors as to principles which should guide them in legislation."[12]

The passage in Austin that Jolowicz refers to is one in which a successful Roman attempt to bind subsequent legislatures is denounced as contrary to logic.[13] The provision involved was evidently the most famous of Roman constitutional rules, that "no law may be passed against an individual" *(Privilegia ne Inroganto).*[14] Jolowicz concedes that this rule was broader than the later prohibitions against attainders, because it suggested a sweeping ban on legislation "used to penalise a particular individual who has not broken some general rule of that community."[15] It does not seem too far-fetched to conclude that, at least in certain periods, the *jus legum* was viewed by many Romans as a kind of unwritten (or semiwritten) constitution, that the senate was conceived as at least a quasi-judicial body capable of enforcing its provisions, and that the question of the compatibility of subsequent legislation with the law of laws therefore was a judicial one. Coxe confirms this proposition in a comparison of the Roman and American systems: "There are thinkers who believe that the best polities are those that have a legislature which is governed exclusively by its own will. Such a view is at variance both with the unwritten republican constitution of Rome and with the written republican constitutions of America."[16]

The final aspect of Roman law relevant to this inquiry concerns the law of mandate. Its importance rests not in its ancient applications—for they were evidently considered to involve matters of private right only—but rather in the claim of George Bowyer, in the midnineteenth century, that the right of American courts to declare legislative acts void can be traced to the Roman principle that the "limits of a mandate are to be diligently preserved; for he who has exceeded them is deemed to do something other than that in the mandate."[17] Bowyer's claim is contingent upon an extension of this principle, originally applied only to administrative officials, to the realm of public law and legislation. The authorities for this alleged extension are Vattel,[18] Puffendorf,[19] and Grotius,[20] all of whom were familiar to the Framers of the American Constitution.

Coxe argues that the following rhetorical assertion of Vattel, quoted by James M. Varnum in his argument before the Superior Court of Judicature of Rhode Island in the 1786 case of *Trevett v. Weeden*,[21] provides the link between the Roman law and some early American decisions rejecting statutes on constitutional grounds.[22] Speaking of those entrusted with legislative power, Vattel says that "the fundamental laws are excepted from their commission. . . . In short, these legislators derive their power from the constitution; how then can they change it, without destroying the foundation of their authority?"[23]

The full force of Coxe's point becomes clear when the foregoing quotation is set beside a passage taken from the opinion of the Superior Court of North Carolina in *Bayard v. Singleton*, decided in 1787 at the onset of the Philadelphia Convention. (Evidently *Bayard* is the first *reported* decision in which legislation was declared contrary to a *written* constitution.) Referring to members of the General Assembly, the court said that "no act that they could pass, could by any means repeal or alter the constitution, because if they could do this, they would at the same instant of time, destroy their own existence as a legislature, and dissolve the government thereby established."[24]

The remarkable similarity of the quotations cannot be overlooked, especially considering that the influence of Vattel's writings on early American political thinkers is well acknowledged;[25] that *Bayard v. Singleton* was reported in the Philadelphia press while the Federal Convention was in session;[26] and that Vattel had been directly quoted in the well-publicized case of *Trevett v. Weeden* the previous year.[27] Neither can we ignore their similarity to certain passages in Marshall's *Marbury* opinion—particularly those involving the relations between constitutions and ordinary legislation[28]—especially in view of Vattel's subsequent *qualification* of his doctrine.

This qualification is stated in the next paragraph of Vattel's great work and clearly foreshadows Marshall's "political questions" doctrine: "But in treating here of the change of the constitution, we treat only of the right: the question of expediency belongs to politics."[29] Interestingly, Coxe completely ignores this stipulation, for it is readily apparent that Vattel intended the two statements to be read together, much as Marshall did the analogous propositions in *Marbury*.

The failure of one so meticulous as Coxe[30] to notice such an obvious connection, in a work devoted to examining the historical antecedents of judicial power in its relation to unconstitutional legislation, raises an interesting aspect of the problem under scrutiny in this study. It suggests that the conception of judicial authority for which Coxe sought historical support was not the same as that entertained by Marshall and his colleagues. This may explain why Coxe, clearly the leading proponent of judicial review in the historic controversy over the role of the Court in the 1890s, was nevertheless no devotee of the Great Chief Justice.[31] Indeed, he could not have been, since the power claimed for the Court by Coxe and his followers was nothing less than that implied in Vattel's proposition, *stripped of its qualification*. The constrained judicial discretion exercised by the Marshall Court in its heyday must certainly have been viewed as a meager foundation for Coxe's theory.

## French, Italian, and English Antecedents

Coxe finds four other cases on the European continent in which judicial bodies determined that acts of legislation were in conflict with a previously acknowledged "binding rule of right."[32] Two of these cases occurred in France,[33] and two in seventeenth-century Italy.[34] The French cases involved invalidation by the parliament (or court) of Paris of legislative acts of the king that had attempted to dilute the power of regency.[35] These apparently helped to provoke so much controversy that the French placed in their first written constitution a provision explicitly denying courts the power to hold laws invalid for any reason whatsoever.[36] According to Article III, Chapter 5, of the French Constitution of September 3, 1791: "The tribunals cannot interfere with the exercise of the legislative power, nor suspend the execution of the laws, nor encroach upon administrative functions, nor cite any administrators to appear before them on account of their functions."[37]

The Italian cases involved application of the canon law by the Court of the Rota Romana. The first of these, decided in 1638, voided the legislative acts of two popes, functioning as temporal authorities, as they affected a third party since the acts were prejudicial to the party's vested contractual rights.[38] The second, decided ten years later, held an act of the Genoan legislature void because it was contrary to the liberty of the church.[39] The court used unequivocal language: "As contrary to ecclesiastical liberty it is null *ipso facto et jure* from defect of the power of the laymen enacting it."[40] In addition, the court cited twenty doctors of canon law in support of this declaration.[41]

These Italian decisions—rulings of an ecclesiastical court applying the canon law—are analogous in at least one respect to the modern constitutional law of federalism, insofar as they sought to regulate the operation of rules promulgated by two overlapping sovereignties upon the same set of individuals. Though in England the working of canon law evidently differed from its application on the Continent, three cases may be cited from the pre-Reformation period in which English statutes were held invalid because they collided with ecclesiastical law.

First, there is the famous condemnation of the so-called constitutions of Clarendon in 1166 by Becket, Archbishop of Canterbury, proceeding under the jurisdiction of the canon law.[42] Six years later, King Henry II effected Becket's declaration of invalidity in a public pronouncement.[43] In the second case, that of the Templars, the pope, acting in his judicial capacity, held English laws prohibiting trial by torture void to the extent that they were contrary to the canons permitting such practices.[44] Here, as in the previous case, the king (Edward II) enforced the ruling of the spiritual authority, disregarding the temporal statutes and, in this instance, Magna Carta as well.[45]

The third case is reported in the Year Book of 21 Henry VII. The Court of Common Pleas ruled that an act of Parliament was void because it purported to make the king parson of a particular church.[46] Such action contradicted a well-acknowledged principle of the canon law: No act of the secular authorities that touched upon spiritual matters could be valid without the pope's consent.[47] Whether such consent had been given was at times considered a judicial question, falling within the jurisdiction of the secular courts. That is shown by Chief Justice Frowick's opinion:

As to the other matter, whether the king can be parson by act of parliament; as I understand, it is not a great matter to argue: for I have never seen that any temporal man can be parson without the agreement of the Supreme Head. And in all those cases which have been put . . . I have seen to the matter; the king had them by the assent and agreement of the Supreme Head; and so a temporal act can not, without the assent of the Supreme Head, make the king parson.[48]

One other English case decided prior to the Reformation is worthy of mention. A certain provision of the statute of Carlisle, held subsequently by Lord Coke to have been a valid act of Parliament in its other aspects,[49] was declared void because it was "impossible to be performed."[50] It is apparently the first recorded instance of the courts of the common law asserting the principle that later appears in Blackstone's Tenth Rule for the construction of statutes: "acts of parliament which are impossible to be performed are of no validity; and if there arise out of them collaterally any absurd consequences, manifestly contradictory to common reason, they are, with regard to those collateral consequences, void."[51]

Blackstone's rule has been viewed historically as the controlling doctrine of English courts from the onset of parliamentary supremacy. However, the cases previously discussed suggest that there was no settled dogma prior to the Reformation. Since Blackstone was not concerned with written constitutions, the interesting question is how to properly apply the "impossible to be performed" portion of the rule in situations where courts do operate in the context of written instruments. The issue is particularly important since opponents of judicial review frequently appeal to Blackstone's authority.

The full force of Blackstone's doctrine concerning the supremacy of "ordinary legislation" when challenged by claims of unreasonableness was not realized until comparatively late in the development of English law (i.e., in the half-century prior to the Puritan Revolution).[52] Probably this had more to do with the lack of clarity throughout much of English history on the exact location of sovereign legislative power than with the existence of a countervailing theory in courts of the common law. However, some attention to the subject is advisable, in view of the tendency initiated in the late nineteenth century by a group of prominent American lawyers and legal writers to cite some early English cases (elaborating dicta of Lord Coke) in support of such a countervailing doctrine.[53]

Apparently the earliest citation of these cases as authority for the *modern* American conception of judicial power is found in the argument of former Associate Justice John A. Campbell before the Supreme Court in the *Slaughterhouse Cases.*[54] According to Benjamin Twiss, this was also the "first argument before a court in which laissez-faire was asserted to be part of the American constitutional law."[55]

The focal point seems to be the famous statement of Lord Coke in *Dr. Bonham's Case* that "in many cases, the common law will control acts of parliament, and sometimes adjudge them to be utterly void: for when an act of parliament is against common right and reason, or repugnant, or impossible to be performed, the common law will control it, and adjudge such to be void."[56] In support of this proposition, Coke refers to several earlier cases in which acts of parliament were allegedly held void for one or more of those reasons.[57]

The trouble with interpreting Coke's dictum as one which lays down a theory opposed to Blackstone's is twofold. First, the language itself does not clearly reveal any such opposition. Blackstone's rule gives two admissible grounds for considering an act of parliament to be either invalid or void, respectively: (1) impossibility of performance; (2) absurdity, which is manifestly contradictory to common reason. Coke's rule gives three such grounds: (1) impossibility of performance; (2) repugnancy; (3) being against common right and reason. Black defines "repugnancy" as an "inconsistency, opposition, or contrariety between two or more clauses *of the same* deed, contract, or statute, or between two or more material allegations *of the same* pleading, or any two writings."[58]

There is little reason to suppose that Coke's idea of "repugnancy" is very different from Blackstone's notion of "absurdity." That evidence to the contrary cannot be discovered in the precedents cited by Coke is made clear when one examines the cases.

In the first of them, it seems that no law was invalidated at all; rather, there is simply a declaration by Justice Herle "that some statutes are made against law and right; which, when those who made them perceiving, would not put them in execution."[59] Two others involved statutes adjudged void because they were alleged to have placed the king in the awkward position of performing services for his subjects, something Parliament could not be presumed to have intended.[60] A fourth case concerned a statute invalidated as "impossible to be performed."[61] In the final case on Coke's list, there were no opinions given, though a law apparently was invalidated.[62]

Similar observations may be made concerning well-known later cases where English jurists cited Coke's *Bonham* dicta approvingly. In *Day v. Savage*, for example, Chief Justice Hobart held "that an Act of Parliament made against natural equity, so as to make a man judge in his own cause, was void."[63] Hobart provided no explanation for this holding, but it was clarified later in an opinion rendered by Chief Justice Holt in the famous case of *The City of London v. Wood.*[64] Referring to Lord Coke's dictum, the chief justice said that "it is a very reasonable and true saying, that if an act of parliament should ordain that the same person should be party and judge, or which is the same thing, judge in his own cause, it would be a void act of parliament; for it is *impossible* that one should be judge and party."[65]

Chief Justice Holt probably meant little more than that Parliament could never be *presumed* by a court to have legislated an impossibility. But this is precisely the doctrine of Blackstone, who, as we have seen, uses the very same example in the paragraph that contains the Tenth Rule, repeated below.

> Thus if an act of parliament gives a man power to try all causes, that arise within his manor of Dale; yet if a cause should arise in which he himself is party, the act is construed not to extend to that; because it is unreasonable that any man should determine his own quarrel. But if we could conceive it possible for the parliament to enact, that he should try as well his own causes as those of other persons; there is no court that has power to defeat the intent of the legislature, when couched in such evident and express words, as leave no doubt whether it was the intent of the legislature or no.[66]

From the review of the opinions in *Dr. Bonham's Case*, the precedents cited therein, and the subsequent cases, it is apparent that none invalidates an unequivocal declaration by Parliament of the legislative will on the ground of unreasonableness. They are thus well within the confines of Blackstone's rule—and were in fact so regarded by Blackstone himself.[67] The matter is nicely summarized by Holdsworth. After mentioning Coke's assertion that some principles of the common law could not be overridden even by an act of Parliament, Holdsworth says that

> Coke, as usual, stated this principle in an exaggerated form. It was quite clear that no one really believed, not even Coke himself, that the principles of the common law could control an Act of Parliament; and it was clear that, if the authority of decided cases could

be disregarded whenever the judge thought that substantial incon-
venience could be caused by following them, very little authority
could be attached to them—a conclusion which was contrary both
to Coke's theory and to his practice. . . . Blackstone admits that the
judges have the power to disregard cases which are absurd or contrary to principle; Parke, B., makes a similar admission; and the
power has been used in modern times. The only question is the extent of this power.[68]

The only clear-cut case prior to the Glorious Revolution in which an
English court invalidated an outright declaration of parliamentary will
is *Godden v. Hales*,[69] but here the court's *ratio decidendi* was far from
anything resembling unreasonableness. Rather, it was the theory "that
the kings of England were absolute sovereigns; that the laws were the
king's laws; that the king had a power to dispense with any of the laws
of government as he saw necessity for it; that he was the sole judge of
that necessity; that no act of parliament could take away that power;
that this was such a law."[70] Two years after the decision in this case,
the theory was put to rest in England by the Revolution of 1688.

### Conclusions

The courts have always been regarded as a branch of the executive in English constitutional theory, but after the Glorious Revolution, even the
Crown itself "was obliged to conform to the common law touching the exercise of the prerogative. Only its purely executive action was unlimited."[71]
By implication, in cases of a purely judiciary nature, the courts had the last
word. In this way a quasi-formal separation between executive and judicial
functions was obtained, although it did not extend to Parliament.[72]

A note of caution is appropriate here, on a point which has been
overlooked by writers determined to find English precedents either for
or against the power of courts to strike down legislation as unconstitutional. Since the time when final appeals were determined to lie in the
House of Lords, the doctrine of parliamentary supremacy has been rooted
in the theory that an act of legislation is a *joint* act of Crown, lords, and
commons.[73] In other words, an act of Parliament is something more than
an act of ordinary legislation in the American sense; for the former
demands a coalescence of legislative, executive, and judicial forces *in
its very enactment*, whereas the latter does not.

The effect of this difference is that ordinary acts of Parliament may become "constitutions," provided they are enforced and applied over a long period of time and stand unrepealed. The situation is neatly described by Meigs.

> It is not unusual to hear or read English discussions as to whether or not such a measure is "constitutional." . . . It appears to mean merely whether the proposed Legislation is in consonance with the spirit of the English system. . . . Should the power contended to be unconstitutional be exercised, the English constitution has undergone a change, and there is no known governmental agency to stop the application and enforcement of the new law or "constitution."[74]

The Framers of the American Constitution were, of course, familiar with this aspect of the English system; they considered it gravely defective and made certain that the mistake was not repeated on this side of the Atlantic by introducing a stricter separation-of-powers concept.[75] Nevertheless, the exact nature of the problem that the Founders thought they were addressing has remained somewhat obscure. Hamilton provides a glimpse of it in a much-ignored passage of the *Federalist*. Arguing for an independent judiciary, Hamilton first points out that nine states already have such and then continues:

> It is not true, in the second place, that the parliament of Great Britain, or the legislatures of the particular states, can rectify the exceptionable decisions of their respective courts, in any other sense than might be done by a future legislature of the United States. The theory, neither of the British, nor the State constitutions, authorizes the revisal of a judicial sentence by a legislative act. Nor is there anything in the proposed Constitution, more than in either of them, by which it is forbidden. In the former, as well as in the latter, the impropriety of the thing, on the general principles of law and reason, is the sole obstacle. A legislature, without exceeding its province, cannot reverse a determination once made in a particular case; though it may prescribe a new rule for future cases.[76]

This passage is striking in view of the persistence with which so many scholars have attempted to give the modern, activist notion of judicial power a Hamiltonian basis.[77] Considering that the Convention appeared to assume that the courts would nullify federal statutes only in cases of a judiciary nature,[78] Hamilton's statement seems to indicate a conception of the judicial function rather more in line with Blackstone than with judges of later eras.[79] It also suggests that the problem with the English system, as perceived by the Founders, was not so much one of theory as of practice. Rather than institutionalizing a new *theory* of government on this side of the Atlantic, perhaps they sought merely to implement the English theory *in a more workable form.*

At any rate, two conclusions may be drawn from the foregoing section. First, the claims made by *proponents*[80] of sweeping judicial power (emergent in the late nineteenth and early twentieth centuries) that they have discovered antecedents in ancient Roman law, canon law, and common law, are without foundation. Second, the claims made by *critics*[81] of such power, that these ancient precedents are "precedents for nothing," are equally unfounded.

When read with the common-law doctrines of Coke and Blackstone, the natural-law doctrines of Grotius and Vattel, and the political doctrines of Locke and Montesquieu, the cases reviewed indicate a developing concern—even preoccupation—with the problem of encapsulating political power, arbitrary in its nature, within some "binding rule of right." This difficulty was inherited in unresolved form by Americans of the Founding Era, and it was they who made the most thorough attempt at its resolution. First, by instituting a stricter separation of powers and an independent judiciary, the Founders themselves extended the English separation principle (of legal control over executive acts in cases of a judiciary nature) to legislatures as well. Second, John Marshall and his Court, through a natural extension of Blackstone's Tenth Rule to an environment constrained by a written constitution, provided the necessary legal framework for implementation of the Founders' solution.

# 3 · The Emergence of an Early American Doctrine of Judicial Power

This chapter will examine American factors bearing upon the evolution of ideas about judicial power in the colonial, revolutionary, and Confederation periods. While the previous chapter discussed important *doctrinal* aspects of the problem, the main concern here involves *experiential* factors, most of which were distinctive to Americans. The legal framework inherited from across the Atlantic by the Founders and the Marshall Court could not have been applied successfully unless shared experiences made its institutionalization seem desirable.

## *The Colonial Period*

Even before the triumph of the doctrine of parliamentary supremacy in Great Britain, many American colonists had come to view their charters in much the same way as later Americans would view their written constitutions.[1] That is, they saw their charters as laws embodying both fundamental principles of government structure and protections for individuals against the arbitrary exercise of power. The foundation for such an attitude is easily traced to the framers of early governing instruments in the colonies, beginning with the New Hampshire Commission of 1679, which declared

> that it shall and may be lawfull from time to time to and for all and every person and persons, who shall think himself or themselves aggrieved by any sentence, judgment or decree pronounced, given or made (as aforesaid) in, about or concerning the title of any land, or other reall estate, or suit above the value of L50 and not under,

to appeal from said Judgement, Sentence, and Decree unto us, Our heirs and successors, and our and their Privie Councell.[2]

A similar provision, applicable to certain kinds of criminal cases, followed.[3]

These clauses were essentially duplicated in the New England Commission of 1686 and the Massachusetts Charter of 1691.[4] The New York Patent of 1664 and the Pennsylvania Charter of 1681 also contained similarly worded provisions regarding appeals, albeit without express reference to the Privy Council.[5] Blackstone asserted that decisions of all the courts in the charter colonies could be appealed to the king in council,[6] and Story inferred that such appeals were considered to be a matter of right in *all* the colonies, given the fundamental nature of the right to appeal in English constitutional law.[7]

That the right of appeal was well used in colonies without express charter provisions to that effect is clearly illustrated by Harold Hazletine's historical spadework in Rhode Island. According to Hazletine, official records revealed no fewer than twenty cases in which such appeals were allowed between 1706 and 1776.[8] Moreover, the Privy Council register recorded fifty-nine appeals from Rhode Island that were decided by the king in council between 1735 and 1776.[9] Notwithstanding the discrepancies in these two records (probably due to lax reporting by the colony), it is a plausible conclusion that the colonists of Rhode Island must have studiously pressed their grievances in court to the fullest extent possible.

Many of the colonial cases decided on appeal by the Privy Council no doubt involved matters of slight importance to the subject of this study; most seem to concern private disputes between aggrieved parties, resolvable on narrow technical grounds.[10] Four decisions, however, stand out because they are rooted in broader principles of individual right and government structure. Since it is the *interweaving* of these two themes that characterizes the political thought of the Founding period, the existence of such cases during the century prior to the framing of the American Constitution is historically significant.

The two most famous of these decisions involved the intestacy laws of Massachusetts and Connecticut, passed in 1692 and 1699, respectively.[11] Both acts contained provisions which divided the property of an intestate among his children, reserving a double portion for the eldest son.[12] In 1724, litigation commenced in Connecticut challenging the law, which was upheld by the superior court in the case of *Winthrop v. Lechmere* two years later.[13] The Privy Council overturned the superior court's decision in 1728, in an opinion that declared the law null and void for repugnancy to the laws of England.[14]

In the second case, the intestacy law of Massachusetts was challenged in 1733 on the very same ground as that in the Connecticut case.[15] However, in 1738, the Privy Council upheld the Massachusetts law by dismissing the appeal.[16] Hazletine accounts for the apparent inconsistency of these two decisions by reference to the Massachusetts charter provision requiring that colonial laws be approved or disapproved, *ab initio*, by the king in council.[17] The Connecticut charter, on the other hand, contained no such provision, so that when the Connecticut appeal came before the council, "they were left free to decide, untrammeled by any previous confirmation of the law in question."[18]

Whether or not this explanation is correct, these cases illustrate the willingness of colonials to question legislation believed in contravention of their basic rights as Englishmen under the protection of the common law. Furthermore, the cases suggest familiarity with the idea of looking, for protection of these rights, to a judicial tribunal completely separate from the lawmaking authority held responsible for their grievances. Thus, the colonists may have become acquainted during this period with a more stringent version of the separation principle than would have been conceivable for their counterparts in England.

In connection with *Winthrop v. Lechmere*, there is an interesting disagreement between Brinton Coxe and James Bradley Thayer during the 1890s, as to whether the decision of the Privy Council in the case was "purely judicial." Coxe apparently thought it was not; Thayer thought that it was.[19] Confirmation of the thesis in this study emerges from the irony of the Coxe-Thayer disagreement. Coxe, clearly a supporter of what I have been calling the modern notion of judicial power, thinks that *Winthrop* is no *real* precedent for judicial review, since the council's order was not purely judicial. On the other hand, Thayer, who is generally *not* regarded as a proponent of the modern view, considers the council's order purely judicial and therefore by implication precedential. Since both agree on the facts and decision, the dispute boils down to the *nature* of the power exercised in the case. Thayer's conception of the judicial function is a narrow one, in accord with the views of most legal writers in earlier times. Coxe, however, wants stronger weapons than *Winthrop* in his historical arsenal.[20]

The two remaining cases in this colonial group involved primarily jurisdictional issues. They are important because they reflect a deepening concern during the period with the problems of establishing controllable boundaries between political authorities and doing so on *purely functional* grounds. As such, they constitute major steps in the development of an idea—fulfilled later by the Founders and solidified in some early decisions of the United States Supreme Court—of the diffusion of power as the most effective safeguard for personal liberty and the most powerful stimulus to good government in the long run. In the words of Robert Ludlow Fowler,

> The framers of the Federal constitution detected the danger of confusing the legislative and the judicial powers of government and their complete separation was a fundamental doctrine of the convention. They not only were aware of the defect in the Constitution of England, but they had seen some confusion ensue in the colonies from vesting an appellate power in the royal governors and councils who comprised the upper legislative houses, at least in the royal governments of America.[21]

One might add to Fowler's statement the observation that upper houses were not the only legislative chambers performing judicial functions during the colonial period. According to Hazletine, the General Assembly of Rhode Island always "regarded itself a judicial tribunal as well as a legislative body, and during practically all of the colonial period exercised an appellate jurisdiction over colonial courts."[22] Evidently this was a matter of great consternation to many colonists and to the lords of trade and plantations as well, who commissioned an inquiry into the practice in 1699.[23] The resulting report contained a declaration that "the General Assembly assume a judicial power of hearing, trying and determining civil causes, removing them out of the ordinary courts of justice, and way of trial according to the course of the common law, alter and reverse verdicts and judgements, *the charter committing no judicial power or authority unto them.*"[24]

The emphasized portion of the declaration is striking indeed, because it acknowledges the idea that the exercise of judicial functions by a legislature constrained by a written instrument is unacceptable unless clear provisions in that instrument speak to the contrary. It also recalls Hamilton's famous statement of the Roman law of mandate in the *Federalist*: "There is no position which depends upon clearer principles than that every act of a delegated authority, contrary to the tenor of the commission under which it is exercised, is void. No legislative act, therefore, contrary to the Constitution can be valid."[25]

Be that as it may, the Rhode Island assembly paid little attention to the report, and in 1705, it decreed that "the General Assembly, at all times convened in general assembly, shall be a court of chancery, as formerly it hath been, until such time as a more proper court may be conveniently erected and settled."[26] This stunning language was too much for the Privy Council; in 1710, in the case of *Brenton v. Remington*, the Council declared a decision on appeal by the General Assembly null and void for want of jurisdiction.[27] After this, the assembly apparently concluded that it had no charter power to constitute itself a court of review, and in 1712, it established a court of chancery.[28] Regardless, according to Hazeltine, subsequent Rhode Island legislatures continued to exercise judicial functions.[29]

The final case to be mentioned concerns a decision of the Superior Court of Massachusetts in the case of *Frost v. Leighton*, rendered in 1739.[30] No colonial legislation was involved here, but the case is significant because the Court refused to issue an execution upon a judgment of the Privy Council, on the ground that it had not been authorized by the Massachusetts charter to issue execution upon the judgment of any court other than itself.[31] Louis Boudin, an early twentieth-century opponent of judicial review, calls the *Frost* precedent "worthless," evidently because the constitutional issue decided was somewhat narrow; he thus reveals an underlying conception of the judicial function remarkably similar to that of his archenemy Coxe.[32]

Boudin notwithstanding, the similarity of the *Frost* holding to that in *Marbury v. Madison* is readily apparent in the following excerpt from the *Frost* opinion:

> The court . . . are of opinion, that they have no authority by any Law of this province, or usage of this Court to order such an Execution. And the Provision made in the Royal Charter respecting appeals to his Majesty in Council, does not as they apprehend, warrant any such Execution but points to a method of another nature in all appeals to be made conformable to the said Charter. . . . By the Constitution of the Courts of Justice in this Province, the action must begin first at an Inferior Court, and so come to this Court by appeal, and the Justices of this Court, when such appeal comes regularly before them will unquestionably endeavor that Justice be done between the said Leighton and Frost.[33]

This case has been much used (and much abused) by twentieth-century analysts of the modern notion of judicial power. Haines, for example, cites the case as an important landmark in the development of the so-called American doctrine of judicial supremacy.[34] Boudin, as noted, declares that Haines's "precedent" is utterly "worthless."[35] Again, the alleged antecedents are seriously misunderstood—as in most of the recent arguments over this question which attempt to provide either side of the dispute with a historical foundation. The misconception of *Frost v. Leighton* is especially important, given the similarity to the distortions about *Marbury v. Madison* which resulted from the virulent attack on that "precedent" in 1895.[36]

Boudin correctly declares that *Frost* is no precedent for any judicial power to void legislative acts, since there was no such act involved.[37] It can therefore constitute no basis whatever for anything like *Pollock* or *Lochner*, as Haines seems to imply.[38] Nor is it sensible to regard the case (as many have also regarded *Marbury*) as a clever legal ploy invented for the purpose of circumventing an embarrassing situation.[39] The obvious observation is that *Frost*, like *Marbury*, is a straightforward example of a court, functioning upon the authority of a written instrument, construing the powers granted to it in that instrument restrictively, so as to safeguard its independence. It is in this sense, and this sense only, that *Frost* appropriately may be viewed as precedential.

## The Revolutionary Period

At the beginning of the revolutionary period, colonists had appealed to the English Privy Council for protection of real or imagined rights against acts of their own legislatures and had appealed to their own courts for protection against the Privy Council itself. Also, in the years immediately preceding the Revolution, colonial experience with the practical consequences of parliamentary absolutism had led more than a few writers to assert the theory that acts of a legislative body which are against constitutional provisions, "natural justice," or the common law are *ipso facto* void.[40]

During and immediately after the Revolution, six cases arose in state courts which, almost forgotten for a century, emerged in the 1880s and 1890s to produce an interminable fifty-year debate. These cases were cited by late nineteenth- and early twentieth-century proponents of judicial power as instances in which state laws were held unconstitutional by the courts.[41] Critics of judicial review again attempted to dismiss the cases as "precedents for nothing."[42] As before, the position of each side at best represents only half-truth.

The earliest of these cases is problematic, since no written opinion of the court (or even any of the justices) has ever been found. However, near the end of the last century, Austin Scott made a strong inferential argument that the Supreme Court of New Jersey in 1780 invalidated an act of that state's legislature that had authorized trial in certain cases by a jury of six.[43] If the case is authentic—although there is no way of knowing this with certainty—then some importance attaches to it. First, David Brearly was the chief justice of the High Court at that time, William Livingston was the governor, and William Paterson was the attorney general.[44] All three of these were delegates to the Philadelphia Convention and were sponsors of the "New Jersey Plan," from which the supremacy clause was ultimately derived.[45]

The now-famous case of *Commonwealth v. Caton*,[46] decided in 1782, is also questionable. It is the first official record of a case in which state legislation was invalidated by a state court. An act of the Virginia House of Delegates pardoned a man who stood convicted of treason. The court of appeals evidently voided the pardon on the ground that the senate had not concurred.[47] The problem with the case, as Boudin pointed out, is that it was not reported until some forty-five years after its decision.[48]

The third and fourth of these cases are absolutely authentic. *Rutgers v. Waddington*, decided in the Mayor's Court of New York in 1784, involved a complicated set of issues centering on how the treaty of peace and the law of nations affected a New York statute, the Trespass Act of 1783.[49] The statute authorized actions by owners against those who had occupied their houses under British orders.[50] The court did *not* hold the statute void; rather, it exempted the parties to the suit from its operation, upon a ground similar to that stated by Chief Justice Marshall a few years later: "An Act of Congress ought never to be construed to violate the law of nations if any other possible construction remains."[51] This rule of construction had long been familiar to English judges and had been applied to an act of Parliament by Lord Stowell.[52]

A brief review of subsequent commentary on this case reveals in a striking fashion the depth of misunderstanding to which judicial decisions of this period have been subjected. The fuss over *Rutgers v. Waddington* dates all the way back to the time of the decision itself, which "excited much ferment, and popular meetings were held to denounce it."[53] It is not clear from the sources whether the public hostility was due to a belief that the court had invalidated a law or was merely a function of more generalized hostility toward Loyalists in the aftermath of the Revolution. Common sense, informed by hindsight, surely counsels the latter view.

However, the confusion over interpretation is even more evident in the various commentaries on the case which emerged during the debates over judicial power in the Populist and Progressive periods. Meigs, for example, says that the court held the Trespass Act unconstitutional on the ground that the act was "against natural reason and justice."[54] Thayer, Fowler, and Elliott follow Meigs in this reading of the case.[55] On the other hand, Coxe (a supporter of judicial power) and later Boudin (an opponent of it) hold that the decision is a precedent *against* judicial authority to invalidate legislation, pointing to the New York court's readiness to adopt a forced construction of the statute so as to avoid striking it down.[56] Professor Crosskey, in a revealing comment on the decision, says that "it seems completely certain that *Rutgers v. Waddington* was well known to the men in the Federal Convention. But precisely because this is true, . . . they could not have relied upon the case as a precedent for judicial review as an ordinary incident of judicial power. For the Mayor's Court, in terms, had . . . disclaimed any right, either in itself or in courts generally, to disregard plain statutes."[57] Does Crosskey mean that "judicial review as an *ordinary* incident of judicial power" consists in the right of courts *generally* to disregard plain statutes? Even so, he and the other debaters have missed the point.

The problem originated in two separate though related ways. First, Alexander Hamilton, counsel for the defendant in *Rutgers*, argued that, among other things, the statute violated "natural justice."[58] Second, in answer to the argument of plaintiff's counsel that Congress had no authority to make a treaty of peace affecting the internal government of the state of New York, the court held that the Confederation gave such authority to Congress and that the exact operation of the treaty inside New York was a proper subject for judicial inquiry.[59]

Since Hamilton's client ultimately won the case and the court did (after a fashion) pronounce upon a "constitutional" question, some have thought that the decision must have been based on the argument for the defense.[60] That this could not have been so is obvious from Judge Duane's opinion. After pointing out that the state constitution had legalized the Confederation in 1777[61] and acknowledging Blackstonian legislative supremacy in cases where the intention of the legislature is manifest,[62] Duane adds that

when a law is expressed in general words, and some collateral matter, which happens to arise from those general words is unreasonable,
then the judges are in decency to conclude, that the consequences
were not foreseen by the legislature; and therefore they are at liberty
to expound the statute by equity, and only QUOAD HOC to
disregard it. When the judicial make these distinctions, they do not
control the legislature; they endeavour to give their intention its
proper effect.[63]

In other words, the court first ruled that the treaty of peace with Great
Britain must be deemed a part of the state constitution, because of the
state's explicit acknowledgement of the peace-making power of Congress.
Then the court applied Blackstone's Tenth Rule for the construction of
statutes to the case at hand, holding that unreasonable "collateral matter" arose from its general provisions.[64] The court buttressed its holding
of unreasonableness on two well-acknowledged principles. The first of
these, rooted in the Roman *Privilegia ne Inroganto,*[65] is the maxim "that
a statute ought to be construed, that no man who is innocent be punished
or endamaged."[66] The second is revealed in the court's opinion: "The
statute under our consideration does not contain even the common
NONOBSTANTE clause, though it is so frequent in our statute books—and
it is an established maxim that where two laws are seemingly repugnant, and there be no clause of NONOBSTANTE in the latter, they shall,
if possible, have such construction, that the latter may not repeal the
former by implication."[67]

Thus the claim of Meigs (and others) that *Rutgers* constitutes precedent for the power of a court to invalidate legislation on the ground of
unreasonableness is erroneous. On the other hand, the claim of Boudin
(and others) that the case is not a precedent for anything is equally unfounded. What the case is, is an early, and possibly the first, example
of an application of Blackstone's Tenth Rule to a situation constrained
by a written constitution.[68] As such, it is ancestral to *Marbury*, when
that case is interpreted according to the logic of this study.

The same may be said of *Trevett v. Weeden*, decided by the Superior
Court of Rhode Island in 1786.[69] In this situation, the General Assembly
had set up special courts for the trial of cases arising from the famous
"paper money" laws.[70] The act contained this language: "The said court,
when so convened, shall proceed to the trial of said offender; and they
are hereby authorized so to do, *without any jury*, by a majority of the
judges present, *according to the laws of the land.*"[71] The court decided

that it could not take cognizance of the case,[72] apparently on the ground that the idea of a trial without a jury by the laws of the land was a contradiction in terms.[73]

The decision was unanimous, and at least three of the five justices clearly viewed the act to be a serious threat to the independence of the courts. Judge Howell, after declaring himself "independent as a judge," held the law to be "repugnant and unconstitutional." Judge Devol concurred.[74] Judge Tillinghast pointed to the "striking repugnancy of the expressions of the act."[75] Later summoned before the assembly to explain the decision, Tillinghast said that he "felt himself perfectly independent while moving in the circle of his duty."[76] Howell explained that "the objectionable part of the act upon which the information was founded, and most clearly demonstrated by a variety of conclusive arguments, that it was unconstitutional, had not the force of a law and could not be executed."[77] He added, speaking of the court, that "for the reasons of their judgement *upon any question judicially before them*, they were accountable only to God and their own consciences."[78]

Much of the subsequent notoriety of *Trevett v. Weeden* has been due, not to the opinions of the judges, but rather to the celebrated argument for the defense made by Gen. James M. Varnum.[79] In language clearly foreshadowing that of Hamilton in the *Federalist* and Marshall in *Marbury*, Varnum plainly adapts Blackstone's rule for use under a written constitution.

> As the legislative is the supreme power in government, who is to judge whether they have violated the constitutional rights of the people? I answer, their supremacy (consisting in the power of making laws, agreeable to their appointment) is derived from the constitution, is subordinate to it, and therefore, whenever they attempt to enslave the people, and carry their attempts into execution, the people themselves will judge, as the only resort in the last stages of oppression. But when they proceed no farther than merely to enact what they may call laws, *and refer those to the judiciary Courts for determination*, then (in the discharge of the great trust reposed in them, and to prevent the horrors of civil war, as in the present case), the judges can, and we trust Your Honors will, decide upon them.[80]

Varnum's quotation is the clearest statement to its date of the doctrine of judicial power which had been slowly developing on the American continent for a hundred years and would remain in force for another hundred years. It is the doctrine of the Convention, set forth in Article III by the union of the "case-controversy" and "arising under" provisions.[81] It is the doctrine of the *Federalist*, which asserts the necessity for an independent judiciary as the most effective guardian of life, liberty, and property this side of the state of nature.[82] It is the doctrine of *Marbury v. Madison*, which attempted to drive a wedge between the domain of *law* (where "binding rules of right" are susceptible to final application by courts) and that of *politics* (where they are not).[83]

Since the theory of judicial function contained in Varnum's argument may be viewed as an appropriate extension of Blackstone's rule to the context of written constitutions that institute full separation of powers, it is merely the *English* theory adapted to American conditions. Alternatively, Varnum's doctrine may well be viewed as the *American* theory, read historically in the light of its authentic antecedents. It follows therefore that the great and longstanding debate between devotees of Blackstonian "legislative supremacy" on the one hand and American "judicial supremacy" on the other, is spurious.

The case of *Bayard v. Singleton*, decided in 1787 and reported in the Philadelphia press while the Convention was in session, involved a statute that required the courts to dismiss all cases concerning disputed property, if the defendant could show by affidavit that he bought the disputed property from a commissioner of forfeited estates.[84] The Superior Court of North Carolina refused to dismiss a particular suit, on the ground that to do so would deprive the plaintiff of his right to a jury trial, which was guaranteed by the state constitution.[85]

The court clearly based its ruling on Vattel's principle that no legislature could repeal a constitutional provision, unless the instrument itself granted express authority. It then pointed out, foreshadowing *Marbury*, that the judiciary was bound to take notice of constitutional provisions as much as any other laws.[86] The court confined its holding to the circumstances at hand: "Notwithstanding the act on which the present motion was grounded, the same act must of course, *in that instance,* stand as abrogated and without effect."[87]

The final case involving judicial declarations on the invalidity of a statute concerned the "Ten Pound Act," which was apparently voided by the Inferior Court of Common Pleas of Rockingham County, New Hampshire, in the early months of 1787.[88] Unfortunately, the precise grounds of decision in the case are unknown, since no opinion of the court was reported. However, the following notice did appear in several Philadelphia newspapers while the Convention was in session: "The

General Court during their late session repealed the ten pound act, and thereby justified the conduct of the Justices of the Inferior Court who had uniformly opposed it as unconstitutional and unjust."[89]

One may only surmise that the decision on the Ten Pound Act might well have rested on grounds similar to those discussed, since the act had provided for trial without jury in actions of debt and trespass where the sum demanded did not exceed ten pounds. In some cases, the act also forbade inferior courts of common pleas to entertain such actions except on appeal from lower courts.[90] The issues in this case, therefore, touched on the procedure and jurisdiction of the courts, which, in the atmosphere I have described, could easily have produced a decision based on grounds similar to those in *Trevett* or *Bayard*.

## Conclusions

Before closing this review of pre-Convention instances of judicial nonapplication of statutes, two observations are in order concerning the alleged antecedents of the Confederation period. First, the disoriented state of scholarship respecting the six cases discussed is apparent from a brief recital of the views of several major authors on how many of these cases they regard as precedents for judicial review. Haines, followed by Wright, claims that all six are precedential; Warren says five; Elliott, four; Meigs, followed by Thayer and Fowler, three; Coxe and Levy, two (though not the same two); Crosskey, one; Boudin, none.

When one considers that the work of this distinguished group represents much of the writing on the subject during the past hundred years, it seems obvious that the inquiry has been seriously misdirected. I believe that the misdirection itself is a function of the modern notion of judicial power. It is no coincidence that such precedent-seeking emerged only when the legal consensus established by the Founders and given institutional expression by Marshall and his Court began to break apart in the era of the Populists and Progressives. When the boundaries between law and politics, so carefully drawn by the early Court, finally succumbed to the confusion of the 1890s, efforts to establish new boundaries inevitably resulted. The failure of these efforts to establish legitimate antecedents thus receives a striking illustration.

Second, four of the six cases in the list involve the right to a trial by jury. Anyone who is interested in the antecedents of judicial power to disregard statutes would do well to notice that the lesson of these cases was not lost on the Founders. In the Constitution, the clause immediately following that which specifies the respective jurisdictions of the Supreme Court provides that "the trial of all Crimes, except in cases of Impeachment, shall be by Jury."[91]

When viewed with Nelson's recent study of the eighteenth-century roots of American constitutional jurisprudence, the significance of the cases becomes perfectly clear. Nelson's thorough survey of the "pervasive and undifferentiated role"[92] of American courts during the colonial period strongly suggests that the jury may well have been regarded then as the true center of gravity in American political life: the institutional locus of a shared system of values which contained, at its heart, incipient notions of individualism and democracy. The history of the American concepts of judicial function is largely the history of a long-standing effort to resolve the inescapable tension between these two ideas.

It is beyond the scope of the present study to unravel the content of this value system and place it in an appropriate historical context. However, if courts and juries during the eighteenth century did provide a unified institutional embodiment of the inevitable conflict between two great ideals, then we may track an unbroken line of development of ideas on the judicial function—which commences in colonial America, proceeds through the "antecedents of judicial power" in the Confederation period, and is brought to fulfillment in the Article III separation concept of the Federal Convention.

The importance of the developing notion of separation of governmental powers according to function—and its close relation to the idea of judicial independence—is crucial to an understanding of the judicial review cases of the Confederation period. Both notions were soon institutionalized in the Federal Convention and enforced by the early Supreme Court, and these cases clearly reveal the two concepts as siblings. All the cases touch on separation questions at some point, and all those in which opinions are reported contain declarations of independence by the judges. The chief object of concern seems to be the problem of delineating authoritative boundaries which will differentiate departments according to function. When the cases are viewed in the perspective provided by the next chapter, it will be fully apparent that the theory of judicial function proposed by the Founders and later expounded by Marshall and his Court was quite well-developed by the 1780s.[93]

# 4 · The Federal Convention

By 1787, at the onset of the Federal Convention in Philadelphia, the idea of limiting legislative power by judicial nonapplication of statutes in certain cases was clearly understood. Such limitation had been accomplished in America by courts operating under both written and unwritten "constitutions" in the colonial and revolutionary periods. These were not merely isolated occurrences, but may be viewed as normal extensions of English rules and practices, applied in the American context.

The relevant features in this American context are: (1) widespread acceptance of Locke's liberal dogma, whereby government exists for the sake of individual well-being, and the resultant perception that it is necessary to institute special protection for individual rights against arbitrary assertions of political power, whether legislative or executive; (2) the peculiar experience of colonists with the institution of courts as *governing* agencies and the prevalent image of courts as *democratic* institutions, due largely to the extensive power of colonial juries; (3) the occurrence of legislative attempts to interfere with the operations of juries (and thereby of courts), leading to widespread support for sharp and formal differentiation of legislative and judicial functions. Reinforcing the third feature is the experience of colonials with the fusion of executive and judicial functions in the English Privy Council, which had seemed an *inadequate* check upon the excesses of both colonial legislatures and Parliament.

The effort to differentiate governmental functions is first apparent in the separation provisions of state constitutions of the Confederation period. The example of Massachusetts attests to the intensity of feeling surrounding these provisions. That state's constitution of 1780 contains remarkable language in its section on the legislative department, which "shall never exercise the executive and judicial powers, or either of them; the executive shall never exercise the legislative and judicial powers or either of them; the judicial shall never exercise the legislative and executive powers or either of them; to the end, it may be a government of laws, and not of men."[1]

James Bradley Thayer, in the late nineteenth century, marvelled at the "curious explicitness" of this provision,[2] but it should come as no great surprise to anyone who has paid close attention to the developments considered previously. The Massachusetts separation provision may be regarded as symbolic of a general attitude toward law, politics, and government prevailing in the 1780s. This attitude, which constitutes an important backdrop for the work of the Federal Convention, helps to explain why the Convention's first plan for limiting potentially arbitrary exertions of national legislative power was ultimately rejected. Called a Council of Revision, the entity was to be composed of executive and judicial authorities.

*The Council Proposal*

The original proposal was part of the Virginia Plan, introduced by Edmund Randolph on May 29.

> Resolved, that the Executive and a convenient number of the National Judiciary, ought to compose a Council of revision with authority to examine every act of the National Legislature before it shall operate, and every act of a particular Legislature before a Negative thereon shall be final; and that the dissent of the said Council shall amount to a rejection, unless the Act of the National Legislature be again passed, or that of a particular Legislature be again negatived by _____ of the members of each branch.[3]

During the Progressive Era conflict over the role of courts, opponents of judicial power claimed that the Convention's repeated rejection of the council proposal proves that the Founders did not intend to establish judicial review of legislative acts.[4] But it seems more reasonable to conclude that the Framers wished only to differentiate clearly the executive function from that of the judicial. The former would be granted the broad, sweeping supervisory power embodied in the executive veto, while the latter would be allotted a more limited (but nonetheless crucial) authority to disregard enactments only when, in cases properly before them, they were thought to encroach upon either judicial functions or individual rights protected by explicit constitutional provisions.

This is perhaps the best explanation of Elbridge Gerry's oft-quoted remark about the state cases of the Confederation period. Opposing the involvement of the judiciary in the proposed Council of Revision, Gerry doubts whether

> the Judiciary ought to form a part of it, as they will have a sufficient check against encroachments on their own department by their exposition of the laws, which involved a power of deciding on their Constitutionality. In some states the judges had actually set aside laws as being against the Constitution. This was done too with general approbation. It was quite foreign from the nature of the office to make them judges of the policy of public measures.[5]

Rufus King then seconded Gerry, observing that "the Judges ought to be able to expound the law as it should come before them, free from the bias of having participated in its formation."[6]

The foregoing remarks occurred during the first of three debates over the council proposal and were followed by an affirmative vote of eight states to two on Gerry's motion to drop the judicial element from the proposed revisionary authority.[7] Immediately after the vote, Edmund Randolph's resolution for the institution of a separate national judiciary was unanimously adopted.[8]

This resolution read as follows:

> Resolved, that a National Judiciary be established to consist of one or more supreme tribunals, and of inferior tribunals to be chosen by the National Legislature, to hold their offices during good behavior; and to receive punctually at stated times fixed compensation for their services, in which no increase or diminution shall be made so as to affect the persons actually in office at the time of such increase or diminution; that the jurisdiction of inferior tribunals shall be to hear and determine in the first instance, and of the supreme tribunal to hear and determine in the dernier resort, all piracies and felonies on the high seas, captures from an enemy, cases in which foreigners or citizens of other states applying to such jurisdictions may be interested, or which respect the collection of the National revenue; impeachments of any National officers, and questions which may involve the national peace and harmony.[9]

Clearly, the prevailing attitude of the Founders, from an early point in the Convention, was decidedly unfavorable toward the blending of judicial functions with those of other departments.

Two days later, Wilson, seconded by Madison, moved to reconsider the defeated council proposal. Pinckney opposed the "introduction of the Judges into the business," and Dickinson thought that the "junction of the judiciary to it, involved an improper mixture of powers." Again, the Convention rejected the proposal, this time by a vote of eight states to three.[10]

The third debate over this question occurred on July 21 and was evidently the critical one, for it is here that the underlying assumptions of both sides in the argument are made fully apparent. As before, Wilson, seconded by Madison, moved "that the Supreme National Judiciary should be associated with the Executive in the Revisionary power." After some remarks concerning previous failures of the proposition, Wilson noted that "it had been said that the Judges, as expositors of the Laws would have an opportunity of defending their constitutional rights. There was weight in this observation; but this power of the Judges did not go far enough. Laws may be unjust, may be unwise, may be dangerous, may be destructive; *and yet may not be so unconstitutional as to justify the Judges in refusing to give them effect.*"[11]

In response to Wilson's point, Gorham remarked that "as Judges they are not to be presumed to possess any particular knowledge of the mere policy of public measures. Nor can it be necessary as a security for their *constitutional* rights."[12] Ellsworth then spoke in support of the motion, because it would impart "wisdom and firmness" to the executive. Madison asserted that it would be useful as a check on "unwise and unjust measures" and that "experience in all the States had evinced a powerful tendency in the Legislature to absorb all power into its vortex. This was the real source of danger to the American Constitutions; and suggested the necessity of giving every defensive authority to the other departments that was consistent with republican principles."[13]

Gerry, however, seemed to think the idea was inconsistent with "republican principles" and stated that "it was combining and mixing together the Legislative and the other departments. It was establishing an improper coalition between the Executive and Judiciary departments. It was making Statesmen of the Judges. . . . *It was making the Expositors of the Laws the Legislators, which ought never to be done.*"[14] Gouverneur Morris supported the motion, suggesting that the idea for the Council of Revision may have come from the historic fusion of executive and judicial functions in the English Privy Council and concurring in Madison's fear that public liberty was "in greater danger from Legislative usurpation than from any other source."[15]

Luther Martin then spoke against the motion, in language as relevant today as it was then.

> A knowledge of Mankind, and of Legislative affairs cannot be presumed to belong in a higher degree to the Judges than to the Legislature. And as to the Constitutionality of laws, that point will come before the Judges in their proper official character. *In this character they will have a negative on the laws.* Join them with the Executive in the Revision and they will have a double negative. *It is necessary that the Supreme Judiciary should have the confidence of the people.* This will soon be lost, if they are employed in the task of remonstrating against popular measures of the Legislature.[16]

After some similar arguments were made by Madison, Wilson, Gerry, and Gorham, a vote was taken and the motion again failed, though only by four votes to three, with two states divided.[17]

Obviously, the Founders were deeply aware of the crucial distinction between policy questions and constitutional questions. Within the constitutional domain, they were sensitive to the distinction between clearly and arguably unconstitutional laws. In addition, the Convention exhibited near-unanimous agreement on the necessity for placing external limitations on the power of Congress. Although it was invited to accept a quasi-policymaking role for the national judiciary, the Convention rejected the role in favor of a qualified executive veto to be combined with a judicial negative, the precise content of which was subsequently clarified during debate on the "arising under" provision of Article III, "it being generally supposed that the jurisdiction given was constructively limited to cases of a Judiciary nature."[18]

### The Judicial Function

At least one additional feature of American experience in the Confederation period is relevant to a complete understanding of the Convention's point of view respecting the role of courts: the efforts of state judiciaries to enforce the treaty of peace between the United States and Great Britain. The treaty was involved, either directly or indirectly, in two of the cases discussed in the previous chapter,[19] and it was a thorn in the side of the Confederation almost from the beginning.[20]

On March 21, 1787, the Continental Congress unanimously adopted a resolution which illustrates its understanding of the distinction between policy and constitutional questions and presages the "pursuance" provision of Article VI in the Constitution.

> Resolved, that the legislatures of the several states *cannot of right* pass any act or acts, for interpreting, explaining, or construing a national treaty or any part or clause of it; nor for restraining, limiting or in any manner impeding, retarding, or counteracting the operation and execution of the same, *for that on being constitutionally made*, ratified and published, they become in virtue of the confederation, part of the law of the land, and are not only independent of the will and power of such legislatures, but also binding and obligatory upon them.[21]

Less than a month later, the same Congress recommended (again, unanimously) that the separate states draft enactments of the following form:

> Be it enacted by _____ and it is hereby enacted by the authority of the same, that such of the acts or parts of acts of the legislature of this state, as are repugnant to the treaty of peace between the United States and his Britannic Majesty, or any article thereof, shall be, and are hereby repealed. And further, that the courts of law and equity within this state be, and they hereby are directed and required in all causes and questions cognizable by them respectively, and arising from or touching the said treaty, to decide and adjudge according to the tenor, true intent and meaning of the same, anything in the said acts, or parts of acts, to the contrary thereof in any wise notwithstanding.[22]

Several remarks are in order concerning these passages. The statement in the first resolution about the relationship between treaties and the "law of the land" was merely an application of Blackstone's doctrine concerning the law of nations—which had already been applied by the Mayor's Court of New York in *Rutgers v. Waddington*, as we have seen.[23] The rule is stated in Blackstone's *Commentaries:* "In arbitrary states this law (i.e., the law of nations), whenever it contradicts or is not provided for by the municipal law of the country, is enforced by the royal power: but since in England no royal power can introduce a new law, or suspend the execution of the old, therefore the law of nations (whenever any question arises which is properly the object of its jurisdiction) is here adopted in its full extent by the common law and is held to be a part of the law of the land."[24]

In other words, where no *political* power exists to suspend the execution of a law that conflicts with the law of nations (or a treaty), then the question of suspension or execution becomes a *judicial* one, to be resolved by the courts in cases otherwise properly before them. This is simply a particular form of the more general principle that defines an essential function of courts: Judicial power is conditioned upon the need to resolve difficulties which are not susceptible to resolution through the regular political process, whatever the particular institutional embodiments of that process may be.[25]

The pursuance provision of the resolution marks a sharp boundary between laws that are binding because of an exercise of arbitrary power by the legislature and laws that are binding "of right" because "constitutionally made." The exact nature of the former kind of "law" is clarified by Congress's use of the term "repugnant" in its subsequent recommendation to the states. As noted before, repugnancy was the usual justification invoked by English courts when refusing to apply statutes in accordance with Blackstone's Tenth Rule, and the relevant portion of the rule operates only on statutes that are held to be *internally* defective. *External* collision with a previously enacted law is normally resolved in accordance with the maxim *lex posterior derogat legi priori.*[26]

The members of the Continental Congress cannot have been unfamiliar with this background, or with Blackstone, or with the fact that each of the decisions in the state cases reviewed previously fall within the confines of Blackstone's Tenth Rule (and no cases to the contrary are apparent). It is therefore reasonable to conclude that the authors of the resolution of March 21 and the recommendation of April 13 must have viewed the idea of unconstitutionality as describing an internal contradiction within a law, not an external collision with another. I suggest that it was precisely this aspect of the situation that made the question of constitutionality seem properly a judicial one to Americans of the Founding period.

The final observation concerns the obvious relationship between the earlier Confederation congressional provisions and the Seventh Resolution submitted to the Committee of Detail on June 20 in the Philadelphia Convention. The resolution read:

> Resolved, that the legislative acts of the United States, made by virtue and in pursuance of the articles of union, and all treaties made and ratified under the authority of the United States, shall be the supreme law of the respective states, as far as those acts or treaties shall relate to the said states, or their citizens and inhabitants; and that the judiciaries of the several states shall be bound thereby in their decisions, anything in the respective laws of the individual states to the contrary, notwithstanding.[27]

This early form of the supremacy clause is clearly a collation of the congressional recommendation to the states and the earlier congressional resolution, the only difference being the Convention's elevation of national laws "made in pursuance of the articles of union" to a status commensurate with that of treaties. The final version, of course, is found in Article VI, where it is provided that "this Constitution, and the Laws of the United States which shall be made in Pursuance thereof; and all Treaties made, or which shall be made, under the Authority of the United States, shall be the supreme Law of the Land; and the Judges in every State shall be bound thereby, any Thing in the Constitution or Laws of any State to the Contrary notwithstanding."[28]

When considered in the context of the Blackstonian doctrines already discussed, this sequence of events, beginning with the resolution of March 21 and ending with Article VI, also helps to explain the Convention's rejection of yet another proposal. In its action, the Convention decided against vesting a power of negative over state laws in the national legislature, reserving that authority to the state (and lower federal) courts instead.

The original proposal read:

> Resolved, that each branch ought to possess the right of originating Acts; that the National Legislative ought to be empowered to enjoy the Legislative Rights vested in Congress by the Confederation and moreover to legislate in all cases to which the separate States are incompetent, or in which the harmony of the United States may be interrupted by the exercise of individual legislation; to negative all laws passed by the several States, contravening in the opinion of the National Legislature the Articles of Union; and to call forth

the force of the Union against any member of the Union failing to fulfill its duty under the articles thereof.[29]

Though it is easy to find political explanations for the Convention's rejection of this proposal, it is likely that functional considerations were also important. A decision concerning the compatibility of a state law with the Constitution involves statutory construction and the *non-obstante* (notwithstanding) provision of Article VI ensures that all valid state laws embody applicable federal constitutional guidelines. Strictly speaking, although a state law incompatible with the Constitution may be *enacted*, it cannot be applied, because such a law is a contradiction in terms. The strongest justification for refusing to apply such a law flows from its lack of internal consistency, and a decision about the internal consistency of a law is most properly rendered by a court. According to the logic of the English precedents, the colonial precedents, the state precedents, the resolutions and recommendations of the Continental Congress, and the supremacy article of the Federal Constitution (along with its antecedents), such a judgment is preeminently *judicial, not political*.

Black defines *non-obstante* to be "words anciently used in public and private instruments, intended to preclude, in advance, an *interpretation* contrary to certain declared objects or purposes."[30] Here it is "interpretations" that are "precluded, in advance" by the notwithstanding clause, *not* a law itself. That the English usage confined the operation of such provisions to particular cases is also indicated by Black: "A clause frequently in old English statutes and letters patent (so termed from its initial words), importing a license from the crown to do a thing which otherwise a person would be restrained by act of parliament from doing. A power in the crown to dispense with the laws in any *particular* case. This was abolished by the Bill of Rights at the Revolution."[31] As we have noted, although the royal power of dispensation was abolished in England after the Revolution, common-law courts nonetheless continued to refuse application of statutes in particular cases where such statutes were thought to be "absurd, repugnant, or impossible to be performed" (see Chapter 2). The practice was replicated by courts on this side of the Atlantic and was further reinforced by written constitutions and statutes containing *non-obstante* provisions (see Chapter 3).

To the legal theorists of the Founding Era, "constitutional adjudication" may be viewed as a special case of *statutory construction*, since it is merely the "performance" of statutes—which presuppose relevant constitutional provisions—that is in question, so long as the judicial power is limited to the disposition of *particular* cases or controversies. Otherwise, the judicial function is either *revisionary* in scope or unable to take account of any constitutional provisions whatsoever in the decision of cases—alternatives which were rejected by the Federal Convention, and later by the Marshall Court.

Similar reasoning applies to the "pursuance" provision of Article VI, whose main thrust seems clear.[32] The "Supreme Law of the Land" is embodied in the constitutions and laws of the respective states by virtue of the notwithstanding provision. At the same time, relevant federal constitutional provisions are embodied in acts of Congress by virtue of the pursuance provision.

The Founders must have intended originally that the state courts could also determine the constitutionality of national laws, since such a determination would have been necessary prior to any ruling on the internal consistency of state laws. Finally, the ultimate appeal to the United States Supreme Court provided in Article III clearly necessitates a secondary determination as to whether a particular federal law has been passed pursuant to the Constitution: "The Judicial Power shall extend to all Cases, in Law and Equity, arising under the Constitution, the Laws of the United States, and Treaties made, or which shall be made, under their Authority."[33] That the pursuance provision is left out of Article III probably indicates a desire on the part of the Framers to extend the judicial power to federal laws generally, whether constitutional or not.

These considerations clarify the rationale underlying the Convention's constructive narrowing of cases "arising under the Constitution" to those "of a Judiciary nature." There could have been little need to make *explicit* provision for such a restriction if it was well understood at the time that *all* questions involving such pursuance provisions were judicial, provided that they arose in cases or controversies otherwise properly before a court (whether state or federal) and were susceptible to a final judicial determination.

Any attempt to determine the sense of the Convention on the role of courts and the exercise of judicial functions must consider Articles III and VI together. The long-standing quest for grounds to distinguish between judicial nonapplication of *state* laws on the one hand, and *national* ones on the other, is simply misguided.[34] The development of the constitutional provisions bearing on these issues reflects their inseparability, since the original explicit ground provided to the Supreme Court for refusing to apply an act of Congress arises from a similar authority in the state courts—an authority which in turn rests upon the *necessity* for the state courts to disregard state enactments which contravene the "Supreme Law of the Land."

This interpretation is further confirmed by the language of Section 25 of the Judiciary Act of 1789, passed by the First Congress under the new Constitution.[35] The section explicitly provides that, when any decision of the highest court of a state that invalidates a federal law or treaty or that challenges a state law as contravening the "Supreme Law of the Land" is upheld, it "may be reexamined and *reversed or affirmed* in the Supreme Court of the United States upon a writ of error."[36] Surely, if doubts existed as to the sense of the Convention on the question of judicial power to invalidate laws, they were put to rest here. According to Benjamin F. Wright,

> This provision would seem to be clear evidence that the members of the first Congress assumed that both state and federal courts would exercise the power to review statutes on the grounds of constitutionality. That Congress contained many members who had served, two years before in the Federal Convention, among them four of the seven members of the Senate Judiciary Committee which drafted the bill. Neither among the former advocates of ratification nor among the Anti-Federalists who were present in the Congress of 1789 was there any openly expressed opposition to the assumption that the power of judicial review was a proper function of the courts.[37]

### The Ratification Struggle

Commentary on the judicial power during the ratification struggle in the states likewise substantiates the reading of the Constitution given above. As with the state cases examined in the previous chapter, there is evident confusion over the import of many of these remarks; as before, the difficulties are traceable to misunderstandings about the doctrine of judicial function which emerged in mature form from the Federal Convention, after at least a century of gestation.

This judicial function, as we have seen, was nonrevisionary in scope. It involved only the discretionary authority to disregard statutes in *par-*

*ticular* cases otherwise properly before a court, *not* a general authority to repeal laws either whole or in part. It approximated a power of repeal only *incidentally*, in cases of a judiciary nature—i.e., where the practical effect of disregarding a statutory provision might lead to a *de facto* (not *de jure*) repeal of the law through application of the doctrine of *stare decisis* in subsequent cases. The act in question had to involve the performance of judicial functions only and was not thereby susceptible of reversal by any other agency of government.

This doctrine was to constitute the general understanding of the role of American courts until after the Civil War, when the modern, more activist, notion of judicial function began to emerge. Attempts by modern legal historians to understand the ratification debates (insofar as they relate to the concept of judicial power) in terms of the modern idea has generated confusion. For example, it has become a commonplace, in the present century, to say that the ratification debates are "inconclusive."[38] They are inconclusive, indeed, if one assumes the modern, activist, supervisory function of courts and then searches for evidence of such authority in ratification-period commentary on the judicial branch. But if this assumption is not accepted, then conclusions are possible.

One of the more interesting aspects of the ratification controversy may be found in remarks made in various state conventions by opponents of the Constitution concerning the judicial power. Almost without exception, these men opposed the instrument because it was defective in providing for adequate control of Congress by state and federal courts. Patrick Henry's remarks in the Virginia convention comparing the state judiciaries with the proposed federal judiciary afford a good illustration. Referring to the Virginia Court of Appeals, Henry declares:

> The honorable gentlemen did our judiciary honor in saying that they had firmness enough to counteract the legislature in some cases. Yes, sir, our judges opposed the acts of the legislature. We have this landmark to guide us. They had fortitude to declare that they were the judiciary and would oppose unconstitutional acts. Are you sure that your federal judiciary will act thus? Is that judiciary so well constituted and independent of the other branches as our state judiciary? Where are your landmarks in this government? It will be bold to say you cannot find any.[39]

Warren goes so far as to claim that "there was no challenge, in any Convention, of the existence of the power of the Court with reference to Acts of Congress."[40] Though Haines says that Gerry, Randolph, and Mason, who refused to sign the Constitution, objected to the judiciary articles because of their "indefinite language,"[41] Wright suggests that such objections had nothing to do with judicial review and were instead based on a fear that the national judiciary would "swallow up the state courts" by assuming jurisdiction in private law cases.[42] Gerry's comments on judicial power in the Federal Convention tend to confirm Wright's observation, as do his later remarks in Congress concerning the president's power of removal: "The judges are expositors of the Constitution and the acts of Congress. Our exposition, therefore, would be subject to their revisal. The Judiciary may disagree with us and undo what all our efforts have labored to accomplish. A law is a nullity unless it can be carried into execution: in this case our law will be suspended."[43] Mason and Randolph objected to the proposed Constitution primarily because it lacked a bill of rights which would be enforceable against Congress, presumably by the courts.[44]

Henry, the leader of Antifederalist forces in Virginia, further illustrates the point. Obviously distrustful of what he thought was excessive centralization of power in the proposed national government, the great orator held it to be "the highest encomium of this country, that the acts of the legislature, if unconstitutional, are liable to be opposed by the judiciary."[45] The context of this remark makes it clear that Henry was referring to the authority of state courts to disregard legislative acts. He goes on to express doubts as to whether federal courts, under the proposed constitution, would render similar protection for individual rights against national legislation, *except in cases involving jurisdictional issues.*[46] In other words, Henry clearly understood the sense of the "Federalist" Convention on the question of judicial power and opposed it, *not* because it conferred upon the Supreme Court broad, supervisory authority over acts of Congress, *but because it did not.*

Similar misgivings were expressed by Antifederalists in other state conventions. Without exception, their fears focused on three concerns: (1) the absence of a bill of rights against Congress in the proposed Constitution; (2) the anticipation that federal courts would dispense with the right of trial by jury in civil suits; and (3) the belief that since the powers of Congress were essentially unlimited, its authority to regulate the appellate jurisdiction of the federal courts would prevent the national judiciary from providing an adequate check on Congress. Nowhere is there opposition in principle to the idea of judicial authority to disregard statutes in particular cases.[47]

Outside the conventions, perhaps the leading critic of the proposed new system was Thomas Jefferson, who has so often been claimed as authority by opponents of judicial review.[48] That such claims are unfounded is obvious from the following statement, uttered during the great debate over adoption of the Constitution. Referring to the executive veto, Jefferson says, "I should have liked it better had the judiciary been associated for that purpose, *or invested with a similar and separate power.*"[49]

The comments of Henry, Jefferson, and others on the role of the courts under the new Constitution show the difficulty of basing arguments against judicial review on their authority. In fact, they were authors of the earliest recorded assertions of the propriety of giving courts a broad negative over the acts of a coordinate branch of government—a paradox, since they were the same authorities who were later so pervasively cited in support of the opposite viewpoint.[50] The authenticity of their position was confirmed during the 1790s, when prominent Antifederalists voiced repeated opposition to federal court decisions upholding acts of Congress.[51]

Another important development during the ratification struggle concerns the appearance in New York of the famous "Letters of Brutus," probably penned by Robert Yates, a prominent Antifederalist.[52] In these letters can be found the most thoroughly reasoned statement of the views held by those who feared that the new national government would ultimately absorb the states.[53] Appropriately, the answer to "Brutus," especially Hamilton's Numbers 78 and 81 of the *Federalist*, constitutes the fullest treatment of the sense of the Convention on the issue of judicial power that emerged during the adoption controversy.[54]

Briefly stated, Yates's argument is twofold. First, the wide latitude given to Congress in Article I—especially the so-called implied power—in conjunction with the broad interpretive authority to be exercised by the Supreme Court under the Article III "arising under" provision, will allow the judiciary to "lean strongly in favor of the general government" and to "give such an explanation to the constitution, as will favour an extension of its jurisdiction," resulting in "an entire subversion of the legislative, executive, and judicial powers of the individual states."[55] Second, speaking of the Supreme Court, Yates argues that there is "no power above them that can correct their errors or control their decisions—the adjudications of this court are final and irreversible, for there is no court above them to which appeals can lie, either in error or on the merits."[56] Yates contrasts the judges of the United States with those in England, who "in no instance assume the authority to set aside an act of parlia-

ment under the idea that it is inconsistent with their constitution."[57]
It is also suggested that if an English court did set aside such an act,
it would be immediately subject to a reversal in Parliament.[58]

Hamilton answers the first of Yates's arguments in *Federalist* Number
78, where, as Publius, he asserts that the "wide latitude" of Article I
will be constrained, rather than enhanced, by the institution of an independent judiciary. Vattel's principle that "every act of a delegated authority, contrary to the tenor of the commission under which it is exercised, is void,"[59] is invoked in derogation of Yates's fear of boundless congressional power. In response to the charge of unrestricted judicial discretion under Article III, Hamilton urges the qualification of Vattel's doctrine (to which I have referred in a previous chapter).

> It can be of no weight to say that the courts, on the *pretense* of a
> repugnancy, may substitute their own pleasure to the *constitutional*
> intentions of the legislature. This might as well happen in the case
> of two contradictory statutes; or it might as well happen in every
> adjudication upon any single statute. The courts *must* declare the
> sense of the law; and if they should be disposed to exercise WILL
> instead of JUDGEMENT, the consequence would *equally* be the
> substitution of their pleasure to that of the legislative body.[60]

Publius thus reassures Brutus that the legislature will be able neither
to exceed the limits of its delegated authority nor to violate the "certain specified exceptions" to its authority which define the nature of
a "limited constitution."[61] The institutional expression of the legislative limitation is found in the role of the judiciary, which is itself
limited by its function. That the judicial limitation is indeed functional
is expressed in Hamilton's differentiation between the exercise of *will*,
which is legislative in nature, and *judgment*, which is the province of
courts. Moreover, he asserts that, *with regard to the function being performed*, courts do nothing very different when deciding constitutional
questions than when deciding merely statutory ones.

The meaning of Hamilton's distinction between will and judgment
is revealed in his answer to the second argument of Brutus in *Federalist*
Number 81. In response to Yates's charge of discontinuity between the
English and American systems, Hamilton counters with the claim that
the "theory, neither of the British, nor the State constitutions, authorizes
the revisal of a judicial sentence by a legislative act. . . . A legislature,

without exceeding its province, cannot reverse a *determination* once made in a *particular* case; though it may prescribe a new *rule* for *future* cases."[62] Answering the allegation that the new constitution authorizes what amounts to an encroachment of the judiciary upon the legislative function, Hamilton calls that a phantom fear, which "may be inferred with certainty from the general *nature* of the judicial power, from the *objects* to which it relates, from the *manner* in which it is exercised."[63]

Therefore, the reason that courts have authority to disregard legislative acts deemed contrary to constitutional provisions when deciding *particular* cases is identical to that which empowers legislatures to prescribe "a new rule for future cases." On the other hand, the reason that legislatures may not overturn *specific determinations* of courts is identical to that which prevents courts from exercising *general, supervisory* power over legislation. The alleged contradiction found by some[64] in the juxtaposition of *Federalist* Numbers 78 and 81 is thus easily resolved if one reads them together in light of the Founders' theory of judicial function.

This interpretation of Hamilton's view on the nature and scope of the judicial function receives additional confirmation from Black's definition of judgment—the key term invoked by Hamilton to describe the judicial function. The dictionary entry reads: "The official and authentic decision of a court of justice upon the respective rights and claims of the parties to an action or suit therein litigated and submitted to its determination. The final decision of the court resolving the dispute and determining the rights and obligations of the parties. The law's last word in a judicial controversy, it being the final determination by a court of the rights of the parties upon matters submitted to it in an action or proceeding."[65]

Black's definition gives specific content to Hamilton's statement about the "nature, objects, and manner" of judicial functioning.[66] Surely, if *Federalist* Number 78 provides the only evidence to support the common argument that Hamilton held an activist view of judicial power,[67] that source should be reexamined in strict accordance with commonly accepted definitions. Furthermore, since Chief Justice Marshall has often been charged with uncritically following *Federalist* Number 78 in his argument for the power of a court to declare a statute void,[68] the correct interpretation of the *Federalist* on this point becomes crucial to a proper understanding of *Marbury v. Madison.*

*The 1790s*

In the 1790s, the pattern of thinking about the role of courts which had emerged during the ratification contest was perpetuated. Federalists generally continued to espouse the narrow view of the Founders on the question of judicial authority to disregard legislative enactments. As noted, this view holds that the power arises necessarily from the duty of a court to apply *statutes* in deciding particular cases or controversies. According to Federalist doctrine, legislative acts under a written constitution presuppose relevant constitutional provisions by virtue of pursuance (in the case of federal laws) or *non-obstante* (in the case of state laws) clauses.

Repugnant statutes—those in which a relevant constitutional provision is adjudged to be in conflict with an explicit statutory provision—cause the court to decide the case at hand by using a discretionary power to disregard either the constitutional or the statutory provision. According to the Federal Convention's constructive narrowing of the "arising under" provision of Article III, the court should disregard the statutory provision in cases of a judiciary nature (those cases susceptible of a final judicial determination) and disregard the constitutional provision in cases which give rise to political questions (those not susceptible to final judicial resolution).

This theory is most evident in decisions of the federal courts. David P. Currie writes that

> two lasting principles of construction were established before 1801: doubtful cases were to be resolved in favor of constitutionality, and statutes were to be construed if possible in a manner consistent with the Constitution. There were intimations of the political question doctrine in the suggestions . . . that some issues, even the constitutional dimension, might be non-justiciable. The informal *Correspondence* settled once and for all that the Court would decide legal questions only in the context of ordinary litigation. There were hints . . . of a coming tendency to construe federal grants of power extensively.[69]

Additionally, Richard Ellis's work on the period indicates that the Federalist conception of judicial authority was shared by most moderate Republicans as well, and that those radicals who opposed it were motivated primarily by a general hostility toward the legal profession, the rule of law, and the idea of an independent judiciary.[70]

There is not even the slightest suggestion in this doctrine that courts have anything approaching a general authority to *repeal* obnoxious legislation, whether in conflict with written constitutions or not. Nor is there a hint of the modern distinction between constitutional and statutory interpretation. Since all statutes presuppose fundamental laws, such a distinction must be arbitrary—a fiction that defines constitutional decisions to be those involving a *collision* of constitution and statute, while holding all others to be "merely statutory." The Federalist theory thus preserves continuity with the English tradition in viewing constitutional adjudication as a special case of statutory construction, according to the logic of Blackstone's Tenth Rule.

On the other hand, some Republicans continued to advocate the more active judicial role expounded by Henry and Jefferson during the ratification struggle. Republicans throughout the 1790s repeatedly challenged the constitutionality of laws passed by the Federalist-controlled national legislature. With regard to the first charter of the Bank of the United States,[71] the Post-Office Bill,[72] the Carriage Tax,[73] the Alien and Sedition Laws,[74] and a host of other measures,[75] Republicans both in and out of Congress asserted the necessity or propriety of judicial intervention. Despite their defeat in the great debate over adoption of the Constitution, many Antifederalists retained substantial hope throughout the decade that state and federal courts would use the power of judicial review to invalidate national laws which they considered oppressive. This was, of course, exactly that hope that Henry and Yates earlier had declared vain.

There was some consensus of opinion between Federalists and Republicans in the aftermath of the ratification struggle, on the question of judicial independence and the need for judicial authority to disregard legislative enactments in order to preserve that independence. That unanimity was revealed in the congressional debate over the president's power of removal, which occurred in June 1789. A proposed bill creating a Department of Foreign Affairs engendered the question of whether Congress could deliver a binding construction of the Constitution by passing a declaratory act (either confirming or disconfirming the executive power of removal). While some thought that Congress had the right to express its opinion on the Constitution through an official declaration, apparently *no one* thought that such a statement could bind a court properly engaged in the performance of its duties. Elbridge Gerry, a Republican who refused to sign the final draft of the Constitution, presaged Marshall in *Marbury v. Madison:*

> If the power of making declaratory Acts really vests in Congress and the Judges are really bound by our decision, we may later alter that part of the Constitution which is secured from being amended by the Fifth Article. . . . I would ask, gentlemen: if the Constitution has given us the power to make declaratory Acts; where is the necessity of inserting the Fifth Article for the purpose of obtaining Amendments? . . . If this is the meaning of the Constitution, it was hardly worthwhile to have had so much bustle and uneasiness about it.[76]

Warren claims that this was the "first great constitutional debate" in Congress, in which "every side of the constitutional question was presented. Nothing in the debate, however, is more striking than the fact the representatives of each side of the constitutional question agreed on one point—namely, that the Court had the power to decide the question of constitutionality."[77] Moreover, this debate was concluded three months *prior* to the passage of the Judiciary Act of September 24, 1789, and appears to explain the paucity of opposition in the First Congress to Section 25 of that act.[78]

Another illustration of Republican attitudes during the period is found in remarks made in Congress on the notorious Alien Act. Gallatin said that "the States and the State Judiciary would, indeed they must, consider the law as a mere nullity, they must declare it to be unconstitutional."[79] Later, after reiterating his view, Gallatin added that "an appeal must be made to another tribunal, to the judiciary *in the first instance*, on the subject of a supposedly unconstitutional law."[80] The emphasized portion of the quotation suggests Gallatin's belief that if the courts failed to invalidate the Alien Act, then the state legislatures should do so, either through nullification or proposal of a constitutional amendment. Nullification, of course, was attempted in Virginia and Kentucky, and their resolutions were subsequently condemned by the legislatures of eleven states.[81] It is significant that at least four of these condemnations rested on the *explicit* ground that the Virginia and Kentucky resolutions constituted legislative usurpations of the judicial power.[82] This reaction of the states seems to indicate that, at least by the late 1790s, there was general acceptance of judicial authority to disregard acts of Congress in cases directly involving certain individual rights and liberties.

Though Republicans and Federalists agreed with that basic idea, the early Republican theory of judicial power was not identical to that advanced by the Founders at the Philadelphia Convention. Some of the differences are evidenced in the attacks on the Bank Act and the Post-Office Bill in 1791 and 1792, respectively.[83] Neither of these laws encroached upon the judicial function per se. Neither was likely to give rise to cases of a purely judiciary nature, nor was it probable that either law would violate rights protected by explicit constitutional guarantees. What then could be the *legal* foundation for a court's invalidation of those acts?

Thomas Fitzsimmons supplied an answer in his argument against a provision of the Post-Office Bill that authorized mail stages to carry passengers without liability to state taxes.

If this were once admitted, the Constitution would be an useless and dead letter; and it would be to no purpose that the States in Convention assembled had framed that instrument to guide the steps of Congress; as well might they at once have said: "There shall be a Congress who shall have full power and authority to make all laws which to their wisdom shall seem meet and proper." . . . In favor of the motion it was urged (that the necessary and proper clause) has conferred on Congress ample powers respecting the point in question. . . . The question could not involve any controversy between the United States and the individual States. *It was merely a judicial question and determinable in a Court of law.*[84]

Likewise, Nathaniel Niles argued that Congress, if it passed the act, would violate state rights and "overleap" its own authority. "This matter may occasion a legal adjudication, in order to which the *Judiciary must determine* whether you have a constitutional right to establish this regulation; and this will depend on the question whether it will be necessary and proper."[85]

If the constitutionality of the Bank Act, the Post-Office Bill, and other such provisions was to Republicans "merely a judicial question determinable in a court of law," then surely their view of the *scope* of judicial power was broader than the view of the Federalists, to whom the institution of the first national government was entrusted. At the same time, the tenor of the Republican remarks indicates that the two factions profoundly agreed on the *nature* (as distinct from the *scope*) of the judicial function. This is most clearly seen in Fitzsimmons's effort to distinguish "controversies between the United States and the individual States," which would presumably constitute disputes of a *political* nature, from those that presented merely *judicial* questions "determinable in a court of law."[86]

In other words, Federalists and Republicans agreed that the judicial function involved the application of statutes in the course of deciding questions "nonpolitical" in nature, but they disagreed about the number and kind of cases which fell within that category. Federalists—at least moderates who dominated national politics throughout much of the 1790s—believed that the class of nonpolitical controversies (i.e., those of a judiciary nature susceptible of final judicial resolution) was *smaller* than leading Republicans of the day conceived it to be. This difference was in turn due to the Republicans' inclusion in the nonpolitical category of disputes over the boundary between state and federal power, as the remarks of Yates, Fitzsimmons, and Niles clearly show.

The more restrictive view of judicial authority instituted by the Founders and propounded by the early Federalists was put into practice by the Supreme and lower federal courts in the 1790s. Without significant exception, these courts steadfastly resisted invitations to interpose themselves between Congress and the Constitution,[87] except in cases bearing directly upon the exercise of their own functions as courts of law.[88] A similar restraint on the part of the Supreme Court is evident when it dealt with the power of individual states to govern themselves through their legislatures.[89] Furthermore, in those cases decided by federal courts in the 1790s, in which the constitutional questions presented were those of a primarily judiciary nature—by far the greater number of constitutional cases in the period—the effect of the decision was, with a single exception, to *narrow* either the scope of jurisdiction or the range of judicial discretion.[90]

The willingness of courts in the pre-*Marbury* period to entertain constitutional questions in the decision of particular cases is as fully apparent at the state level as it is at the federal. In a succession of cases decided in Virginia,[91] South Carolina,[92] Pennsylvania,[93] Kentucky,[94] Maryland,[95] and North Carolina,[96] such questions were raised and in some instances were actually decided.[97] Interestingly, in one of the Virginia cases, Spencer Roane, that archenemy of the Federalists (and later of Marshall), enunciated the doctrine later made famous by Marshall in *Marbury v. Madison:*

It is the province of the judiciary to expound the laws. . . . The
Judiciary may clearly say, that a subsequent statute has not changed
a former for want of sufficient words, though it was perhaps intended
it should do so. It may say, too, that an Act of Assembly has not
changed the Constitution, though its words are expressly to that
effect. . . . In expounding laws the judiciary considers *every* law
which relates to the subject. Would you have them to shut their eyes
against that law which is of the highest authority of any, or against
a part of that law, which, either by its words or by its spirit, denies
to any but the people the power to change it?[98]

Roane's statement is a conclusive illustration of the congruence of
early Federalist and Republican thought on the relation between judicial
and political power, for he was probably the most important exponent
of Jeffersonian views to sit on the bench of any court in the early years
of the American Republic.[99] Here, Roane declares: (1) for the power of
courts *generally* to take account of constitutional as well as statutory
provisions when deciding cases, since *both* are law; (2) that the power
of a court to say "that an Act of Assembly has not changed the Constitution" (constitutional adjudication) and the power of that same court to
say "that a subsequent statute had not changed a former for want of sufficient words" (statutory construction) were powers *identically* derived;
(3) that the *source* of the derivation is the judicial *function* itself, whose
province it is "to expound the laws"; and (4) that a constitution, being
the act of the people, may only be changed by the people themselves—*not*
by their representatives. As we shall see in the next chapter, Marshall
himself claimed nothing more or less than this.

# Part Two · A Precedent
for All Seasons

Chapters 5 through 8 examine important aspects of *Marbury v. Madison*.
Though some of these have already been suggested in previous sections,
they have been treated as peripheral to the background materials which
were the primary subject of Part I. The case will now be analyzed ex-
egetically, along with its contemporaneous history and its subsequent
development by the Supreme Court of the United States.

Chapter 5 focuses on *Marbury* itself and contains a detailed analysis
of the Court's opinion in the case. I argue that the textbook version of
the case, which is usually drawn from the last few pages of the opinion,
bears little resemblance to what was actually said and decided there.
Nothing in the opinion contradicts the restrictive conception of judicial
power which is embodied in the Constitution. Specifically, I contend
that *Marbury* was not a political decision but was based on sound constitutional doctrine and existing legal precedent. In short, it was precisely
the sort of case that the Founders considered appropriate for the exercise of judicial review. A failure to exercise authority in that case would
surely have impaired the Court's ability to properly perform its own
functions.

Chapter 6 surveys important commentaries on the Marshall Court and
judicial review, along with references to *Marbury v. Madison*, through
the Civil War. Special attention is given to the famous partisan attack
on Marshall and *Marbury* penned by former President Martin Van Buren
in 1862 and first published in 1867. Van Buren's broadside is most important to Part III of this study, for it is the first scathing attack on *Marbury*
(Jefferson notwithstanding) and foreshadows the kind of criticism levelled
at Marshall and his Court in the 1870s, respecting contract-clause decisions, and in the 1890s, respecting the exercise of judicial review. Van

Buren's critique is a precursor of J. Allen Smith's conspiracy theory of the Federal Convention, published some forty years later. The chapter closes with a look at the views of Andrew Jackson and Abraham Lincoln on the subject of judicial review.

Chapter 7 explores what is perhaps the strongest argument in support of the restrictive interpretation of *Marbury* and judicial review: that *Marbury* is not cited as a precedent for judicial review at all until the late nineteenth century, and only ten times by justices of the Supreme Court prior to 1958. All pre-1983 *Marbury* citations in the Supreme Court are classified and analyzed, divided roughly into thirty-year periods beginning in 1803. *Marbury* was not mentioned in support of the idea that the Supreme Court's determination of constitutional questions is conclusive on the other branches of the national government until the decision of *Cooper v. Aaron* in 1958. I contend that the Court's attitude toward this supposed finality of judicial declarations is a distinguishing factor between modern judicial review and the older variety.

Chapter 8 analyzes the famous dissenting opinion of Justice John Gibson of the Pennsylvania Supreme Court in *Eakin v. Raub* (1825). Since the late nineteenth century, Justice Gibson's opinion has been thought by many commentators to constitute the strongest contemporaneous rebuttal to Marshall's conception of judicial review. My argument is that there is no incompatibility between *Eakin* and *Marbury*. Careful reading of the Gibson dissent reveals that his argument is explicitly confined to a point that has nothing whatever to do with *Marbury v. Madison*. Modern constitutional scholars apparently have placed undue reliance on Gibson's offhand reference to *Marbury* in the opening section of his *Eakin* opinion. The idea of an *Eakin-Marbury* conflict is based on misunderstandings regarding the content of both opinions, the actual scope of the decision in *Marbury*, and the fact that, in the American constitutional system, the national government is one of delegated power, whereas state governments are not.

# 5 · The Case of
# *Marbury v. Madison*

## Background

When the United States Supreme Court convened on February 9, 1803, to hear arguments in the case of *Marbury v. Madison*,[1] it found itself in a problematic situation. The reasons were primarily political. As we have seen, Antifederalists and Republicans throughout the 1790s believed that the courts would protect individuals and states from encroachments of the federal legislature. When their hopes failed to materialize, many Republicans adopted the view later expressed by Jefferson, that federal judges were "a subtle corps of sappers and miners."[2] This incongruity of Republican views *held by the same people at different times* reveals the difficulty experienced by Jeffersonians in establishing a coherent perspective on the proper scope of the judicial function during the early years of the American Republic.

No doubt some frustration was a result of the tendency of Jeffersonians to evaluate institutions on the basis of their ability to bring about a speedy realization of cardinal principles (as they understood them) in society. When an institution did not live up to its promise, as in the bank and post office instances, Republicans often rejected it in favor of another institution. This orientation is confirmed even by prominent writers who are sympathetic to the Jeffersonian persuasion. For example, Dumas Malone, speaking of the nullification tactic embodied in the Virginia and Kentucky resolutions, says that emphasis "should be laid not on the weapon he [Jefferson] used, but on the ends he sought, and he should be recognized as a champion of rights which he deemed universal."[3]

At any rate, by 1803, Jeffersonian disillusionment had produced an unprecedented attack on the federal judiciary.[4] When a few Federalist judges attempted to enforce the Alien and Sedition Acts, their improper behavior kindled intense hostility toward the courts.[5] By 1803, the Republican-controlled Congress had: (1) repealed the Judiciary Act of 1801;[6] (2) impeached a federal judge;[7] and (3) suspended the 1802 term of the Supreme Court, perhaps anticipating that the Court might declare the repeal act unconstitutional.[8]

It is hardly surprising that one of the most bitter conflicts in the early Republic involved the role of courts.[9] The Republicans, who had to challenge the original Federalist consensus in order to obtain political power, emerged naturally as opponents of the national judicial establishment. Successful institutionalization of the rule of law demands a general willingness on the part of the citizenry to accept peacefully the resolution of some acrimonious disputes by adjudication and others by legislation. The crucial element is a stable agreement on the respective parameters of these two forms of conflict resolution—in other words, the relative scopes of the adjudicative and legislative functions. The consensus that had been formed at the Philadelphia Convention now faced the Republican challenge at the onset of Jefferson's administration.

## The Case

In February 1801, a Congress dominated by lame-duck Federalists passed two laws which created new positions within the federal judiciary.[10] Four of the new appointees, including William Marbury, failed to receive their commissions, and on December 17, 1801, they sued for a writ of mandamus compelling delivery of the commissions in an original action before the Supreme Court.[11] Before the case came to trial, Congress, with a newly elected Republican majority, passed an act repealing one of the two laws, though not the one under which Marbury and the others were appointed.[12] Shortly thereafter, Congress passed a law that eliminated the June and December terms of the Supreme Court.[13] The measure was probably an attempt by Congress to prevent the Court from ruling on the constitutionality of the Repeal Act, and it resulted in the postponement of Marbury's case until the Court's February term in 1803.[14] By that time, James Madison—absent at the commencement of the lawsuit—had assumed his office as secretary of state.

Prior to initiation of the suit, the four plaintiffs—William Marbury, Dennis Ramsay, Robert Townsend Hooe, and William Harper—had applied to both the secretary of state and the secretary of the Senate for information regarding the commissions. On January 31, 1803, the Senate had refused to allow its secretary to produce copies from the journal reflecting its "advice and consent to the appointments."[15] According to the testimony of Jacob Wagner, a subpoenaed witness from the State Department, Marbury and Ramsay had been referred to him by the secretary of state. Wagner told the applicants that "two of the commissions had been signed, but the other had not." Wagner then stated that this fact had been communicated to him by others but declined to reveal the identity of the informants. A second employee of the State Department, Daniel Brent, testified that he was "almost certain" that Marbury's and Hooe's commissions had been completed, but not Ramsay's; and that he (Brent) had been the person who "made out the list of names by which the clerk who filled up the commissions was guided." Brent did not believe that any of the commissions had been recorded; but Wagner believed that some of them had.[16] Apparently neither Brent nor Wagner had been granted access to the relevant ledgers in order to confirm their beliefs.

The only other administration witness called was Attorney General Levi Lincoln, who had been acting secretary of state when Marbury and Ramsay first made their application to the department. At first, Lincoln declined to answer questions because he "did not think himself bound to disclose his official transactions while acting as secretary of state" and "ought not to be compelled to answer any thing which might tend to criminate himself." Later, Lincoln agreed to entertain several questions, though he stated that he would not answer the crucial question as to "what had been done with the commissions."[17] Lincoln's about-face was evidently in response to an argument made by Charles Lee, counsel for the plaintiffs, which concerned the duties of the secretary of state under the two acts of Congress then dealing with that subject.[18]

The first of these acts had been passed on July 27, 1789, and had created the Department of Foreign Affairs, with the secretary as its head. Under this act, the secretary was to "perform and execute such duties as shall from time to time be enjoined on, or entrusted to him by the President." The scope of the act was explicitly confined to matters "respecting foreign affairs," as the title of the agency suggested. Lee conceded that, in regard to "the powers given and the duties imposed by this act, no mandamus will lie," since the secretary is here "responsible only to the President."[19]

The second act was passed on September 15, 1789, and its purpose was to provide for the safekeeping of official documents of the United States.

This act changed the name of the Department of Foreign Affairs to the Department of State and charged the secretary with the duty to publish, print, preserve, and record all bills, orders, resolutions, and notes of Congress which have been signed by the president, and to "make out," "record," and "affix the seal of the United States to all civil commissions, after they have been signed by the President." Respecting the judicial process, the act also stated that all copies of official documents, including commissions, "shall be as good evidence as the originals." According to Lee, the duties of the secretary embodied in this act, unlike those in the earlier act, must be performed independently of the president and may therefore be compelled by mandamus in the case of nonperformance, "in the same manner as other persons holding offices under the authority of the United States."[20]

The last quote was a clear reference to Section 13 of the Judiciary Act of 1789 and indicated that Marbury and the other plaintiffs brought their complaint directly to the Supreme Court in reliance on the act.[21] Later, in oral argument, Lee quoted the relevant sentence of Section 13.

The supreme court shall also have appellate jurisdiction from the circuit court, and courts of the several states, in the cases hereinafter specially provided for; and shall have power to issue writs of prohibition to the district courts, when proceeding as courts of admiralty and maritime jurisdiction; and writs of mandamus, in cases warranted by the principles and usages of law, to any courts appointed, or *persons holding office*, under the authority of the United States.[22]

That Lee interpreted the last phrase concerning mandamus as pertaining to the Court's *original* jurisdiction was apparent from his next remark: "Congress is not restrained from conferring original jurisdiction in other cases than those mentioned in the constitution."[23] Lee's accompanying citation was *United States v. Ravara,* a 1793 decision of the circuit court for Pennsylvania involving prosecution of a German consul for extortion.[24] The consul's lawyers had argued against the circuit court's jurisdiction, relying on the provision of Article III which gives to the Supreme Court original jurisdiction in cases affecting consuls. Justices Wilson and Peters rejected this argument (Iredell dissenting), since Congress, in Section 13 of the Judiciary Act, had specified the Supreme Court's jurisdiction in cases involving consuls to be original, but not exclusive.[25] (Lee must have misinterpreted *Ravara* on the point in question, since that case involved no statutory enlargement of the Court's original jurisdiction, but only a clarification.) Lee then moved on to cite several cases where the Court earlier had entertained jurisdiction on prohibition or mandamus. In each case the requested writ was denied.[26]

Two additional witnesses submitted affidavits which supported the claims of the plaintiffs. The first was James Marshall, brother of the chief justice, who had acted as a courier for the State Department in the delivery of several of the commissions. Marshall stated that he had been unable to deliver all the commissions and that two of those left undelivered belonged to Hooe and Harper.[27] Hazen Kimball, who had been a clerk in the department on March 3, 1801, the day before Jefferson's inauguration, stated that in the office that day there were "commissions made out and signed by the president, appointing William Marbury a justice of peace for the county of Washington; and Robert T. Hooe a justice of the peace for the county of Alexandria, in the District of Columbia."[28]

Several observations arise from this brief survey of the preliminaries. First, the existence of the commissions of Marbury, Hooe, and Harper were reliably established, though not that of Ramsay. Second, none of the evidence was challenged by any of the witnesses examined—not even those presumably hostile to the cause. Third, no significant response to the Court's original order to "show cause why a mandamus should not issue"[29] was entered either by Madison himself or by any of his subordinates. Finally, the issue of the constitutionality of Section 13 was raised, albeit obliquely, in oral argument.

Lee's argument, devoted to persuading the Court that it was entitled to issue a mandamus to the secretary of state, stressed the equity of the proceeding and its basis in English law. According to Blackstone, a writ of mandamus is

a command issuing in the king's name from the court of king's bench, and directed to any *person,* corporation or inferior court, requiring them to do some particular thing therein specified, *which appertains to their office and duty,* and which the court has previously determined, or at least supposed, to be consonant to right and justice. It is a writ of a most extensively remedial nature, and issues in all cases where the party has a right to have any thing done, *and has no other specific means of compelling its performance.*[30]

According to Lee, since the secretary in the *Marbury* situation was acting merely as recorder of laws, deeds, letters patent, and commissions, he was controlled only by the laws imposing such duties and was subject to indictment for refusal to perform them. "A prosecution of this kind might be the means of punishing the officer, but a specific civil remedy to the injured party can only be obtained by a writ of mandamus."[31] After noting the threat posed by the arbitrary acts of the administration to an independent judiciary, Lee concluded by presenting a number of English cases designed to show that mandamus is appropriate where there is "no other *adequate, specific, legal* remedy," thereby rendering the issuance of the writ consistent with "the principles and usages of law," as required by Section 13.[32]

As we have seen, the first section of Marshall's opinion dealt with Marbury's right to receive his commission and the appropriate legal remedy that attaches to such a right.[33] The Court ruled that Marbury had been duly appointed and that the secretary of state had improperly withheld the commission.[34] After discussing at some length the duty of a government of laws to supply remedies for violated rights,[35] the Court then held the writ of mandamus to be an appropriate legal remedy for resolving Marbury's dilemma.[36] This section of the opinion thus followed closely the lines of argument laid down by Charles Lee in his presentation of Marbury's case.

Not so with the second section of the opinion. Examining the power of the Court to issue the requested writ, the Court reduced the question to whether it may exercise original jurisdiction in the case.[37] The Court answered negatively, holding that the act on which Marbury relied was one that unconstitutionally enlarged the original jurisdiction of the Supreme Court, a jurisdiction which is spelled out clearly in Article III of the Constitution.

The relevant phrase in Article III extends the Court's original jurisdiction to cases affecting "Ambassadors, other public Ministers and Consuls, and those in which a State shall be Party."[38] Although this provision was designed to protect the dignity of American states and foreign nations when sued, Lee had premised Marbury's original action in the Supreme Court on the idea that the secretary of state could be compelled by mandamus "in the same manner as other persons holding offices under the authority of the United States" per Section 13 of the Judiciary Act.[39] The Court thereby rejected Lee's assertion that Congress may confer original jurisdiction in cases other than those mentioned in the Constitution.[40]

The dominant modern view of *Marbury v. Madison* rests on several contentions regarding alternative ways in which the Court might have handled the case. Most of them were advanced in an article, now a classic, penned some years ago by William Van Alstyne.[41] Lief Carter has claimed that Van Alstyne's dissection of the opinion reveals on Marshall's part "a lack of legal integrity bordering on fraud."[42] Many others have echoed similar sentiments.

First, it has been suggested that, since the Court ultimately declined to issue the requested writ of mandamus, it might as well have done so without opinion—or at least without expressing an opinion on either Marbury's "rights" or the theoretical power of the federal courts to enforce such rights by issuing mandatory injunctions to executive officials.[43] After all, a no-opinion approach would have circumvented Jefferson's charge that the Court had "travelled beyond its case to prescribe what the law would be in a moot case not before the court."[44] Likewise, summary dismissal would have comported nicely with such modern maxims of judicial restraint as nonanticipation of constitutional questions and decision of constitutional cases whenever possible on other than constitutional grounds.[45]

Closely related is the contention that the Court could have construed Section 13 narrowly, thereby avoiding the necessity of declaring the law unconstitutional. The Court might have assumed that Congress could not have meant to enlarge the original jurisdiction and thereby resolved the matter on statutory grounds. Alternatively, the Court might have ruled that the culpable mandamus provision could apply in either original or appellate jurisdiction, so long as the assumption of jurisdiction was justified on other grounds.[46] By this strategy, the Court would have avoided imputing either bad motives or poor draftsmanship to the national legislature, whose decisions are entitled to the utmost respect.

Also, since Congress is empowered to make exception to the Court's appellate jurisdiction, some have said that the distribution of jurisdiction in Article III might have been merely provisional.[47] Moreover, it has been claimed that Marshall himself later rejected the implication of *Marbury* on this point and thereupon threw out the baby with the bath water.[48]

Finally, the famous argument in support of judicial review, found in the closing paragraphs of Marshall's opinion, has been criticized for asserting judicial supremacy over Congress and the president in constitutional matters.[49] In the words of Judge Learned Hand, "It will not bear scrutiny."[50] Suspecting that the modern interpretation may bear it no better, I shall now examine relevant portions of the *Marbury* opinion in

the light of that critique, hoping at least to provide a more balanced view
of the case.

## Summary Dismissal

Under normal circumstances, where the law is considered settled, it is
appropriate for the Supreme Court to dismiss a claim for want of jurisdiction without expressing opinion on the merits of the dispute. In appellate
jurisdiction, denial of the writ of certiorari, a discretionary authority
granted to the Court by statute in 1891, may accomplish this result.[51]
The procedure was, of course, unavailable to the Court in Marbury's day
and remains inapplicable in matters of original jurisdiction. Thus, at least
prior to 1891, the Court's discretionary authority was greater in original
than in appellate jurisdiction, and the Court might, with more justification in the former instance than the latter, regard itself bound to explain
its refusal to employ its jurisdiction in a particular way. When the Court
is invited to exercise original jurisdiction, it is essentially being asked
to perform the functions of a trial court, the most important of which
is the determination of the rights and responsibilities of parties who have
not had their claims previously adjudicated.

These considerations apply with even greater force when the Court
is asked to invoke its equity powers while sitting as a court of original
jurisdiction. Since the issuance of a writ of mandamus is an equitable
remedy, the Court undoubtedly recognized this as the situation in *Marbury* when it declared its threefold obligation: (1) "solely, to decide on
the rights of individuals";[52] (2) to consider whether a specific duty has
been "assigned by law"; and (3) to determine whether "individual rights
depend upon the performance of that duty."[53]

To be sure, the case had implications extending far beyond Marbury's
personal dilemma. As we have seen, the federal courts were under siege
throughout the entire period in which Marbury's case was before the
Court.[54] The Judiciary Act of 1801 had been repealed, a federal judge had
been impeached, and the 1802 term of the Supreme Court had been
suspended.[55]

With the judiciary so embroiled, it is understandable that the Court
would have been chagrined at the refusal of the secretary of state to appear in order to "show cause why a mandamus should not issue."[56] The
separation doctrine of the Federal Convention surely enabled the Court
to defend itself against brazen attempts by coordinate branches of govern-

ment to impair the capacity of the judiciary to perform its functions properly. This was probably the Convention's primary rationale for judicial review in the first place, reflected in its narrowing of the power to cases of a judiciary nature, of which, I have argued, *Marbury* is an example.[57]

The *Marbury* situation is somewhat analogous to that in *United States v. Nixon*. There the Court unanimously held that documents in the custody of executive officials, including the president, are subject to judicial process whenever they are essential to appropriate adjudication of the rights and duties of parties to a case pending in federal court, absent a clear showing of the necessity of their exemption.[58] Notwithstanding the obvious factual and legal differences between the two cases, in both *Marbury* and *Nixon*, important documents sorely needed by the courts were withheld without any showing of necessity. Furthermore, in *Marbury*, the executive refusal had occurred in the face of an act of Congress which *required* that the requested information be produced. At any rate, the Court's declaration of the law respecting whether, and in what circumstances, a right to a commission stemming from a judicial appointment "has vested or not" must be understood against this threatening background.[59]

According to the Court, the answer depends upon the separability of the acts of appointment and commission. Since "the power to perform them is given in two separate and distinct sections of the constitution," and since one of those sections imposes without qualification a duty upon the president to "commission all the officers of the United States," some of whose appointments may be vested by Congress "in the President alone, in the courts of law, or in the heads of departments,"[60] it follows that the acts must be deemed separable and that the commission is merely evidence of an appointment, not "itself the actual appointment."[61]

Furthermore, "the verity of the Presidential signature" demands that "the great seal is only to be affixed to an instrument which is complete," and Congress has imposed upon the secretary of state, independent of presidential authority, the duty to "make out," "record," and "affix the said seal to all civil commissions to officers of the United States."[62] Therefore, delivery of the commission is merely incidental to the acts of appointment and commission. The failure of the secretary either to produce evidence of an appointment (a commission) or to "show cause why a mandamus should not issue" seriously intrudes upon the Court's power to perform one of its most important functions: determining when the legislature has imposed upon a government official a duty to perform certain ministerial acts on which the rights of individuals are dependent. Under those conditions, "he is so far an officer of the law; is amenable to the laws for his conduct; and cannot at his discretion sport away the vested rights of others."[63]

In view of the attention that has been focused on the Marshall-Jefferson conflict,[64] and the usual reading of these portions of the *Marbury* opinion as a veiled attack upon the president, it should be noted that all the remarks quoted above are prefatory to the Court's invocation of Blackstone. The Court cites that "injuries to the rights of property can scarcely be committed by the crown without the intervention of its officers, for whom the law, in matters of right, entertains no respect or delicacy; but furnishes various methods of detecting the errors and misconduct of those agents, by whom the king has been deceived and induced to do a temporary injustice."[65]

In this context also, the Court enunciates the distinction which is at the heart of the doctrine of political questions.

> By the constitution of the United States, the President is invested with certain important political powers, in the exercise of which he is to use his own discretion, and is accountable only to his country in his political character, and to his own conscience. To aid him in the performance of these duties, he is authorized to appoint certain officers, who act by his authority and in conformity with his orders. In such cases, their acts are his acts; and whatever opinion may be entertained of the manner in which executive discretion may be used, still there exists, and can exist, no power to control that discretion. The subjects are political. They respect the nation, not individual rights.[66]

In other words, the first portion of the *Marbury* opinion is not a lecture to the chief executive by way of dicta.[67] Nor is it an example of a Court's "travelling beyond the confines of the case," or reaching out to decide "issues that did not have to be decided."[68] The secretary had exhibited behavior unbecoming the dignity of his office; he had failed to perform duties that had been assigned to his office by statute independently of his responsibility to the chief executive; and he had thereby implicated the presidency itself in an illegal effort to suppress information relevant to the determination of the rights and duties of parties to a lawsuit—a determination which the courts are duty-bound to make.

Summary disposition of Marbury's complaint would therefore have been disingenuous on the part of the Court. Marbury had relied upon a presumably valid statute, which had not been previously construed by the Court on the point in question.[69] Had the Court chosen to deny Marbury his remedy without apprising him of his right to pursue the cause in another court, Marbury's fate would have, in effect, been determined by a legal technicality, which seems inconsistent with the fairness expected of courts when they render judgment on the rights of individuals respective to the powers of government.

On the other hand, the Court could not reach the constitutional issue without ruling on these questions—without carefully distinguishing the acts of a subordinate official which are assumed to be the acts of the executive itself, from the acts of such an official operating on his own. Otherwise, the Court would have rightly been charged with disrespect toward a coordinate agency of government. In the case that Section 13 was void and the writ could not be issued, the Court would have acquiesced in an executive usurpation of judicial functions, since the outcome would have seemed dependent upon the arbitrary will of a *subordinate* executive official. In the case that Section 13 were valid and the writ could be issued, the Court would have intruded upon the prerogatives of the president, by issuing the writ when it was unclear whether the "failure to show cause" was properly within the executive discretion or not.

### Statutory Construction

In Marbury's case, the Court refused to apply the following portion of Section 13 of the Judiciary Act of 1789:

> The Supreme Court shall also have appellate jurisdiction from the circuit courts and the Courts of the several states, in the cases hereinafter specially provided for; and shall have power to issue writs of prohibition to the district courts, when proceeding as courts of admiralty and maritime jurisdiction, and writs of mandamus, in cases warranted by the principles and usages of law, to any courts appointed or persons holding office under the authority of the United States.[70]

One possible basis for a narrow interpretation of the provision would be that, since the mandamus provision is part of a sentence that commences with a statement about the appellate jurisdiction, the intent of Congress may be construed as applicable only in that jurisdiction.[71] In response, the phrase "in the cases hereinafter specially provided for" does not seem to refer to the mandamus provision at all, but suggests application to subsequent sections of the act, where appellate procedures are "specially" delineated. The most likely reference is to Section 25, which authorizes Supreme Court review of decisions of state courts of last resort.[72] Additionally, the first three sentences (the remainder) of Section 13 are devoted *entirely* to original jurisdiction, suggesting again that the subsequent "appellate" phrase is merely a forethought and not determinative of the whole fourth sentence.

Those three sentences read as follows:

And be it further enacted, that the Supreme Court shall have exclusive jurisdiction of all controversies of a civil nature, where a state is a party, except between a state and its citizens; and except also between a state and citizens of other states, or aliens, in which latter case it shall have original but not exclusive jurisdiction. And shall have exclusively all such jurisdiction of suits or proceedings against ambassadors, or other public ministers, or their domestics or domestic servants, as a court of law can have or exercise consistently with the law of nations; and original, but not exclusive jurisdiction of all suits brought by ambassadors, or other public ministers, or in which a consul or vice consul, shall be a party. And the trial of issues in fact in the Supreme Court, in all actions at law against citizens of the United States, shall be by jury.[73]

The purpose of the first two sentences is clearly to distinguish those instances where the court's original jurisdiction is exclusive from those where it is not. The third sentence says that, when the Court exercises its original jurisdiction in actions at law against United States citizens, the determination of fact must be made by a jury.

Another basis for a narrow view would be that the mandamus provision is intended to apply in either original or appellate jurisdiction, so long as the assumption of jurisdiction is justified on other grounds.[74] In reply, one should be reminded of Marshall's tendency to read legal provisions literally, at least whenever language is relatively unambiguous. For example, Marshall read the term "contracts" in Article I, Section 10, to include "public" as well as "private" ones (see Chapter 9).[75]

Since the mandamus provision in Section 13 lists no specific jurisdiction, a literal reading renders the following plausible conclusions: (1) that the provision applies generally to *any* "persons holding office, under the authority of the United States";[76] and (2) that the writ therefore may be issued in *both* appellate *and* original jurisdiction.[77] So read, the provision enlarges the Court's jurisdiction. It is thus unconstitutional, and the Court is at liberty to refuse it application.

In justifying its refusal to apply Section 13, the Court through Marshall wrote the most famous portion of its *Marbury* opinion. The Court had established Marbury's right to his commission, the propriety of the writ of mandamus as a remedial device in situations where no other remedy is available, and the appropriateness of its issuance against an executive official who "commits any illegal act, under color of his office, by which an individual sustains an injury," and who cannot therefore pretend "that his office alone exempts him from being sued in the ordinary mode of proceeding."[78] Now it turned to an examination of relevant constitutional doctrine bearing on its denial of the requested writ.

The Court first states that the instant case is one to which the judicial power of the United States applies, since this power "is expressly extended to all cases arising under the laws of the United States; and consequently, in some form, may be exercised over the present case; because the right claimed is given by a law of the United States."[79] This law imposes upon the secretary of state the ministerial duty to "make out," "record," and "affix" the seal of the United States to all civil commissions.[80] It does not impose upon the secretary the obligation to deliver a commission, "but it is placed in his hands for the person entitled to it; and cannot be more lawfully withheld by him, than by any other person."[81] Marbury's claim "respects a paper, which according to law, is upon record, and to a copy of which the law gives a right, on the payment of ten cents."[82]

This point has been overlooked in contemporary discussions of *Marbury*. Marbury's notorious right is not to *delivery* of the commission, but rather to a mere copy from the record on demand. The right is therefore *statutory* (not constitutional), arising from the duty imposed by Congress upon the secretary "to do a certain act affecting the absolute rights of individuals, in the performance of which he is not placed under the particular direction of the President, and the performance of which, the President cannot lawfully forbid, and therefore is never presumed to have forbidden."[83] In other words, the secretary's duty is to perform a purely ministerial act not within executive discretion. It is within the power of a court to supply a remedy for an individual who has been harmed by the minister's failure to do his duty. That is the main reason why delivery of a commission cannot be considered essential to the completion of an appointment. "The transmission of the commission, is a practice directed by convenience, but not by law. It cannot therefore be necessary to constitute the appointment which must precede it, and which is the mere act of the President."[84]

In sum, the case falls squarely within the scope of Article III's "arising under" provision,[85] in that: (1) the plaintiff is potentially a judicial officer of the United States; and (2) the defendant's response (or lack thereof) amounts at best to executive interference with the Court's effort to perform its own proper function, or at worst to executive usurpation of judicial authority. It is therefore a case of a judiciary nature in the strongest sense.

The problem for Marbury, however, is that when Section 13, the provision that supposedly authorizes the mandamus remedy in his case, is construed literally, it runs afoul of Article III's distribution of federal judicial power. The second clause of the Article's second section reads:

> In all cases affecting ambassadors, other public ministers and consuls, and those in which a state shall be a party, the Supreme Court shall have original jurisdiction. In all the other cases before mentioned, the Supreme Court shall have appellate jurisdiction, both as to law and to fact, with such exceptions, and under such regulations as the Congress shall make.[86]

The "other cases before mentioned" refers back to the first clause of the same section, which spells out the various kinds of cases over which the Court has jurisdiction, including the grants of original jurisdiction in the second clause.[87] A straightforward reading of the text therefore demands the conclusion that the Founders specified the appellate jurisdiction quite as clearly as they had the original, subject only to the qualification that empowers Congress to make "exceptions" to the former.

## The Exceptions Clause

The *Marbury* opinion has been subjected to a variety of criticisms which revolve around the "exceptions" provision. Van Alstyne has suggested that the Founders intended nothing more by the original/appellate division than to provide a guideline for the Court if Congress failed to act.[88] David P. Currie has claimed that such a "provisional distribution" is "precisely what they [the Framers] did with respect to the appellate jurisdiction by empowering Congress to make 'exceptions.'"[89] The upshot of such arguments is succinctly expressed by William Winslow Crosskey: "The only legitimate question in *Marbury v. Madison* was whether Congress had made such an exception, by Section 13, in a constitutional manner. And that the answer to this question should have been in the affirmative is clear."[90] In other words, by drafting Section 13, Congress had merely "made an 'exception' to the appellate jurisdiction by providing original jurisdiction instead."[91]

These notions, if taken seriously, reduce the entirety of the second clause in Article III, Section 2, to superfluity. The Court certainly realized as much in *Marbury* and said so unequivocally: "That they [the Supreme Court] should have appellate jurisdiction in all other cases, with such exceptions as Congress might make, is no restriction; unless the words be deemed exclusive of original jurisdiction."[92]

Currie adds confusion to contradiction when he says that Marshall "was to reject the implications of his Marbury reasoning in *Cohens v. Virginia,* where he declared that Congress could grant appellate jurisdiction in cases where the Constitution provided for original."[93] Yet, as Currie himself points out, Alexander Hamilton had outlined reasons why original jurisdiction was provided in those cases involving the dignity of a state, whether domestic or foreign.[94] However, Currie fails to notice that Hamilton also spelled out the logic of attaching the exceptions clause to the appellate jurisdiction. It involved an effort on the part of the Founders to counter widespread public fear that the appellate jurisdiction "both as to law and fact" would empower the Supreme Court to overrule determinations of fact rendered by juries below.

The relevant language in the *Federalist* is the following:

To avoid all inconveniences, it will be safest to declare generally that the Supreme Court shall possess appellate jurisdiction both as to law and fact, and that this jurisdiction shall be subject to such exception and regulations as the national legislature may prescribe. This will enable the government to modify it in such a manner as will best answer the ends of public justice and security. The view of the matter, at any rate, puts it out of all doubt that the supposed abolition of the trial by jury, by the operation of this provision, is fallacious and untrue. The legislature of the United States would certainly have full power to provide that in appeals to the Supreme Court there should be no re-examination of facts where they had been tried in original causes by juries. This would certainly be an authorized exception; but if, for the reason already intimated, it should be thought too extensive, it might be qualified with a limitation to such causes only as are determinable at common law in that mode of trial.[95]

If Hamilton's interpretation is correct, there is no incompatibility between *Marbury* and *Cohens*, since the appellate jurisdiction would be subject to either enlargement or restriction, depending on what the "ends of public justice and security" require in the particular instance. To "grant appellate jurisdiction in cases where the Constitution provided for original," is therefore not equivalent to granting the reverse.

Marshall and his Court must surely have known this at the time of the *Marbury* decision, for the first two sentences of Section 13 differentiate between those instances where the Court's original jurisdiction is exclusive from those where it is not. In effect, those sentences "enlarge" the appellate jurisdiction of the Court. The inescapable logic of the Section 13 division is pointed out by the Court later in *Cohens*, via *reductio ad absurdum*.

Can it be affirmed, that a State might not sue the citizen of another State in a Circuit Court? Should the Circuit Court decide for or against its jurisdiction, should it dismiss the suit, or give judgement against the State, might not its decision be revised in the Supreme Court? The argument [of counsel] is, that it could not; and the very clause which is urged to prove, that the Circuit Court could give no judgement in the case, is also urged to prove, that its judgement is irreversible. A supervising Court, whose peculiar province it is to correct the errors of an inferior Court, has no power to correct a judgement given without jurisdiction, because, in the same case, that supervising Court has original jurisdiction. . . . It is, we think, apparent, that to give this distributive clause the interpretation contended for, to give its affirmative words a negative operation, in every possible case, would, in some instances, defeat the obvious intention of the article. . . . It must, therefore, be discarded. . . . The Court may imply a negative from affirmative words, where the implication promotes, not where it defeats the intention.[96]

In other words, in *Cohens*, the Marshall Court refuses to "imply a negative from affirmative words," because there the implication "defeats the intention." On the other hand, in *Marbury*, the implication promotes the intention, and thus a negative may be inferred. The Court addresses the issue squarely in *Marbury*.

> If it had been intended to leave it in the discretion of the legislature to apportion the judicial power between the supreme and inferior courts according to the will of that body, it would certainly have been useless to have proceeded further than to have defined the judicial power, and the tribunals in which it should be vested. The subsequent part of the section is mere surplusage, is entirely without meaning, if such is to be the construction.[97]

These remarks are unimpeachable. But in what immediately follows, it must be conceded that Marshall made a mistake: "If congress remains at liberty to give this court appellate jurisdiction, where the constitution has declared their jurisdiction shall be original; and original jurisdiction where the constitution has declared it shall be appellate; the distribution of jurisdiction, made in the constitution, is form without substance."[98] The mistake, however, is one of inappropriate expression, not of logic. Taken at face value the statement is entirely true. It is merely a hypothesis with two premises, both of which must be true if the conclusion is to follow. Since the first premise ("congress remains at liberty to give this court appellate jurisdiction, where the constitution has declared their jurisdiction shall be original") is *true*—as we have seen and as the Court later held in *Cohens*—it follows that the second premise ("congress remains at liberty to give this court original jurisdiction where the constitution has declared it shall be appellate") must be *false*. Were it true, then a faulty conclusion ("the distribution of jurisdiction, made in the constitution, is form without substance") would also have to be true. And the Court held to this logic in *Marbury*. Later, in *Cohens*, Marshall says that the "general expressions in the case of *Marbury v. Madison* must be understood with the limitations which are given to them in this opinion; limitations which in no degree affect the decision in that case, or the tenor of its reasoning."[99]

## Judicial Review

After demonstrating the incompatibility of Section 13 with the constitutional distribution of judicial power, the Court entertains the question of whether a jurisdiction inappropriately conferred may nevertheless be exercised. For its answer, the Court has recourse in the underlying premise of Article V.

> That the people have an original right to establish, for their future government, such principles as, in their opinion, shall most conduce to their own happiness, is the basis, on which the whole American fabric has been erected. The exercise of this original right is a very great exertion; nor can it, or ought it to be frequently repeated. The principles, therefore, so established, are deemed fundamental. And as the authority, from which they proceed, is supreme, and can seldom act, they are designed to be permanent. . . . It is a proposition too plain to be contested, that the constitution controls any legislative act repugnant to it; or, that the legislature may alter the constitution by an ordinary act.[100]

At this point the Court reaches the issue that eventually generated the great controversy over judicial review which has yet to subside. Granted that "the constitution is either a superior, paramount law, unchangeable by ordinary means, or it is on a level with ordinary legislative acts," does it nonetheless follow that an act, "repugnant to the constitution, . . . notwithstanding its invalidity, bind the courts, and oblige them to give it effect?"[101] Answering this crucial question, the Court articulates the theory of judicial function for which *Marbury* is celebrated.

> It is emphatically the province and duty of the judicial department to say what the law is. Those who apply the rule to particular cases, must of necessity expound and interpret that rule. If two laws conflict with each other, the courts must decide on the operation of each. So if a law be in opposition to the Constitution; if both the law and the Constitution apply to a particular case, so that the court must either decide that case conformably to the law, disregarding the constitution; or conformably to the constitution, disregarding the law; the court must determine which of these conflicting rules governs the case. This is the very essence of judicial duty.[102]

Since these lines have frequently been cited as precedent for a view of the judicial power which renders the Supreme Court ultimate arbiter of constitutional questions, it is equally important to assess what is *not* said in them. No exclusive power to interpret the fundamental law is claimed for the Court, here or anywhere else in *Marbury*. To be sure, it is "the province and duty of the judicial department to say what the law is"—but only "of necessity," whenever those "who apply the rule to particular cases" *must* determine which of two "conflicting rules governs the case." This portion of the *Marbury* opinion seems directed primarily toward justification for the idea that, in *some* cases, "the constitution must be looked into by the judges."[103] There is no denial of the legislature's power to do likewise; that is made clear a few paragraphs later in the opinion: "It is apparent, that the framers of the constitution contemplated that instrument, as a rule for the government of courts, as well as of the legislature."[104]

Even less does the language of *Marbury* suggest that the Court's determinations may legitimately transcend the confines of the particular case before it. After all, the Court has already said that its province is "solely, to decide on the rights of individuals."[105] And faced with a "repugnancy," it only has to "disregard" either statute or constitution to determine "which of these conflicting rules governs the case."[106] In other words, the power of review claimed by the Court in *Marbury* is merely a power of discretion to disregard existing laws in the decision of particular controversies, provided that the constitutional and statutory provisions involved are, like those in Article III and the Judiciary Act, *addressed to the Court itself*. If the provisions are *not* addressed to the Court itself, then the court is not *compelled*, as a matter of *logic*, to choose between them *in order to decide the case*. Since precedents are created by holdings on points of law *necessarily* decided in particular cases, the Court's choice between constitutional and statutory provisions, one or both of which are *not* addressed to the Court, should not control the decisions of subsequent cases. Nor should such unconstrained choices be read speculatively into the Court's opinion after the fact by historians, when the words of the Court itself are expressly to the contrary.

*Marbury* thus affords no basis for inferring that the Court is *bound* to disregard a statutory provision in conflict with the Constitution, except in that relatively small number of instances where the Constitution furnishes a direct rule for the courts. Indeed the *Marbury* Court suggests precisely this view in its reference to the idea of political questions. Therefore, when the Court declares the superiority of the Constitution over ordinary legislation in *Marbury*, it does so not in derogation of legislative power, but only in justification of its judgment in that case, which is the determination of the respective rights and duties of Marbury and Madison.

## Conclusions

The foregoing observations imply that the twentieth-century *Marbury* is largely a myth. Far from constituting an innovative decision, each important aspect of the opinion is grounded on familiar principles of legal interpretation. First, the Court's rendering an opinion apprising Marbury and Madison of their respective rights and duties was appropriate. The relief requested by Marbury was equitable in nature (since a mandatory injunction directing specific performance is an equitable remedy), and the function of a court of equity is to do as much justice as can be done under the circumstances of the case, when no adequate legal remedy is available. Since the court was powerless to issue the writ while sitting as a court of original jurisdiction, the maxim that wrongs are not to be without remedies demanded at least a statement of the law of the case. Despite Jefferson's retort, the opinion was not advisory, in the sense in which the doctrine proscribing *ex cathedra* pronouncements on constitutional questions has since been developed. The purpose of that doctrine is accomplished when a court refuses to interpret constitutional provisions in the *absence* of a bonafide case or controversy. There is no question concerning Marbury's standing to litigate. The only question concerns the appropriate forum.

Second, three familiar principles of construction fully account for the Court's handling of the law issues in *Marbury:* (1) interpret unambiguous language in a literal manner, unless such an interpretation would (2) render some other provision in the same document meaningless, or (3) defeat the intention of the drafters in some obvious way. Since literal interpretation of the fourth sentence in Section 13 does no violence to the remainder of the section in the sense of the second or third principles, the Court is fully justified in adopting the first principle as its rule of construction. The familiar conclusion that the *Marbury* Court went out of its way to invalidate Section 13 is therefore questionable. To be sure, one might criticize the Court for failure to adopt a *strained* construction of the provision in order to avoid declaring it unconstitutional. But saying that the Court failed to follow modern maxims of judicial restraint to the limit in a particular decision is not the same as saying that the decision amounted to gross abuse of judicial authority. In Marbury's case, the charge of gross abuse has frequently been made.

A similar analysis may be applied to the Court's interpretation of the distributive jurisdictional provisions in Article III. Even though these provisions appear to spell out the respective original and appellate jurisdictions so as to leave no overlap in the categories, the Court showed convincingly in *Cohens* that a literal reading of the clause pertaining to appellate jurisdiction would defeat the obvious intention of the drafters, thus violating the third of the principles stated above. The Court had already demonstrated in *Marbury* that nonliteral application of both clauses (original and appellate) *simultaneously* would reduce the entire section to superfluity, thereby violating the second principle of construction; further, if nonliteral application is required in *Cohens*, then literal interpretation is required in *Marbury*. And that is precisely the holding of the Court.

Finally, the Court's argument on judicial review in *Marbury* is defensive in character and appropriately restricted to the circumstances of the case at hand. Assuming that an act in violation of the Constitution is a nullity as a matter of law (which few have questioned), the Court proceeds to argue that, in *some* cases, it may say so. The cases in which it may say so are those (like *Marbury*) where the performance of essential judicial functions would be impaired if it said otherwise. Anything less would destroy the separation of powers so carefully established in the Constitution, thereby rendering much of its language pointless, and defeating the purposes of its drafters in a most obvious way.

It is time to substitute history for mythology and to reclaim the tradition for which *Marbury* once stood. Having examined the background of this tradition, subsequent sections will discuss its development and ultimate transformation.

# 6 · Judicial Review
# in the Marshall and Taney Periods

*Contemporaneous Reaction to* Marbury

Scholars have long agreed that contemporaneous reaction to the Court's assertion of its duty to disregard an unconstitutional statute in *Marbury v. Madison* was very mild.[1] Marshall's most prominent biographer, Albert J. Beveridge, was "dumbfounded by the apparent disinterest in the case."[2] He complained that Marshall's first great decision "received scant notice at the time of its delivery. The newspapers had little to say about it. Even the bench and the bar of the country, at least in the sections remote from Washington, appear not to have heard of it, or if they had, to have forgotten it."[3] Such newspaper coverage as there was tended to be reports rather than editorials, as is evidenced by articles in the *National Intelligencer* and the *Washington Federalist*, the most prominent Republican and Federalist papers, respectively, in the District of Columbia.[4] To the extent that the public paid heed to the decision, the focus was primarily on Marshall's indication that courts had power to issue writs of mandamus to executives in appropriate circumstances.[5] For the most part, the Court's refusal to enforce Section 13 of the Judiciary Act of 1789 was either approved or ignored.[6]

Though scholars have generally agreed that there was a dearth of contemporaneous criticism, they have disagreed about the explanation. Dewey, for example, believes that the cause lies in a general public failure to understand the opinion.[7] Coverage by the *Alexandria Gazette* the day after the opinion was rendered is a case in point: "The judges of the Supreme Court have given it as their opinion, in the case of the Mandamus, that the justices are entitled to their commissions, but, that they have not the power to issue a mandamus in the District of Columbia, it not being a State."[8] On the other hand, George Haskins suggests that the decision did not evoke much hostility because the Court, "only six days later, in *Stuart v. Laird,* . . . declared constitutional the repeal of the Judiciary Act of 1801."[9]

Whatever the force of truth contained in these observations, previous sections of this study have indicated that both are incomplete. Since the Court's refusal to apply Section 13 in *Marbury* was consistent with Lockean values, existing legal precedent, and the theory of judicial function embodied in the Constitution, it is more plausible to assume that the lack of public controversy derives from the general acceptability of the decision itself and the opinion that justified it. The surprise of Beveridge and others testifies that, by 1895, the case had taken on a symbolic significance which it did not possess at the hour of its decision and which surely neither the Court nor its critics envisioned in 1803. After all, from the period immediately following adoption of the Constitution to the election of 1800, the most prominent advocates of judicial power to invalidate acts of Congress had been Republicans (see Chapter 4). Likewise, in *Cooper v. Telfair,* decided by the Court only three years prior to *Marbury,* four justices, in separate opinions, had affirmed the general power of courts to invalidate legislation that was clearly contrary to constitutional provisions.[10]

It is difficult to understand how scholars have been able to argue that *Marbury,* now everybody's favorite precedent for judicial review, was itself unprecedented.[11] Nevertheless, Alexander Bickel can remark, as late as 1960, that "if any social process can be said to have been 'done' at a given time and by a given act, it is Marshall's achievement. The time was 1803; the act was the decision in the case of *Marbury v. Madison.*"[12]

## Legal Treatises during the Marshall and Taney Periods

Professor Bickel's assertion seems doubly difficult to maintain in view of major legal treatises published during the remainder of the Marshall and Taney periods. Perhaps the strongest affirmation that *Marbury* was generally accepted during Marshall's tenure as chief justice is found in contemporaneous writings of those who might have been expected to be his most vitriolic detractors. John Taylor, for example, in a book[13] largely devoted to an attack on the Court's opinion in *McCulloch v. Maryland,*[14] nonetheless reiterates approvingly a portion of *Marbury v.*

*Madison* that describes how the Founders' theory of judicial power applies to unconstitutional laws passed by Congress. Referring to the second paragraph in Article VI of the Constitution, Taylor remarks that

> as the constitution embraced our whole system of government, both state and federal, by delegating and reserving powers, the supremacy bestowed on it was intended equally and coextensively to protect and secure the powers delegated to the federal government, and those reserved to the states. In this construction of the word "supreme," the court itself has literally concurred, in asserting "that it would be its duty to declare an unconstitutional law void." The right of doing this arises from the supremacy of the constitution over law; from the restriction it imposes upon political departments on spheres to confine themselves within their limited orbits; and from its intention that each department or sphere should control another, if it transgresses its boundary. Upon this ground the court has asserted this constitutional power *in its own sphere. It can be defended upon no other.*[15]

Thomas Cooper, an even more extreme states' rights advocate than Taylor, also expressly conceded the correctness of the Court's reasoning in *Marbury*. Prior to recommending a constitutional amendment to overrule "mistakes of the Judiciary," Cooper addresses the question of the extent of federal jurisdiction.

> Much of it has been assumed for the most part, not merely on plausible but on undeniable legal conclusions. The Constitution of the United States, is the paramount law of the Union: the Constitution of each particular State, is the paramount Law of that State; for the legislatures and their laws, are of a derivative character, and inferior to that Supreme Law under which they hold their tenure, and from which they ultimately derive their authority. Of this supreme Law, the Judges sworn to decide according to law, must upon their oaths take notice; they cannot shut their eyes to it; and in cases of doubt or conflict it is their duty to determine. There is no gainsaying the able argument of Chief Justice Marshall on this point in *Marbury v. Madison.*[16]

Likewise, Benjamin Oliver, in a treatise on states' rights, cites *Marbury* as precedent for the principle that "the person applying for a mandamus must be without any other remedy, and the officer to whom it is directed, must be one to whom such direction may be legally made."[17] A few paragraphs later, Oliver adds: "If, in a case depending before any court, a legislative act shall conflict with the constitution, it is admitted that the court must exercise its judgment on both, and that the construction must control the act. The court must determine whether a repugnancy does or does not exist, and in making this determination must construe both instruments."[18] Finally, Peter Du Ponceau, in a famous discourse on the Constitution, does not even mention judicial review in a section entitled "Judicial Power."[19]

Throughout the entirety of his career, Marshall's most outspoken opponent was Thomas Jefferson. Yet, in his earliest recorded mention of judicial review after the *Marbury* decision, Jefferson made no reference to the case. In a letter to Abigail Adams, written some eighteen months after *Marbury*, he comments on judicial review of the Sedition Act, declaring that "nothing in the constitution has given them a right to decide for the executive, more than to the Executive to decide for them. Both magistracies are equally independent in the sphere of action assigned to them."[20] Dewey—a modern-day Marshall detractor who has stated that "once Marshall's judicial philosophy coincided with political advantage, there was sure to be an exercise of judicial review"[21]—nonetheless concludes from Jefferson's letter that "as he did not bring up the *Marbury* case, it is evident that, at least in 1804, the judicial review exercised in *Marbury v. Madison* was acceptable to Jefferson because the Supreme Court was interpreting legislation involving its own judicial sphere."[22] Even after Jefferson's attacks on Marshall and his Court intensified in later years, Jefferson never denied the power of courts to perform the limited type of review exercised in *Marbury*.

In a letter to George Hay during the trial of Aaron Burr, Jefferson said of *Marbury* that "the judges in the outset disclaimed all cognizance of the case; altho' they then went on to say what would have been their opinion, had they had cognizance of it."[23] He then revealed what was most upsetting to him in the opinion: Even if jurisdiction had been granted, a mandamus could not have issued, for "to a commission, a deed, a bond, *delivery* is essential to give validity."[24] No mention was made of that portion of the opinion where the Court refused to apply an unconstitutional statute.

Jefferson continued to refer to these same points throughout the remainder of his life, with minor variations. In 1823, he wrote to Justice Johnson, alluding to *Marbury*:

This practice of Judge Marshall of travelling out of his case to prescribe what the law would be in a moot case not before the court, is very irregular and very censurable . . . the question before them was ended, but the Chief Justice went on to lay down what the law would be, had they jurisdiction of the case, to wit, that they should command the delivery. The object was clearly to instruct any other court having the jurisdiction, what they should do, if Marbury should apply to them. Besides the impropriety of this gratuitous interference, could anything exceed this perversion of law?[25]

Consider also the remarks of Spencer Roane, chief justice of Virginia's Court of Appeals during most of Marshall's tenure on the Supreme Court. Roane, a bitter opponent of Marshall as well as confidant to Jefferson, aggressively supported expansive judicial review throughout his life, so long as the judge's gavel was in the hands of the *state* judiciary. In *Hunter v. Martin*, the Virginia Court of Appeals unanimously asserted its power to disregard an act of the United States Congress: "The appellate power of the Supreme Court of the United States does not extend to the Court under a sound construction of the Constitution of the United States; that so much of the twenty-fifth Section of the Act to establish the Judicial Courts of the United States as extends the appellate jurisdiction of the Supreme Court to this Court, is not in pursuance of the Constitution of the United States."[26] Judge Roane further declared in a separate opinion that "this Court is both at liberty and is bound to follow its own convictions on the subject."[27]

Finally, there is Brockenbrough's second "Amphictyon" essay, which appeared in the *Richmond Enquirer* on April 2, 1819, and attacked the Supreme Court for its *failure* to invalidate the law creating the Second Bank of the United States in *McCulloch v. Maryland*.[28] As had been the case in the 1790s, this attitude toward the Court remained characteristically Republican throughout the Marshall period.

Joseph Story, Marshall's respected colleague on the Court, remarked on the early Republican theory of judicial power in contrasting Jefferson's view with that of the Federalists. According to Story, the "power of interpreting the laws involves necessarily the function to ascertain, whether they are conformable, to declare them void and inoperative."[29] Elsewhere, Story articulates what I have referred to as the Founders' theory of functional coordinate review, explicitly distinguishing it from Jefferson's arbitrary coordinate review.

So, if a proposition be before Congress, every member of the legislative body is bound to examine and decide for himself, whether the bill or resolution is within the constitutional reach of the legislative powers confided to Congress. And in many cases the decision of the executive and legislative departments, thus made, become final and conclusive, being *from their very nature* and character incapable of revision. . . . yet cases may be readily imagined, in which a tax may be laid, or a treaty made, upon motives and grounds wholly beside the intention of the constitution. The remedy, however, in such cases is solely by an appeal to the people at the elections; or by the salutary power of amendment, provided by the constitution itself. But, where the question is *of a different nature*, and capable of judicial inquiry and decision, there it admits of a very different consideration. . . . Mr. Jefferson carries his doctrine much further, and holds, that each department of government has an exclusive right, independent of the judiciary, to decide for itself, as to the true construction of the constitution . . . and he proceeds to give examples, in which he disregarded, when president, the decisions of the judiciary.[30]

Considering Judge Roane's view, Jefferson's theory might well have been considered applicable to states as well as to presidents.

On the other side, the Federalist attitude toward *Marbury* and its progeny during the Marshall period may be aptly demonstrated by Chancellor Kent's famous overstatement. Kent asserts that, in *Marbury*, "the power and duty of the judiciary to disregard an unconstitutional act of Congress, or of any state legislature, were declared, in an argument approaching the certainty of a mathematical demonstration."[31]

Whatever the partisan perspective on the issue, the institution of judicial power to invalidate laws in appropriate circumstances (the appropriateness being dependent on the perspective), as articulated by Marshall's Court in *Marbury*, remained essentially unquestioned during the Marshall era. I have found only four statements throughout the entire period that take a negative view of the Court's authority to refuse to apply congressional statutes. The first of these is part of a letter from John Steele, a former United States comptroller and a prominent Federalist, to Nathaniel Macon, Republican Speaker of the House. Steele denounced the "fashionable doctrine . . . that the Courts have power to pronounce acts of Congress unconstitutional and void." In response,

Macon disagreed.[32] The second statement is contained in one of the letters from "An Unlearned Layman," a series printed in the *Washington Federalist* from April 20 through April 29, 1803. "Layman" pointed out the "danger and inconsistency of such a power residing in the judges," and argued for the "supremacy of the legislature" instead.[33] Another anonymous letter, to the *Aurora* on March 6, 1804, contended that the "claim of a power of suspending laws to be exercised by the judiciary was a part of the 'Federalist system of aristocracy.'"[34]

The remaining assertion is reported by Haines from the *Memoirs* of John Quincy Adams. According to Haines, Adams referred to *Marbury v. Madison* as follows: "It was generally believed that 'if the judges of the Supreme Court should dare as they had done, to declare an act of Congress unconstitutional, or to send a mandamus to the Secretary of State as they had done,' it would be the duty of the House of Representatives and the Senate to remove them for exceeding their constitutional limits."[35] Needless to say, four statements—one by a Federalist, two anonymous, and another by a former president who apparently did not remember exactly what was decided in the case—constitute poor evidence of widespread disaffection with *Marbury*'s holding.

As previously suggested, "unreconstructed" Republicans insisted on a wider scope for the application of judicial power,[36] and their attacks on the Court were directed at its *failure* to invalidate national laws in specific instances.[37] The image of the Court in the mind of one of its most stubborn opponents was that of flatterer, not of usurper: "Let us not act like Cambyses's Judges, who when their approbation was demanded by the prince, to some illegal measure, said, that, *though there was a written law, the Persian Kings might follow their own will and pleasure.*"[38]

The general acquiescence in *Marbury*'s version of judicial power was sustained until the end of the Civil War. Even the Court's most vehement critics apparently accepted its principle of limited judicial review, and some ventured so far as to distinguish carefully *Marbury*'s holdings from whichever later decisions had become the focus of their attacks. This impression is strongly reinforced when attending to the most famous anti-Court treatise of the period, Benton's *Examination of the Dred Scott Case.*[39]

In *Dred Scott*, the Court had invalidated the Missouri Compromise of 1820 on substantive due-process grounds.[40] According to Benjamin F. Wright, Chief Justice Taney's opinion for the Court made "the first judicial assertion of a general supervisory jurisdiction over Congress."[41]

Both Benton and the Court failed to mention *Marbury*, yet the basis of Benton's argument against Taney's opinion is clearly the logic of *Marbury*. Referring to some rulings in *Dred Scott* which bear on congressional authority to prohibit slavery in the territories, Benton says that "these decisions upon their face show themselves to be political, and tried by the test of enforcement, they are proved to be so. The Supreme Court cannot enforce these decisions; and that is the test of its jurisdiction. Where it cannot enforce, it cannot try."[42]

Examination of other important legal commentaries published during the Taney period reveal similar acquiescence in (or ignorance of) the opinion in *Marbury* v. *Madison*. Some of these works reflect the increasing militancy of the states' rights school of constitutional jurisprudence. Calhoun, for example, explicitly affirms the Court's power to invalidate *national* laws in cases that embrace "such questions as are of a judicial character;—that is, questions in which the parties litigant are amenable to the process of the courts."[43] Then, in disregard of Article VI, Calhoun asserts that "there is nothing in the constitution which vests authority in the government of the United States, or any of its departments, to enforce its decision against that of a separate government of a State."[44]

On the other hand, in discourses unencumbered by the states'-rights perspective, unquestioning adherence to *Marbury* (and to *Cohens* as well) is in evidence everywhere. Parsons, for example, cites *Marbury* as authority for the proposition that "the people have an original right to establish, for their future government, such principles as, in their opinion, shall most conduce to their own happiness";[45] and likewise, that a court is obliged to disregard an unconstitutional statute whenever there is no other way to decide a case that is properly within its jurisdiction.[46] Duer, in one of the most thoroughly documented treatises of the time, does not cite *Marbury* as precedent for judicial review of Congress, but rather in support of its jurisdictional holding,[47] and as authority for the rule that "if two statutes conflict with each other, the Courts must decide upon the operation of each, and endeavor, if possible, to harmonize their provisions."[48]

## Van Buren's View of Marbury

The only serious critique of *Marbury v. Madison* committed to writing during the entire period of Taney's tenure is found in a portion of the memoirs of Martin Van Buren.[49] These were published in 1867, five years after their author's death and two years past the closing of the period discussed in the present chapter. However, it is appropriate to consider Van Buren's thoughts at this point, since he was, after all, firmly rooted in the Taney era. Van Buren had served with Taney in Andrew Jackson's cabinet, and Taney, of course, sat on the Court throughout Van Buren's presidency.

Van Buren's book is significant for this study, because it contained the lengthiest discussion of *Marbury* to its date. Virtually an entire chapter was devoted to a recounting of the context and decision of the case.[50] Van Buren's description was highly partisan—as might be expected, since the overall plan of the work was to trace the rise of political parties in the American Republic. *Marbury* was thus interpreted from the standpoint of its contribution to the partisan political controversy of its day, rather than from a legal perspective. That surely accounts for Van Buren's focus on the mandamus aspect of the case, which had generated most of the contemporaneous criticism of *Marbury* in the first place.[51] To some extent, the treatment of this aspect was a repetition of earlier criticisms: that Marshall had manipulated the order of questions presented in the case so as to discuss issues not properly before the Court; and that such behavior exhibited "a culpable want of courtesy on the part of one of the three great departments of the Federal Government toward a coordinate member."[52] In that last quote, Van Buren (like Jefferson before him) failed to notice that, in the *Marbury* situation, the observation cuts both ways.

More interesting for our purposes is Van Buren's insistence that the Court should have renounced jurisdiction of *Marbury*'s case on statutory grounds alone, since in his view the "plain intention" of Section 13 had been

> to extend the right of issuing a mandamus, in the exercise of its *appellate jurisdiction*, to any subordinate authorities upon whom Congress might confer judicial power, whether that power was given to a court, or to a single officer not constituting a court according to the ordinary interpretation of that word. . . . To think otherwise is to suppose that the men who framed the Judiciary Act of 1789 designed by the terms they employed to give to the Supreme Court original jurisdiction in cases in which it was denied to it by the Constitution—a design too absurd and too disingenuous to have found even a momentary resting-place in the minds of those great men.[53]

That this difficulty with the decision in *Marbury* is removed when the whole of Section 13 is read in context has already been shown.[54] Nor is it necessary to impute malicious design to those who penned the act; poor legislative draftsmanship is a more likely possibility. Yet Van Buren's curious reversal of the *argumentum ad hominem* turned out to constitute the downfall of his argument. A few paragraphs later, he claimed that Section 25 of the Judiciary Act of 1789, giving power to the Supreme Court to "reexamine" and "reverse" decisions of state courts of last resort,[55] was unconstitutional, "an idea never broached in the Federal Convention, or in the slightest degree alluded to in the Constitution it adopted."[56]

Now, if it is "absurd" and "disingenuous" to attribute to the drafters of the Judiciary Act an intent to confer unwarranted enlargement of the Court's original jurisdiction, then how much more so is it to attribute to them a desire to enlarge the Court's authority to review state decisions beyond proper constitutional bounds? Surely the latter is a far more significant expansion than the former and would have been proportionately more difficult to perpetrate on an unwilling public, given the temper of the times. In truth, however, Van Buren's theory demanded this incongruity, for it was his view that *both* Marbury *and the Judiciary Act* had been but singular steps in an overarching Federalist conspiracy to "select some department, or some nook or corner in our political system, and to make it the depository of power which public sentiment could not reach nor the people control."[57]

The difficulties with all this are that Section 25 is deduced *from the letter* of Articles III and VI[58] and that *Marbury* is fully consistent with the Founders' theory of judicial function.[59] Van Buren's theory thus falls victim to the classic problem of conspiratorial theorizing about political origination. If Section 25 and *Marbury* are in fact usurpations, then so must have been the Federal Convention itself, a point evidently not lost on J. Allen Smith a half-century later.[60] On the other hand, even if the Federal Convention were a usurpation, the people nevertheless ratified its fruits *together* with their manifest implications, and so the Judiciary Act and *Marbury* must be regarded as legitimate. The conspiracy theory thereby dissolves into a contradiction which issues from its own origins.

Nowhere did Van Buren deny the power of the Court (or of courts generally) to set aside statutes in the decision of particular cases. To the contrary, he tacitly approved it in his obvious disenchantment with Section 25. Neither did he deny the invalidity of Section 13, when read the way the *Marbury* Court construed it. The importance of his commentary therefore lies, together with the contract-clause critiques of the 1870s, in its contribution to an atmosphere of increasing hostility toward the Marshall Court among liberal intellectuals in the late nineteenth century. This hostility was to erupt into a chorus of boos in the 1890s (see Chapter 11). Ultimately, the guns were turned upon the Constitution itself in the full-blown critiques of Progressive historians during the first two decades of the twentieth century. But for now, Van Buren is a voice in the wilderness, a throwback to the days when Jefferson talked of "sappers and miners."

## Jackson and Lincoln on Judicial Review

Before closing this chapter, it is appropriate to take account of the remarks of Andrew Jackson and Abraham Lincoln on the relationship of the Supreme Court to the other branches of government in the matter of constitutional interpretation. Neither Jackson nor Lincoln had specific comments on *Marbury v. Madison*, but each confirms, albeit in different ways, the theory of review that has been developed here.

Jackson's view was articulated best in his message to Congress of July 10, 1832, vetoing the bill that renewed the charter of the Bank of the United States.[61] The Supreme Court had affirmed the bank's constitutionality some thirteen years previously, in *McCulloch v. Maryland*.[62] Denying that the *McCulloch* decision had put to rest the constitutional squabble for all time, Jackson declared that all three branches of the federal government were under a solemn duty to consider (and reconsider) any constitutional question raised by measures properly brought before them. Thus admitting the power of judicial review, Jackson wrote, "It is as much the duty of the House of Representatives, of the Senate, and of the President to decide upon the constitutionality of any bill or resolution which may be presented to them for passage or approval as it is of the supreme judges when it may be brought before them for judicial decision."[63]

Jackson drew upon a theory of balanced government to support his coordinate constitutional review, rightly contending that the mere existence of a previous Supreme Court decision upholding a law does not *obligate* Congress or the president to *approve* such a law if it comes before either of them again in an official capacity.[64] At most, a previous Court decision *invalidating* a law might deny Congress effective authority to *pass* such a law in the future. But these two situations are not remotely analogous.

The constitutional portion of Jackson's veto message was controversial, but hardly unprecedented. Remini reports that, from the time the Constitution went into effect until 1832, presidents had employed the veto nine times, three of which involved important issues. "In every instance the President claimed that the offending legislation violated the Constitution. It was therefore generally accepted that a question of a bill's constitutionality was the only reason to apply a veto."[65] In other words, it was understood from the beginning that Congress and the president shared responsibility for interpreting the Constitution with the Supreme Court. Taney later confirmed Jackson's position respecting executive interpretive authority and qualified the doctrine somewhat by restricting it to situations where the president is "acting as part of the legislative power—and not of his right or duty as an executive officer."[66]

Lincoln articulated his position on the division of responsibility for constitutional interpretation amid the controversy over the *Dred Scott* decision.[67] Lincoln's views mostly parallel those of Jackson, though Lincoln's primary focus was on congressional, rather than presidential, authority. In a series of speeches and letters delivered in 1857 and 1858, Lincoln reiterated the power of the legislative department to interpret the Constitution.[68] Reacting to the Court's holding in *Dred Scott*, that blacks could not be citizens and thus were not entitled to sue in courts of law, Lincoln indicated his willingness to acquiesce in the decision, so far as the actual litigants were concerned.

> I do not resist it. If I wanted to take Dred Scott from his master, I would be interfering with property, and that terrible difficulty that Judge Douglas speaks of . . . would arise. But I am doing no such thing as that, but all that I am doing is refusing to obey it as a political rule. If I were in Congress, and a vote should come up on a question whether slavery should be prohibited in a new territory, in spite of that Dred Scott decision, I would vote that it should.[69]

Lincoln thus agrees with Jackson on the power of Congress to repeal laws that previously have been validated by the Court, and goes further by affirming its powers to pass laws of a kind already invalidated by the Court.

That he also agreed with Jackson (and with Taney) on the extent of the president's power to interpret the Constitution while performing a veto is apparent from a speech delivered on July 17, 1858. Responding to the charge that he had counseled disobedience to law by opposing *Dred Scott*, Lincoln says:

I am opposed to that decision in a certain sense, but not in the sense which he [Douglas] puts on it. I say that in so far as it decided in favor of Dred Scott's master and against Dred Scott and his family, I do not propose to disturb or resist the decision. I have never proposed to do any such thing. I think, that in respect for judicial authority, my humble history would not suffer in a comparison with that of Judge Douglas. He would have the citizen conform his vote to that decision; the Member of Congress, his; the President, his use of the veto power. He would make it a rule of political action for the people and all the departments of the government. I would not. By resisting it as a political rule, I disturb no right of property, create no disorder, excite no mobs.[70]

Elsewhere, Lincoln tacitly approves the constitutional basis for Jackson's bank veto and reminds Douglas that he also supported the veto on the same ground.

Do not gentlemen here remember the case of that same Supreme Court, some twenty-five or thirty years ago, deciding that a National Bank was constitutional? . . . Such is the truth, whether it be remembered or not. The Bank charter ran out, and a re-charter was granted by Congress. That re-charter was laid before General Jackson. It was urged upon him, when he denied the constitutionality of the bank, that the Supreme Court had decided that it was constitutional; and that General Jackson then said that the Supreme Court had no right to lay down a rule to govern a co-ordinate branch of the government, the members of which had sworn to support the Constitution—that each member had sworn to support that Constitution as he understood it. I will venture here to say, that I have heard Judge Douglas say that he approved of General Jackson for that act. What has now become of all his tirade about "resistance to the Supreme Court"?[71]

In sum, both Jackson and Lincoln accepted a power of judicial review in the Supreme Court. Lincoln went even further, denying explicitly any countervailing authority in the government to disregard Court decisions insofar as they applied to particular litigants. Lincoln made a sharp distinction between the aspects of judicial decisions that "absolutely determine the case decided" and those that "indicate to the public how other similar cases will be decided when they arise."[72] For Lincoln, no person or agency of government is entitled to interfere with the binding effect of a court's decision on the parties to a lawsuit. On the other hand, acquiescence in the *stare decisis* effect of a judicial decision may vary with the circumstances of the case. Even as to *Dred Scott,*

> If this important decision had been made by the unanimous con- currence of the judges, and without any apparent partisan bias, and in accordance with legal public expectation and with the steady prac- tice of the departments throughout our history, and had been in no part, based on assumed historical facts which are not really true; or, if wanting in some of these, it had been before the court more than once, and had there been affirmed and re-affirmed through a course of years, it then might be, perhaps would be, factious, nay, even revolutionary, to not acquiesce in it as a precedent.[73]

Jackson did not go so far, but rather contended that the authority of the judiciary must not "be permitted to control the Congress or the Execu- tive when acting in their legislative capacities, but to have only such influence as the force of their reasoning may deserve."[74] Jackson's con- stitutional doctrine thus seems more like that of Jefferson than does Lincoln's. By suggesting that he would have disobeyed judicial orders in *Marbury* and other cases, Jefferson tacitly asserted the right of the pres- ident to disregard court decisions he disagreed with. However, these dif- ferences should not obscure the more crucial congruity: that both Jack- son and Lincoln claimed for the Congress and the executive the right "to think and act as equal and independent members of the government."[75]

# 7 · The Strange History of *Marbury* in the Supreme Court

History is fraught with paradox. For the proverbial "man on the street," the subject tends to be viewed as a collection of stories about the past, and the demands of academic specialization have encouraged a somewhat similar attitude among professionals in the twentieth century. Yet, when seen from a wider perspective, history is the study of the movement of human institutions through time. As such, it is a process whose constitutive events or aspects are never complete at any given point in time. In the language of modern existentialism, it is always "becoming," not merely "being."

That observation is especially appropriate in the context of Anglophilic legal history. The fundamental premise of systems based on common law is that *stare decisis*, not political philosophy or social policy, is the primary justification acceptable for most court decisions. It follows that historical treatment of a legal doctrine in America involves preeminently its unfolding as precedent. As noted before, then, the history of *Marbury v. Madison* is largely a history of judicial review in the United States.

Though the Supreme Court has not always adhered to precedent, it has always adhered to the principle of *stare decisis* in its constitutional decisions. Indeed, the preponderance of opinions emanating from that distinguished body of jurists for the past two hundred years has been devoted to the task of making the Court's decisions appear compatible with previous ones. Even those justices who question the role of precedent in constitutional adjudication strive to square present rulings with existing law, although such attempts frequently amount to the squaring of circles. The Court's treatment of *Marbury* during various historical periods is indicative of how it conceived its own power during those eras. With these thoughts in mind, I shall now examine the history of *Mar-*

*bury v. Madison* in the Supreme Court of the United States. Special attention will be paid to the Court's attitude regarding two currently accepted presuppositions: (1) that *Marbury* "established" the power of judicial review; (2) that judicial review is a power in the Supreme Court to issue "final" interpretations on constitutional questions generally.

## Marbury *in the Supreme Court, Nineteenth Century*

The Supreme Court must have agreed, throughout most of the nineteenth century, with the view of *Marbury v. Madison* advanced in this study. During the remainder of Marshall's tenure as chief justice, ten separate opinions contain references to *Marbury*. Nine are purely jurisdictional in nature, buttressing the distribution of jurisdiction contained in Article III.[1] The remaining reference is made to support the ruling that writs of mandamus may issue to executive officials only when engaged in the performance of purely ministerial duties.[2] Not only is the authority of *Marbury* not questioned in any of these instances, but the Court's power to invalidate laws is not mentioned at all.

The idea that the Court's decision in *Marbury* was viewed by Marshall's contemporaries as only a step in the continuous clarification of the restrictive theory of judicial function—and not as an "explosive" decision "establishing the power of judicial review"[3]—is further supported by the character of other constitutional decisions rendered by Marshall's Court. As Professor Currie has pointed out, the "entire constitutional output of the Court between 1801 and 1810," with the exception of two cases, dealt with purely jurisdictional issues.[4] Four involved the federal diversity jurisdiction;[5] three (including *Marbury*) decided questions pertaining to Article III's original/appellate distribution;[6] three involved the general jurisdiction of the federal courts.[7] Eight of these decisions (again including *Marbury*) may be plausibly construed as effectively narrowing the scope of federal judicial power,[8] lending credence to the observation of Haskins and Johnson that "self-restraint and extreme caution in asserting jurisdiction characterized the Supreme Court from 1801 to 1815."[9]

Examination of constitutional cases throughout the remainder of the Marshall period tends to confirm the pattern of the Court's early years. In the resolution of jurisdictional questions, the Court adhered, as it had in *Marbury*, to narrow views respecting the range of judicial discretion,[10] unless Congress had clearly provided for the assumption of appellate jurisdiction via statute.[11] In substantive areas, the Court allowed wide latitude to the discretion of the people's representatives in Congress[12] and also in the states,[13] unless there were explicit violations of relatively unambiguous constitutional limitations.[14] Most of these decisions hardly reveal a Court desirous of expanding its authority at the expense of either Congress or the states. Rather, they depict a Court deferential to democracy, yet prepared to defend the rights of individuals against clear-cut excesses of government.

The patterns of commentary on *Marbury* and judicial review, established during Marshall's tenure as chief justice, remained virtually intact until the end of the Civil War. From 1835 to 1865, *Marbury* is cited in fifteen separate opinions in the *United States Reports*. As before, the largest number of citations is in the jurisdictional area.[15] Six concern nuances in the mandamus remedy.[16] One refers to a well-known passage in *Cohens v. Virginia*, where Marshall had clarified some loose language in *Marbury* which was unnecessary to the decision in that case.[17] Again, there is no hint of a critical attitude toward *Marbury* or any of its holdings in these citations, nor is judicial review mentioned.

Neither is a sharp divergence of views between the Marshall Court and the Taney Court apparent in cases involving important constitutional issues.[18] Robert G. McCloskey remarks, while commenting on the overall tenor of constitutional decision making in the Taney era, that

> as the decisions were finally read and compared with those of Marshall's time, as the whole doctrinal course of the Taney Court was traced, it became apparent that . . . the old jurisprudence had not been broken down after all, or even very greatly altered: the claims of property were still well-protected, the nation was not constitutionally fragmented, judicial power was not surrendered . . . the basic dogmas of Marshall's contract clause interpretation were not challenged . . . the national government's supremacy over the states was repeatedly upheld.[19]

In the jurisdictional area, David Currie has pointed out that "the principal departure of Marshall's successors in this field would be to take a still broader view of federal jurisdiction in diversity and admiralty cases."[20] During Taney's years as chief justice, the Court, for the first time, took jurisdiction of a boundary dispute between two states;[21] held that, for diversity purposes, a corporation[22] and its members[23] are presumed to be citizens of the state of incorporation; upheld a congressional extension of federal admiralty jurisdiction to the Great Lakes[24] and to navigable rivers beyond "the ebb and flow of the tide";[25] and declared that, in a case involving bills of exchange, the Court could apply "general commercial law," rather than the law of the state as interpreted by its own courts.[26]

In cases touching on the relationship of the Supreme Court to coordinate branches of the national government, the Taney Court generally held to its predecessor's sharp distinction between policy and legal questions, suggested early in *Marbury*[27] and later in two other Marshall opinions.[28] The most famous example of that adherence is found in *Luther v. Borden.* The Court refused to determine which of two contending factions was the legitimate government of Rhode Island, because the president had already resolved the dispute, which was of a "political" nature.[29]

The only serious breakdown in this continuity of outlook was *Dred Scott v. Sanford*, where the Court, among other things, invalidated the Missouri Compromise of 1820.[30] For our purposes, the most interesting aspect of the holding is the Court's striking failure to cite *Marbury v. Madison* as precedent for its exercise of judicial review. No doubt the absence of a *Marbury* reference derived from the fact that *Dred Scott* was the first time that the Supreme Court invalidated national legislation in a case unequivocally *not* of a judiciary nature.[31]

To summarize, between 1803 and 1865, the Court had set aside only two acts of Congress—one in an opinion containing a restrictive interpretation of judicial authority *(Marbury)*, the other in an opinion involving a sweeping denial of legislative power *(Dred Scott)*. Throughout the entire period and without exception, the Court had read *Marbury v. Madison* as having settled either a narrow jurisdictional question or a technical issue relating to the mandamus remedy. *Marbury's* importance as a precedent for judicial review of legislation was never mentioned by the Court, not even in the only other case of the period in which the Court invalidated an act of Congress.

This pattern continued during the period from 1865 through 1894, the year before the fateful *Pollock* and *Knight* decisions.[32] During these years, the Court invalidated national laws in no fewer than twenty cases,[33] yet *Marbury* is mentioned in none of them. As before, those instances where *Marbury* is cited relate primarily to the jurisdictional area[34] or to the mandamus remedy.[35] A few of the citations invoke *Marbury's* distinction between "political" and "ministerial" acts of administrative officials.[36] Two refer to the technical finality of acts within the executive discretion.[37] One quotes the equitable "right/remedy" maxim announced in the first section of the *Marbury* opinion.[38] One mentions the *Cohens* clarification of *Marbury* dicta.[39] Finally, for the first time in the history of the Supreme Court, *Marbury v. Madison* is cited as precedent for the idea that courts may enforce constitutional limitations on legislative bodies. This citation is found in the Court's opinion in *Mugler v. Kansas*, decided in 1887.[40]

The *Mugler* reference is significant, because it involves two important misrepresentations of *Marbury*. First, quoting *Marbury*, the *Mugler* Court asks:

> To what purpose . . . are powers limited, and to what purpose is that limitation committed to writing, if these limits may, at any time, be passed by those intended to be restrained? The distinction between a government with limited and unlimited powers is abolished, if those limits do not confine the persons on which they are imposed, and if acts prohibited and acts allowed are of equal obligation.[41]

This segment of Marshall's argument is used in *Marbury* to support the conclusion that legislative acts contrary to the Constitution are void, not that courts have the power to refuse to apply them.[42] But the *Mugler* Court uses the passage to propose that "the courts must obey the Constitution rather than the lawmaking department of government, and must, upon their own responsibility, determine whether, in any particular case, these limits have been passed."[43]

Second, adding insult to injury, the *Mugler* Court then employs *Marbury* in the service of the developing doctrine of substantive due process: "The courts are not bound by mere forms, nor are they to be misled by mere pretenses. They are at liberty—indeed, are under a solemn duty—to look at the substance of things, whenever they enter upon the inquiry whether the legislature has transcended the limits of its authority."[44] All this occurs in a passage which is essentially obiter dicta, since the actual decision in *Mugler* merely upheld a state prohibition on manufacture and sale of intoxicating beverages. Yet the use of *Marbury* in a foreshadowing of *Lochner* gives one pause and clearly indicates the direction in which the Court is moving at this stage in its history. According to Corwin, the *Mugler* passage is the earliest indication of the Court's acceptance of substantive due process as Fourteenth Amendment doctrine.[45]

That *Marbury* was cited only once in support of judicial review between 1865 and 1894 is even more striking in view of the Court's contemporaneous invalidation of ten times as many congressional statutes as had been voided by both the Marshall and Taney Courts together.[46] On the other hand, only a handful of these cases actually involved constitutional questions bearing directly on the performance of judicial functions.[47] Thus Wright observes that, during this period, "the Court is beginning to . . . act as a supervisor of legislative righteousness and as a guardian of the spirit of the Constitution,"[48] which suggests that the Court had already begun to prefer the logic of *Dred Scott* over *Marbury*, without saying so.

Finally, in 1894, the Supreme Court for the first time cited *Marbury* in support of an actual exercise of its power to invalidate acts of Congress in *Pollock*, the famous Income Tax Case.[49] There the Court declares that *Marbury* confirms the idea that "it is within judicial competency, by express provisions of the Constitution or by necessary inference and implication, to determine whether a given law of the United States is or is not made in pursuance of the Constitution, and to hold it valid or void accordingly."[50] After quoting extensively from the *Marbury* opinion, the Court qualifies its reading of the case by restricting the exercise of judicial review to "proper" cases, without indicating precisely what that means.[51]

## Marbury *in the Supreme Court, Twentieth Century*

In light of the era of judicial assertiveness that was on the horizon and the Court's "discovery" of *Marbury*'s judicial-review component, one might have expected to find extensive development of the "precedent" in the years after 1894. Such is not the case. Between 1895 and 1957, *Marbury* is cited only thirty-eight times, hardly more often than during the thirty-year period preceding 1895.[52]

As before, most of the citations have nothing to do with judicial review. Five refer to the "right/remedy" maxim.[53] Four support the holding that writs of mandamus may be issued only as an exercise, or in aid, of appellate jurisdiction.[54] Four refer to the "ministerial/discretionary" distinction made in *Marbury*.[55] Four confirm that acts in violation of the Constitution are not law, without citing *Marbury* to show that courts may refuse to enforce them.[56] Three pertain to questions about the removal power of the president.[57] Two refer to sections of the *Marbury* opinion which imply that courts may resolve only "cases or controversies" instituted according to the regular course of judicial procedure.[58] Two concern Marshall's remark in *Cohens* that general expressions (in *Marbury*) are to be taken "in connection with the case in which they are used."[59] Two involve the relationship between executive appointments and commissions.[60] Two utilize *Marbury* to support the principle that no words in the Constitution should be presumed to be without effect.[61] One maintains that constitutional language should receive a liberal construction whenever individual rights are at stake.[62] Another supports the idea that the national government is supreme within its lawful sphere.[63]

Eight of the *Marbury* citations during this period pertain to the judicial power to invalidate laws, and four of these occur between 1900 and 1926. The first follows the pattern of the *Pollock* reference, stating that the power of judicial review is drawn by implication from the nature of a written constitution, but only in clear cases.[64] Again, exactly what is meant by "clear" is not disclosed—although in 1901, *Marbury* is used to support a hypothetical judicial invalidation of an Article I, Section 9 violation.[65] The third reference to *Marbury*'s judicial-review holding is in the famous *Muskrat* case, where the Court employs a restrictive interpretation to show that courts have no "general veto power" over legislation, but may invalidate laws only in proper cases, when forced to choose between the Constitution and the law.[66] Sixteen years later, in the equally famous *Myers* case, *Marbury* is applied to defend the view that courts possess the power "to consider and pass upon the validity of acts of Congress enacted in violation of the limitations of the Constitution, when properly brought before them in cases in which the rights of the litigating parties require such consideration and decision."[67]

After *Myers*, *Marbury* is not cited again in support of judicial review until 1946. Justice Black, in his well-known *Adamson* dissent, said that, since constitutional interpretation affects policy, courts should not pass upon the validity of laws except "by looking to the particular standards enumerated in the Bill of Rights and other parts of the Constitution."[68] Justice Black probably meant here that the exercise of judicial review should be restricted to situations where literal interpretations of the Constitution are possible. There are three other judicial-review references to *Marbury* during the next twelve years. In *United States v. Commodities Corp.*, *Marbury* is held to impose upon the Court the obligation to "interpret the law," but only in "proper" cases.[69] In *Touhy v. Ragen*, the Court merely notes the petitioner's argument that *Marbury* requires that "the Executive should not invade the Judicial sphere."[70] And in *Textile Workers v. Lincoln Mills*, Justice Frankfurter, dissenting, mentions *Marbury* as one of a long line of cases in which legislation was declared unconstitutional "because it imposed on the Court powers or functions that were regarded as outside the scope of the 'judicial power' lodged in the Court by the Constitution."[71]

It is a fair conclusion, therefore, that although the Court began to notice *Marbury*'s judicial-review holding during the first half of the present century, it recognized fully the restrictive nature of that holding. Nowhere is there anything approaching a declaration that the Court is the final arbiter of constitutional questions. *Fairbank* is the only case of the period which used *Marbury* to hold that the power to invalidate laws is drawn by implication from the "nature of a written constitution" (an erroneous interpretation of Marshall's argument, as I have suggested); even there, the power is restricted to "clear cases."[72] The remaining references reflect even narrower perceptions of the case. All told, of the ninety-two citations of *Marbury* by justices of the Supreme Court between 1803 and 1957, only *ten* refer to that portion of the Marshall opinion that has been said to have established the power of judicial review. *Marbury*, at least throughout most of its history in the Supreme Court of the United States, has been thought primarily to have settled other matters.

All this stands in marked contrast with the Court's treatment of *Marbury* from 1958 to 1983. There are *eighty-nine* separate citations of *Marbury* in less than three decades, which almost equals the total of the previous 154 years.[73] Of these eighty-nine, *fifty* utilize *Marbury* in support of some kind of judicial review.[74] Of these fifty, at least *eighteen* read *Marbury* as having justified sweeping assertions of judicial authority.[75] Of these eighteen, *nine* apply *Marbury* to support the idea that the Court is the "final" or "ultimate" interpreter of the Constitution, with power to issue "binding" proclamations to any other agency or department of government respecting any constitutional issue.[76] That notion was hardly one established by the Marshall Court and developed in subsequent years; rather, it was one established by the Warren Court and subsequently developed by the Burger Court.

Of those thirty-nine references not concerned with judicial review, the largest number are made to *Marbury*'s "right/remedy" maxim, perhaps reflecting the expansion of the Court's equity powers in recent years.[77] Seven support purely jurisdictional holdings.[78] Five confirm holdings which involve executive discretion and accountability.[79] Four point out

*Marbury*'s reference to Article III's "case-controversy" provision.[80] Two reassert the judiciary's power to "say what the law is" applied to statutory construction.[81] Two refer to *Marbury*'s "government of laws not men" rhetoric.[82] One accuses Marshall of starting the American obiter dicta tradition in *Marbury*.[83] One cites *Marbury* in support of constitutional supremacy.[84] One refers to Marshall's statement that no phrase in the Constitution is presumed to be without effect.[85] The remaining citation remarks on Attorney General Levi Lincoln's objection to answering certain questions in *Marbury*, on the ground that the answers "might tend to criminate" him.[86]

In the judicial review category, as indicated before, eighteen of the citations support expansive views of judicial authority,[87] nine of which declare the Supreme Court to be the "ultimate" expositor of the Constitution.[88] The other references in this group make a variety of claims in regard to *Marbury*'s holding. Two assert, without qualification, that the Court may invalidate acts of Congress that exceed its delegated authority.[89] Two describe the Court as the "constitutional watchdog," or the "guardian of individual rights."[90] Two others claim, somewhat astonishingly, that *Marbury* conforms to the idea that no deference is due to Congress or the president in constitutional cases.[91] One regards *Marbury* to be an example of the Court's deciding a constitutional question not necessary to the decision of the case.[92] Another considers *Marbury* as a precedent for the principle that the Supreme Court must "supervise" the states in order to ensure "consistent" policy.[93] A final example declares *Marbury* to support the idea that judicial review is "legitimate by implication," without adding the qualification suggested in the earlier citations on this point—that the exercise of the power is restricted to "clear cases."[94]

Of the remaining thirty-two citations, sixteen read *Marbury* to embody a broad theory of judicial power, but place some qualification on the doctrine.[95] Examples are: declaring the Court "guardian of individual rights," but not a "superlegislature";[96] declaring the Court's decisions in constitutional cases "binding" on other departments, but acknowledging that such decisions should be made with "self-restraint";[97] declaring that the mutual intransigence of Congress and the president on an issue of grave national importance would require the Court to resolve the issue, subject to its power to "say what the law is."[98] Also placed in this category are unqualified assertions of the Court's power to "say what the law is";[99] and some other interpretations of *Marbury*'s significance that are admittedly difficult to classify, such as the assertion that *Marbury* stands for the proposition that the Court may over-turn state laws.[100]

The last sixteen citations are appropriately restrictive interpretations of *Marbury*'s judicial-review holding.[101] These include confining the Court's constitutional adjudication function to a "power over laws, rules, and remedies" not involving "supervision" of other branches of government;[102] affirming the Court's power to "say what the law is," but narrowing the scope of such authority to strictly "legal," as opposed to "policy," questions;[103] avowing performance of constitutional review, but only when necessary to decide a case.[104] This group of references follows the traditional, pre-1950's view of *Marbury v. Madison*.

## Conclusions

The foregoing survey has brought into focus two historical presuppositions in the field of contemporary American constitutional law, which were stated previously: (1) that *Marbury v. Madison* established the institution of judicial review in the United States; and (2) that judicial review is a power in the Supreme Court to issue final interpretations on constitutional questions generally. After disentangling these two propositions, it may now be concluded that, so long as the first proposition is defined in terms of the second, both are flatly false.

The Court's historic hesitancy to use *Marbury* as a precedent for judicial review lies in a conception of the judicial function that was both the doctrine of the Federal Convention and the guiding principle of *Marbury*'s judicial-review holding: that the Court may invalidate federal laws with finality only when to allow such laws to stand would impair the performance of judicial functions. *Marbury*, little noticed during the first century of our national existence, was elevated by proponents and opponents of judicial power in the late nineteenth and early twentieth centuries into the primordial symbol that it remains today.

Yet the Court's traditional discomfort has not completely subsided. Even though *Marbury* has been claimed precedential for a judicial power of infallible resort in nine separate opinions, only four of these have been in opinions "for the Court."[105] Leaving aside *Cooper* and its attendant difficulties, examination of the other opinions in this set reveals that each case involved either the internal functioning of Congress,[106] the internal functioning of the executive,[107] or the relationship between the two.[108] In other words, each appears to constitute precisely the sort of case to which the historical *Marbury* did not pertain. In essence, *Marbury* has become a myth—one which, like Plato's noble lie, imparts the flavor of time-honored truth to what is really a modern idea of judicial guardianship. Consider the significance of a mythology which enables a small group of fallible persons to impose policies on others to whom they are politically unaccountable; or entertain for a moment the discard of the myth, leaving modern judicial review grounded on what would be its primary progenitor were it not for *Marbury*'s existence: *Dred Scott v. Sanford*, the first case in which the Supreme Court set aside a national law on substantive policy grounds alone.[109]

Whether or not the Supreme Court is uncomfortable with the *Marbury* Myth, academe, surely among the Court's most important constituencies, is not. Long before the Court accepted the revisionist *Marbury*, Beveridge reported that Marshall had used the case "to announce that the Supreme Court was the ultimate arbiter as to what is and what is not law under the Constitution."[110] Beveridge's view of the case has been handed down to several generations of political scientists, lawyers, and students of American government. Yet another generation is being nourished by it now.

As recently as 1987, Archibald Cox declared that *Marbury* was a "cornerstone of judicial supremacy in applying the Constitution."[111] A few years earlier, an important text had claimed that "judicial review elevates the judicial to a position of supremacy over the action of the other two branches of the national government with regard to the Constitution. This power was asserted by the Supreme Court in deciding the case of *Marbury v. Madison* in 1803."[112] Still another stated that "the decision in *Marbury* says that the final judgement as to what the Constitution means rests not with the legislative or executive branches but with the Supreme Court."[113] Such quotations could be multiplied endlessly. It is therefore not surprising that Beveridge's *Marbury* finally found its way to the Court.

It is salutary that academic disputes, no less than political ones, proceed under the guise of generally accepted presuppositions. Indeed, if they did not, rational debate would be impossible. Some suppositions (such as that which holds argument preferable to war in the resolution of conflict) are so fundamental that they safely may be left unquestioned. Others are left unexamined only at peril. Nowhere is the latter more true than in the study of the legal dimensions of politics, where yesterday's fact often becomes today's doctrine. "One precedent creates another—they soon accumulate and constitute law."[114] So long as the

United States Supreme Court practices law as institutionalized history, building on the common-law tradition of establishing continuity by the creation, dissemination, and dissolution of precedent, intellectual honesty requires that such accumulations be the stuff of constitutional development.

Perhaps the mythical *Marbury* is destined to carry the day. That may even be for the best. But the ultimate triumph should not be realized until the historical *Marbury*, and the tradition for which it stands, are first accorded, in the words of Justice Harlan on another matter, "a more respectful burial."[115] If the modern theory of judicial review is based on historical revisionism, then that is a reproach to the theory. Perhaps a tale of Justice Story should be borne in mind: "how slow every good system of laws must be in consolidating; and how easily the rashness of an hour may destroy what ages have scarcely cemented in a solid form."[116]

# 8 · *Eakin v. Raub:*
# Refutation or Justification
# of *Marbury v. Madison?*

Twenty-two years after the decision of *Marbury v. Madison,*[1] Justice John Gibson of the Pennsylvania Supreme Court penned a now-famous dissenting opinion in the case of *Eakin v. Raub,* treating extensively the issue of the relationship between courts and legislatures in a democracy.[2] The dissent, obscure until its rediscovery late in the nineteenth century by James Bradley Thayer,[3] has come to be regarded by many scholars as the most elaborate, if not the only, contemporaneous rebuttal to the views expressed by the Court in the final pages of its *Marbury* decision.[4] These pages contain the famous argument, per Chief Justice Marshall, in support of judicial power to disregard legislation in the decision of particular controversies.

Allegations of the *Marbury-Eakin* collision are so numerous as to defy computation. For example, Donald O. Dewey, who has written the only full-length book devoted exclusively to the subject of *Marbury v. Madison,*[5] claims that "by 1825, when Justice John B. Gibson of the Pennsylvania Supreme Court undertook a refutation of Marshall in *Eakin v. Raub,* he complained that judicial review had become 'a professional dogma' resting on faith rather than reason."[6] Rocco Tresolini and Martin Shapiro, in an important constitutional law text of the 1970s, remark that "the most effective answer to Marshall's argument was given in a dissenting opinion written by Justice Gibson of the Supreme Court of Pennsylvania in the relatively unimportant case of *Eakin v. Raub,* decided in 1825."[7]

More recently, Stanley I. Kutler says that Judge Gibson's dissent constitutes the "classic judicial refutation" of Marshall's position and may be viewed as a "point-by-point refutation of Marshall's rationale and as a rejoinder in logical reasoning."[8] According to Robert F. Cushman, Gibson's opinion is perhaps "the most lucid and carefully reasoned answer to Marshall's argument in *Marbury v. Madison.*"[9] Rossum and Tarr claim that Gibson "effectively presents, in a dissenting opinion, the opposite side of the argument made by Chief Justice Marshall in *Marbury v. Madison.*"[10]

Feeley and Krislov appear to perceive a less violent contradiction between *Marbury* and *Eakin*, when they say that "Gibson was dealing with the Pennsylvania Constitution."[11] The implication is that Marshall was dealing with the United States Constitution, which is an altogether different matter. Albert B. Saye seems to have a similar idea in mind: "In a dissenting opinion Justice Gibson begins by pointing out that at common law the English judges had no power to pass upon the validity of statutes and that no express grant of such power is found in the Constitution."[12] Saye does not, however, indicate which constitution he thinks Gibson is referring to. John Schmidhauser, after commenting on the dearth of contemporaneous criticism of *Marbury's* judicial-review holding, asserts that judicial review in relation to the separation of powers was fully discussed in *Eakin*.[13] Like Saye, Schmidhauser does not reveal which separation doctrine he believes Gibson discussed. Finally, Peter Woll, who perhaps is least convinced of the complete incompatibility between *Marbury* and *Eakin*, nonetheless reads Gibson's argument as a rebuttal to Marshall's alleged implication of "a general judicial power of review over legislative acts under all circumstances."[14]

In short, *Marbury-Eakin* commentary falls into two general categories. One group of writers discovers in the two opinions a stark confrontation between contending judicial philosophies. The other group finds a less complete contrariety, yet enough to justify setting the two cases alongside one another as representing different concepts of the judicial function in the United States. Harboring no disrespect for either of these groups, I shall nevertheless attempt to provide an alternative account of the relationship between the two cases, which not only renders them consistent with one another, but also suggests that the infliction of an *Eakin-Marbury* dichotomy upon several generations of students in constitutional-law courses may have contributed more to misunderstanding of the two cases than to enlightenment. In order to establish the plausibility of such an interpretation, it is necessary to compare the two opinions more closely and to perform some rudimentary exegesis on each.

## Justice Gibson's Dissent

*Eakin v. Raub* involved disputed land titles.[15] The question presented to the Court concerned the effect of Pennsylvania's statute of limitations on the plaintiff's recovery.[16] Plaintiff's counsel had suggested during oral argument that to interpret the statute by the defense's contention would render it unconstitutional, obliging the Court to rule accordingly.[17] The Court declined, however, to adopt such an interpretation and so avoided passing upon the constitutionality of the law.[18] Refusing to skirt the issue completely, Judge Tilghman offered the following dicta in his opinion for the court:

> I adhere to the opinion which I have frequently expressed that when a judge is convinced, beyond doubt, that an act has been passed in violation of the constitution, he is bound to declare it void, by his oath, by his duty to the party who has brought the cause before him, and to the people, the only source of legitimate power, who when they formed the constitution of the state, expressly declared that certain things were excepted out of the general powers of government and should forever remain inviolate.[19]

Judge Gibson begins his response to Judge Tilghman by explicitly addressing his argument to the dicta. The reply is confined to the question of whether the Supreme Court of Pennsylvania may refuse to enforce an act of the state legislature because it conflicts with the state constitution, presuming, for purposes of argument, the unconstitutionality of the act:

> But it is said . . . the latter act would be unconstitutional; and, instead of controverting this, I will avail myself of it, to express an opinion which I have deliberately formed, on the abstract right of the judiciary to declare an unconstitutional act of the legislature void. It seems to me, there is a plain difference, hitherto unnoticed, between acts that are repugnant to the constitution of the particular state, and acts that are repugnant to the constitution of the United States; my opinion being, that the judiciary is bound to execute the former, but not the latter.[20]

With considerable deference, Judge Gibson then cites *Marbury*, saying that "although the right in question has all along been claimed by the judiciary, no judge has ventured to discuss it, except Chief Justice Marshall (in *Marbury v. Madison*, 1 Cranch 176); and if the argument of a jurist so distinguished for the strength of his ratiocinative powers be found inconclusive, it may fairly be set down to the weakness of the position which he attempts to defend."[21]

The argument continues with its major premise, which consists in the division of judicial powers into those that are "ordinary" and those that are "extraordinary." The former power derives from the common law and exists with or without express constitutional grants. The latter exists only in consequence of express constitutional grants, or by "irresistible implication from the nature of the government." Since every power "by which one organ of the government is enabled to control another, or to exert an influence over its acts, is a political power," and since the "political powers of the judiciary are *extraordinary* . . . such, for instance, as are derived from certain peculiar provisions in the constitution of the United States," then judicial annulment of legislation is "extraordinary." That power should be eschewed except when expressly granted by the constitution or by "irresistible implication from the nature of the government."[22]

An example of the last phrase is later described as what would arise from a legislative usurpation of the right of citizens so "monstrous" as to work a change "in the very structure of the government," and bring about a revolution: "By this, I mean, that while the citizen should resist with pike and gun, the judge might co-operate with *habeas corpus* and *mandamus* . . . but this is far from proving the judiciary to be a *peculiar organ*, under the constitution, to prevent legislative encroachment on the power reserved by the people; *and this is all that I contend that it is not.*"[23] In other words, Judge Gibson flatly addresses his entire argument to Judge Tilghman's notion that judges are peculiarly bound by their oaths and their duties to prevent legislative tyranny, even in the absence of explicit constitutional authorization. His famous opinion is thus narrowly circumscribed, a fact that proponents of the *Marbury-Eakin* dichotomy generally have overlooked.

Judge Gibson places an additional qualification on the doctrine that courts may not invalidate legislation, when he recognizes that there are cases of a "judiciary nature" for which "the constitution furnishes a rule for the judiciary" and which the "legislature cannot alter because it cannot alter the constitution." Only in such instances is the constitution justly said to be "a law of superior obligation" for the courts.[24] In all other cases, since the "constitution of Pennsylvania contains no express grant of political powers to the judiciary," Pennsylvania courts may not invalidate state laws on the ground of their incompatibility with the state constitution.

> For, after all, there is no effectual guard against legislative usurpation, but public opinion, the force of which, in this country is inconceivably great. . . . The constitution of this state has withstood the shock of strong party excitement for thirty years, during which no act of the legislature has been declared unconstitutional, although the judiciary has constantly asserted a right to do so in clear cases . . . for these reasons, I am of the opinion, that it rests with the people, in whom full and absolute sovereign power resides, to correct abuses in legislation, by instructing their representatives to repeal the obnoxious act.[25]

In the course of his opinion, Judge Gibson successfully refutes several contentions which have been advanced to support the doctrine that judicial power to nullify statutes may be drawn *by implication:* (1) that a constitution is a law of superior obligation and that judges must strike down violations whenever possible;[26] (2) that judicial nullification is necessary to uphold a "written constitution," by the very nature of the instrument;[27] (3) that legislative power derives only from express grants in the constitution and that unconstitutional acts are therefore *ipso facto* void;[28] (4) that judges take oaths to support the constitution, and therefore must enforce it in preference to countervailing laws;[29] (5) that it is the business of the judiciary to "say what the law is," and the constitution is law.[30]

Judge Gibson's response to these assertions is that each begs the question.

> The foundation of every argument in favor of the right of the judiciary, is found at last to be an assumption of the whole ground in dispute. . . . The constitution and the right of the legislature to pass the act, may be in collision; but is that a legitimate subject for judicial determination? If it be, the judiciary must be a peculiar organ, to revise the proceedings of the legislature, and to correct its mistakes: and in what part of the constitution are we to look for this proud preeminence?[31]

Though warrant for such preeminence is not discoverable in the state constitution, Judge Gibson is confident that exactly the reverse is true "in regard to an act of assembly, which is found to be in collision with the constitution, laws or treaties of the United States." He justifies this proposition using the clear logic of Article VI: "By becoming parties to the federal constitution the states have agreed to several limitations of their individual sovereignty, to enforce which, it was thought to be absolutely necessary, to prevent them from giving effect to laws in violation of those limitations, through the instrumentality of their own judges."[32]

And in the event of an infraction of the limits imposed upon the states:

> By the third article and second section, appellate jurisdiction of all cases arising under the constitution and laws of the United States, is reserved to the federal judiciary, under such regulations as congress may prescribe; and in execution of this provision, congress has prescribed regulations for removing into the supreme court of the United States, all causes decided by the highest court of judicature of any state, which involve the construction of the constitution, or of any law of the United States.[33]

Although Judge Gibson is commenting above on the power of the United States Supreme Court to invalidate state laws which are found to be in violation of the Constitution, there is no reason to believe that he was not thoroughly familiar with the "removal" provision of which he spoke: that is, the Judiciary Act of 1789, Section 25.[34] This provision granted to the Court the power to reverse or affirm any decision of a state court of final resort where the validity of a federal law, among other things, is questioned. If the Supreme Court affirms a lower court's invalidation of federal law, the result is a final declaration of unconstitutionality. The Court therefore had such authority long before its decision in *Marbury v. Madison*. Judge Gibson was probably aware of this implication of the Judiciary Act and thus would not have been disturbed by the power of the Supreme Court to invalidate federal laws in appropriate circumstances. And the circumstances of *Marbury* were most likely those that Judge Gibson would have considered appropriate.

## Marbury *Revisited*

However persuasive Justice Gibson's *Eakin* dissent was, it would be of little relevance today had it not taken on new meaning lately as an at-

tack on that part of the *Marbury* opinion that justifies the Supreme
Court's refusal to apply an unconstitutional statute.[35] To review the relevant portion of *Marbury*, the first segment is an argument supporting
the conclusion that "an act of the legislature, repugnant to the constitution, is void."[36] The second argues that "courts, as well as other
departments, are bound by that instrument."[37] Marshall thus explicitly
recognizes the distinction at the heart of the *Eakin* dissent: between (1)
a law being a *nullity* due to its collision with the constitution, on the
one hand, and (2) a court's having the power to *nullify* such a law, on
the other.[38] Judge Gibson's opinion is devoted entirely to the task of
disproving the contention that the *second* conclusion may be drawn by
*implication* from premises which are truly capable of supporting only
the *first*.[39]

Marshall's first argument invokes three of the principles which Gibson later challenges in *Eakin:* (1) the constitution is a law of superior
obligation; (2) the nature of the written constitution; and (3) repugnant
legislative acts are *ipso facto* void.[40] Since Marshall uses none of these
notions to support his *second* argument, they have no application to *Marbury* when challenged from Gibson's viewpoint.

Two of the principles challenged in the *Eakin* dissent remain, both
of which are utilized in Marshall's second argument, albeit with the appropriate qualifications suggested by Judge Gibson. Marshall begins this
segment of *Marbury* with the rhetorical question: "If an act of the
legislature, repugnant to the constitution, is void, does it, notwithstanding its invalidity, bind the courts, and oblige them to give it effect?" His
famous answer—"It is emphatically the province and duty of the judicial
department to say what the law is"[41]—is followed by an often-ignored
qualification: "Those who apply the rule to particular cases, must of
necessity expound and interpret that rule. . . . So . . . *if* both the law and
the constitution apply to a particular case, . . . the court *must* either
decide that case conformably to the law, disregarding the constitution;
or conformably to the constitution, disregarding the law."[42]

In other words, the answer to Marshall's rhetorical question is both
affirmative and negative. The courts are not obliged to give effect to an
unconstitutional law whenever *both* the constitution *and* the law are
applicable to a *particular* case which the court has a *duty* to decide. Judge
Gibson held exactly that view in *Eakin*, while pointing out the only provision in Pennsylvania's constitution that "furnishes a rule for the
judiciary," and that "the legislature cannot alter because it cannot alter
the constitution. In all other cases, . . . the constitution and act of

assembly . . . do not furnish conflicting rules *applicable to the point before the court;* nor is it at all necessary that the one or the other of them should give way."[43]

The only remaining ground of implication challenged by Judge Gibson, which Marshall used in *Marbury,* concerns the oath of judges to support the constitution. Marshall explicitly confines this directive to the conduct of the judges "in their official character."[44] But again, that is exactly what Judge Gibson does: "granting it [the oath] to relate to the official conduct of the judge, as well as every other officer, and not to his political principles, still it must be understood in reference to supporting the constitution, *only as far as that may be involved in his official duty;* and consequently if his official duty does not comprehend an inquiry into the authority of the legislature, neither does his oath."[45] Therefore, the grounds for implication of judicial power to invalidate legislation, challenged by Judge Gibson, are inapplicable to the opinion in *Marbury v. Madison.*

What of the other arguments utilized by the Great Chief Justice to support his conclusion that "in some cases then, the constitution must be looked into by the judges"? These are, in the order in which the Court discusses them: (1) Article III, Section 2, extending the "judicial power of the United States . . to all cases arising under the constitution"; (2) Article I, Section 9, prohibiting passage of a "bill of attainder or ex post facto law," and likewise prohibiting taxes or duties "laid on articles exported from any state"; (3) Article III, Section 3, prohibiting conviction for treason "unless on the testimony of two witnesses to the same overt act, or on confession in open court."[46]

On the last of these, Marshall provides the same justification as had Gibson, for that provision regulating "the style of process" and establishing "an appropriate form of conclusion in criminal prosecutions."[47] The treason clause, says Marshall, is "addressed especially to the courts. It prescribes, directly for them, a rule of evidence not to be departed from."[48] And according to Judge Gibson, whenever "the judiciary, and not the legislature, is the immediate organ to execute" a constitutional provision, "they are bound by it, in preference to any act of assembly to the contrary; in such cases, the constitution is a rule to the courts."[49] In other words, such provisions only give rise to cases of a judiciary nature, and therefore *all* cases arising under them are cases of that type by strict definition.

As to Article III's "arising under" provision, we have already observed its explicit affirmation by Judge Gibson as authority for Section 25 of the Judiciary Act of 1789. Section 25 contains an express authorization of the Supreme Court of the United States to review any "final judgment or decree . . . in the highest court of law or equity of a state . . . where is drawn in question the validity of a treaty or statute of, or an authority exercised under the United States, and the decision is against their validity."[50] Such a decision may, on reexamination, be "reversed or affirmed in the Supreme Court of the United States upon a writ of error."[51] If the highest court of a state enforces against Congress, for example, the Article I, Section 9 prohibition that "no tax or duty shall be laid on articles exported from any state," the Supreme Court may *affirm* the judgment of that state court, thereby invalidating the act of a coordinate branch of government.

Judge Gibson surely knew this. Perhaps it is why he so carefully confined his opinion "on the abstract right of the judiciary to declare an unconstitutional act of the legislature void," to the "plain difference, hitherto unnoticed, between acts that are repugnant to the constitution of the particular state, and acts that are repugnant to the constitution of the United States," his opinion being "that the judiciary is bound to execute the former, but not the latter."[52] Elsewhere, while commenting on the allegation that judicial power to nullify statutes is legitimate because, when exercised, "the judiciary does no positive act, but merely refuses to be instrumental in giving effect to an unconstitutional law," Judge Gibson remarks that this

> is nothing more than a repetition, in a different form of the argument—that an unconstitutional law is ipso facto void; for a refusal to act under the law must be founded on a right in each branch to judge of the acts of all the others, before it is bound to exercise its functions to give those acts effect. No such right is recognised in the different branches of the national government, except the judiciary (and that, too, on account of the peculiar provisions of the constitution).[53]

These peculiar provisions are not identified, but it is reasonable to assume that they are the same ones Marshall invokes in *Marbury* to support the notion that the Constitution may be "looked into by the judges."[54] This inference is plausible because, in the American federal system, the national government is one of purely delegated authority, whereas state governments are not.[55] Since the Tenth Amendment reserves *all* "powers not delegated to the United States by the Constitution, nor prohibited by it to the States," to the "States respectively, or to the people," acts of national legislation not pursuant to the Constitution are, indeed, *ipso facto* void.[56]

However, such is not the case with acts of state legislation, which, according to Judge Gibson, "are, in no case, to be treated as ipso facto void, except where they would produce a revolution in the government; and that, to avoid them, requires the act of some tribunal competent, under the constitution (if any such there be), to pass upon their validity. All that remains, therefore, is, to inquire whether the judiciary or the people are that tribunal."[57] Certainly Judge Gibson's great opinion is worthy of respect as an exegesis of the Tenth Amendment, rather than as a quibble with *Marbury v. Madison*.


## Conclusions

The foregoing analysis raises several questions. First, from his off-hand remark about the *Marbury* opinion, it appears that Judge Gibson himself must have misinterpreted *Marbury*. Surely that is unusual for so learned a judge, assuming a careful reading of the latter opinion. However, Gibson's authority might not have been *Marbury* itself, but rather Judge Tilghman. After all, Gibson neither quotes from nor cites *Marbury v. Madison*, except in the casual reference already mentioned.[58] And that reference is not made to support any substantive point, but rather to illuminate the uncontroversial nature of the subject in general.

On the other hand, Judge Tilghman's cousin Edward Tilghman had been counsel before the United States Supreme Court in the case of *Cooper v. Telfair*, decided just three years prior to the decision in *Marbury*, and had argued at that time that it was the duty of a court to declare legislation void when convinced beyond doubt of its incompatibility with the Constitution.[59] The Court must have accepted the argument, since four justices, in separate opinions, affirmed the power of courts to invalidate in particular cases legislation clearly contrary to constitutional provisions.[60]

A certain irony attends *Cooper*, in that perusal of the *United States Reports* for examples of the use of *Marbury v. Madison* as a precedent for judicial power to invalidate laws reveals only one instance prior to the Court's 1887 decision in *Mugler v. Kansas*,[61] and that is *Cooper v. Telfair*. The trouble is, of course, that *Cooper* was decided three years *in advance* of *Marbury*. The citation appears in a footnote to the opinion of Justice Chase, evidently added by the reporter after the decision of *Marbury v. Madison*.[62]

The second question concerns the adoption by James Bradley Thayer of the *Eakin* dissent as a rebuttal of *Marbury*. Here the answer seems clear, because the rise of *Eakin* corresponds with the rise of *Marbury* as a precedent for judicial power to invalidate laws. *Marbury*, shrouded in relative obscurity until its resurrection in 1868 by Thomas M. Cooley in the most important legal treatise of the period,[63] was cited with increasing frequency by a group of legal writers bent upon providing an adequate legal foundation for the developing doctrine of Fourteenth Amendment substantive due process.[64] This movement touched off a furious debate over the role of the judiciary in American society, one of the high points of which was the appearance of Thayer's classic article in 1893.[65] It is significant not only that the Supreme Court's first citation of *Marbury* as a precedent for judicial power to nullify laws occurred in the midst of this controversy, but also that the reference itself was used in dicta to support the Court's power to strike down *state* laws on grounds of *substance* alone—a blatant misrepresentation of *Marbury's* holding.[66]

The third and final question raised by this analysis relates to the continuing viability of the revisionist view of *Marbury*—and of *Eakin*—throughout the present century. Here some speculation is required. Beginning in 1895, the left wing of the American Bar Association launched a concerted attack on the *Marbury* decision, declaring that the doctrine of judicial nullification had not been intended by the Framers and consequently had been an invention of the Marshall Court.[67] This outburst was matched blow-for-blow by the conservative wing of the Bar, which by 1903 had managed to elevate the *Marbury* case to a status commensurate with the Declaration of Independence and the Constitution itself.[68] Neither side questioned the adequacy of the historical premise that *Marbury* was an example of raw judicial aggression.

Given that mistaken assumption, it was but a short step to the famous claim of Albert J. Beveridge that *Marbury*, "for perfectly calculated audacity, has few parallels in judicial history."[69] On the way to Beveridge, Edward S. Corwin coined the phrase "judicial review" in an article published in 1910.[70] The conjunction of Beveridge's view of *Marbury* and Corwin's phrase has been passed on to generations of students in the fields of American politics and constitutional law. The myth it embraces likewise imparts a flavor of legitimacy to the modern, activist conception of judicial review. So it is that Judge Gibson's mighty treatise endures, reconstituted as the contemporaneous contrary of the mythical *Marbury*, and a curious reminder of the infirmities of the noble lie.

# Part Three · The Creation of a Judicial Myth

Part III elaborates the conversion of *Marbury v. Madison* into a mythical symbol of modern judicial review. Chapter 9 examines the revisionist critique of the Marshall Court's contract-clause decisions, which first appeared in the 1870s. This critique is important as an initial step toward the ultimate revision of American constitutional history, completed by the Progressive historians in the early twentieth century. The principal issue concerned the meaning of the term "contracts" in Article I, Section 10 of the Constitution. In a series of early decisions, the Court read the term broadly, so as to include so-called public, as well as private contracts. Few, if any, seemed to mind, until a small group of relatively obscure writers began to take Marshall to task for it shortly after the Civil War. The main trouble with the revisionist argument is that the Founders had explicitly rejected the invitation to qualify "contracts" with the adjective "private," thereby rendering Marshall's interpretation highly plausible. The commentaries of court-watchers throughout the remainder of the Marshall and Taney periods provide additional support for this view. Yet Marshall-bashing was fashionable in some circles during the late nineteenth and early twentieth centuries, and the revisionist view carried the day—as indicated by its somewhat uncritical acceptance in 1938 by Benjamin F. Wright, author of this century's most influential study of the contract clause.

The purpose of Chapter 10 is to explore the fascinating controversy which erupted among legal scholars in the 1880s about the role of courts in the United States. Following publication of Thomas M. Cooley's treatise on constitutional limitations in 1868, and alongside the contract-clause critiques, rumblings from another corner of the legal establishment began to be heard. A group representing the laissez-faire wing of the Bar championed a more expansive idea of judicial power than that which characterized earlier periods. Whereas John Marshall had become something of a scapegoat for the contract-clause critics who wished to limit judicial power with respect to legislative bodies, he was to become a heroic example of judicial statesmanship for those who advocated the more expansive view. These incompatible strains of thought converged in the mid 1880s, marking the commencement of the first extensive scholarly debate on the judicial function in the United States. Among the participants were James Bradley Thayer, William Meigs, George Bancroft, and Brinton Coxe. The controversy raged in law reviews, academic journals, books, and pamphlets for about ten years. It is during this period that *Marbury v. Madison* emerged as a precedent for judicial review.

Chapter II describes the bitter dispute over *Marbury* and judicial review which arose in the wake of the Supreme Court's decision in the Income Tax Case (*Pollock v. Farmers' Loan & Trust Co.*, 1895). Both proponents and opponents of the federal income tax were poised to ground their respective views on historical authority, and Marshall's Court, by this time, was the likeliest candidate. When the Fuller Court invalidated the tax in the *Pollock* case, supporters of the tax seemed cornered. Attacking the very idea of judicial review, these critics uncovered the source of the trouble, not in the Court that nullified the tax, but with the "ghosts of Marshall and Hamilton" emanating from the final pages of *Marbury* and *Federalist* Number 78. Marshall's defenders came quickly to the rescue, ignoring for the moment that nothing in *Marbury* could plausibly be construed to justify the Court's decision in *Pollock*. By 1903, friends of the Court had elevated *Marbury* to a status commensurate with the Declaration of Independence! What had once been a relatively obscure precedent embodying a fairly restrictive conception of judicial authority was subtly transformed into an all-encompassing symbol of the full-blown modern doctrine of judicial review. Unfortunately, this version of *Marbury* was accepted by such Progressive writers as J. Allen Smith, Charles Beard, and Vernon Parrington. Though these men were not in perfect accord on the question of the proper scope of judicial authority, they did believe that the "mythical" *Marbury* represented the true constitutional doctrine of judicial review in America.

Chapter 12 completes the historiography of *Marbury v. Madison* with a survey of modern commentary on the case. Such a survey necessarily must be a mere representative sampling, since *Marbury* has now become the seminal case in American constitutional law. Virtually no important work in the field can be done without paying homage to it. In the chapter, I discuss the relationship between the mythical *Marbury* and contemporary perceptions of judicial power in the United States, along with the broader mythology to which *Marbury* is central. Also covered are the origins of the two most important constitutional doctrines of the twentieth century respecting judicial review of state laws: substantive due process and selective incorporation of the Bill of Rights. Finally, I undertake a survey of the Court's twentieth-century decisions invalidating acts of Congress. The reader is encouraged throughout to keep in mind the vacillations of academicians in the present century toward the institution of judicial review. I contend that the confusion has resulted directly from the adoption of a misleading version of American history, and that confusion will continue to characterize the field so long as we hold fast to the myth.

# 9 · Public and/or Private Contracts

It is now common to think that, when the clause prohibiting states from passing laws "impairing the obligation of contracts"[1] was adopted at the Philadelphia Convention in 1787, the Founders intended the prohibition to extend only to contracts between private individuals, and not to contracts between individuals and states; in other words, not to "public" contracts.[2] Yet, this was not the understanding of the Marshall Court in the formative years of the Republic, when the meaning of the clause was first questioned from a legal viewpoint. The main purpose of this chapter is to explore the apparent shift in legal scholarship on the original meaning of the contract clause. The shift took place in the 1870s and constitutes the beginning of a major transformation in academic attitudes toward the early Supreme Court, a transformation that culminates some forty years later. Before reaching the 1870s, a brief historical survey is in order.

## The Contract Clause in the Founding Era

There was very little discussion of the contract clause at the Philadelphia Convention of 1787, and equally little at the various state ratifying conventions that followed. Rufus King introduced the original motion in Philadelphia on August 28. Its terms were virtually identical to those used in Article II of the Northwest Ordinance, passed by the Confederation congress earlier in the same year after prodding by "land speculators in and out of Congress who wished to make the western areas attractive to prospective settlers."[3] The clause in the ordinance read:

in the just preservation of rights and property, it is understood and declared, that no law ought ever to be made or have force in the said territory, that shall, in any manner whatever, interfere with or affect private contracts, or engagements, bona fide, and without fraud previously formed.[4]

After a brief discussion, during which members of the Convention raised several objections to King's motion, James Wilson argued that the "answer to these objections is that retrospective interferences only are to be prohibited." Madison responded that retrospective interferences with contracts would be handled by the prohibition of *ex post facto* laws, which he apparently thought covered both civil and criminal cases. Madison's view was not challenged at that time, so Rutledge moved to replace King's original motion with one prohibiting retrospective laws, and the new motion passed without further discussion. However, Madison had been wrong about the equivalence of "retrospective" and *ex post facto*, for Dickinson had searched Blackstone's *Commentaries* that evening and announced on the following day that *ex post facto* referred to criminal cases only. About two weeks later, Elbridge Gerry moved to extend the provision to civil cases, but his motion was defeated.[5]

The final development in the Convention occurred on September 12, when the Committee on Style presented its report, having changed the wording of the clause to read that no state shall pass laws "altering or impairing the obligation of contracts." Two days later, the word "altering" was dropped without discussion, leaving the clause in its present form.[6] The conclusion from this brief review is that the proceedings at Philadelphia, per se, offer no basis for the belief that the Founders intended to make a sharp distinction between public and private contracts. In fact, the annals indicate the opposite, since the word "private" in King's initial motion was subsequently deleted from the clause.

The record is equally scanty respecting subsequent discussions in the various state ratifying conventions and in the press. The only straightforward mention of the clause in the *Federalist* is made by Madison in Number 44, in which he says that "laws impairing the obligation of contracts, are contrary to the first principles of the social compact, and to every principle of sound legislation. . . . Very properly, therefore, have the convention added this constitutional bulwark in favor of personal security and private rights."[7] This tells us very little, since the rights affected by state impairment of public contracts are always private ones, except in the unusual case of contracts between governmental units.

Another reference to contracts in the *Federalist* is in Number 7, where Hamilton remarks on "private contracts." He does so, however, *not* while discussing the *contract* clause, but rather while discussing the monetary clauses in general.[8]

There are only two relevant debates over the clause in state ratifying conventions, one favorable to each interpretation. In Virginia, Patrick Henry argued that the clause "includes public contracts, as well as private contracts between individuals." Governor Randolph answered that he was "still a warm friend of the prohibition, because it must be promotive of virtue and justice, and preventive of injustice and fraud."[9] Although Randolph subsequently pointed to state interferences with private contracts as a source of great calamities, he nowhere denied Henry's contention as to the meaning of the clause.

In the North Carolina state ratifying convention, the question was raised whether the clause had reference to contracts of the states. W. R. Davie, a member of the Federal Convention, answered that it did not.[10] I believe that Davie's statement is the only *definite* reference in this period by a member of the Philadelphia Convention that took this position as to the *intentions* of the Framers. The last item which might be cited is Luther Martin's address to the Maryland legislature, in which he explained that he voted against the adoption of the clause because he wanted the states to have the power to pass debtor's relief legislation in extreme circumstances and he thought the clause would prevent that.[11] However, Martin nowhere mentioned state or public contracts in the course of his address.

## The Contract Clause in the Early Supreme Court

The United States Supreme Court had its first occasion to interpret the contract clause with respect to public contracts in 1810, when it decided the important case of *Fletcher v. Peck*. In the majority opinion of the Court, John Marshall held that a state legislature's grant of land to an individual, which was completed by a conveyance from the governor, was a contract within the meaning of the obligation clause and that a subsequent statute repealing the grant was therefore unconstitutional.[12] Two crucial principles were established here: (1) a grant, completed by a conveyance, is an executed contract, giving rise to an implied "executory" contract on the part of the grantor, to refrain from reasserting his right to the thing granted; and (2) a contract between a state and an individual is a contract within the meaning of the Constitution. At the root of the second holding is the idea that there is no distinction between public and private contracts.

Between 1810 and 1823, the United States Supreme Court handed down several important interpretations of the contract clause, all of which expanded the *Fletcher* doctrine to some extent. In *New Jersey v. Wilson,* the Court held that a state's grant of immunity from taxation was a contract within the meaning of the obligation clause.[13] In *Trustees of Dartmouth College v. Woodward,* the Court held that a charter of incorporation was a contract within the meaning of the clause, thereby extending *Fletcher*'s protection of the contract rights of "natural" persons to "artificial" ones as well.[14] Finally, in *Green v. Biddle,* a contract between two states was protected from impairment.[15]

Juxtaposed to the cases involving public contracts were some involving private ones. The Court, in *Sturges v. Crowninshield,* held a state bankruptcy law unconstitutional as it respected contracts made *prior* to its enactment;[16] and in *McMillan v. McNeill,* the Court did the same for contracts made *subsequent* to a state's insolvency law,[17] a principle that was overruled in *Ogden v. Saunders* over Marshall's dissent.[18]

There were few objections from the bench to the Marshall Court's early interpretations of the obligation clause as it related to public contracts. Justice Johnson dissented from the Court's reasoning, but not from its decision in *Fletcher;* while he had no problem declaring that a state could not revoke its grants, he would do it "on a general principle, on the reason and nature of things: a principle which will impose laws even on the Deity."[19] In other words, Johnson believed that the Constitution incorporated natural law, and thus the security of contracts, whether public or private, would be better insured by invocation of general principles, than by resort to a clause that contained words of "equivocal signification."[20] There was one other dissent—by Justice Duvall in *Dartmouth*—but without opinion.[21]

Early decisions of the Marshall Court which held that the clause protected public contracts as well as private ones were not without precedent. Although the Court did not base its decisions in *Fletcher, New Jersey,* and *Dartmouth* directly on these grounds, there were "several early cases in the Federal circuit courts and at least one of importance in the state courts which throw light upon the attitude of the bench toward the contract clause long before Marshall was given the opportunity in *Fletcher v. Peck* to express his interpretation of that part of the Constitution."[22] For example, in *Vanhorne's Lessee v. Dorrance,* a

Pennsylvania statute that confirmed the title of some claimants to land in that state was later repealed. Justice Paterson, an influential member of the Federal Convention, spoke for the circuit court and held that the repeal was invalid as violative of the obligation clause.[23] The similarity of this ruling to Marshall's in *Fletcher* is obvious.

In 1799 another circuit court case, of which there is evidently no official record, invalidated on contract-clause grounds a Vermont law authorizing town selectmen to seize church lands.[24] Some similarity with *Dartmouth* is apparent here. In *Wales v. Stetson*, a case not decided on contract-clause grounds, Chief Justice Parsons of the Massachusetts Supreme Court said that "rights legally vested in a corporation cannot be controlled or destroyed by a subsequent statute, unless a power be reserved to the legislature in the act of incorporation."[25] Even Benjamin Wright, clearly an opponent of Marshall's early contract-clause decisions, cannot find a *single* early case in the state or lower federal courts to support his position that Marshall stepped out of line in his contract-clause holdings. All of the cases he cites in this era would have bolstered *Marshall's* position, had Marshall chosen to use them.[26]

## The Contract Clause in the Late Marshall and Taney Eras

If the years between the drafting of the United States Constitution and 1827 represented a period when application of contract-clause doctrine was broadened with respect to public contracts, then the period from 1827 to the Civil War was a time when its applicability was somewhat narrowed. The 1827 *Ogden v. Saunders* has already been mentioned, but it did not involve a state contract. Beginning in 1829, before the end of the Marshall era, the Court began to limit the operation of the contract clause within the developing doctrine of reserved state powers: police, taxation, and eminent domain.

The first case worthy of mention is *Willson v. Blackbird Creek Marsh Co.*[27] Although not itself a contract-clause case, Marshall's opinion upholding a state-authorized swamp drainage scheme foreshadows the subsequent development of the state "police power" doctrine, much later articulated in *Stone v. Mississippi.*[28] In *Providence Bank v. Billings*, the Court (per Marshall) held that a state's relinquishment of the power of taxation over a corporation is never to be implied, since a corporate charter merely gives "individuality" to a group; "any privileges which may exempt it from the burthens common to individuals do not flow necessarily from the charter, but must be expressed in it, or they do not exist."[29]

In *Charles River Bridge v. Warren Bridge*, Chief Justice Taney's first important contract-clause decision, the Court applied the principle enunciated in *Providence* to cover state grants of monopolistic privileges, saying that public grants are to be strictly construed, with nothing passing by implication.[30] Finally, in *West River Bridge Co. v. Dix*, the Court held that all contracts are subject to the state's power of eminent domain.[31]

There were many other important contract cases during this period, but the foregoing suggest the main lines of development in early nineteenth-century law respecting state contractual obligations. The crucial point is that, far from being neglectful of the need for states to possess adequate powers to govern, as some of his latter-day detractors have suggested, John Marshall himself laid the foundation for the subsequent development of the doctrine of reserved power. Moreover, in none of the pre–Civil War cases that imparted broader scope to these powers was the notion of the applicability of the obligation clause to public contracts seriously questioned.[32]

The same may be said of treatises written by legal scholars on both constitutional and contract law in the period from 1820 to 1870. No statements are found that directly challenge Marshall's assertion of the Framers' intention to include public contracts within the scope of the obligation clause. In general, the scholarly evaluations of the early contract-clause decisions are positive, though some do not take a clear-cut position on the question of the Founders' intent.

For example, John Taylor suggested in 1820 that the contract clause, along with prohibitions on bills of attainder and *ex post facto* laws, was introduced to prevent "usurpations" and "evils," without saying exactly what these were.[33] In 1828, Theron Metcalf claimed that the Framers intended to prevent not only the recurrence of evils already endured (most of which evidently had to do with a shortage of capital as a result of the Revolutionary War), but "also to guard against the happening of similar evils; to establish justice, and the most perfect faith in agreements, and to ensure the sanctity of private property, so far as these objects can be secured by legislative enactments."[34] Peter Du Ponceau, in 1834, suggested an even broader reading of the clause, holding that it was intended to apply to all contracts "absolutely and unconditionally."[35]

Chancellor Kent seemed in full agreement with the early Court's view of the contract clause. He summed up his discussion of the *Dartmouth* decision in 1826:

> The decision in that case did more than any other single act, proceeding from the authority of the United States, to throw an impregnable barrier around all rights and franchises derived from the grant of government; and to give solidity and inviolability to the literary, charitable, religious, and commercial institutions of our country.[36]

In fact, Kent thought not only that public contracts properly fell within the meaning of the clause, but also that the principle of strict construction of state grants, announced in the *Charles River Bridge* case, was "deeply to be regretted."[37]

Joseph Story, while speaking of the *Dartmouth* case, said that the preservation of corporate rights may not have been directly contemplated by the Framers—they might have had in mind more "pressing" mischiefs. But he added, quoting from *Dartmouth*, that the contractual prohibition itself was made more general.

> It is applicable to all contracts, and not confined to the forms then most known, and most divided. Although a rare or peculiar case may not of itself be of sufficient magnitude to induce the establishment of a constitutional rule; yet it must be governed by that rule, when established, unless some plain and strong reason for excluding it can be given. It is not sufficient to show, that it may not have been foreseen, or intentionally provided for. To exclude it, it is necessary to go further, and show, that if the case had been suggested, the language of the convention would have been varied so, as to exclude and except it.[38]

There are also later references—such as Francis Hilliard, who said in 1848 that the obligation clause "received from the Supreme Court its fullest and most satisfactory exposition, in vindicating the charter of Dartmouth College from legislative interference and assumption."[39] Timothy Walker discussed the contract clause extensively, along with its basis in the Northwest Ordinance, and wrote as if there was never any doubt about its application to state contracts.[40] William Duer, in 1856, thought that the Framers intended an even broader scope for the clause than that given to it by the Marshall Court.[41]

The only writers in this period whose statements might (with some imagination) be interpreted as reflecting doubt that the Framers intended to include public contracts within the scope of the obligation clause are Theophilus Parsons (1855), George Ticknor Curtis (1858), and Thomas M. Cooley (1868); and in each instance, the case for such an interpretation is weak. Parsons simply said that the Framers' intent is not certain on this point, but that, whatever their motives, no distinction between public and private contracts exists, so far as the Constitution is concerned.[42]

Curtis claimed that the contract clause in the Northwest Ordinance is more "stringent" than that in the Constitution.[43] Some have interpreted that as a denial that the Founders intended state contracts to be covered by the constitutional clause, since it was apparently "modelled" after the ordinance clause.[44] However, there is a more straightforward explanation available, in that the Framers used the term "impairing" in the Constitution instead of the words "in any manner whatever, interfere with or affect," which appeared in the ordinance.[45] Clearly, the latter phrase is more stringent than the former; yet, in the ordinance, this stringency is applied only to *private* contracts, not to public ones. Because the Founders deleted the word "private" from the original clause, it is reasonable to assume that Curtis meant only to say that there are many ways to interfere with contracts (public and private) that would *not* also impair them.

At first Cooley did not address the question of the Founders' intentions. In discussing *Fletcher*, he said only that the decision settled the crucial points that both executed contracts and a state's contract with an individual are within the operation of the clause.[46] However, in a short treatise written some twelve years later, Cooley said, in reference to the Constitutional Convention, that "apparently nothing was in view at the time except to prevent the repudiation of debts and private obligations, and the disgrace, disorders, and calamities that might be expected to follow."[47] Now, this statement may be interpreted in the same way as Story's, that what was "in view" is not necessarily what was "intended."[48] Yet the absence of the remark in the earlier treatise is interesting, especially considering the shift in attitudes toward the contract clause that took place in the intervening period.

## The Shift

As we have seen, prominent legal treatises written prior to the Civil War reveal no clear-cut challenge to the Marshall Court's view that the obligation clause bound the states to performance of their contracts. Apparently, state and lower federal courts in the pre-*Fletcher* era adopted this theory as well. But after the Civil War and Reconstruction, the view was brought into question. The first definitive statement in a major legal discourse is evidently that of Cooley in 1880, mentioned above, to the effect that the Framers intended the clause to apply only to "private debts and obligations." After 1880, numerous such statements may be found in treatises, articles, textbooks, and judicial opinions.

What seems to have happened is the following. Between 1874 and 1879, a number of articles appeared in the *American* and *Southern Law Reviews*, all of which were highly critical of the Marshall Court's early contract-clause decisions. The first, published in 1874 in the *American Law Review*, was authored by Clement H. Hill, assistant attorney-general of the United States in the Grant administration.[49] The second, written by R. Hutchinson, was published in the *Southern Law Review* in 1875.[50] That journal also published the rest, in a series of articles between 1875 and 1879 written by John M. Shirley—all of which, with some additional materials, were published in book form in 1879.[51] Taken together, these works embody a plethora of arguments designed to show that Marshall's early contract decisions (especially *Fletcher, New Jersey,* and *Dartmouth*) were misinterpretations of the Constitution from several standpoints. Since each work contains most of the negative judgments (especially those of Hill and Shirley), they constitute together the turning point in the scholarly interpretation of the obligation clause in nineteenth-century law.

One line of argument against Marshall's early view (found in both Hill and Shirley) centers on the assertion that James Wilson was the real author of the obligation clause. The basic idea is that, since Wilson was the only Founder thoroughly conversant with the civil-law tradition, and since the phrase "obligation of contract" apparently had its *linguistic* origin in the Latin *obligatio ex contractu*, Wilson must have authored the clause. Furthermore, he must have intended the adoption of the civil-law *meaning* of the phrase, which was widely used in early Roman law and referred only to "private debts and obligations."[52] To support their claim, Hill and Shirley refer to the argument of Mr. Hunter, counsel in *Sturges v. Crowninshield*, who urged this view—for the first time, I believe—upon the Court. The argument was rejected by Marshall and his colleagues.[53]

A second argument concerns an implication of the civil-law obligation. In the civil law, there are only contracts and quasi-contracts; no "real" obligation arises from a quasi-contract, and "implied" contracts are merely a species of quasi-contract. Therefore, no real obligation can arise from an implied contract. This logic contends that the implied executory agreement, which Marshall said arose out of the *Fletcher* land grant, was really no contract at all and therefore should not have been protected by the Constitution, regardless of whether state contracts were within the scope of the clause.[54] In other words, any *additional* obligation which arises from an executed contract must itself be by express covenant and cannot be implied. Narrowed to public contracts, the gist of this argument seems to be that, if Marshall had not made a fundamental mistake on executed contracts, then he would not have been able to set the precedent on state contracts for which *Fletcher* became justly famous and which served as the major groundwork of the *Dartmouth* decision—the decision that both Hill and Shirley are most interested in attacking.

The third type of assault on Marshall's view pertains to the *source* of the distinction between public and private contracts. Both Hill and Shirley hold that this distinction is based *not* on the *origin* of the contract, but rather on the *objects* for which it was created. This view was expressed by Mr. Sullivan (counsel for Woodward) in his argument before the New Hampshire Supreme Court; was accepted by Chief Justice Richardson in his majority opinion there; and was later overruled in Marshall's *Dartmouth* opinion.[55] According to this theory, if a charter of incorporation (or a land grant, perhaps) is granted for the accomplishment of important public purposes, then it is a public contract and, in their view, is not protected by the obligation clause. Conversely, if there are no significant public purposes involved, then it is a merely private contract, even if a state is one of the parties. Hill makes the latter point in his discussion of *Fletcher*, arguing that the land grant *might* be construed as a private contract in this sense, though it seems quite evident to him (and to Shirley) that the Dartmouth charter *cannot* be so construed.[56]

Related to the objects-versus-origins argument is a fourth type conceived by Marshall's critics: No matter what constitutes the obligation of a contract, it is a creature of positive law; and therefore it is absurd to hold that a state, which, after a fashion, creates *all* contracts since all contracts are made subject to its laws, can be obligated by its own contracts. It would be analogous to saying that God is obligated by the Ten Commandments. This view implies that a state cannot contract respecting objects within its sovereign powers and would seem to question especially Marshall's holding in *New Jersey v. Wilson*, that a state may grant perpetual tax exemptions.[57] The real point seems to be that Marshall must have based his early contract decisions on *natural law*, rather than positive law, and that such a basis for judicial decisions could never have been intended by those at the Philadelphia Convention. For empirical evidence to support this position, Marshall's critics often refer to his famous statement in the *Fletcher* opinion, that "the State of Georgia was restrained, either by general principles which are common to our free institutions, or by the particular provisions of the Constitution of the United States."[58]

The fifth argument is one put forward by Hutchinson: The Founders (or perhaps those in the various state ratifying conventions) could not possibly have intended *both* (1) that the obligation clause would have the effect of binding the states to perform their contracts, *and* (2) that the federal courts would possess the sort of jurisdiction over state courts that Marshall held them to have, according to Section 25 of the Judiciary Act of 1789, in *Cohens v. Virginia*.[59] The idea seems to be that the Founders could not have expected the states to willingly surrender so much power to the national government in general, and to the federal courts in particular. In other words, from the states' viewpoint, one might concede either *Fletcher* or *Cohens*, but not both.

Finally, Shirley adduces a large and complex set of historico-biographical arguments against Marshall's *Dartmouth* ruling, most of which are hardly worth considering. Here is a sample of these arguments: (1) The king never really granted the Dartmouth charter; rather, it was granted by the royal governor without the king's knowledge.[60] (2) Webster and Mason (counsel for the college) never really had much faith in the obligation-clause argument, since only about one-tenth of Webster's argument before the Court was devoted to it.[61] (3) The Dartmouth dispute was not really a "legal" one at all, but rather a *political* dispute between Federalists and Antifederalists (or a religious dispute between Calvinists and non-Calvinists), resulting in a perversion of the Constitution in favor of the "Federalist" notion of the sanctity of private property.[62]

Here, then, are the major arguments expressed by our trilogy of critics. Clearly, their real concern is not with the *substance* of the Marshall Court's early contract-clause decisions, but with their *consequences* in terms of legal, political, and economic developments later in the nineteenth century.[63] Whatever one thinks about such consequences—and before the Marshall Court is held responsible for them—the arguments should be evaluated on their own merits.

## The Argument against Marshall's Critics

First, there is no real evidence of Judge Wilson's alleged authorship of the contract clause. Neither Hill, Shirley, nor Hutchinson cite any source other than "tradition" to support this view, and it seems implausible since Wilson was *not* a member of the Committee on Style at the Philadelphia Convention, from which the clause emerged in its final form. Moreover, Rufus King, who introduced the clause as it appeared originally in the Northwest Ordinance, *was* a member of this Committee.[64] In fact, Curtis believed that King's authorship of the clause was unquestioned.[65]

Nor is it clear what would be proved if Wilson were the author of the clause. Although Wilson had no opportunity while on the bench to construe the clause directly (which both Shirley and Hill bemoan), a passage from his *Works* shows a marked affinity for the view later expressed by Marshall. Speaking of the state, Wilson says:

> It is an artificial person. It has its affairs and its interests; it has its rules; it has its obligations; it has its rights. It may acquire property, distinct from that of its members; it may incur debts, to be discharged out of the public stock, not out of the private fortunes of individuals: it may be bound by contracts and for damages arising quasi ex contractu.[66]

And in arguing against repeal of the Charter of the Bank of North America in 1785, he says:

> I am far from opposing the legislative authority of the state: but it must be observed, that, according to the practice of the legislature, publick acts of very different kinds are drawn and promulgated under the same form . . . surely it will not be pretended, that, after laws of those different kinds are passed, the legislature possesses over each the same discretionary power of repeal. In a law respecting the rights and properties of all the citizens of the state, this power may be safely exercised by the legislature. . . . Very different is the case with regard to a law, by which the state grants privileges to a congregation or other society. . . . Still more different is the case with regard to a law, by which an estate is vested or confirmed in an individual: if, in this case, the legislature may, at discretion, and without any reason assigned, divest or destroy his estate, then a per-

son seized of an estate in fee simple, under legislative sanction is, in truth, nothing more than a solemn tenant at will.[67]

Wilson himself was a product of the Scottish moralist school of philosophy, and following this tradition, he held a profound belief in natural law, which recognized no distinction between obligations arising out of public, as contrasted with private, contracts.[68] The quotations certainly confirm that. It is therefore not clear, all things considered, why Marshall's critics think that they gain anything by the claim that Wilson authored the contract clause, even if he was familiar with the civil law. Perhaps Hill, Shirley, and others can cite Wilson's civil-law training while ignoring his natural-law background only because virtually everyone in the late eighteenth century shared a belief in natural law, which has been pointed out in many scholarly works devoted to understanding the moral basis of early American law.[69]

However, the most definitive rebuttal of the implications of Wilson's alleged authorship is found in his own concurring opinion in *Chisholm v. Georgia*. Though the obligation clause was not directly before the Court in that case, Wilson buttresses his argument by reference to it: "What good purpose could this constitutional provision secure if a state might pass a law impairing the obligation of its own contracts, and be amenable, for such a violation of right, to no controlling judiciary power?"[70] This statement appears to be conclusive evidence that, given the opportunity, Wilson would have construed the clause in precisely the same way as Marshall—as indeed most would have in that time. Far from refuting Marshall by recurring to Wilson, the critics have refuted *themselves*, since Wilson's statement in *Chisholm* is probably the first mention of the contract clause from the federal bench, and it comes from one whose prestige at the Philadelphia Convention was second to none, save perhaps Madison.

The argument derived from the civil-law understanding of contractual obligation is self-defeating from the outset. Even if Wilson were the only Founder familiar with this tradition (which seems implausible), then how could the Convention, taken as a whole, have "intended" such a meaning? It would signify that the Framers adopted a reading of the clause of which they were only dimly aware, considering the paucity of discussion on it. Such a notion of intention is hardly comprehensible, let alone sufficient as a basis for constitutional interpretation.

Finally, even a cursory reading of the development of the civil law from ancient to modern times fails to support the idea of civil-law obligation put forward by Hill and Shirley. In early Roman law, *obligatio ex contractu* did refer only to private debts; yet, according to at least one prominent modern authority, the civil-law obligation of contracts developed *away* from the strict Roman-law tradition to a much broader notion, which gradually subsumed the concept under natural law sometime between the thirteenth and seventeenth centuries.[71] It would be unwise to rest fundamental principles of American constitutional law on ancient precedents, without recognizing their subsequent development. Thus the Hill-Shirley theory is simply unfounded.

Even if the Founders were not cognizant of the development of the civil-law tradition, they were certainly familiar with the theory of contract in the common law. While it may be true that quasi-contract and implied contract are the same in the civil-law tradition, this is *not* the case in the common law.[72] In civil law, only express contracts give rise to real obligations; in common law, both express and implied contracts are obligatory. This difference may explain why Hill and Shirley rely so much on the civil law, for the only other possibilities are the *common* law, in which case Marshall was right in saying that grants give rise to implied executory agreements; or *natural* law, in which case Marshall was right in saying that states are obligated by their contracts. Hill and Shirley must deny *both* of these points in order to make their argument plausible.

Actually, the development of civil- and common-law contract doctrines between the thirteenth and seventeenth centuries tended toward increasing acknowledgement of *autonomy* (free will) as the basis for obligation.[73] During most of this period, however, absolutism prevented inclusion of the state into the widening domain of responsibility. With the demise of absolutist rule, government itself came to be seen increasingly as a kind of autonomous entity capable of making contractual agreements and being held accountable for them. This "Kantian" development was retarded somewhat in continental Europe, though not completely so.[74] In England, it took the form of the principle that the *Crown* could not revoke its grants and charters. Fullest expression of autonomy was realized in the United States, in the idea that even *legislatures* could not impair the obligations arising from contracts they themselves had entered into.

As to the objects-versus-origins argument, its ahistoricity is evident. To hold that a public contract is one in which public, as distinct from private, purposes are manifest is to presuppose a world view that sharply distinguishes between public interests and private rights. By contrast, the Founders probably shared the opinion "that society existed to preserve the rights an individual possessed before he entered society and the corollary that society benefitted and prospered in direct proportion to the protection afforded individual rights."[75] According to Francis Stites,

> Protection of the basic right, property, either of private individuals or groups of private individuals would encourage the productive labor necessary to open the continent and develop the economy. Nineteenth-century American law absorbed this belief in the tie between individual rights and public welfare.[76]

In short, if the Founders believed that the *public* interest was best served by construction of a legal and political framework for protection of *private* rights (recalling Madison's statement about the obligation clause in *Federalist* Number 44), then no sharp distinction between public and private contracts was possible. The Hill-Shirley view finds such a separation only because it assumes attitudes widely shared in their age, but not in 1787.

The argument drawn from the positive-law theory of obligation fares no better, and for the same reason. The idea that a state cannot contract regarding its essential powers of sovereignty is closely related to the idea that contracts embodying important public purposes are subject to impairment by the state. For what are "essential powers of sovereignty" if not those which may, at all times and places, override private claims in the public interest? As Nathan Isaacs has shown, the Framers were steeped in the natural-law tradition of the eighteenth century, and Marshall's early contract decisions must be read in that light.[77] Even Professor Corwin, not one of Marshall's greatest admirers, criticizes those who would blame all the social and economic ills of the late nineteenth century on these decisions.[78] Indeed, Marshall himself laid some of the groundwork for the later development of reserved state powers in the *Willson* and *Providence* decisions,[79]—well before the revolution in nineteenth-century jurisprudence led by John Austin and his followers.[80]

Nevertheless, Marshall's late nineteenth-century critics insist on the Great Chief Justice's complicity (conscious or otherwise) in a conservative scheme for "subordinating the public good to the benefit of a privileged few."[81] Shirley's view is extreme, and while Hill is more moderate, he leaves little doubt as to where his concerns lie.

> A legislature, in a fit of benevolence, inserts in the charter of a charitable institution . . . that it shall be exempt from taxation. A

great railway company Wheedles . . . privileges,—perchance coupled with a release from public burdens,—which enables it to hold whole communities in a state of vassalage more galling and more durable than any established by the feudal system; or it combines with a ring of bad men, corrupts the judiciary, and plunders the commercial capital of the country at pleasure. Or, to use a more painful illustration, the perhaps most shamelessly corrupt and contemptible body of men that ever called themselves a legislature, grant to a corporation . . . the exclusive monopoly . . . of killing butchers' meat in a great city and its suburbs. To rescind the exemption from taxation, when it proves burdensome to the State; to attempt to limit the powers uncautiously granted to the railway company, when shown to be mere instruments of oppression and extortion; to repeal the monopoly of furnishing an essential article of food, even to save two hundred thousand people from starvation,—are not wise and beneficent acts of legislation, but laws impairing the obligation of contracts, breaches of public faith so contrary to sound principles of government that they are classed with ex post facto laws and bills of attainder! Chief Justice Marshall did not mean this; but his decision means this to the present generation.[82]

But apparently the Great Chief Justice did mean that. And so, it seems, did the Founders. Madison himself made no clear-cut distinction between *ex post facto* laws and laws impairing the obligation of contracts. Be that as it may, one must interpret the foregoing passage in light of Hill's role as assistant United States attorney-general during a period when the proportion of contract-clause cases that resulted in holdings of unconstitutionality reached an all-time high—the period between 1865 and 1873.[83] During those years state governments began to suffer the consequences of ill-advised concessions granted to private corporations prior to the Civil War (such as huge land grants to railroad companies, some of which never built the railroads). Considering the ever-present human temptation to blame the dead for the sins of the living, the Hill-Shirley view is at least understandable, albeit incorrect.

Finally, the doctrine of "police" powers as a qualification of the contract clause had not received its clearest formulation at the time Hill and Shirley wrote their works. That happened in *Stone v. Mississippi*, just one year after the publication of Shirley's treatise.[84] Thus the critics of the 1870s were attacking the contract-clause doctrines of the Marshall Court because their application was unfit for the period in question, and the Supreme Court had not yet developed a proper "fit." Underlying this view is an idea that the judicial process embodies an essentially *legislative* function, one ever-ready to respond to changing circumstances, according to perhaps novel conceptions of what is "just" or "prudent."

Little discussion seems necessary on the argument that the Founders could not have intended the *conjunction* of federal jurisdiction over state courts (*Cohens*) with the principle that states were obligated by their contracts. If the Framers had intended that federal courts would exercise such jurisdiction, the content of their intention must have been such specific provisions of the Constitution as the limitations set forth in Article I, Section 10. On the other hand, if they had intended that states should be obligated by their contracts, it is absurd to think that they would then have sought to render such obligation nugatory through deprivation of enforcement potential. Wilson's opinion in *Chisholm* seems definitive on this point.[85]

## Effects of the Shift

In summary, the origin of the modern idea that the Founders intended a sharp distinction to be drawn between public and private contracts is discovered in the writings of some relatively obscure authors whose works appeared between 1874 and 1879. Likewise, this idea is based on serious misinterpretations of early sources, misconceptions about the nature of the judicial process, and an undisguised preoccupation with the ultimate effects (some merely imagined) of the Marshall Court's obligation-clause decisions.

When viewed from the perspective of the late nineteenth-century reformers, such preoccupations are easily understood. These critics were responding partly to the widespread economic insecurity and consequent agitation for monetary reform occasioned by the currency crises of the early 1870s,[86] and partly to the willingness of the Supreme Court to use the contract clause to protect the fruits of improvident legislative grants made, for the most part, prior to the Civil War.[87]

At the same time, ideas respecting the nature of judicial decision making were changing. The Court's 1869 decision in *Hepburn v. Griswold*, invalidating a *federal* law on contract-clause grounds,[88] had given way to a dramatic reversal just two years later,[89] and had caused many to question the traditional notion that judicial decisions are based on "findings" of the law.[90] In the early 1870s, Oliver Wendell Holmes had proposed that the process of judging was complex and that there was a sense in which judges had "made" the law, as well as a sense in which they had "found" it.[91] Armed with hostility toward the contemporaneous Supreme Court and a new theory of judicial law-making that was rooted in an over-simplification of the Holmes idea, Hill, Shirley, and Hutchinson read their own experience and theory into their commentaries on Marshall. They concluded that when Marshall's Court rendered its famous contract decisions, it "made the law" in activist fashion.[92]

And the critics had their effect. Numerous statements reflecting the Hill-Shirley-Hutchinson "private debts and obligations" version of the Marshall Court's contract decisions appear after Cooley's apparent adoption of the view in 1880.[93] Between 1880 and 1938—the year in which Benjamin F. Wright's influential book on the contract clause was published[94]—Marshall's approach was challenged in treatises on the law of corporations,[95] contracts,[96] and the Constitution.[97] A number of authors continued to applaud him,[98] but after 1938, the cheering stopped, perhaps in testament to the influence of Wright's book.[99] Only recently has there been discernible movement toward refurbishing Marshall's reputation in this area.[100]

In conclusion, the issues debated here have great relevance for this study. Technically, the Marshall Court's contract decisions have little to do with *Marbury v. Madison* or with any of *Marbury*'s holdings, yet the significance of the Hill-Shirley-Hutchinson critiques in setting the tone for subsequent criticism of the Marshall Court cannot be overlooked. The assertion of the critics that Marshall and his Court "read" public contracts "into" Article I, Section 10, in order to lay a foundation for legal protection of property rights, contrary to the intentions of the Framers, parallels the later claim that Marshall read the idea of judicial review into the Constitution in order to bring other branches of government under judicial control. The objective was to pin the activist label on Marshall. The fruits of this endeavor will be reflected clearly in the chapters to follow.

# 10 · The Great Debate on the Judicial Function

*Background*

At the close of the Civil War, the doctrine of judicial power that has been ascribed to the Founders in 1787, to moderate Republicans and moderate Federalists in the 1790s, and to Marshall's Court in 1803, remained the controlling principle of American constitutional law regarding the role of courts. The narrow conception of judicial review over Congress embodied in *Marbury v. Madison* was derivative from that doctrine and stood essentially unquestioned throughout the Marshall and Taney periods. Both periods witnessed a virtual absence of disagreement with the idea of judicial review *in principle*, and the preponderance of criticism was directed at the Court's *failure* to invalidate acts of Congress. Not until after *Dred Scott* did there emerge any significant critique of the Court's invalidation of an act of Congress; even then, there was no denial of its power to do so in appropriate circumstances.

During the Marshall period, hostility toward the Court no doubt reflected the clash between a newer, more "partisan" style of politics that surfaced in the 1790s, and an older, more "consensual" style rooted in colonial America. Negative commentary on the Court grew increasingly bitter throughout the first two decades of the nineteenth century and reached a climax in the extensive critiques of the Court's opinions in *McCulloch v. Maryland*[1] and *Cohens v. Virginia.*[2] In those cases, the assailants read the Court's deference to Congress as an unwarranted "enlargement by construction" of the legislative power (see Chapter 6). In the Taney period, criticism of the Court reflected the increasing sectionalism and polarization of the country, the gradual breakdown of the constitutional compromises regarding slavery,[3] and the Jeffersonian failure to give up the idea that the Confederation had never really been abolished.[4]

Meanwhile, between 1803 and 1865, the Court itself had set aside only two acts of Congress,[5] one in a case of a judiciary nature.[6] Likewise, throughout the entire period and without exception, it had regarded *Marbury v. Madison* as having settled either a narrow jurisdictional question or a technical issue relating to the mandamus remedy.[7] Its importance as a precedent for judicial review of congressional authority was never mentioned by the Court—not even in the only other case of the period where the Court invalidated an act of Congress.[8]

This pattern continued from 1865 through 1894, the year before the *Pollock* and *Knight* decisions.[9] During these years, the Court cited *Marbury* in *none* of the twenty decisions invalidating national laws.[10] Those instances in which *Marbury* is cited relate primarily to the jurisdictional area or to the mandamus remedy. All but one of the citations refer to subjects which have no bearing on judicial review.[11] Finally, for the first time in the history of the Supreme Court, *Marbury v. Madison* is cited in 1887 as precedent for the idea that courts may enforce constitutional limitations against legislative bodies.[12]

Whatever the reason for the Court's exclusion of *Marbury* in connection with judicial review until 1887, the Court's more aggressive post-– Civil War stance had a marked effect on the most prominent legal writers of the day. This stance was as evident respecting state cases as it was respecting national legislation. According to Wright, between 1865 and 1898, the Court invalidated state laws in some 171 cases,[13] nearly *tripling* the number of such decisions in the Court's entire history prior to 1865.[14] Forty-six of this number occurred during the period of Justice Chase's tenure as chief justice (1865–1873).[15]

This period seems to have generated the historiographical critique of the Marshall Court on the contract clause, under which the Chase Court's nixing of state laws reached an all-time high.[16] Enraged over some of these decisions, a small group of critics inappropriately lambasted the Marshall Court for having laid the foundation by "reading" public contracts "into" Article I, Section 10, contrary (in the critics' view) to the intentions of the Framers (see Chapter 9).

### Post–Civil War Treatises

In contrast to the virulent contract-clause critiques of the 1870s and aside from Van Buren's work, treatises published during the Chase period

and the first decade of Chief Justice Waite's tenure (1874–1883) uniformly support the decision and the opinion in *Marbury v. Madison*. Thomas
M. Cooley's famous *Constitutional Limitations*, which was published
the year the Fourteenth Amendment was adopted, refers to *Marbury* only
once, listing it as one of the "very numerous authorities upon the subject" of the "right and power of the courts" to determine the "invalidity"
of a "law, direction, or decree," which is "applicable to the facts, but
on comparison with the fundamental law . . . is found to be in conflict."[17]
This citation is significant because it appears to be the first instance
where *Marbury* is used to support a power of judicial annulment drawn
*by implication* from the fact that "the Constitution is the fundamental
law of the State,"[18] rather than from specific constitutional authorization. Cooley thus presages the error that the Court itself would later
commit in *Mugler v. Kansas*.[19] The entire text of Cooley's argument
reads:

> The administration of public justice is referred to the courts. To
> perform this duty, the first requisite is to ascertain the facts, and
> the next to determine the law that is applicable. The constitution
> is the fundamental law of the State, in opposition to which any other
> law, or any direction or decree, must be inoperative and void. If,
> therefore, such other law, direction, or decree seems to be applicable
> to the facts, but on comparison with the fundamental law it is found
> to be in conflict, the court, in declaring what the law of the case
> is, must necessarily determine its invalidity, and thereby in effect
> annul it. The right and power of the courts to do this are so plain,
> and the duty is so generally—we may now say universally—
> conceded, that we should not be justified in wearying the patience
> of the reader in quoting from the very numerous authorities upon
> the subject.[20]

Then follows the citation of *Marbury*. To reiterate the previous discussion of Justice Gibson's opinion in *Eakin v. Raub*, any argument, from
a premise such as "the Constitution is fundamental law" to the conclusion that "the courts have the power to annul statutes," essentially
begs the question; in other words, the validity of the argument depends
on the use of the conclusion as an unstated premise. Moreover, no such
argument was made by Chief Justice Marshall in *Marbury v. Madison*.[21]
Cooley's citation of *Marbury* is therefore inappropriate, and his argument unfounded.

Ten years after publication of Cooley's treatise, Irving Browne provided a similarly laudatory account (and another significant misrepresentation) of *Marbury v. Madison* in a widely read collection of articles from the *Albany Law Journal*. Alluding to the Marshall Court, Browne remarks:

> Some of the questions decided by that court are so elementary that it now seems strange that they should ever have been debated. The earliest and most important of these decisions is the case of *Marbury v. Madison*, 1 Cranch 137, decided in 1803, where it was for the first time held that it is the right and duty of the judicial department to determine the constitutionality of a legislative act, and if such act be found repugnant to the provisions of the constitution; to declare it null and void. Under *this* doctrine no less than twenty-six *State* laws were overruled.[22]

The carte blanche for such uncritical usage of the *Marbury* decision was delivered by Edward J. Phelps in an address to the second annual meeting of the American Bar Association in August 1879. In the most thorough overstatement to its date of *Marbury*, Phelps praises the Marshall Court for establishing the principle

> that the construction of the constitution of the United States, for all purposes for which it requires construction, belongs *everywhere* and *always* to the jurisprudence of the country, and not to its politics, or even to its statesmanship. The lawyer or the student, who shall set himself down to follow the labors of that great tribunal from beginning to end, to learn on what foundation they rested, and what was the guide through the maze that proved as unerring as the mariner's compass in the storm, will find in it that salutary principle, set forth with the utmost clearness and unanswerable force in the early case of *Marbury against Madison*, followed up from time to time by repeated decisions, and adopted by all courts and all jurists ever since, that the constitution of this country has *by an inevitable necessity*, reposed in the judicial department of the government, *the sole determination and construction of the fundamental law of the land*.[23]

Phelps's assertion is extremely startling, considering the Founders' narrow conception of the judicial function; *Marbury*'s restatement of it and its continued acceptance throughout the pre-Civil War period; and the fact that the Court itself, despite having invalidated national legislative provisions in fourteen cases prior to 1879,[24] had *never* yet cited *Marbury* in support of any such holding. His statement is apparently the very first instance of *Marbury*'s use to defend a sweeping (and exclusive) power of nullification in courts generally, which is now recognized as the full-blown doctrine of judicial review.[25] Coming from so influential a member of the Bar, the point could hardly have been lost on those who, only five years later, began to question the role of the judiciary in the American Republic.

The remaining reference to *Marbury* during the period 1865–1883 is somewhat ironic. John M. Shirley, in a book otherwise devoted to excoriating the Marshall Court for its contract-clause decisions, nevertheless provided the most accurate discussion of the case in the entire period. Citing *Marbury* to illustrate the point that the vast preponderance of early Supreme Court decisions "were of no greater consequence than those which came before the Supreme Court of the several States," Shirley says:

> The issue, in a legal sense, was exceedingly narrow. The vital and decisive question which confronted the petitioners . . . was, whether the court had jurisdiction; and this depended upon another, whether Congress could annul the Constitution, or authorize or compel the court to disregard its provisions. . . . The question was neither new nor difficult, nor did Marshall so regard it. . . . He simply reiterated what had been previously said by Hamilton, Wilson, and by many other eminent statesmen and jurists.[26]

Shirley then argues that the power of courts to set aside unconstitutional statutes is confirmed by pre-Constitution precedents in the state courts, by "the most eminent" members of the Federal Convention, and by "Judges of the Supreme Court, sitting at the circuit. . . . It is no wonder, then, that Marshall regarded the point clear and unquestionable, or that the court decided it had no jurisdiction, and ordered the rule discharged."[27]

To summarize, then, to 1883, the Supreme Court had never cited *Marbury v. Madison* in support of judicial authority to disregard statutes, yet no one had challenged the *Marbury* holding that courts could do so "in some cases."[28] Virtually everyone supported *at least* the minimal, narrow theory of judicial function propounded by the Founders at Philadelphia in 1787, which acknowledged the Court's power to disregard congressional enactments in cases of a judiciary nature. On the other hand, references to *Marbury* (except Shirley's) throughout most of the two decades following the Civil War grossly overstate what was decided in *Marbury*, unlike the references examined for the period prior to the war. Thus it is possible to detect a nascent movement, beginning with Cooley's treatise in 1868, toward legitimization of a broader notion of judicial power than that conceived by the Founders and by the Marshall Court. At the same time, the eruption of a historical broadside between 1874 and 1879, aimed at the Marshall Court's contract decisions, could only have helped to accustom later critics of the Court to the expediency of blaming present woes on generations past.

## The Great Debate

The Court, too, had done its part. Just as its voiding of some twenty state laws during Chase's tenure had played a significant role in bringing about the contract-clause critiques, so its nullifications of congressional statutes between 1873 and 1883—*all six* of which were in cases decidedly *not* of a judiciary nature[29]—must have been an important factor in the emergence of an extensive debate on the judicial function. That debate was set in motion by Judge Robert Street, in a paper read before the American Bar Association in August 1883.[30] With this event, the acquiescence in *Marbury* and its narrow holding came to an end; and for the first time, a negatively critical misinterpretation of the *constitutional principle* of that decision was effected.[31] On the other hand, a new period in American constitutional historiography was ushered in. Prior to 1883, there is no evidence of a single published book or article devoted *entirely* to the subject of judicial power to invalidate acts of coordinate agencies of government. In the decade following Street's paper, at least a dozen such treatises appeared.[32]

Street begins by making a mistake similar to that made by Phelps some four years earlier: "From *Marbury v. Madison* down to the present time, the judiciary department of the Federal Government has been the final resort of political parties on the greatest questions of public policy that have agitated the country."[33] The emphasis, however, is different, because Street believes that "the judiciary has become a factor in the political power of the government, never contemplated in its origin."[34] No doubt this much was true, given previous Supreme Court decisions invalidating congressional provisions. Attacking the Court's inconsistency in the earlier legal-tender decisions, Street claims that its notorious reversal in *Knox v. Lee*[35] proved that *Hepburn v. Griswold*[36] was nothing more "than the mere expression of opinion." He then invokes the theory of coordinate review, saying that "the judiciary can no more annul an act of Congress on the ground of its unconstitutionality than Congress can set aside a decree of the courts without jurisdiction."[37]

Less than a year later, James Bradley Thayer, in a letter to the editor of *The Nation*, developed the famous "reasonableness" test out of a version of the two questions treated by Marshall in the final pages of his *Marbury* opinion: (1) Is the law constitutional? (2) May the Court declare it so?[38] Citing "recent decisions," and making special reference to the Court's decision in the *Civil Rights Cases*, Thayer points out that "the difficulty with this form of question—viz. Is the act constitutional?—is that it steadily tempts the court into stating its own opinion on questions that may be purely legislative or political, instead of fixing its attention upon the precise judicial function, that, namely, of determining whether the Legislature has transgressed the limits of reasonable interpretation."[39]

In other words, Thayer, albeit without citing *Marbury*, believes that "recent decisions" indicate a propensity in the courts to confuse the two questions distinguishable in the "constitutional" portion of that opinion. The "test" is a heuristic device for bringing proper focus back to the second of these questions, since, in most constitutional cases, the function of the court "is not that of declaring the true construction of the Constitution, but that of deciding whether another department has acted unreasonably."[40]

One year after the appearance of Thayer's article, William Meigs, writing in the *American Law Review*, endorsed Street's argument on coordinate review, again citing *Marbury* to support a *stronger* version of binding judicial power to invalidate national laws.[41] After stating that the doctrine of *Marbury* "is now so entirely interwoven with and become an integral part of all our forms and processes of reasoning that we never stop to question, or in any way examine, the basis of reasoning on which it rests," Meigs observes that "it was by no means so entirely free from question as is assumed."[42] He then argues (in line with Street) that constitutional interpretations by the courts are not conclusive upon other agencies of government, referring to the "sociology of judges" and attacking the decision in the *Civil Rights Cases*.[43]

On February 5, 1886, the famous historian George Bancroft issued a pamphlet attacking the Court's decision in *Juilliard v. Greenman*, the last of the legal-tender decisions.[44] According to Charles Warren, this decision, upholding the power of Congress to "make the notes of the Government a legal tender in payment of private debts," contained "the most sweeping opinion as to extent of Congressional power which had ever theretofore been rendered."[45] The Court had ruled similarly some thirteen years before, but it was generally thought that the earlier holding had been confined to the circumstances of a wartime emergency.[46] With this basis no longer available, the Court rested its holding in *Juilliard* on the ground that the power, "not being prohibited to Congress by the Constitution, . . . is included in the power expressly granted to borrow money on the credit of the United States." Perhaps if the Court stopped here, public criticism of its decision might have been less severe, but it chose instead to further assert that the power was one "universally understood to belong to sovereignty, in Europe and America, at the time of the framing and adoption of the constitution of the United States." The Court then cited an English case involving "the Emperor of Austria, as King of Hungary," in support of the proposition.[47]

That was more than the Jeffersonian spirit of George Bancroft could tolerate. Echoing John Taylor's remarks on *McCulloch* a half-century before, Bancroft charged that the *Juilliard* opinion was an "enlargement by construction" of the powers of Congress and urged the Court to reconsider its decision.[48] Richard C. McMurtrie, described by Arnold Paul as the "dean of the Philadelphia bar,"[49] answered the great historian in the autumn of 1886, claiming that it was highly questionable whether the Court could invalidate the Legal Tender Acts.[50] McMurtrie charges the critics of *Juilliard* with inconsistency, because their argument that the Court should declare the tender acts void is asserted on the ground that congressional authority to pass them is based entirely on implication and inference. In fact, the Court's power of voiding a legislative act is *itself* based exclusively on inference and implication, since "there is no reference whatsoever to any such power in the text of the constitution," and "no such exercise of judicial power has ever been heard of before in civilized countries."[51]

McMurtrie then lays complete responsibility for the power "of declaring void a legislative act" at Marshall's doorstep.

Is there any such grant in the constitution, or any allusion to it? Since C. J. Marshall's judgement in *Marbury v. Madison*, I should have said, but for the facts contradicting me, that no one probably has been able to question that the power does not exist, and that it was created by the constitution. But it is a mere deduction of logic. Impossible (to my apprehension) for a sane mind to question, but still derived by *tacit implication*, a process which one of the most conspicuous members of the Convention assured the most important of the communities that enacted the instrument, *could not be a ground for asserting a grant*.[52]

In the following year, coincident with the Philadelphia Convention's centennial, the debate on the judicial function culminated in the appearance of several important treatises. Dr. Hermann von Holst published, for the first time in English, his famous book on American constitutional law.[53] *Marbury* is not mentioned in the work, but von Holst does refer to Thayer's article and to Cooley's treatise.[54] Using language strikingly similar to that in *Marbury*, von Holst states that "the task of the court is to say what *is* law under the constitution, the federal laws and treaties." He carefully distinguishes the judicial function from the legislative, the latter consisting in a decision as to "what *shall be* law under the constitution."[55] At root is the distinction between politics and law—one of the main grounds of the separation doctrine of the Federal Convention.[56]

On the other hand, Alexander Johnston, in an article commemorating the Constitution's centennial, declares that the power of a court to determine the constitutionality of legislation is "inseparable from the adoption of a written constitution as the permanent exponent of a purely popular will." According to Johnston, courts in the United States are different from those in other countries because the former must "deal with the will of the real sovereign, the people, put into permanent shape in a written constitution; and they have to consider, when *any* law is pleaded before them, whether that law is in accord with the will of the real sovereign, and valid, or opposed to it, and 'unconstitutional.' "[57] Thus emerges the "guardianship" theory of judicial function, whereby courts are regarded as "stand-ins" for "the people," ever vigilant to protect the people against incursions upon their will by their own elected representatives. Appropriately, *Marbury* is not cited in support of the doctrine.[58]

*Marbury* is, however, used to corroborate the most extreme notion of judicial power to be advanced during the centennial year—or, indeed, during the first hundred years of the Constitution's existence. In an article published in the *Chicago Law Times*, James R. Doolittle referred to the Supreme Court's authority to disregard legislative enactments as a "veto" power "greater than that of the president." Comparing the respective authorities, Doolittle points out that the president "has power to require a law to be passed by two-thirds of each house of Congress. That court has power to veto a law if passed by both houses unanimously. It vetoes the laws of the federal legislature not authorized by the Constitution, and it vetoes laws made by State legislatures when they encroach upon the domain of national sovereignty."[59] After likening the Court's veto to that of the Roman tribunes,[60] Doolittle then remarks:

> In 1803, in the case of Marbury against Madison, . . . that high tribunal . . . for the first time exercised its great tribunitian power, and declared an act of Congress repugnant to the Constitution null and void. It was its first veto upon the usurpation by Congress of unconstitutional power. This case also recognized that tribunal as the one to hold the balance of power, to decide what is within and what is without the domain of federal sovereignty.[61]

Thus the first talk appears of the Court's role as "umpire" of the federal system.[62]

During the centennial year, perhaps the soundest piece of work on the judicial role was by Sydney Fisher in the *American Law Review*. Fisher takes issue with Street and Meigs, claiming that their theory of coordinate review is a perversion of the separation doctrine of the Federal Convention.[63] According to Fisher, their ideas are based on the old Jeffersonian doctrine that holds *each* branch of government to be the *final* judge of its own *constitutional* authority and therefore legally *entitled* to override decisions of other departments whenever in possession of the raw power to do so—*whatever* the type of case involved.[64] In other words, Street and Meigs suppose that the three branches of government are "absolutely independent" of one another.[65]

Fisher believes, as I do, that such a concept is grossly oversimplified and prefers to call the relationship "distinct," rather than "independent."[66] He lists the ways in which each branch of government is, or is not, independent of the others. Included in the list are the following four propositions:

> 1. The President is independent of the judiciary in vetoing a bill, in making a treaty, in pardoning a prisoner, and in executing an act of Congress. 2. But he is not independent of the judiciary with respect to their decrees and judgements. He must enforce them whether he thinks them constitutional or not. 3. The President is

independent of Congress in vetoing a bill, in pardoning a prisoner, and in removing from office. In negotiating a treaty he is independent of the House of Representatives, but not of the Senate. 4. But he is not independent of Congress in executing the laws. He must enforce the laws which Congress has enacted, whether he thinks them constitutional or not.[67]

Fisher then cites *Marbury v. Madison* to support the second and fourth propositions, adding that "the Supreme Court have several times held that the officers of the executive department, though beyond judicial control in discretionary duties, could be compelled by process to perform ministerial acts which were required by law; as, for example, to deliver a land patent, or an officer's commission, or to credit a person with money due him."[68]

The issue reached its climax that year on December 5, when the Supreme Court handed down its decision in *Mugler v. Kansas*, using *Marbury* for the first time in support of judicial authority to invalidate legislation.[69] In 1888, nothing of particular relevance occurred, and only Cooley's *Constitutional History* in 1889, which treats *Marbury* somewhat more narrowly than in the earlier *Limitations*.[70] In 1890, Charles B. Elliott published an article examining the historical roots of the doctrine of judicial power to invalidate legislation, both in England and America. Its importance here lies in its assertion that the power is based on the "idea of a written constitution," which Johnston had stated earlier, and its proposal that the decision in *Marbury* is grounded on that theory, which had not been suggested before.[71] Elliott prefaces his discussion of *Marbury* with Kent's famous description of the case, in which "the power and duty of the judiciary to disregard an unconstitutional act of Congress or of any state legislature were declared in an argument approaching to the precision and certainty of a mathematical demonstration."[72] Elliott concludes, "The power was never seriously questioned in the federal courts after the decision in *Marbury v. Madison*, and was gradually established in all the states."[73]

One other significant work which appeared in 1890: Christopher Tiedeman's little book, in which he suggests that judicial power to set aside statutes is part of the "unwritten Constitution," and that the "real value of a written constitution" lay in its making possible this feature.[74] *Marbury*, however, is not cited. The following year witnessed the publication of Hampton Carson's volume on the Supreme Court, which included essays by Edward J. Phelps and William A. Butler.[75] Phelps reiterates the earlier points made before the American Bar Association in 1879, adding an assertion of the guardianship theory articulated by Johnston.[76] Butler declares that the Court has "the final rights of determining whether *any* act of Congress contravenes the Constitution, and whether *any* Constitution or statute of a State contravenes the Constitution or the laws of the United States."[77]

After another brief respite in 1892, the dialogue resumed with the publication of the first full-length treatise *entirely* devoted to the question of judicial power to disregard legislative enactments. Its author was Brinton Coxe, a distinguished member of the Philadelphia Bar, and its purpose was indicated by the question inscribed on the title page: "Does the Constitution express or imply the truth that its *jus legum*, which binds legislators in legislating, also binds judges in deciding?"[78] According to Thayer, the work

> is a posthumous fragment from the hand of the lamented translator of Guterbock's "Bracton, and His Relation to the Roman Law"— published in 1866. It is edited by William M. Meigs, of the Philadelphia Bar, a writer favorably known to the profession and to students of constitutional law by various publications. . . . The main proposition of it is that the Constitution of the United States *expressly* gives to the courts the power of disregarding unconstitutional Acts of the legislature.[79]

Coxe must have begun the work sometime after 1886, for his point of departure is the Bancroft-McMurtrie disputation of that year.[80] His quarrel is with the Court's opinion in *Juilliard v. Greenman* and with McMurtrie's defense of it.[81] According to Coxe, the doctrine of *Juilliard* is that Congress has, constructively and as incidental to its express powers, all the powers "which the national legislatures of foreign sovereign and civilized governments have and use," unless withheld by the Constitution.[82] McMurtrie's argument is that the Court's power to disregard statutes is based on implication and inference.[83]

For Coxe, the effect of the two doctrines,

> when taken together, seem to undermine the foundations of the judicial power as hitherto understood. . . . If . . . the U. S. Congress were to enact a statute prohibiting the Supreme and Inferior Courts from declaring any act of Congress in any case to be unconstitutional and void, it seems impossible to understand how such a

statute would not be valid, supposing the doctrine in *Juilliard v. Greenman* and Mr. McMurtrie's doctrine to be both wholly correct. If they both be wholly correct, the power to enact such a law can not be expressly withheld, must be unknown in every civilized country, and must be incidental to the express legislative powers of Congress, among which is that of making all laws necessary and proper for carrying its *other* powers into execution.[84]

Coxe regards such a result as absurd, and if "the conclusion be absurd, there is a *reductio ad absurdum* of some part or parts of one or both the premised doctrines."[85]

Thus begins his effort to refute McMurtrie's contention that the power of courts to disregard legislation is grounded on tacit implication—and the first victim is Marshall, singled out by Coxe as the original perpetrator of McMurtrie's "fallacy."[86] After a line-by-line examination of the constitutional portion of *Marbury v. Madison*, Coxe concludes "that any writer who maintains that such a judicial competency (the power to declare a law unconstitutional and void) is matter of express import according to the constitutional text, must proceed otherwise than Marshall, and must reason upon a basis different from the opinion in *Marbury v. Madison*."[87] In view of the purpose of Coxe's enterprise, this must be taken as strong criticism, indeed.

Thayer, who doubts that Coxe has "established" his "main point,"[88] nonetheless agrees with him in finding the *Marbury* opinion somewhat inadequate. Thayer mentions *Marbury* in a reference to Judge Gibson's dissenting opinion in *Eakin v. Raub*, remarking that the dissent "has fallen strangely out of sight. It has much the ablest discussion of the question which I have ever seen, not excepting the judgement of Marshall in *Marbury v. Madison*, which, as I venture to think, has been overpraised."[89] (Thayer's is the first mention of Judge Gibson's opinion in any of the treatises under scrutiny here, and it is significant that he does *not* say that the Court's opinion in *Marbury* is inconsistent with Judge Gibson's dissent, unlike most, if not all, contemporary commentators.) Thayer next argues that the "American doctrine" is derived from the colonial experience of an external sovereign replaced by "the people" at the Revolution and from the separation of powers, but it cannot be drawn from the "idea of a written constitution" per se, contra Johnston and Elliott.[90]

In addition to the famous works of Coxe and Thayer, three more contributions to this ongoing discussion appeared during 1893. Walter D.

Coles, in a curious article encouraging people to "look to the Supreme Court to stay the tide which is running so strongly towards centralization," assails the Court's opinion in *Juilliard v. Greenman* for being "weak, incoherent, and uncandid." He also predicts that Marshall would have dissented along with Field, had he been on the Court when that case was decided—despite Coles's own declaration that most decisions of the Marshall Court resulted more from the "Federalist proclivities of the judges" than from anything else.[91] *Marbury* is not cited.

Finally, McMurtrie reenters the debate in December, claiming (presumably in response to Coxe, though he does not say so) that Marshall's "doctrine," set forth in *Marbury v. Madison*, "cannot be successfully controverted." The contents of this doctrine are then explicated. The basic idea, as Elliott had suggested, is that Marshall's theory arises from the "idea of a written constitution"—and McMurtrie's is the first *clear* assertion to that effect. The authority justified in *Marbury*, then, must be deduced from the "idea" by "necessary implication." This is acceptable because, when the Great Chief Justice "established" the power to disregard acts of legislation, he transcended the bounds of mere legality and became a "statesman."[92] The author concludes with a reminder of the constraints placed on the judicial role by the Marshall Court and warns that the old "natural law" jurisprudence (à la Chase and Johnson) might be finding its way back into the courts, resulting in a "surrender of sovereignty" by the people.[93]

The great debate ended on a bizarre note. Commenting on some recent decisions with which he was dissatisfied, McMurtrie seized an opportunity to further clarify his perspective on *Marbury*. He was evidently aware that the problem with the tacit-implication position is its propensity for abuse by judges. So, McMurtrie attempts to distinguish between Marshall, who "recognizes the State restraining its officers by a document to be construed and understood," and others, who find "the restraint in the views that may be entertained as to the inconsistency of the law with an unwritten and undefined code of ethics, political economy or policy."[94]

William Draper Lewis, editor of the *Register*, took issue with McMurtrie's distinction, arguing that his position is really based on the principle that a statute interfering with "natural justice," "fundamental principles," and the like, must be shown (either expressly or implicitly) to be *prohibited* (not merely unauthorized) before a court can invalidate it. Using the Marshall Court as his lynchpin, Lewis suggests that such a principle is of comparatively recent vintage and that "undoubtedly the quantity and quality of judicial opinion, prior to the days of TANEY, is in favor of [the position] that a statute interfering with natural rights must be shown to be authorized, not that it must be shown to be prohibited."[95] With some confusion, it seems, Lewis then cites *Fletcher v. Peck* as an illustration of the Court's invalidating a statute on the ground of "natural law" and asserts, at the same time, that *Dartmouth College v. Woodward* was the culprit case which established the contrary principle.[96]

## The Aftermath

With Lewis, the ongoing dialogue, which had begun ten years earlier in the address of Judge Street, draws to a close. During that decade, crucial issues had been raised for the first time in a highly articulate form, and *Marbury v. Madison* had been moved from a place of relative quiet to the center of a storm. The decade had witnessed the first citation by the Supreme Court of *Marbury* to support a doctrine of judicial review (though the phrase itself had not yet been used);[97] the appearance of the first full-length work devoted entirely to that subject;[98] and the first public criticism of *Marbury*'s "constitutional" holding (though by way of misinterpretation).[99] For the first time in *each* of the following instances, *Marbury* had been cited to support: a "veto" power in the Supreme Court;[100] the Court's newly achieved status as "umpire" of the federal system;[101] the doctrine that judicial power to disregard statutes is based on "inference and implication,"[102] and on the "idea of a written constitution."[103] Marshall had been called "more of a statesman than a lawyer";[104] and his opinion for the Court in *Marbury* had been, again for the first time, compared unfavorably with Judge Gibson's dissenting opinion in *Eakin v. Raub*.[105] Most of the above are straw men. But these arguments, taken together, comprise a substantial portion of important twentieth-century ideas about *Marbury* and judicial review. In this chapter, we have observed the genesis of these straw men. In the next, we shall bear witness to their incendiary nature, when confronted with an appropriate catalyst.

# II · A Reinterpretation of American Constitutional History

Prior to the Court's decision in the Income Tax Case,[1] *Marbury* had been cited both to support and to derogate concepts of judicial power that cannot fairly be drawn from it. No one, however, had presumed to question the fundamental constitutional doctrine of *Marbury*: that the Supreme Court possesses authority to disregard acts of Congress "in some cases."[2] Likewise, no one had ventured to suggest that such an authority was not entirely consistent with the intentions of the Founding Fathers.

Between 1868 and 1895, both sides of the controversy applied their arguments mainly to the idea of judicial power that had emerged *in that period*, a power that Wright has appropriately called "supervisory."[3] On May 20, 1895, when the Court declared the entire federal income tax law unconstitutional (the "most decisive and dramatic" culmination of "the advance of judicial supremacy," according to Arnold Paul),[4] the era of moderate debate came to an end. So did the long-standing acquiescence in the constitutional doctrine of *Marbury v. Madison*. Sylvester Pennoyer, former Democratic-Populist governor of Oregon, initiated a series of attacks on the Court in the July–August issue of the *American Law Review*.[5] In his broadside, Pennoyer utilized the public attention which had previously been focused on *Marbury* and perhaps responded to the Court's apparent acceptance of the views advanced by Joseph H. Choate, chief counsel for the winning side in *Pollock*, who had made reference to *Marbury* in his successful oral argument against the constitutionality of the tax.[6]

## The Attack on Marbury *and Judicial Review*

Pennoyer begins by asserting the total "independence" of the three branches of national government, providing the most extreme version

176

of the theory of arbitrary coordinate review to date.[7] The implications of this position are apparent a few pages later: "if there be a difference of opinion between the departments of the Federal government in regard to the constitutionality of a measure, the opinion of Congress, and not the opinion of the court, must prevail."[8] In other words, to Pennoyer, coordinate review means congressional review.

Between the two statements is Pennoyer's claim, appearing perhaps for the first time since *Marbury*, that the Founders had not intended that courts should have the power to set aside acts of Congress.[9] The corollary is that, in *Marbury*, the Supreme Court first assumed without warrant the "right to supervise the laws of Congress." According to Pennoyer, "Ever since 1803, . . . we have had a substituted government, under which Congress has abrogated the exclusive prerogative of making laws conferred upon it by the Constitution. We have, during this time, been living under a government not based upon the Federal Constitution, but under one created by the plausible sophistries of John Marshall." Pennoyer concludes with the charge that the Court's nullification of the income tax is a usurpation of an "exclusive power of Congress," that the "nullifying judges" should be impeached and removed from office, and that the president should be instructed to "enforce the collection of the income tax."[10]

In the November–December issue of the *Review*, Lafon Allen responded to Pennoyer, calling his argument "somewhat confused" and at times, "childishly vicious."[11] Allen believes that Article III, Section 2 is a "lettered warrant" authorizing courts to disregard legislative enactments, and even if it were not, Congress cannot be the final judge of its own acts because "interested parties cannot judge themselves." Since the "interpretation of laws is a judicial power in this and in every civilized country," according to Allen, "to say that this is a creation of John Marshall is to compliment even John Marshall too highly."[12] After suggesting that the mere existence of a written constitution gives courts the power to nullify statutes, Allen assails Pennoyer's idea of complete independence of the departments with rhetorical flourish.

> When Montesquieu and his disciples contended for the independence of the three governmental departments, they did not mean that they should know nothing of one another; that the government of our country, for example, could be most successfully administered with the White House and the houses of Congress at the two poles, and the Supreme Court holding its sittings in the palace of the Khan Kublai at Xanadu.[13]

Pennoyer wasted no time in answering Allen's criticisms. Attempting to bolster his viewpoint with historical documentation, he claims that the Federal Convention's repeated rejection of the proposal to vest some of the executive revisionary authority in "a convenient number of the national judiciary" proves that courts were not intended to have the power to invalidate statutes.[14] Turning to the *Federalist*, Pennoyer says that Hamilton is no authority for determining the Framers' intentions, since he was a "monarchist,"[15] whose plans for placing government "beyond the control of the people" were carried into execution by Marshall.

> In the case of *Marbury v. Madison*, the foundation of a government was laid, entirely different from that which was laid by the framers of the constitution. With sophisticated reasoning which may perhaps have been equalled, but which certainly was never excelled, Chief Justice Marshall educed a thesis changing our constitutional form of government into a judicial oligarchy, with such adroitness and such exploitation as to win the sanction of the thoughtless, many of whom still believe that it is a true interpretation of our constitution.[16]

Another article appears in that same volume of the *American Law Review*, clearly related to the *Pollock* controversy. Robert Ludlow Fowler, exclaiming that the income tax decision "emphasizes the great power of the judicial establishment in this country of limited legislative powers," adds that the "power of declaring acts of the legislature void because in conflict with the constitution of government—is very ancient in America."[17] Fowler cites English and American "precedents" to support his view, concluding that the Founders intended the judiciary "to be the conservator of the constitutional rights of the people."[18] As further evidence, Fowler advances the somewhat daring idea that "the people who made, as well as those who adopted, the Federal Constitution of 1787 had long lived under a form of government where the judiciary were supreme over the legislature *ex natura rerum*"; and "if the legislature transcended their power, the courts of first instance in the colonies were bound *by the very nature of things* to adjudge the fact."[19]

According to Fowler, this idea of "transcendent judicial power" was accepted by Americans prior to 1787. Since written constitutions cannot "create a sovereign power," but can only "declare where that power is lodged, and if they misstate the fact, the document and not the power, will in the course of events first disappear," then either the Constitution of 1787 incorporates transcendent judicial power, or it has in fact "disappeared" and been replaced by an "unwritten" constitution which does "vest this transcendent power in the judicial branch of the Federal government."[20] Previously, Tiedeman had suggested that a judicial power of nullification might be drawn from an "unwritten constitution," yet he had derived this "unwritten constitution" from the written one.[21] Fowler's notion thus may be the earliest suggestion on record that such authority may be drawn, not from the idea of a written constitution, but rather in *defiance* of it.

This phase of the controversy reached its climax in the following year, with the appearance of the first full-length article devoted exclusively to *Marbury v. Madison*. Predictably, its author was Sylvester Pennoyer, who had by now discovered Van Buren. Beginning with the bald assertion (another "first") that *Marbury* is the most important case in the history of jurisprudence, the former governor reiterates all the points he had previously made concerning the case and adds most of Van Buren's criticisms as well.[22] The first culprit is Hamilton, who "controlled" both the administrations of Washington and Adams, "and the legislation of Congress, for the first twelve years of our national existence." Borrowing Jefferson's famous phrase, Pennoyer charges that the Federalist party had been a host of "sappers and miners, busily engaged in undermining our constitutional fabric." Evidence lies in the passage of the Judiciary Act, the bank bill, and the notorious Alien and Sedition Acts—all of which, Pennoyer claims, were unconstitutional.[23]

After declaring that the election of 1800 "must necessarily be considered as the best and soundest interpretation of the constitution, which was ever given to it, or which could possibly ever be given to it," Pennoyer calls the Judiciary Act of 1801 a plot of the aristocratic Federalists, "anticipating the incoming administration, and strengthening the judicial department of government, the power of which was to be enlarged by usurping powers never conferred; thus endeavoring, by hiding behind the gowns of the judiciary and pleading the sanctity of judicial proceedings and determinations, to render powerless and ineffective the verdict of the people at the ballot box."[24] This explains to Pennoyer's satisfaction the reversal of the order of counsel's questions in *Marbury*—treating the jurisdictional question last, so as to make it possible to declare Section 13 unconstitutional, thus "overthrowing" the constitution and "completely destroying the coordination of the three great branches of the government, by rendering the legislative subservient to the judicial."[25]

Why then did the Court not follow up its own lead and invalidate more laws passed by democratically elected Congresses? Why did the Court "remain quiescent" in this area until 1857? According to Pennoyer, they were silent "for fear that they might be deprived of the unconstitutional powers conferred upon them by the Judiciary Act of 1789, if they proceeded any further." He reveals what the "verdict" of 1800 really was: that the claim of the Court to overturn state laws was unfounded, due to the unconstitutionality of Section 25; and that "the true constitutional doctrine was that contained in the Kentucky Resolution of 1798." Pennoyer closes with the plea that Congress abolish the inferior federal courts, since they have made "the free people of this country the bond slaves of the insatiate greed of mammon and the unbridled lust of corporations."[26]

Pennoyer was answered again, this time by Junius Parker, who retorted that the Court's power to "sit in the quietest room in the Capitol at Washington, and quietly make naught a law which Congress has with long and noisy travail, brought forth, . . . is an absolutely logical and necessary consequent to our system of government, and that its being realized and acquiesced in has been most fortunate to our institutions and general welfare."[27] Parker bases his argument on the erroneous hypothetical that, if "an act of an agent beyond the scope of his authority and contrary to it *is void*," then "courts can do no less than so declare." He contends that it "is not only incorrect historically, but it is disrespectful, to say the least, to the intelligence and acumen of the framers of the constitution; and the men who after so long and earnest discussion, adopted it, to say that this thoroughly logical result was not apparent to them, and intended by them."[28] Parker cites *Marbury v. Madison* as hardly an "unprecedented" decision and suggests that its "precedents" might be precisely those earlier "declarations" which grounded the theory of judicial nullification in the idea that unauthorized national legislation was *ipso facto* void. All of which means, to Parker, that the function of the judiciary is to "survey the work of the legislature, and the limits which have been imposed on its power."[29]

The flurry of commentary on *Marbury*, contained in two volumes of the *American Law Review* and authored in response to the *Pollock* controversy, had given the debate a decidedly different tone. In marked contrast with the commentators of 1883–1893, Pennoyer and his critics increasingly relied on *ad hominem* arguments and rhetorical flourishes. In Pennoyer's case, such reliance might best be described as vitriolic scapegoating and grotesque oversimplification. Gone are the areas of agreement which imparted to the earlier debate its academic flavor and left some basic questions open for future resolution. *Marbury* might have been a fulcrum from which that resolution would be accomplished, given thorough historical and jurisprudential investigation of its place in American constitutional law. However, once engulfed in the flames of *Pollock, Knight,* and *Debs,* the destiny of that long-obscured case was finally divorced from its origin, and it became a primal symbol of the great national political conflict which would not subside until 1937—and perhaps did not subside even then.

## *A Marbury Centennial!*

The tendencies of the *Marbury* commentators of 1895–1896 were perpetuated by others for the rest of the nineteenth century and the first five years of the next. Continuing in the critical vein of Pennoyer, John W. Akin delivered an address before the Georgia Bar Association on July 7, 1898, in which he charged the federal courts with various "aggressions" in the fields of labor relations, interstate commerce, municipal and state government, and personal liberty. Claiming that "the Federal judiciary, . . . is the sole repository of ultimate power in this republic," and that "no greater power has ever been vested in any officials or in any department of any government than is now exercised by the Federal judiciary," Akin admonishes Judge William Howard Taft for having once said that "by the verdict and acquiescence of the people John Marshall had been vindicated and the criticisms of Thomas Jefferson have been refuted."[30]

Turning his wrath on Hamilton and Marshall, Akin says that "centralization, absolutism, and, if you please, imperialism, owe more to these than any other two Americans, and hence they stand out boldly and prominently in the perspective of our history." Akin charges that both "believed in the government of the many by the few," "doubted the ability of the people to govern themselves," "were not willing to trust the States or the plain people of the land," and "believed not only in the sacredness of property but in the natural right of wealth and classes to control the destinies of the nation."[31] He concludes:

Between these on the one hand, and Jefferson and his school on the other, there was—and still is—an irreconcilable conflict. It has been fondly dreamed that Jefferson and his school won, and that absolutism in this republic was forever made impossible by the growth of that democracy whose expounder and author was Jefferson. But the frightful ghost of Marshallism and Hamiltonism is resurrected in the modern Federal Judiciary and stalks abroad unmasked.[32]

Two years later, at the century's turn, Henry Flanders reiterated the argument that the Supreme Court has no constitutional power to declare void an act of Congress.[33] Writing in the *American Law Register*, he based his assertion solely on two arguments: (1) Since Congress and the president take an oath to support the Constitution, the passage of a bill implies that the question of its conformity with constitutional requirements has been fully considered. (2) If such question has been fully considered, then the argument is at an end, because there is no express clause in the Constitution empowering the Court to "interpose a judicial veto."[34] Of most interest is Flanders's extensive quotation from Judge Gibson's dissent in *Eakin v. Raub*, which he described as little more than an extended commentary on, and rebuttal of, the constitutional holding in *Marbury v. Madison*.[35] Thayer had compared *Marbury* with *Eakin* in his famous 1893 article, but had not discovered an incompatibility.[36] It therefore appears that Flanders is the author of the modern view of the relationship between the two cases.

The vehement attacks on Marshall and *Marbury*, which had been advanced by Pennoyer and Akin, were finally answered in no less exaggerated a fashion by the memorialists at the centennial of Marshall's appointment to the Supreme Court.[37] According to Dewey, the three-volume set of orations spawned by this celebration "devoted nearly twice as much attention to *Marbury v. Madison* as to the vitally important *McCulloch v. Maryland*, *Cohens v. Virginia* or *Gibbons v. Ogden*. Some of the speakers on Marshall implied that there must perforce be another centennial in 1903 to celebrate *Marbury v. Madison* properly."[38] John Dillon's introduction to the set contains the following exaggeration:

Marbury's Case opened a new chapter in the history of constitutional governments. That decision said to Congress, that is to the people's department, to the law-making power, "if you enact a law in conflict with the Constitution it is utterly void, and the court, although only a coordinate department, has the right under the Constitution so to decide, and such decision is authoritative and final, binding throughout the land upon States and people." But that decision also said to the head of one of the executive departments, acting under the immediate orders of the President, "You, too, are subject to the Constitution and are amenable to judicial authority whenever you deny or violate the legal rights of any individual, for be it known this is a Government of laws, and not of men." Verily a new charter of individual rights and liberties was here proclaimed.[39]

Others were even less restrained. Jeremiah Smith, perhaps the most objective of the lot, nonetheless declares that "if an addition is ever made to the number of days celebrated as national anniversaries, I submit that the twenty-fourth of February [the date of the *Marbury* decision] may well be added to the list."[40] Burton Smith exclaims that *Marbury* was "an epoch in the world's history! . . . A bulwark of liberty and civilization, towering above all others erected by the Anglo-Saxon race!"[41] Judge U. M. Rose says that next to "the formation of our government the decision in *Marbury v. Madison* is perhaps the most important event in our history. It established the only distinctively original principle in our institutions."[42] Horace G. Platt calls *Marbury* "as great a document as the Bill of Rights, as far-reaching as the Declaration of Independence, as essential to the healthy development of our Government under the Constitution as the Constitution itself."[43]

The hagiography contained in these volumes represents the high tide of *Marbury* exultation and completes the process that was set in motion by the address of Edward Phelps before the American Bar Association in 1879.[44] The idea, which Thomas Cooley's innocuous little footnote had first mentioned some thirty-five years before, had finally borne fruit.[45] In an amazing transformation of American constitutional history, Cooley's suggestion that *Marbury* grounded the power of judicial nullification on the maxim that "the constitution is the fundamental law of the State" had led finally to Dillon's notion that *Marbury* proclaimed "a new charter of individual rights and liberties."

## Prelude to the Progressive Revision

In their creation of the *Marbury* straw man, the leaders of the conservative wing of the American Bar Association had unwittingly provided their antagonists the leverage with which to overthrow long-accepted views on American constitutional history. Once the polarization of attitudes on Marshall and *Marbury* had reached the extremes of Pennoyer and Akin on the one side, and those of Dillon and the memorialists on the other, rational debate on the judicial function was exhausted, and argument could proceed in only one direction. That direction had first been heralded by Van Buren's "voice in the wilderness," and its lonely suggestion would now become the basis for a wholesale reinterpretation of American constitutional foundations by Populist and Progressive intellectuals.

Van Buren had insisted that both *Marbury* and the Ellsworth Judiciary Act of 1789 had been singular events in an overarching Federalist conspiracy to "select some department, or some nook or corner in our political system, and to make it the depository of power which public sentiment could not reach nor the people control."[46] As noted earlier, such an assertion contains a manifest contradiction. If the Ellsworth Act was an effort by Congress to increase the power of federal courts beyond constitutional bounds, then Section 13 was part of that effort. *Marbury* was therefore correctly decided and cannot be considered part of the "conspiracy." Reasoning the other way, if the *Marbury* decision was incorrect, then either the Ellsworth Act was *not* a product of "conspiracy," or it was—*and so was the Federal Convention.*

Neither Van Buren nor his follower Pennoyer had ventured to suggest the latter logic, yet their arguments imply it.[47] Beginning in 1905, a series of writings appeared which moved toward the ultimate acceptance of the proposition. The first of these was authored by Camm Patteson in the *Virginia Law Register* and was a throwback to Akin's article seven years previously. Patteson charges Marshall with rabid nationalism in "almost every decision he made," reiterates the well-worn connection between *Marbury* and *Pollock*, and says that "the greatest danger which threatens the American Republic is the judicial usurpation of powers."[48] After tracing the origin of that usurpation to the date of Marshall's installment into judicial office, Patteson turns to the Federal Convention, asserting that "the *fatal mistake* of the Federal Constitution was the life tenure of judicial office."[49]

In the same year, two important works appeared which took opposing positions on *Marbury* and judicial power to disregard statutes. In Andrew McLaughlin's volume in The American Nation series, the power of review is deduced from Article III, Section 2, and derived, if not from the "conscious purpose" of the Framers, then by "force of logic."[50] Contra McLaughlin was Joseph Cotton's edition of Marshall's constitutional decisions.[51] Cotton writes that there is "no express warrant" for the power of judicial review in the Constitution, that its existence "was denied by every other branch of the government and by the dominant majority of the country," and that "no such power had been clearly anticipated by the framers of the Constitution, nor was it a necessary implication from the scheme of government they had established."[52] He also states that *Marbury* "is the beginning of the American system of constitutional law. In it Marshall announced the right of the Supreme Court to review the constitutionality of the acts of the national legislature and the executive, the coordinate branches of the government." The last sentence apparently contains the original usage of the word "review" to describe the Court's power of constitutional nullification.[53]

The following year, Edward Corwin announced the need to reconsider the Court's power to "supervise" national legislation, due to the contrary views of McLaughlin and Cotton.[54] Corwin agrees mainly with Cotton, but adds some novel views of his own. He concurs that the Framers could not have intended to give the Court power of nullification, because there is no express declaration in the Constitution; nor is it a necessary derivation of the form of government therein established. Corwin adds a third, somewhat startling, rationale: the Constitution is not a "paramount" law, but rather is mere "ordinary legislation."[55] To defend this, Corwin attacks the *first* of Marshall's two constitutional arguments in *Marbury* and denies that "an act of the legislature, repugnant to the constitution, is void."[56] It will be recalled that *all* the previous attacks on the constitutional portion of Marshall's opinion had been directed toward the *second* conclusion: that courts have the power to *declare* unconstitutional legislation void.[57] Corwin's assault on Marshall's *first* argument therefore appears to be an original.

Corwin next turns to a discussion of the Constitution itself and overtly suggests the conspiracy theory of the Federal Convention, saying that the power to nullify statutes rests upon a "concealed premise" of "Lockean individualism," and that the "checks and balances" system is a device to counteract "popular sovereignty." He advances a plethora of arguments against *Marbury* and the judicial power to nullify statutes, claiming that Judge Gibson in *Eakin* "overrode and denounced the doctrine," that *Marbury* had "settled the question" only so far as courts and lawyers are concerned, and that, regardless, the Constitution is merely what the judges say it is. Corwin concludes the article curiously with an attack on Jefferson, since he never denied the power of the courts to disregard statutes and his dogma of coordinate departments, concurred in by Madison, Jackson, and Lincoln, had in reality been one of the main pegs upon which the doctrine of judicial nullification had hung.[58]

Judge Walter Clark, writing in the *Yale Law Journal* in 1906, took another stride in the direction of the conspiracy view of the Constitution, by suggesting (another original) a radical incompatibility between the Constitution and the Declaration of Independence.[59] Claiming that the Declaration was "frankly democratic," Clark follows Corwin (and presages Smith) in proposing that the Constitution was designed to "take government from the people" and that the best evidence of such an intention is the "undemocratic" character of the federal judiciary.[60] He then pursues Patteson's suggestion that federal judges should be elected and advocates repeal of the Fourteenth Amendment, to eliminate the idea of substantive due process from the field of American constitutional law.[61] Although, according to Clark, the judiciary was *intended* to comprise the most undemocratic aspect of the federal establishment, he nonetheless believes that, in *Marbury*, the Court "assumed" the power to invalidate statutes "without a line in the Constitution to authorize it, either expressly or by implication."[62]

The last article to appear in 1906 was authored by William Trickett in the *American Law Review*.[63] Trickett reiterates several of the old criticisms of *Marbury*: that the decision rests solely on the idea that the Constitution is a "written document"; that since legislators as well as judges take an oath to support the Constitution, the "oath" theory cannot support judicial nullification; that judges cannot claim infallibility, and so other departments are not bound to follow their constitutional interpretations.[64] What is more interesting are two additional assertions. The first is that "the theory of *no body* except Chief Justice Marshall and American Judges who have followed him, is, that a law repugnant to a written constitution is void."[65] Trickett has apparently accepted Corwin's position—and thinks everyone else has, too—that the conclusion of Marshall's first argument in the final portion of *Marbury* is faulty. Trickett's second suggestion is that the judiciary—*in America*, as in Great Britain—is merely a division of the executive.[66] In that case, the judiciary is not "coequal," and thus it has no power to adjudge the constitutionality of legislative acts.

In an article that appeared in 1907, in the next volume of the *American Law Review*, Trickett continues the reasoning set in motion by the subsumption of the courts within the executive function.[67] Turning to the Federal Convention, the problem becomes explaining what is meant by the Founders' "constructive narrowing" of the "arising under" jurisdiction to cases of a "judiciary nature." Trickett's answer begins a startling succession of original constitutional interpretations. First, the Article III jurisdiction was intended to extend only to "judicial cases involving the statutory validity of executive acts performed under a statute," not to judicial cases "which involved the constitutional validity of legislative acts enacted under the Constitution." But then why the phrase "arising under the *Constitution*" (in addition to "laws" and "treaties")? Trickett replies that this language only applies to situations where *state* laws contravene the Constitution (for example, Article I, Section 10 prohibitions), but no *federal* law applies. And what of the "pursuance" language of Article VI? "Every law is in one sense, enacted in 'pursuance of the Constitution,' when it is enacted by Congress. The Congress exists, in pursuance of it; its legislative power exists in pursuance of it."[68] In other words, so far as Professor Trickett is concerned, the "pursuance" provision is superfluous.

Trickett then attempts to refute some precedents advanced by Coxe and Meigs, asserting the "sheer imbecility" and "ineptitude" of adopting their view that the Framers intended the courts to have the power to nullify statutes. He suggests that Judge Gibson's *Eakin* dissent was wholly a refutation of *Marbury* and points out that *Marbury* and *Cohens* were inconsistent, probably because the chief justice "forgot" his earlier "mistake."[69] Now back at the Federal Convention, Trickett asserts (as if all the foregoing arguments were beside the point) that "whatever the criterion may be, of the intention of the *enactors* of the Constitution; the intention of the *framers*, not being *their* intention, is *unauthoritative.*"[70]

Oddly enough, Trickett continued his assault in yet another article, with an entirely different set of arguments. Despite the statement quoted above, his purpose is to show that the *Framers* (as opposed to the enactors) of the Constitution could not have intended that the courts should have power to invalidate legislation.[71] After reasserting that the judiciary is merely an adjunct of the executive, Trickett argues that, if the Framers had wished the Court to have the power of nullification, they would not have left it vulnerable to "congressional vengeance" via impeachment, or given Congress the power to regulate either its appellate jurisdiction or size.[72] In addition, surely the Framers could not have intended to give *one man* (in the event that the Court is evenly divided) power to determine the policy of the country in defiance of legislative unanimity! Nor could they have intended to institutionalize *ex post facto* laws—which is what Professor Trickett thinks judicial nullification of statutes amounts to.[73] Trickett concludes with a nod in the direction of an emerging philosophy of legal realism, and a touch of disrespect for the Framers.

The power authoritatively to interpret the Constitution is virtually the power to make it. Practically, so far as many of the functions of government are concerned, the Constitution is made for us, from time to time, by the nine lawyers who are judges of the Supreme Court. They make it, while, like the Roman haruspices, they think, as do others, that they are only divining the intention of the Numen, the dead men of 1787.[74]

The final pertinent writing to appear in 1907 was authored by Judge Robert Street, who had led off the great debate some twenty-four years previously.[75] Street announces the presence of an "irreconcilable conflict" (Akin's phrase) between the forces of stability and change in early twentieth-century America. Insisting that the common-law doctrine of *stare decisis* is irrevocably at odds with the "rediscovered doctrine of the inherent powers of the nation, existing outside of the enumerated powers," Street notes the trend toward abolishing traditional canons of constitutional interpretation: "Hitherto construction has aimed at the right interpretation of the intention of the makers, but in the departure proposed the intention of the makers becomes a negligible factor."[76] The "departure proposed" had been delivered in an address to the Boston University Law School by Professor Melville M. Bigelow late in 1906: "The Faculty oppose the doctrine both of abstract Principles and of the law as a system of precedents in the books, governing of their own force alone, *propriore vigore*, or pointing the way for governing, all questions that may now or hereafter arise; in other words, *that the past governs the present*."[77]

Street believes that, in the face of this irreconcilable conflict, the American doctrine of judicial power, which "confides the proscription of the limits of the political power of the country to that most rigid and inelastic branch of the Government—its judiciary," is a prescription for disaster. He suggests: (1) that the American doctrine was evolved by "Marshall, and his associates to meet certain conceived exigencies, party predilections"; (2) that the political-questions doctrine is defective, since "the distinction between judicial and political questions is one incapable of being drawn with accuracy"; and (3) that it is "deeply to be regretted" that Marshall did not uphold Section 13 and issue the writ of mandamus in *Marbury*, since Jefferson "would have disregarded the decision in executive action, confidently asserting as he did that the Act was unwarranted by the Constitution."[78]

## The Progressive Revision

Street's article marks the end of the decade of extensive *Marbury* criticism which had followed the appearance of Pennoyer's seminal writings in 1895–1896. Subsequent commentary on the case during the remainder of the Progressive Era includes little more than restatement of the views already presented.[79] The explanation for this abrupt conclusion is probably threefold. First, the ultimate implications of Van Buren's views on the relationship between the Ellsworth Judiciary Act and *Marbury v. Madison* were fully realized by the end of 1907 with the publication of J. Allen Smith's *Spirit of American Government.*[80] Smith's thesis was the distinction that first Corwin and then Clark had advanced the year before: that the respective "spirits" of the Declaration of Independence and the Constitution were radically at odds.[81] Accordingly, Smith argued that the idea of judicial power to nullify statutes was not generally recognized during the Confederation period, but that the Federalists at the Philadelphia Convention had "conspired" to "incorporate" the power into the Constitution—without actually saying so. The reason for this "silence" was that providing for such a power expressly would have revealed the "undemocratic reactionary character of the proposed government."[82]

These views had largely been anticipated in the writings of *Marbury* critics during the two years prior to the publication of Smith's work. In those critiques, the Constitution had been held to contain a "fatal" flaw—the federal courts; the idea of judicial nullification had been predicated on a "concealed premise"—Lockean individualism; the system of "balanced government" had been called a "device to counteract popular sovereignty"; and a distinction had been fixed between the "framers" and the "enactors" of the Constitution. This sequence evolved from the idea that the federal judiciary is "undemocratic," to encompass the whole system of checks and balances, and finally the Constitution itself. Once the end of this progression was reached, there was no reason to argue about *Marbury* any further, and in fact, Smith did not even cite the case.

A second likelihood for the scaling-down of *Marbury* censure was that one of the main critics abruptly reversed his earlier position. In a 1910 article that coins the phrase "judicial review," Edward Corwin declares that "there can be no doubt . . . that the idea of judicial review, within narrow limits, and particularly as a weapon of self defense on the part of the courts against legislative encroachment, had made considerable headway among the membership of the Constitutional Convention."[83] Corwin does not explain this curious reversal, but perhaps a dose of Smith prompted additional homework. At any rate, he does not repeat the earlier suggestion that the Constitution is mere "ordinary legislation"; on the contrary, he asserts that the idea of a constitution as "fundamental law" is the legitimate historical basis for judicial review![84]

The abrupt end of the *Marbury* controversy may also be attributed to Charles Beard, who accomplished in 1912 a moderately successful refutation of the remaining *Marbury* critics. In a little book, whose sole purpose was to show that the exercise of judicial review is entirely compatible with the intentions of the Founders, Beard challenges the views of Clark, Trickett, and Louis Boudin.[85] Since seventeen of the twenty-five most influential Founders declared—directly or indirectly—for judicial control,[86] Beard claims that *Marbury* could hardly be viewed as "unprecedented."[87] His fundamental point, to be reiterated the following year in the famous *Economic Interpretation*,[88] is that the American constitutional system was "designed primarily to commit the established rights of property to the guardianship of a judiciary removed from direct contact with popular electorates."[89] Turning once again to *Marbury*, Beard says that "the general principles on which Chief Justice Marshall rested his argument are laid down in the following extracts from his opinion in the case. By comparing them with the doctrine already enunciated by Hamilton, Paterson, and other leaders in the convention, one can see how closely Marshall caught the spirit of the Constitution."[90] Beard then quotes directly the entire final portion of *Marbury*.[91]

## *Beveridge's* Marbury

At this point, scholarly attention turns, at least temporarily, from *Marbury* and judicial review to the broader implications of the Progressive reinterpretation of American constitutional history. The relationship between that and *Marbury v. Madison* has been examined. We have observed the crucial role that *Marbury* and the judicial function played in the development of the views of the Progressive historians. We have witnessed the transformation of an essentially obscure case, whose holdings were very narrow, into an all-encompassing symbol of the modern doctrine of judicial review. *Marbury* stands today as that symbol, as a cursory glance through almost any American government text will confirm.

It is ironic that perpetuation of this distortion should be due largely to the influence of Marshall's greatest admirer. In his classic biography, Albert J. Beveridge forged together the *arguments* of the *Marbury* critics and the *sentiments* of the memorialists at the Marshall centennial of

1901.[92] Extolling Marshall's "statesmanship,"[93] Beveridge suggests that the decision was fabricated in order to announce the Supreme Court as exclusive interpreter of the Constitution.[94] According to Beveridge, the idea that Section 13 was unconstitutional was a "pretext . . . which, had been unheard of and unsuspected hitherto . . . as daring as it was novel . . . the only original idea that Marshall contributed to the entire controversy."[95] Beveridge concludes that

> by a coup as bold in design and as daring in execution as that by which the Constitution had been framed, John Marshall set up a landmark in American history so high that all the future could take bearings from it, so enduring that all the shocks the Nation was to endure could not overturn it. Such a decision was a great event in American history. State courts, as well as National tribunals, thereafter fearlessly applied the principle that Marshall announced, and the supremacy of written constitutions over legislative acts was firmly established.[96]

After all this, it is no wonder that Vernon Parrington, though from a different viewpoint, would suggest that Marshall went "far out of his way"[97] to bring the Constitution "under the sovereignty of the judiciary,"[98] for the purpose of "devising legal springes to catch unwary democrats."[99] Parrington elsewhere describes Marshall without the slightest equivocation: "No man in America was less democratic in his political conviction . . . as stalwart a reactionary as ever sat on the Supreme Court bench . . . utterly indifferent to popular views . . . who calmly overturned the electoral verdicts of his fellow Americans with the deliberateness of a born autocrat."[100]

Nowhere is the observation of Cushing Strout more appropriate than when applied to the historiography of *Marbury v. Madison*: "Disagreeing on every issue of politics and economics, conservatives and reformers nevertheless agreed on a version of history fraught with profoundly different meanings for both sides."[101] The process by which that version of the history of the case ultimately came to be reflected in the view of Beveridge—the most influential Marshall scholar of the twentieth century—has been the main concern of this chapter. How it has been handed down to subsequent generations of Americans will constitute the primary subject of the next.

# 12 · Beyond the Mythical *Marbury*

The reputation of John Marshall and his Court has not yet recovered from the misrepresentations of the late nineteenth and early twentieth centuries. The bulk of post-1920s scholarship on the Marshall Court has been conducted within a framework that superimposes the Beveridge view of *Marbury v. Madison* on the Parrington view of Marshall himself.[1] It is no wonder that Professor Wolfe can assert that a view of Marshall "which dismisses his own statements as words 'well and finely said' but not to be taken seriously, is the prevalent, almost unchallenged understanding of Marshall today."[2]

The view is notably cynical and has generated predictably inconsistent attitudes toward judicial review throughout the present century. After all, if *Marbury* was an "audacious" decision, fabricated in an effort to hoodwink Republicans into tacit acceptance of an institution that would later be used for Federalist political purposes, then judicial review is of doubtful legitimacy. With such ancestry, justification of review by reference to public-policy considerations appears as plausible as justification by any other standard. Hence, "result-oriented" constitutional jurisprudence has become the order of the day, as courts are now widely regarded as political institutions, not much different from other policymaking agencies of government.[3]

That partly explains the peculiar shifts within both liberal and conservative camps during the past fifty years on the propriety of judicial review. In the early twentieth century, conservatives defended court supervision of legislation as essential for protection of institutional property rights.[4] On the liberal side, before 1937, "historians and politicians were 'proving' that judicial review was a usurpation of power defeating the original intent."[5] After 1937, the positions began to shift, and by the 1960s liberals had begun to argue that review was necessary either for protecting[6] or for countering[7] the democratic process. Conservatives, on the other hand, argued that judicial review was just plain "undemocratic."[8]

Severance of judicial review from its institutional moorings in the Constitution, via the cynical reading of *Marbury* and an incoherent view of the Marshall Court, has also generated the main categories of debate among those who support judicial review: judicial "activism" and "restraint." In the absence of institutional constraints on the behavior of judges (such as those stemming from, say, the "departmental" theory of review), there remains—aside from the unlikely threat of impeachment—little indeed to check the judicial will save the "self-restraint" of the judges themselves. Yet it seems clear that this would have been unacceptable to the makers of the Constitution, who believed that government functionaries could *never* be trusted to govern themselves and their constituents at the same time. Persistence of a controversy between proponents and opponents of judicial activism can only be regarded as important evidence, as well as an important result, of a modern departure from one of the first principles of American governance.

The academic community's cynicism toward the very foundation of judicial review has finally cast the judicial function adrift in contemporary constitutional debate. If review itself is based on an unwarranted constitutional revision by the Marshall Court, then the hope for future revisions is that they will conform to favored policy preferences. More importantly, legitimization of constitutional "interpretation" by reference to policy outcomes becomes acceptable. So much recent controversy in the field, especially over important judicial appointments, has been so transparently a reflection of such hopes (and fears) that one is tempted to conclude that the Supreme Court has been deprived of rational criticism of the performance of its functions.

Those who read and write about judicial opinions form a major portion of the Court's constituency and have a great impact on the views of the general public toward the Court as an institution. The lay public can hardly be expected to be sensitive to the subtleties of the separation of powers without guidance from the experts. Yet without an informed citizenry, judges have little incentive to apply the strictures of self-restraint in constitutional cases. They have even less if it is widely believed that the Great Chief Justice himself failed to apply those strictures. How we view our heroes and villains has much to do with how we behave.

## Nationalism and the Marshall Court

The dominant contemporary view of the Marshall Court originates from that Court's supposed abuse of the judicial function in cases involving property rights and federalism. As Wallace Mendelson has pointed out, this perception contains three components. First, judicial review was "in an artful opinion foisted upon the nation"; second, review was then used "to promote nationalism at the expense of local self-government"; and third, it was used to promote "property at the expense of human or personal rights."[9] This study concerns primarily the first of these components, but the others should not be overlooked. As to the third, the evidence in Chapter 9 casts serious doubt on the charge that the Marshall Court perverted the contract clause out of an overarching concern for the rights of property.

What of the possibility that the Marshall Court "established" judicial review over Congress—and by implication, the states—in order to position itself as a "referee" in conflicts between state and nation, and resolve them in favor of the latter? Was the Marshall Court guilty of overbearing "nationalism"—a disposition to use federal judicial power to weaken, or destroy, the position of the states in the federal system—as Yates had feared?[10] A complete answer to these questions would take us far beyond the scope of this study; let me here suggest briefly what I think the answer might include.

Aside from *Marbury v. Madison*, perhaps the most famous (and certainly the most contemporaneously controversial) Marshall opinion is that rendered in *McCulloch v. Maryland*.[11] Faced with a call to restrict the elastic power of Congress to such means as are "absolutely necessary" to the fulfillment of its other powers, the Court decided in *McCulloch* that Article I, Section 8, Clause 18 gave the national legislature sufficient authority to establish the Second Bank of the United States and that a state could not tax the legitimate operations of such an instrument of the national government.[12] The *McCulloch* holding is usually said to have rested on a theory of "broad" or "liberal" construction of the Constitution, in contrast to the so-called strict constructionism of the argument for the state of Maryland. Marshall's approach is further said to reflect a "nationalist" bias, an eagerness to "expand," or "enlarge," the powers of Congress beyond the scope clearly provided in the Constitution. In other words, the enlargement in *McCulloch* was supposedly accomplished "by construction," not by a fair reading of the text.[13]

The logic of this argument leads from expressed powers through implied powers to a federally chartered private corporation, and reasonable people might surely question such a progression. However, a contrary decision in *McCulloch* would have involved the federal courts in determining how much legislative necessity is required to justify laws that are designed to implement other policies passed in pursuance of enumerated powers. The "necessary" (as distinct from the merely "convenient") would be defined largely by the individual judge's calculations of the long-range effects of policy, combined with his or her beliefs regarding the proper boundaries between state and national authority—a contentious subject in Marshall's day. Thus such an interpretation would have placed the Court squarely in the most dangerous political thicket of that time, compelling it to make policy determinations bearing on the wisdom of legislation.

Much the same would have followed from a contrary decision on the state's power to tax the bank, since the courts would have been required to locate precisely the line between allowable and destructive taxation of federal instrumentalities by states. The only alternative to judicial discretion is the allowance of any tax whatsoever, in which case the power to tax is indeed the "power to destroy."

The charge of nationalism is difficult to sustain in the face of these considerations. If it has any merit, it is only because the Court's process of reasoning, which purportedly justifies the bank, is arguably weak. Yet that difficulty was resolved, in accordance with one variant of the departmental theory of review, by President Jackson's *constitutional* veto of a subsequent act of Congress rechartering the bank.[14] From an institutional standpoint, the *McCulloch* decision represents judicial deference to an elective national legislature in an important policy area and is fully consistent with other decisions of the Marshall era. In the theory of judicial review that I have claimed was held by the Founders and the Marshall Court, *McCulloch* is a case of "nonjudiciary" nature; and for the Court to have invalidated the act chartering the bank would have amounted to a gross usurpation of legislative power. If Marshall made a mistake, it was emphatically *not* in the direction of nationalism but rather in his suggestion that in some future case the Court might be entitled to invalidate national laws merely on the ground that such laws transcended the legislature's power to enact them.

In addition to the Court's narrow reading of its own power to interfere with congressional enactments in *McCulloch*, its opinion indicates an awareness of the importance of leaving the taxing power of states unmolested when it is consistent with the health of national institutions. This attitude is manifest in Marshall's intimation that the prohibition of state taxes on federal instrumentalities should be confined to taxes on the operations of those agencies, not to taxes on all federal property whatsoever.[15] So read, *McCulloch* establishes a boundary between permissible and impermissible taxation based on differences in kind, a distinction more amenable to judicial standardization than one based on degree.

A similar approach is evident in *Gibbons v. Ogden*, the Marshall Court's leading opinion in the field of interstate commerce.[16] In that opinion, the Court held that "commerce," within the meaning of Article I, Section 8, Clause 3, was "intercourse" which affected more than one state; that Congress was therefore empowered to legislate on any subject of commercial activity which extended in its nature and effect beyond the boundaries of a single state; and that a state law conflicting with a legitimate federal regulation was null and void, at least to the extent of the conflict. Following more closely than in *McCulloch* the idea that its power to invalidate congressional acts was severely limited, the Court reasoned that the legislative power over objects within its competence was "plenary."[17]

Here, more so than in *McCulloch*, a contrary ruling on any of these points would have left open to the states many opportunities for harming each other, without neutral provision of recourse for those harmed. As in *McCulloch*, the Court was mindful of legitimate state interests. Rather than grounding its judgment on an alleged exclusive national power of commercial regulation, as it had been urged to do, the Court instead chose to base its decision on the federal Coasting Act, under which Gibbons held a license to navigate.[18] Had the Court done otherwise, it could have hamstrung future efforts to reach accommodations between state and national authority in the field of commercial regulation. When *Gibbons* is read together with *Willson v. Blackbird Creek Marsh Co.*,[19] decided just a few years later, the Marshall Court's commerce-clause jurisprudence seems more in line with the Taney Court's famous compromise in *Cooley v. Board of Port Wardens*[20] than has generally been thought. By conceding a dormant power of regulation to Congress without altogether denying to the states power to pass appropriate regulatory statutes, Marshall and his colleagues laid down the boundaries of future constitutional debate on the commerce problem. At the same time, they reinforced the idea that constitutional questions should never be decided except on the narrowest of possible grounds.[21]

In *Cohens v. Virginia*, the Marshall Court decided that Congress could give the Supreme Court authority to review final state-court decisions that reject claims based on the "Supreme Law of the Land" (the Constitution, federal laws pursuant to the Constitution, and treaties) set forth in Article VI.[22] In this instance, a contrary ruling would have fundamentally altered the nature of the federal system established in the Constitution. If Congress could not establish procedures for federal-court review of state-court decisions that fail to obey the mandate of Article VI, then the system created in 1787 would be, from a legal standpoint, "confederal," not "federal"—since there could be as many different "federal" constitutions as there are state courts of last resort. In reaching its decision, the Court again marked out boundaries between state and national authority by invoking the principle that, if a federal statute can be construed so as not to collide with a state law, then it should be so construed.[23] The Court then upheld the state law, which a Virginia court had previously affirmed as well.[24]

Whatever this is, it is surely not rabid nationalism; and if such a charge cannot be sustained by resort to this trio of cases, it is doubtful that others will serve any better. After all, *McCulloch*, *Gibbons*, and *Cohens* are those decisions most often cited as examples of the Marshall Court's broad construction of the powers of the national government to overcome state authority. Yet each of the cases may be accounted for more plausibly, by viewing it as the result of judicial deference toward Congress in a case not of a judiciary nature. Such an accounting has distinct advantages over the nationalist and broad-construction theories. First, it explains *all* the decisions of the Marshall era where the Court upheld national laws, as well as the single case in which it did not, *Marbury v. Madison*. Second, it is logical, since the Court's reading of the powers of Congress in *McCulloch* was more *restrictive* than what is suggested by the broad-construction theory. Third, unlike the nationalist theory, it requires no murky speculation concerning the motives and predispositions of the justices.

The final decision which deserves mention in any discussion of Marshall's alleged nationalism is from *Barron v. Baltimore*.[25] In *Barron*, the Court was squarely presented for the first time with the question of the applicability of a federal Bill of Rights provision to the states. The case developed out of Baltimore's effort to pave its streets, which meant diverting several streams from their natural course and resulted in the destruction of the commercial value of Barron's wharf. Barron alleged that the action of the city, a municipal corporation whose existence derived solely from the authority of the state of Maryland to charter such entities, violated the Fifth Amendment's prohibition on taking property for public use without just compensation.[26]

The Court's well-known response to Barron's plea was negative. Since the Constitution was framed by the whole people of the United States solely for their own government, not that of individual states, the provision could have no application to Barron's problem, the "taking" notwithstanding.[27] This decision was reaffirmed throughout the half-century that followed its announcement and ultimately came to stand for the principle that the federal Bill of Rights has no application at the state level. As late as 1887, the Court held that "the first ten Articles of Amendment were not intended to limit the powers of the state governments in respect to their own people."[28] And in 1893, it said that "the Fifth Amendment operates exclusively in restriction of Federal power, and has no application to the States."[29]

If Marshall had been determined to enlarge the powers of national government to protect the rights of property from state interference, why did he not broadly construe the Bill of Rights to protect Barron's commercial property from virtual confiscation by the city of Baltimore? After all, those who accuse Marshall of overzealousness in the protection of property assume that the Great Chief Justice had no trouble broadly construing the contract clause to include public contracts within its scope (see Chapter 9). Marshall himself thought that *Barron* presented a question "of great importance, but not of much difficulty."[30] Perhaps it was obvious to him that, had the Founders wished to apply the compensation principle to the states, they could have specified it in Article I, Section 10 (a section devoted to explicit restrictions on the states), rather than in the federal Bill of Rights. Yet Marshall's antiproperty critics seem to think that *Fletcher* and *Dartmouth* should have been just as easy. Previously, Marshall had used analogous reasoning in *McCulloch*, holding that, had the Founders meant the necessary and proper clause to limit rather than enlarge the powers of Congress, they could have placed the provision in Article I, Section 9 (devoted to explicit restrictions on the national government), rather than in Article I, Section 8.[31] The Marshall critics question *McCulloch, Dartmouth*, and *Fletcher*, yet *Barron* stands foursquare against that critique. These inconsistencies reveal the state of confusion in Marshall scholarship, which originated in the late nineteenth century and persists even today.

*Barron* is important for other reasons as well. Its subsequent demise in the late nineteenth century coincides precisely with the great debate on the judicial function, discussed in Chapter 10, and with the emergence of the two most controversial, and probably most important, constitutional doctrines of the twentieth century: substantive due process and the incorporation of the Bill of Rights. Nationalism's ascendance, from a legal standpoint, resulted largely from the advent of these two doctrines. Far from being the product of the Marshall Court's alleged nationalism, the creed required for its very existence the overruling of one of the Marshall Court's most important decisions.

While the doctrines of incorporation and substantive due process are nowadays regarded as quite distinct, the impression is misleading. In the mind of today's student of constitutional law, the latter doctrine is closely tied to the economic conservatism of the Nine Old Men, and the former, to the more recent civil libertarianism of the Warren Court. Yet their genesis is easily discovered in the ashes of *Barron v. Baltimore*. Furthermore, despite a temporary estrangement, their reunion is apparent in a line of recent decisions involving the concept of privacy.[32] To fully understand the origin and development of these two doctrines, we must attend to their peculiar interrelatedness in the period following the adoption of the Fourteenth Amendment.

## Substantive Due Process and Selective Incorporation

In the earliest decisions bearing directly on the adoption of the Fourteenth Amendment, there seemed to be virtually unanimous opinion among jurists that the due-process clause entailed no general protection for property rights. These decisions were consistent with what the majority of the Court evidently thought was the main purpose of the amendment: protection of newly-freed slaves from *de jure* race discrimination. Justice Miller said as much in his opinion for the Court in the *Slaughterhouse Cases*, while holding that none of the three main clauses in the first section of the Fourteenth Amendment protected property rights of businessmen contending against a state-licensed monopoly.[33] A similar decision was reached four years later in *Munn v. Illinois*, where a state's regulation of rates in the grain warehousing and railroading businesses was upheld in the face of Fourteenth Amendment and commerce-clause challenges.[34] These decisions were rendered with Justice Field's rancorous dissenting opinions, joined by Justice Bradley in *Slaughterhouse*.[35] Two years after the decision in *Munn*, the Court reaffirmed the race-discrimination understanding of the Fourteenth Amendment in *Strauder v. West Virginia*, holding that the conviction of a black man for murder by a jury from which blacks had been excluded by state law could not stand.[36] The following year, the practice of excluding blacks from juries by commissioners in Delaware was invalidated.[37]

In 1883, however, the tide began to turn, when the Court declared that the Fourteenth Amendment did not authorize Congress to make it a crime for a private individual to discriminate on the basis of race, thereby restricting the means available to Congress for enforcement of the amendment's key provisions.[38] Three years later, the Court extended the protection of the due-process and equal-protection clauses to corporations[39] and, in 1890, invalidated on Fourteenth Amendment grounds a state legislature's delegation of final rate-making authority to an administrative tribunal.[40] Finally, in 1896, *de jure* racial segregation in public accommodations was held *not* to violate the Fourteenth Amendment, a holding which signalled the demise of the race-based understanding of *Slaughterhouse* and *Munn*.[41]

In the post-1868 era, the first case in which the Supreme Court had the opportunity to determine the effect of the Fourteenth Amendment on the *Barron* ruling was *Twitchell v. Pennsylvania*.[42] In *Twitchell*, an appeal by a petitioner who had been sentenced to death for murder listed denial of Fifth and Sixth Amendment rights by a state court. The Court, citing the *Barron* rule, dismissed the appeal without dissent. As Professor Mendelson points out, "Counsel and all of the Justices had just lived through the era of the drafting, discussion, and public adoption of the Fourteenth Amendment. Yet none of them seemed aware of what later became the doctrine of incorporation (i.e., that somehow the Fourteenth Amendment 'reverses' *Barron* and imposes the Bill of Rights on the States)."[43] *Twitchell* was reaffirmed some eighteen years later in a case stemming from the famous Haymarket riots.[44]

The same attitude is apparent respecting the "just compensation" provision of the Fifth Amendment. The first relevant post-1868 decision is *Pumpelly v. Green Bay Co.*, rendered in 1871.[45] Pumpelly brought an action of "trespass on the case" against a canal company for overflowing a section of his land, which had been sanctioned by an act of the Wisconsin legislature. The Court sustained Pumpelly's plea, but *not* on the ground that the Fifth Amendment was applicable to the states by virtue of the Fourteenth. Rather, the Court rested its decision on an interpretation of the state constitution and its reading of prior decisions of Wisconsin's Supreme Court. On the question of federal Bill of Rights applicability, Justice Miller remarks that "though the Constitution of the United States provides that private property shall not be taken for public use without just compensation, it is well settled that this is a limitation on the power of the Federal government, and not on the States."[46]

However, some curious dicta in the succeeding portion of Justice

Miller's opinion should not be overlooked, due to its suggestion of a broader ground of judgment. After denying the applicability of the Fifth Amendment's provision to the states, the Court says: "The Constitution of Wisconsin . . . has a provision almost identical in language. . . . Indeed this limitation on the exercise of the right of eminent domain is so essentially a part of American constitutional law that it is believed that no State is now without it."[47] Justice Miller was wrong, since North Carolina had no such provision.[48]

This language is both qualified and clarified six years later in *Davidson v. New Orleans*, in an opinion also written by Justice Miller.[49] Here the city of New Orleans had made an assessment (authorized by state statute) on property owned by Mrs. Davidson for $50,000, for the improvement of swamplands by drainage. The owner refused to pay, claiming among other things that, since the price was exorbitant, her property (money) was being "taken" for the public use of general land improvement without "just compensation" (i.e., specific benefit to her own property in the amount taken). Justice Miller's response is worth quoting in full.

> If private property be taken for public uses without just compensation, it must be remembered that, when the fourteenth amendment was adopted, the provision on that subject, in immediate juxtaposition in the fifth amendment with the one we are construing, was left out, and this was taken. It may possibly violate some of those principles of general constitutional law, of which we could take jurisdiction if we were sitting in review of a Circuit Court of the United States, as we were in *Loan Association v. Topeka* (20 Wall. 655). But however this may be, or under whatever other clause of the Federal Constitution we may review the case, it is not possible to hold that a party has, without due process of law, been deprived of his property, when as regards the issues affecting it, he has, by the laws of the State, a fair trial in a court of justice, according to the modes of proceeding applicable to such a case.[50]

In other words, the Supreme Court may enforce compensation according to "general principles of constitutional law," when reviewing adverse decisions of a lower *federal* court, but when reviewing adverse judgments of the highest court of a *state* (as in *Davidson*), the meaning of due process reverts back to the ancient requirement of "fair trial." This conclusion clearly implies that the *Barron* rule had remained intact with respect to the Fifth Amendment's compensation provision, as well as all the others, through the *Davidson* decision in 1877.

Justice Bradley, however, did not agree. In his *Davidson* concurrence, he says:

> It seems to me that private property may be taken by a State without due process of law in other ways than by mere direct enactment, or the want of a judicial proceeding. If a State, by its laws, should authorize private property to be taken for public use without compensation (except to prevent its falling into the hands of an enemy, or to prevent the spread of a conflagration, or, in virtue of some other imminent necessity, where the property itself is the cause of the public detriment), I think it would be depriving a man of his property without due process of law.[51]

This statement is the first clear intimation from the federal bench of a willingness to enforce the compensation principle on the states by due process of law. And despite the unequivocal line of decisions supporting Miller's view, it was Bradley's opinion that soon became, and remained, the law of the land.

The turning point occurred eleven years after *Davidson* with the decision of the U. S. District Court for the Northern District of Ohio in the case of *Scott et al. v. City of Toledo*.[52] By ordinance, the city had not only appropriated real estate belonging to Scott and others for laying out a street, but had also assessed the plaintiffs for "the entire costs and expenses incident to and resulting from said appropriation, together with all expenses of laying off, opening, extending, widening, straightening, and improving said extended avenue."[53] The plaintiffs applied for an injunction to restrain the city, claiming that it had taken their property without providing just compensation and hence deprived them without due process of law.

The court (per Justice Jackson) began its opinion with a detailed examination of the ordinances in question, relevant state constitutional provisions, and state court decisions bearing on the case. Finding the latter inconclusive, the court faced the issue of the applicability of the Constitution:

> The single question is therefore presented, whether, in the taking of private property for public use, "due process of law" requires that compensation shall be made to the owner for property so appropri-

ated. In other words, may a state, or any subordinate division thereof, since the adoption of the fourteenth amendment to the constitution of the United States, take the property of its citizen for public purposes without making him compensation therefor?[54]

After stating wrongly that the United States Supreme Court had not yet passed on the question, the court rejected the city's claim that "the fourteenth amendment does not prohibit the taking of private property by a state without compensation." Citing with approval the dictum of Justice Bradley in *Davidson*, Justice Jackson boldly declared:

Whatever may have been the power of the states on this subject prior to the adoption of the fourteenth amendment to the constitution, it seems clear that, since that amendment went into effect, such limitations and restraints have been placed upon their power in dealing with individual rights that the states cannot now lawfully appropriate private property for the public benefit or to public uses without compensation to the owner; and that any attempt so to do . . . would be wanting in that "due process of law" required by said amendment. The conclusion of the court on this question is that since the adoption of the fourteenth amendment compensation for private property taken for public uses constitutes an essential element in "due process of law," and that without such compensation the appropriation of private property to public uses, no matter under what form of procedure it is taken, would violate the provisions of the federal constitution.[55]

The *Scott* decision was reaffirmed in at least two subsequent cases prior to its ultimate ratification by the Supreme Court of the United States. The first was decided in the Supreme Court of Massachusetts in 1893. A state law required the city of Boston to transfer the Mount Hope Cemetery to a private corporation without compensation. In an opinion in which Justice Holmes himself (who was on the Massachusetts court at the time) apparently acquiesced, the court held that "the cemetery falls within the class of property which the city owns in its private or proprietary character, as a private corporation might own it, and that its ownership is protected under the Constitutions of Massachusetts and of the United States so that the Legislature has no power to require its transfer without compensation. Const. of Mass., Dec. of Rights, Art. X. Const. of U.S., Fourteenth Amendment."[56]

The second case arose in the U.S. District Court for the Southern District of Ohio in 1896 and involved a situation virtually identical with that in the *Scott* case. After applauding Justice Bradley's *Davidson* dictum, the court rendered judgment for the plaintiff, remarking that the "whole subject was considered by Judge Jackson in *Scott v. City of Toledo,* 36 Fed. 385. He held that such proceedings as are complained of in this bill were in violation of the provision of the fourteenth amendment of the constitution of the United States, that no state shall deprive any person of life, liberty, or property without due process of law."[57]

The Supreme Court was finally forced to reconsider the issue in the landmark case of *Chicago, Burlington, & Quincy R.R. v. Chicago,* decided in 1897.[58] The city had sought, by condemnation proceedings, to open a street across tracks owned by the railroad company. Illinois law provided for assessment of compensation by a jury, which was impaneled and awarded the company one dollar for the property taken. This judgment was affirmed by the state supreme court, and the railroad company appealed, alleging that the compensation was not "just" and that it had thus been deprived of its property without due process of law.[59]

In his argument, counsel for the city contended that the Court had no jurisdiction to reexamine the final judgment of the Illinois Supreme Court, since the latter had not expressly referred to the federal Constitution in its opinion. According to the city, the amount of compensation was a matter of local law, so long as the company had been given adequate notice and provided an opportunity for a fair hearing.[60] In fact, that was exactly the holding of Justice Miller in *Davidson*—that only procedural issues would be considered when reviewing decisions of *state* tribunals.[61]

The Court (per Justice Harlan) rejected the city's claim—and with it, the *Davidson* rule—finding it necessary to "inquire at the outset whether 'due process of law' requires compensation to be made to the owner of private property taken for public use, and also as to the circumstances under which the final judgement of the highest court of a State in a proceeding instituted to condemn such property for public use may be reviewed by this court."[62] And in language befitting the era into which it was about to embark, the Court said that in "determining what is due process of law regard must be had to substance, not to form. . . . If compensation for private property taken for public use is an essential element of due process of law as ordained by the Fourteenth Amendment, then the final judgement of a state court, under the authority of which the property was in fact taken, is to be deemed the act of the state within the meaning of that amendment."[63]

The Court then cited *Scott v. Toledo, Baker v. Norwood,* and *Mount Hope v. Boston* to support its view that the

> judgement of a state court, even if it be authorized by statute, whereby private property is taken for the State or under its direction for public use, without compensation made or secured to the owner, is, upon principle and authority, wanting in the due process of law required by the Fourteenth Amendment of the Constitution of the United States, and the affirmance of such judgement by the highest court of the State is a denial by that State of a right secured to the owner by that instrument.[64]

This view, the view of Justice Bradley as set forth in his *Davidson* concurrence, has never since been seriously questioned.

Justice Bradley figured prominently in another portentous case, decided on March 1, 1897—the same day as *Chicago, Burlington & Quincy R.R. v. Chicago*. That case was *Allgeyer v. Louisiana,* in which the Supreme Court first invoked the doctrine of "economic" substantive due process to strike down a state law.[65] Adopting a strained construction of a contract for insurance (holding that the final notification of acceptance was merely "collateral matter," not part of the contract itself), the Court invalidated a state law which prohibited the making of marine insurance contracts with companies not in compliance with "the laws of the State." The Court believed that the statute violated the Fourteenth Amendment, "in that it deprives the defendants of their liberty without due process of law."[66]

What the Court meant by "liberty" is subsequently held to include "the right of the citizen to be free in the enjoyment of all his faculties; to be free to use them in all lawful ways; to live and work where he will; to earn his livelihood by any lawful calling; to pursue any calling or avocation, and for that purpose to enter into all contracts which may be proper, necessary and essential to his carrying out to a successful conclusion the purposes above mentioned."[67] This peroration is reminiscent of language in Field's famous *Slaughterhouse* dissent, which first articulated the theory imbedded in the notion of substantive due process: that the Fourteenth Amendment incorporates the "pursuit of happiness" provision in the Declaration of Independence.[68]

By 1897, this theory had been pressed unsuccessfully on the Court for twenty-five years by leaders of the American Bar Association.[69] Justice Bradley, who had dissented along with Field in *Slaughterhouse*, had also endorsed the theory in a concurring opinion in *Butchers' Union Co. v. Crescent City Co.*, decided in 1884.[70] To support its holding in *Allgeyer*, the Court quoted from Justice Bradley's *Crescent City* concurrence.

> The right to follow any of the common occupations of life is an in-alienable right. It was formulated as such under the phrase "pursuit of happiness" in the Declaration of Independence, which commenced with the fundamental proposition that "all men are created equal, that they are endowed by their Creator with certain in-alienable rights; that among these are life, liberty and the pursuit of happiness." This right is a large ingredient in the civil liberty of the citizen. . . . I hold that the liberty of pursuit—the right to follow any of the ordinary callings of life—is one of the privileges of a citizen of the United States. . . . But if it does not abridge the privileges and immunities of a citizen of the United States to pro-hibit him from pursuing his chosen calling, and giving to others the exclusive right of pursuing it, it certainly does deprive him (to a cer-tain extent) of his liberty; for it takes from him the freedom of adopt-ing and following the pursuit which he prefers; which, as already intimated, is a material part of the liberty of the citizen.[71]

The *Allgeyer* Court then concludes by declaring that Justice Bradley's remarks "well describe the rights which are covered by the word 'liberty' as contained in the Fourteenth Amendment."[72]

Decision of the *Chicago* and *Allgeyer* cases completed the Court's late nineteenth-century overthrow of John Marshall's constitutional juris-prudence. Only two years before, the Court had emasculated the com-merce power of Congress in *Knight*, the Sugar Trust Case, on a theory that the Tenth Amendment worked positive restrictions on that power—thereby overturning the fundamental premises of both *Gibbons* and *McCulloch*, that the powers of national government were unrestricted regarding their assigned objects and that Congress, not the Court, was the proper judge of the reach of such powers.[73] In *Chicago*, the Court's rebuttal of *Barron* cleared the way for later "selective" application of the Bill of Rights to the states and instituted the Court itself as the primary selector.[74] Finally, in *Allgeyer*, the Court's equally selective incorpora-tion of the Declaration of Independence, based on the due-process approach of *Dred Scott*, abolished the narrow-gauge judicial review embodied in *Marbury* and established the Court as ultimate guarantor of the wisdom of laws. All that remained was the contract clause, which would be put to sea in the early decades of the twentieth century.[75]

All this is familiar enough. What generally passes without notice is revealed whenever the Court's late nineteenth-century decisions are contrasted with the landmark precedents that they overturned. The thrust of Marshall Court jurisprudence was mainly to restrict, wherever possible, the range of judicial discretion. Such an attitude also was characteristic of the Taney Court, with a single large exception.[76] By comparison, the result of the Court's decisions in *Knight, Chicago,* and *Allgeyer* was exponential enlargement of that discretion and enhancement of the Court's power to act as that very Council of Revision which had been so emphatically rejected at Philadelphia in 1787.[77] It is sad irony that in *Mugler v. Kansas*—a decade prior to the decision in *Allgeyer*— the Court had already appropriated Marshall's name and reputation to support a judicial hegemony that he disavowed.[78]

## Judicial Review in the Twentieth Century

The magnitude of the transformation which resulted from the overthrow of Marshall's jurisprudence and the institution of the Muglerite *Marbury* as the model for judicial review becomes fully apparent when one examines the cases where the Court set aside state and federal laws in the early twentieth century. Between 1897 and 1937, almost as many state laws were invalidated on Fourteenth Amendment grounds alone as had been struck down *in toto* during the previous 110 years.[79] Once the rights of blacks had been "read out" of the Fourteenth Amendment in *Plessy v. Ferguson,*[80] the Court's primary target became statutes regulating various forms of business activity. During that forty-year period, the Court struck down some 209 state laws on Fourteenth Amendment grounds.[81] By the most liberal estimate, only *nine* of these laws had anything whatever to do with race discrimination.[82] On the other hand, at least 176 were business regulations invalidated on substantive due-process or substantive equal-protection grounds.[83]

As to federal laws, the Court overturned some fifty-five acts of Congress between 1896 and 1936, nearly tripling the previous number.[84] Of these, only *eight* occurred in cases of a judiciary nature—i.e., in cases where the law was invalidated because of its collision with a constitutional restriction on *judicial* power.[85] Four decisions invalidated laws that the Court thought reduced the salaries of federal judges;[86] four adopted strained constructions of Article I, Section 9, to invalidate taxes on exports.[87] Of the remaining thirty-nine holdings, twelve overturned laws on Fifth Amendment substantive due-process grounds,[88] eight on the theory that the reserved power of the states in the Tenth Amendment invoked positive restrictions on the powers of Congress—the theory of "dual federalism."[89] The other cases negated laws thought by the Court to constitute excessive uses of various congressional powers.[90]

The inescapable conclusion to be drawn from this brief review is that, under the constitutional doctrines of the Marshall Court, roughly 85 to 90 percent of the state cases, and 70 to 85 percent of the federal ones, would have been decided very differently. Indeed, the Court itself subsequently has overturned, either directly or indirectly, most of these decisions—decisions, so deplorable to liberal intellectuals of the pre-1937 era, that would never have been rendered under Marshall's jurisprudence.[91] Clearly, a constitutional theory that confines the exercise of judicial review to cases of a purely judiciary nature would have produced outcomes more to the liking of Populists, Progressives, and other reformers of bygone days. It would have happened not out of any particular result-orientation, but because such a theory has the effect of limiting the range of judicial discretion by assigning a larger measure of constitutional responsibility to other agencies of government.

Though perhaps less obvious, I also believe that such a theory might have prevented the half-century of legal stagnation in race relations which followed on the heels of *Plessy v. Ferguson*.[92] Surely a Court operating under Marshall's principles would have found it difficult, if not impossible, to emasculate the power of Congress "to enforce, by appropriate legislation," the provisions of the Fourteenth Amendment, as it had done in the *Civil Rights Cases* of 1883.[93] And a Court less inclined to employ the due-process and equal-protection clauses in the service of business interests might well have invoked those provisions in pursuit of the purposes for which they were designed.

After 1937, the Supreme Court retreated from the constitutional doctrines of the Nine Old Men, as demonstrated by the Roosevelt Court's invalidation of only three federal laws between 1938 and 1953.[94] Moreover, since each of the laws set aside in these cases was incompatible with constitutional provisions involving restrictions on judicial power, they may be regarded as cases of a judiciary nature, and thus acceptable from the standpoint of Marshall Court jurisprudence.[95] During this period, the

Court also began to return to the old *Slaughterhouse* understanding of the Fourteenth Amendment,[96] clearing the way for the ultimate, but long overdue, demise of *Plessy v. Ferguson.*[97]

Beginning in 1954, the Court again assumed a more aggressive posture. From 1954 through 1969, twenty-three provisions in acts or resolutions of Congress were overturned. Though it may come as a surprise to some, the Warren Court gets fairly good marks by the standards of this study, at least in constitutional decisions involving coequals. The majority of these decisions were based on procedural, due-process-related provisions,[98] and as many as eighteen may be regarded as cases of a judiciary type.[99] Several are difficult to categorize, since they involve either the Uniform Code of Military Justice or the issue of citizenship—both of which subjects are textually committed to Congress in Article I, Section 8.[100]

As to the other cases, two should be regarded as precursive and well beyond the acceptable range of judicial discretion. In the first, the Court incorporated the Fourteenth Amendment's equal-protection clause into the Fifth Amendment's due-process clause, in order to eliminate segregated elementary and secondary schools in the District of Columbia.[101] While one can only applaud the intent of this decision, it is simply impossible to reconcile with the theory of judicial review put forward in this study or with any other theory of constitutional interpretation that does not permit Court supervision of coequal branches of government. Had the old Court resisted supervising Congress in the *Civil Rights Cases*, it might never have been necessary for the Warren Court to supply its corrective in *Bolling v. Sharp.*[102]

The second case involved the Court's invalidation of a resolution of the U.S. House of Representatives expelling one of its members.[103] Here, the Court thrust itself into the internal affairs of a coequal agency of government by adopting a strained construction of two constitutional provisions addressed to the national legislature.[104] The remaining decisions under consideration during the Warren years struck down laws in cases not "of a judiciary nature" on various substantive policy grounds.[105]

*Bolling* and *Powell* are portentous because they laid the foundation for several of the more excessive examples of judicial policymaking by the Burger Court. Between 1970 and 1986, that Court invalidated national laws in no fewer than twenty-seven cases, most of which were decidedly *not* of a judiciary nature. Nine of these followed the "reverse incorporation" doctrine of *Bolling v. Sharp*, negating federal laws that were held to establish impermissible classifications in the denial of certain benefits.[106] One decision was grounded in the logic of Fifth Amendment substantive due process;[107] one resurrected,[108] and another suggested,[109] the discredited theory of dual federalism. One, picking up where *Powell v. McCormack* left off, adopted a strained interpretation of the presentment clauses in Article I, Section 7, in order to strike down a "legislative veto" provision.[110] The reasoning of the Court in *Immigration and Naturalization Service v. Chadha*, if carried to its ultimate conclusion, might well necessitate the invalidation of more than two hundred national laws—more than the Court has overturned in its entire history.[111] In the remaining cases—only two of them clearly of a judiciary nature— the Court struck down laws mostly on due-process or First Amendment grounds.[112]

One additional line of decisions should be mentioned. The Warren Court, best known for its activism in state policy through the use of the doctrine of incorporation, established a "zone of privacy" in 1965, while striking down a Connecticut law prohibiting the use of contraceptives.[113] As the old Court had done in *Chicago, Burlington & Quincy R.R. v. Chicago* in 1897, the Warren Court joined the doctrines of selective incorporation and substantive due process to fashion a new set of constitutional rights.[114] This approach generated the Burger Court's decision in *Roe v. Wade*, probably the most controversial constitutional decision of the past two decades.[115] Whatever one thinks about the moral and policy implications of *Roe* and similar decisions, we have clearly returned to the situation described by Holmes in his famous *Lochner* dissent: a case decided on a "theory which a large part of the country does not entertain."[116]

This review of post-1937 decisions suggests a slow but steady return to judicial activism.[117] Furthermore, the pattern of its modern development is remarkably similar to that of the late nineteenth and early twentieth centuries. The process begins haltingly (the Marshall and Taney Courts in the early period; the Roosevelt Court in the modern era), continues through periods of heightened self-assurance characterized by an increased number of judicial nullifications, though many in cases of a judiciary nature (the Chase and Waite Courts in the early period; the Warren Court in the modern era), and culminates in judicial supervision of coequal branches of government in those substantive policy areas most dear to the respective courts (the Fuller Court in the early period; the Burger Court in the modern era).

This analysis suggests, not that the Court has already become the Nine Old Men, but that it may be on the brink. Whether or not history repeats itself, institutional practices are certainly strengthened through repetition. Given the apparent inclination of Americans to seek an ever-increasing array of legal solutions for social, economic, and political problems, and the transparent self-interest of an ever-increasing number of lawyers in helping them find such solutions, the Court's susceptibility to cyclic judicial activism is not difficult to comprehend.

Added to these considerations is the fact that the Court nowadays operates largely under the influence of one of its most important constituencies—academe—which has itself been strongly influenced by the Warren Court. Since that Court laid the groundwork for much of the more pronounced activism of its successor in the separation-of-powers field and was itself an activist Court in state civil-liberties cases, it appears that two of the Court's most important constituencies—lawyers (by interest) and professors (by inclination)—currently support judicial supervision in some policy areas. Yet close scrutiny of the Court's most recent decisions strongly suggests that Warrenism (whether interpreted as civil-liberties activism or separation-of-powers moderation) is not now, any more than it was a hundred years ago, the direction in which the Court is moving.

## Marbury *Commentary in the Twentieth Century*

The mythical *Marbury* was in place by the 1920s. Even before the publication of Beveridge's massive biography of John Marshall, Horace A. Davis wrote, in a series of essays designed to show that judicial review was a "political," not a "legal" function, that Marshall's opinion in *Marbury* "was a shrewd political manifesto, rather than a logical foundation for the decision of that highly technical case."[118] On the other side of the debate, Robert von Moschzisker, chief justice of Pennsylvania and a strong proponent of judicial review, asserted in 1923 that Marshall had made "official pronouncement of a judicial guardianship of the Constitution in *Marbury*."[119]

In 1924, Dormin J. Ettrude, an opponent of judicial review, said that the importance "of the judiciary in the government was unexpectedly created in 1803 by a decision of the Supreme Court of the United States, without a line in the Constitution to authorize it, when that body assumed the right to nullify and veto any act of Congress that they chose to hold unconstitutional. This astonishing declaration was made in the case known as *Marbury v. Madison*, by Chief Justice Marshall."[120] Writing in 1928, Charles Evans Hughes, former associate justice and later chief justice of the United States, said that the "finality" of the Court's determinations of constitutional questions was decided by "the Supreme Court itself" in *Marbury v. Madison*.[121] Despite this statement, Hughes never asserted the principle from the bench, even during his eleven years as chief justice.

In an important book published in 1930, Charles Grove Haines joined several aspects of the mythical *Marbury*.[122] Relying heavily on Judge Gibson's *Eakin* dissent, which had been rediscovered by Thayer in 1893,[123] Haines maintained that Marshall's *Marbury* doctrine had been inappropriately drawn by implication from the nature of written constitutions generally.[124] Furthermore, Haines connected *Marbury* with the doctrine of "vested rights" that Corwin and others had championed previously. Haines declared that "Chief Justice Marshall indicated his adherence to the doctrine as early as 1803, when he observed 'the government of the United States has been emphatically termed a government of laws, and not of men. It will certainly cease to deserve this high appellation, if the laws furnish no remedy for the violation of a vested legal right.' "[125] That interpretation of the quote was, of course, erroneous, since Marbury's "right" was *statutory*, derived neither from natural law nor from the Constitution, as we have seen.[126] Also, the *Eakin* critique was based on a misreading of Marshall's argument in support of judicial power to disregard acts of Congress (see Chapter 8).

Finally, Haines fortified the vested-rights interpretation of *Marbury* by reference to several Marshall Court contract-clause decisions, suggesting that "vested rights" was a "Federalist principle." Paradoxically, the statement that Haines relied on most heavily is the famous one by Justice William Johnson, the Marshall Court's leading Republican: "I do not hesitate to declare . . . that a state does not possess the power of revoking its own grants. But I do it on a general principle, on the reason and nature of things; a principle which will impose laws even on the Deity."[127] The natural-law reading of the Marshall Court's contract decisions is highly questionable, at best (see Chapter 9). Nonetheless, that view, succinctly articulated here by Haines, was echoed a year later by Benjamin F. Wright. Ultimately incorporated into twentieth-century judicial mythology in Wright's famous treatise on the contract clause, it has since remained virtually unquestioned.[128]

By the mid 1930s, the attention of most commentators had turned from arguing over the legitimacy of judicial review to the question of how to curtail the Court's exercise of that power in cases affecting the New Deal

recovery program. Despite this change of emphasis, the *Marbury* Myth
continued as the touchstone of American constitutional law. In a 1936
article, which offered "clarifying amendments to the Constitution" to
retire the Court "from the fields of constitutional construction in which
it faces the greatest difficulty and incurs the sharpest criticism," Robert
E. Cushman asserted that the Court "boldly announced in 1803 in the
case of *Marbury v. Madison* that it was the organ of government to maintain the supremacy of the Constitution."[129]

The following year, in a scathing attack called *The Nine Old Men*,
Drew Pearson and Robert S. Allen regurgitated the political aspects of
the *Marbury* Myth, suggesting that the Court's present troubles were
not unlike those that Marshall had faced in 1803.[130] According to Pearson and Allen, Marshall had "inserted his wedge" in "one of the most
adroit politico-legal maneuvers in history" by declaring that "the entire
Judiciary Act of 1789 was unconstitutional." Weaving an amazing web
of contradiction and innuendo, these erstwhile muckrakers contended
that the Marshall Court was cowardly in its failure to invalidate even
more national laws, despite the authors' apparent belief that the power
to do so had been unfounded in the first place; and that Marshall himself
had, "with customary negligence," failed to deliver the commissions
while acting as secretary of state, so that he could use Marbury's case
"as a vehicle to put across his thesis, now almost an obsession on his
part, that the Supreme Court must have final power to pass upon the
constitutionality of acts of Congress." Adding further insult to injury,
Pearson and Allen asserted that criticism of *Marbury v. Madison* was
"echoed by succeeding Presidents, by members of Congress, state
legislatures, and from a thousand political platforms. Even judges joined
in the dissent. In 1815 [sic] Justice Gibson of the Pennsylvania Supreme
Court handed down his famous opinion in the case of *Eakin v. Raub* emphatically refuting Marshall's dictum."[131] Needless to say, none of this
prattle was accompanied by a single footnote.

In a milder vein, Isidor Feinstein recognized that the *Marbury* decision was subject to a much narrower reading than that proposed by Pearson and Allen, but still declared that "the Court's view of itself as the
final interpreter of the Constitution was summed up in *Marbury v.
Madison*."[132] Dean Alfange, another opponent of the Court during the
New Deal era, stated that "the far-reaching power by which a Court, or
even a single judge, may veto an act of Congress and stem the tide of
popular will without accounting to any constituency was masterfully
engrafted upon our constitutional system by the eminent Chief Justice

John Marshall through a series of decisions beginning with the famous case of *Marbury v. Madison* decided in 1803."[133] In formulating the doctrine of judicial review, Alfange said, Marshall "went beyond the necessities of the case" and "affirmed as an inherent power of the courts under a written constitution their right to void laws passed by Congress." Calling the decision exemplary of Marshall's "political-mindedness," Alfange connected his discussion of *Marbury* with an earlier remark of Chief Justice Hughes that "judicial review has established itself as a historical necessity imposed by the inner logic of the American system."[134] The following year, Hughes himself suggested a portion of Stone's famous footnote in the *Carolene Products* case, signalling the end of the era of judicial activism on behalf of laissez-faire economic philosophy and laying the foundation for a new era of activism on behalf of "personal" rights.[135]

After the threatened Court-packing scheme of 1936 and the Court's subsequent retreat from its New Deal posture, commentary on judicial review substantially subsides—but not before publication of the most vicious diatribe to date against the character and career of John Marshall. This attack, published in 1941, was penned by Beryl H. Levy,[136] and his purpose was clearly to vindicate the *Carolene Products* approach to judicial review. The result is the first comprehensive defense of a doctrine that took hold in the Warren era: judicial activism in personal rights and liberties, coupled with judicial restraint in substantive economic policy—in other words, the flip side of the judicial approach of the Nine Old Men. Levy's method was to contrast the judicial and political philosophy of Marshall with that of Taney, Holmes, and Brandeis, and to establish that the former's was the very embodiment of judicial activism, whereas the latter group's reflected judicial restraint. To Levy, ultimate responsibility for the judicial fiascos of laissez-faire jurisprudence rested squarely on the shoulders of the justices of the Marshall Court.[137]

Levy first connects the most important aspect of the *Marbury* Myth with Marshall's alleged nationalism and pro-property stances: "The Supreme Court becomes a final authority, private contract rights are sanctified, and the Union takes precedence, through the determination of a party man little learned in the law."[138] After the usual incantation of the *Marbury* decision as "a master stroke of political strategy," Levy declares that its primary consequence was to establish a principle "by which the Court was exalted to a pedestal of pre-eminence. Final veto power with respect to Congressional legislation . . . was thenceforth to reside in the Court." The point is reiterated:

The real audacity of Marshall's opinion lies not so much in his claim that statute must give way to Constitution as in his general claim that the Court should be the one—the only one—to say when they do clash. . . . But the judicial branch has no basis for maintaining that it has the sole authority to determine constitutionality in *every* case, no matter what branch of the government is affected. Marshall, however, contended . . . that the judicial branch was to have exactly that full power.[139]

Levy suggests that Marshall was unethical for not disqualifying himself from the case; that *Marbury* was not based on the Constitution but was drawn by inference from it; that *Dred Scott* would have been decided differently had it not been for the "foundation precedent" of *Marbury*; that *Marbury* was an example of "judicial imperialism"; that Marshall "went out of his way" to establish final judicial review; and that Marshall's opinions generally prove that ours is a government of men, not of laws.[140] Like Pearson and Allen, Levy does not support a single line of this with references.

In the same year, a famous book was published by soon-to-be Associate Justice Robert H. Jackson, who had also written the introduction to Levy's book.[141] Jackson expends few words on *Marbury*, saying only that it was the "first step in establishing supremacy of the judicial over both other departments in constitutional matters."[142] He leaves little doubt that he believes such supremacy is justified: "Such power should be promptly exercised by a court of finality as well as one of a high sense of responsibility and a national outlook in those cases where the power is properly invoked, and self-restraint should lead to prompt and final declination to interfere with the legislative process in those cases where the lawsuit is inappropriate to overrule statecraft."[143] Clarifying the distinction, Jackson says:

It is always the dynamic party of change which is frustrated by the Court's attitude, for the conservative party, resting on the policy of letting well enough alone, presents for review little legislation that is untried or novel. Liberal leadership exhausts its power to persuade the discontented and the have-nots to accept ballot-box disappointments or compromises if their victories are to be nullified and if elections are effective in shaping policy only when conservatives win.[144]

Elsewhere, Jackson asserts that "the search for Justices of enduring liberalism has usually ended in disappointment." As a fundamentally conservative institution, the Court therefore should employ its power of review only in pursuit of the liberal ends for which it is best fitted: the protection of individual rights and minority interests.[145]

The paradox inherent in Jackson's view of the Court's role is most striking when contrasted with the devastating critique of judicial review that Judge Henry Edgerton had offered just a few years before.[146] In a book published the year after Jackson's, Robert K. Carr claims that Edgerton countered the argument that the Court protects civil liberties against congressional encroachment, by denying "the existence of a single *bona fide* decision protecting an individual's civil liberties against adverse federal action. He [Edgerton] points out, interestingly enough, that in the very case in which the right of judicial review was first asserted by the Supreme Court [*Marbury*] the Court refused to protect a helpless individual against arbitrary action by officers of the federal government."[147] Carr's study primarily defends the thesis that "the Supreme Court is more readily studied and understood as a political agency, sharing with the President and Congress the power to govern, than it is as a judicial body applying strictly legal rules to constitutional questions."[148] Predictably, then, Carr's treatment of *Marbury* stresses the political background of the case and the ultimate political consequences of the decision—which he believes flow from Marshall's choice to base his decision "upon the much broader ground that the Court must refuse to enforce any act of Congress which it considers contrary to the Constitution, regardless of whether the act is one pertaining to the work of the judiciary or dealing with some other matter altogether."[149]

The treatises of Jackson and Carr point to a trend that would be realized only after the preoccupation with World War II and its immediate aftermath subsided. The mid and late 1940s are notable in the absence of extensive commentary on the role of courts and judicial review, but a momentous shift had already occurred in the early years of the decade. Commentaries in the 1920s and 1930s had mostly disputed the very *legitimacy* of judicial review, much as they had in the preceding two decades. On the ascendancy of the Roosevelt Court, that disputation altogether disappears, and the focus of court-watchers turns to the proper *application* of review in constitutional cases, its legitimacy having been presupposed. That this switch in academic opinion was not the result of overwhelming historical evidence has been shown clearly in the previous review of commentaries. Additional insight may be obtained from Robert G. McCloskey's 1967 introduction to a reprint of B. F. Wright's 1942 work on the development of American constitutional law.[150]

According to McCloskey, in 1941, the year when Justice McReynolds (the last of the Four Horsemen) retired, the demise of a 150-year-old jurisprudence was signalled. "[The] fundamental bias had favored property owners. . . . The Court had unanimously resolved that property rights would be given less, and civil rights more, constitutional protection than they had enjoyed in the past. The judges had proposed (though here not so unanimously) a rationale to support such a 'dual standard.' " As a result, McCloskey concludes that the Court "can no longer be regarded simply as an undemocratic institution" and points out that Wright himself had asserted in 1942 that "the doctrines of the Court are again 'in substantial accord with the main currents of national life.' "[151]

On the other hand, there is no change in the distorted version of *Marbury v. Madison* that was universally accepted by the early forties. Wright sums up the main thrust of the *Marbury* Myth, holding that the *Marbury* opinion advances "a theory of the judges as the only true guardians of the permanent will of the people which is incorporated in the Constitution. The assumption throughout is that the Congress and President cannot be trusted to interpret that will. It is assumed that if the Court believes that an act is not in harmony with the Constitution then it is most certainly inconsistent with that document."[152] In fact, no such doctrine was announced by the Court prior to 1958 (see Chapter 7).

Wright also repeats several other aspects of the *Marbury* Myth, claiming that Marshall was a "supreme conservative," a "superb strategist" who sought to "write his theory into the law of the land";[153] that "no one, before Marshall conceived his brilliant tactical maneuver, had ever suspected that it was unconstitutional to vest the power to issue writs of *mandamus* in the Supreme Court";[154] that judicial review would not have had so broad a scope had Jefferson, rather than Adams, been able to make the appointment to Marshall's seat;[155] and that "what we have in this most famous of constitutional decisions is not protection of the original Constitution but a judicial revision of its meaning."[156] Like Haines and others before him, Wright treats *Marbury* as the first step toward the establishment of judicial supremacy in the United States.

In the 1950s and beyond, commentators, rather than questioning the *Marbury* Myth, would attempt to enlist it in the service of particular causes, much as their predecessors in the era of laissez faire had done for very different goals. One of the first steps was taken by Edmond Cahn, in a book reporting on a 1953 conference that celebrated the sesquicentennial of *Marbury v. Madison*.[157] Cahn believes that, whether or not judicial review was intended by the Framers, the Constitution would have been a dead letter without it.[158] He attaches *Marbury* to the theory of legal positivism, suggesting that the primary contribution of the decision was to alter the constitutional theory embodied in the document. This alteration was a "historic turn" from the Founders' view of the Constitution as perpetual, immutable, and divinely sanctioned, to Marshall's view of it as efficacious, adaptable, and sanctioned by the Court.[159] "What was needed was a change to the law of the land or *lex terrae*, a change from higher-than-positive law to higher, positive law. This, of course, is the very change that Marshall consummated in *Marbury v. Madison*: by legitimizing the appeal to the courts he presumably bastardized any possible 'appeal to heaven.' " Cahn locates the basis for this appeal in Marshall's alleged reading of Article V: Since the people "can seldom act" to amend the Constitution, the Court must stand in for them whenever the Article V process is too much of "a very great exertion."[160] Thus is Hughes's famous dictum engrafted upon the mythical *Marbury*.[161] In Cahn's view, *Marbury v. Madison* did nothing less than to introduce

> an unending colloquy between the Supreme Court and the people of the United States, in which the Court continually asserts, "You live under a Constitution but the Constitution is what *we* say it is," and the people incessantly reply, "As long as your version of the Constitution enables us to live with pride in what *we* consider a free and just society, you may continue exercising this august, awesome, and altogether revocable authority."[162]

Picking up where Cahn left off, Charles P. Curtis elaborates the newly discovered cooperative relationship between the Supreme Court and people of the United States: "I suggest that what *we* have persuaded the Court to do is nothing less than this: interpret *for us* and declare *to us* the immanent component in our constitutional law. We have persuaded the Court to mediate between this immanent component and the other component which is imposed upon us by the rule of a sometimes hasty, occasionally hysterical, and too often selfish majority."[163] Elsewhere, Curtis suggests that in the evolution of judicial review, "the Constitution becomes, not a voice, but the trumpet through which we are constantly speaking to a listening Court."[164] These cryptic remarks are accompanied by equally curious references to *Marbury v. Madison*. According to Curtis, Marshall's doctrine in *Marbury* was premature—a "trick" reflecting that its author "was as cautious as he was audacious." Despite the difficulty Curtis has with believing "that Marshall had any idea of the magnitude of what he and his fellow justices had done," he believes that Marshall, revising Franklin, "might equally have said that he had given us judicial supremacy, if we could take it."[165] Discounting the historical approach to constitutional adjudication, Curtis quotes from Montaigne that "laws take their authority from possession and usage; it is dangerous to trace them back to their birth."[166]

Likewise, John P. Frank, eschewing the "detailed steps" in Marshall's *Marbury* opinion, declares that "while his [Marshall's] logic has been exposed to much scholarly criticism, his faithfulness to the historical design of the Constitution seems so well established as to be *no longer a fruitful subject of discussion*. . . . The real task of scholarly thought at this late date is to appraise not the history or logic of Marshall's opinion, but the *consequences* of this judicial function [review] in American life."[167] Frank's conclusion about these consequences, announced at the end of a survey of Supreme Court decisions affecting civil liberties, is that the Court's record has not been very good.[168] However, unlike Judge Edgerton, who had deduced the same fifteen years before, Frank proposes to retain judicial supremacy—albeit with a dose of liberal vengeance. He recommends that the Court contract the area of nonjusticiability (political questions), revise the doctrine of standing, and reverse the presumption of constitutionality in cases involving basic liberties.[169] According to Frank, due to the self-imposed limitations on the Court which are embodied in the restrictions on access, "*Marbury v. Madison*, and the system of review of acts of Congress which it represents, has not been of any great significance to the civil liberties of the American people." Removal of these restrictions will impart perfection and proper function to that system: "The potential use of *Marbury v. Madison* is not yet wholly lost; it could still become a cornerstone of American liberty."[170]

The most significant feature of the previous survey is the utter imperviousness of the *Marbury* Myth. Despite the seismic changes in perspective on judicial review throughout this century (especially from 1937 to 1942) and the wide differences of opinion among proponents and opponents of review at almost any given time, the version of *Marbury* summarized in Beveridge's biography of Marshall has remained the starting-point of discussion.[171] According to this construction, since judicial review originated from a coup d'etat, engineered for political purposes, *Marbury* is the primary antecedent for judicial policymaking in the modern era. Since the Beveridge view rested the case on a doctrine of the Court as final, infallible interpreter of the Constitution, *Marbury* has become shorthand for judicial supremacy, as well.

The main consequence of the widespread acceptance of this view of *Marbury* has been to banish discussion of the proper scope of the judicial function from constitutional discourse. This has, in turn, polarized debate on constitutional review to two extremes: either judicial supremacy (with concomitant, and intermittent, judicial activism in the areas of economic and/or social policy) or *nothing at all* (anarchy in constitutional law). Thus constitutional interpretation is reduced to questions about what the Supreme Court should do or, more often, what it should have done. The self-appointed elite who read and write about court decisions may find this salutary, but it is hardly a prescription for robust, public debate on constitutional issues in America. An astute observer might reasonably ask professors Cahn and Curtis exactly who is the "we" that speaks to the Court?[172]

Whatever the answer, there can be little doubt that, on occasion, the Supreme Court has listened. The Court adopted the theory of its own supremacy in constitutional interpretation in 1958, after some years of urging, and grounded that adoption on *Marbury v. Madison*.[173] It has since reiterated the doctrine several times.[174] The process seems not unlike what transpired in the late nineteenth century, leading to the Court's acceptance of substantive economic due process.[175] On the other hand, despite the continual recitation of the mythical *Marbury*, there are at least two novelties in the commentary on judicial review throughout the 1950s and 1960s, both of which are evident in the Cahn volume.[176] The first attempts to discount the importance of the historicity of *Marbury v. Madison* and the *historical* legitimacy of judicial review. The second proposes that the Supreme Court is not really an undemocratic institution, and so legitimizes review without reference to history.

The former tendency is well illustrated by a comment of Thomas Reed Powell in the first of the famous Carpentier Lectures delivered at Columbia University in 1955. After recounting most of Beveridge's *Marbury*, Powell says that "there have been arguments aplenty that Marshall's assumption of the power [of review] was judicial usurpation, but they do not interest me. However initially indefensible that first seizure might have been, the power has now been duly sanctioned by a century and a half of sufficient national acquiescence."[177] Three years later, the distinguished jurist Learned Hand, in his Oliver Wendell Holmes Lectures at Harvard University, suggests that Marshall's alleged declaration of judicial supremacy in *Marbury* ran directly counter to contemporaneous doctrine, but that the Court must possess such ascendancy, due to "the necessity, in such a system as ours of some authority whose word should be final as to when another 'Department' had overstepped the borders of its authority."[178]

In a 1960 book largely devoted to the proposition that judicial review "must be and can be justified not as a means of defeating but as a means of fulfilling the will of the people," Charles L. Black apologetically agrees with Thayer that the *Marbury* opinion has been "overpraised" and then asks rhetorically, "does that make it any the less authentic as precedent?"[179] Elsewhere, Black says that *Marbury* prepared the way for "liberal utilization of the 'necessary and proper' clause," though by means of a nationalism of vile origin entwined with "the power of money." But no matter, for we may "rejoice that good has come of evil, and live in the well-joined house that was built, doubtless, for another tenancy."[180] Similarly apologetic, Eugene V. Rostow, in an attack on Herbert Wechsler's "neutral principles," asserts:

> Generations of writers about law, and of law teachers, have dissected the erratic reasoning of *Marbury v. Madison.* . . . So be it. It is too bad. . . . We must accept the fact that under the best of circumstances judges will often write opinions which fail to convince many, or all, or the best lawyers of their time, or of later times. Their decisions may nonetheless turn out to have been right or wrong, with the benefit of hindsight—in error or in creative anticipation of a principle theretofore unsensed.[181]

Rostow concludes by declaring the need for "a more coherent and explicit doctrine of judicial action in advancing the cause of constitutional democracy."[182] That the quest embodied in Rostow's call has persisted well into the 1980s is apparent in the attention received by John Hart Ely's now-famous "representation-reinforcing" theory of judicial review.[183]

As Leonard Levy pointed out in 1967, the concept of judicial review as a democratic institution represents a sharp break with the historical past: "A single generation's experience with judicial review over Congress does not wipe out the experience of a century and a half."[184] Understandably, the rise of such a belief in the 1950s and 1960s coincides with an effort to deflate the importance of history (and consequently, precedent) as the primary basis of legal reasoning in constitutional cases. Furthermore, since *stare decisis* traditionally has been the foundation of the judiciary's claim to objectivity in common-law systems, the idea of review as democratic, and the corresponding devaluation of historical approaches, has been accompanied by an all-out assault on the very principle of objectivity in judicial decision making. This attack, penned largely by the proponents of judicial democracy, initially takes on Herbert Wechsler's "neutral principles of constitutional law."[185] A late development of American legal realism, it dovetails with a number of contemporary notions, such as those that hold courts to be "political" institutions and judges to be "lawmakers."

For now, let it suffice to say that all this converges in the mythical *Marbury*. After all, in the Beveridge version, the case is the epitome of judicial decision without benefit of history—a coup so "bold in design" as to have been "unprecedented." Just as surely is *Marbury* a "political" decision, in which John Marshall "made some law." Indeed, Rostow himself uses the career of Marshall as an ultimate refutation of Wechsler's objectivism.

> The Great Chief Justice . . . is the classic exemplar and exponent of political prudence in the employment of the Court's powers. Wisely judging the strength of the conflicting forces whose conjecture influenced the growth of the law, carefully husbanding the Court's strength for the crucial issues, shrewdly choosing among alternative possible premises for its opinions, he still had the energy, vision, and courage to make the written Constitution into the constitution-in-fact for a nation.[186]

A reconstituted *Marbury* has become the symbol of the spirit that considers the search for objectivity to represent "a repudiation of all we have learned about law since Holmes published his *Common Law* in 1881, and Roscoe Pound followed during the first decade of this century with his path-breaking pleas for a result-oriented, sociological jurisprudence, rather than a mechanical one."[187]

Thus the *Marbury* Myth was likely to remain cemented for some time, since the glue was nothing less than a new theory of judicial decision making. As late as 1978, William F. Swindler says that what *Marbury* decided was that "neither the executive nor the legislative branches of government could be the final arbiters of their own constitutional powers."[188] According to Swindler, *Marbury* "settled the principle that Congressional action was to be tested against the Constitution by the judiciary."[189] This distinguished author also remarks that "upon what were rather tenuous premises, the concept of judicial review was pronounced as an inherent, or 'necessary and proper,' power of the judiciary."[190] Former Chief Justice Warren E. Burger, who composed the introduction to Swindler's volume, has recently said that, in *Marbury*, "the great war over the supremacy of the Supreme Court in constitutional adjudication, has been won by Marshall—and by the United States."[191]

In a less friendly tone, Rexford G. Tugwell suggests that *Marbury* accomplished an attenuation of the Preamble's "We, the people," to "We, the justices."[192] And in 1981, Thomas J. Higgins, another staunch critic of judicial review, relied heavily on Beveridge to establish that "the first taking of power [in *Marbury*] was irregular because the action of the Court in assuming power to declare acts of Congress null was not justified by the nature of judicial power, by pertinent precedent, or by grant of the Constitution."[193] There can be little wonder why Julius J. Marke chose to close his chapter on *Marbury* with the observations of J. A. C. Grant, that "nothing remains of *Marbury v. Madison* except its influence"; and of Max Lerner, that "everything else has been whittled away. But its [*Marbury's*] influence continues to grin at us from the Cimmerian darkness like the disembodied smile of the Cheshire cat."[194]

## Conclusions

Myths do not flourish in isolation. The *Marbury* Myth has sustained the Court's modern experiments with judicial policymaking, by providing the precedential foundation required in a legal system based on common law. It is therefore a necessary, but not a sufficient, condition for modern judicial activism. The *Marbury* Myth symbolizes a more general mythology fired by the fusion of law and politics which followed the breakdown of the Marshall Court's jurisprudence in the late nineteenth and early twentieth centuries. From this mythology, several modern maxims about judges, courts, and constitutions are derived, which legitimize, and are in turn legitimized by, the mythical *Marbury*.

First among these is the idea that judges "make" law. This maxim should not be confused with its ancestral counterpart, born in the response of legal realism to the old natural-law myth that judges "find" the law. The realists objected to the natural-law premise that the source from which law springs is human nature, and they feared the subjective consequences of erecting a legal system on a doctrine of judicial self-reflection. As G. Edward White points out in his excellent study of the intellectual development of tort law in America, early exponents of legal realism disavowed the universalistic abstractionism of nineteenth-century legal scholarship but were objectivist in their methodology.[195] White's comment about Roscoe Pound furnishes a good example: "He was not skeptical about the derivation of rules, merely offended by the social implications of certain rules that had been derived. His goal was to have 'fresh illustrations of the intelligent application of a principle to a concrete cause, producing a workable and a just result.'"[196]

Yet, as Professor White has also suggested, maintaining objectivity was a continuing problem for legal realists. "By demonstrating an enlightened skepticism about the permanency or even the comprehensibility of values," some were led ultimately to embrace moral relativism—[197]the variant of realism from which the contemporary myth of judicial legislation (i.e., that judges are always "policymakers") is derived. Its factual basis is therefore as patently flawed as that of an extremist natural-law counterpart.

The early realists rightly perceived that personal bias and policy preference often interfere with judicial objectivity and that explaining court decisions solely by abstract principle was misleading. They recognized that a judge can be as blind as anyone, especially when values held dear are at stake. However, they did not deny that objectivity was a desirable goal, even if its perfection were unattainable in practice. Nor did they deny the existence of a functional difference between law and politics, or between judges and lawmakers. The suggestion that Justice Holmes, when dissenting in *Lochner v. New York*, was engaged in the same kind of "result-oriented" jurisprudence as the Court was when deciding that case, simply will not do.[198] But it is precisely such suggestions, and corresponding denials of objectivity, that are revealed in the persistence of the *Marbury* Myth and in the repeated incantation that judges make law. When we say that John Marshall, without appropriate constitutional foundation, reached out to establish judicial review in *Marbury*, thereby rendering a political decision, we are not simply commenting on the action of a judge in a particular case. We are also *legitimizing* the notions that judges make law, and that courts are political institutions, by throwing the weight of precedent behind those maxims.

The predominant contemporary understanding of judicial lawmaking is illustrated by Leonard Levy's editorial comment on Eugene V. Rostow's attack on Herbert Wechsler's famous argument for "neutrality" in constitutional adjudication. Levy says that

Rostow very nearly accused Wechsler of treason to the legal profession for having suggested that the Supreme Court should not use principles instrumentally as do politicians, but should decide on "genuinely principled" or "entirely principled" grounds of "neutrality and generality"—a neutrality that transcends "any immediate result that is involved" and a generality that applies consistently in all cases. . . . Rostow was not wrong in declaring that "the goal which Professor Wechsler makes his only test for judicial propriety is impossible to achieve; that it never has been achieved by any common law court, nor by any other court; *and that it can never be achieved, in the nature of the judicial process.*"[199]

These comments, especially the emphasized phrase, indicate the depth of modern cynicism toward the plausibility and desirability of attempting to formulate objective standards for evaluating judicial decisions. They reveal a great deal more than an ordinary and healthy skepticism regarding the human propensity to rationalize rather than to reason, or to justify particular results in universal precepts. The denial of objectivity inherent in the assertion that the *nature* of the judicial process precludes neutrality has become an article of *faith* for its adherents. As such, it may not be accorded scientific status—i.e., a hypothesis advanced for testing by unfolding experience and thus open to question. The adherents of non-neutrality regard their cardinal precept as having been already "proved" by earlier "advances" in the "sociology of knowledge."[200] The precept is therefore a myth—a fundamental presupposition which must be believed before inquiry can proceed.

The extent to which the myth of non-neutrality has undermined the constitutional system established in the Federal Convention may be seen by recalling Alexander Hamilton's celebrated argument for judicial independence in *Federalist* Number 78. Hamilton's defense rests entirely on the premise that an independent judiciary could—and would—exercise only "judgement," not "will."[201] The distinction is clarified in *Federalist* Number 81, where the meaning of judgment is referred to the nature, objects, and manner of the judicial process.[202] In other words, the fundamental rationale for the institution of Article III courts was the belief of the Founders that impartiality, neutrality, and objectivity *were plausible and worthwhile goals for independent judges.* Since it is exactly that proposition that is denied by modern proponents of judicial non-neutrality, adoption of that myth undermines *in toto* the conventional foundation of judicial independence.

Furthermore, because calls for a "purposive" jurisprudence rest on the belief that impartiality, neutrality, or objectivity "can never be achieved, in the nature of the judicial process," such exhortations undermine judicial review as well as judicial independence.[203] As Judge Frank H. Easterbrook has recently put it, "A theory of meaning that treats a legal text as if it were a poem or appeals to philosophy and hopes for a better future destroys the basis of judicial review. We cannot simply assume review and then argue about meaning. We must choose a theory of meaning that simultaneously allows review."[204]

I have attempted in this work to articulate a theory of the judicial function in constitutional cases that provides for judicial review without undermining its basis. This theory, rooted in a constitutional understanding of Blackstone's Tenth Rule of Statutory Construction, would allow the Supreme Court to disregard acts of coordinate agencies of government with finality only when such acts contravene constitutional restrictions on judicial power. Throughout the study, such instances have been referred to as cases "of a judiciary nature," following language used at the Federal Convention to describe the scope of Article III's "arising under" jurisdiction. The confinement of judicial power to invalidate laws to cases of a judiciary nature implies a theory of departmental review that I have called "functional coordinate review," in contrast to the "arbitrary coordinate review" that, since Jefferson, has been synonymous with "departmental review." Functional review in turn implies a derivative discretion in Congress—and, to an extent, in the president—to disregard judicial decisions which set aside laws on the basis of constitutional provisions not addressed to the courts.

Such a theory has a number of distinct advantages over theories that rest final authority to interpret constitutional provisions in the courts alone. First, it is fully consistent with the text of the Constitution and with the historical evidence of the Framers' (and ratifiers') intentions about the scope and nature of the judicial function (see Chapter 4). It thus satisfies those who support a jurisprudence of original intent, broadly conceived—a jurisprudence, it might be added, which has never been disavowed by the Court itself.

Second, the theory is consistent with virtually all cases of the colonial, revolutionary, and Founding periods, where courts—federal and state—set aside acts of coordinate agencies of government (see Chapter 3). It is also consistent with similar decisions in the federal courts during the Marshall and Taney periods (see Chapter 6). It should therefore appeal to those who urge that constitutional decisions should be firmly grounded in the doctrine of *stare decisis*. In case some counter that such a theory comes too late in the day, it should be recalled that the vast majority of the Court's decisions setting aside federal laws in the pre-1937 period have, in effect, been overruled.[205] Since all invalidations of federal law by the Roosevelt Court, and most by the Warren Court, were handed down in cases of a judiciary nature, those most influenced by this analysis are the twenty-odd decisions of the Burger Court discussed earlier in this chapter.[206] Surely the weight of these "precedents" is not so great as to counterbalance a doctrine grounded in 180 years of American constitutional history.

That observation suggests a third advantage of the ideas advanced here. The theory is not merely a set of propositions about what the Court should do in future cases, but also a statement of what the Court has in fact done in the past. Since most of the Court's pre-1970 nullifications of federal law in cases *not* of a judiciary nature are no longer followed, the remaining cases of a judiciary nature constitute the greater (and better) part of the Court's *effective* exercise of judicial review over Congress. A theory of judicial review that preserves continuity with our constitutional tradition stands a better chance of public acceptance in the long run than one that exposes the judicial process to the cyclic fluctuations accompanying political, economic, and social instability.

Finally, the theory satisfies the demand for objectivity inherent in a conception of courts as organs of government exercising judgment rather than will. It is neutral with respect to *particular* results. Congress may exercise its plenary powers in pursuit of liberal, conservative, reactionary, or progressive ends; as long as it does so without encroaching on judicial functions, the Court has no power to prevent enforcement of the legislative will. Under this approach, for example, Congress would no more be prevented from establishing segregated schools in the District of Columbia (a reactionary end) than from utilizing its commerce powers to curtail the use of child labor in factories (a progressive end). On the other hand, if Congress should forbid the Court to exclude coerced confessions in criminal cases, pursuant to its power to regulate the Supreme Court's appellate jurisdiction, the Court would justifiably disregard the enactment. Indeed, it could not do otherwise, for applying the statute would directly contravene the Fifth Amendment's ban on such confessions (which is a restriction on judicial power addressed to the courts) and place the Court in contradiction with itself. Moreover, the Court's decision would be final, since lower courts would be bound by it in subsequent cases and hence be bound to disregard the statute in every case where it applied. Congress would have no recourse, save impeachment.

Despite these advantages, two major policy arguments might plausibly be directed against the type of theory propounded here. First, a theory of constitutional review based on an extension of Blackstone's approach to statutory construction might have the ultimate effect of liberating judges, rather than constraining them.[207] This paradox might follow if constitutional adjudication were reduced to statutory interpretation, thereby leading judges to regard the former activity as merely ordinary, rather than extraordinary. After all, throughout much of our history, constitutional questions have been regarded as elevated and unusual. Such a perspective would seem to justify a special hesitancy on the part of judges when they are entertaining the possibility of refusing to apply laws on constitutional grounds. This attitude might be undermined if judges began to consider constitutional decision making as a routine aspect of everyday judicial process.

Given the propensity of judges (and other officials) to enlarge discretion wherever possible, it would be foolish to deny the plausibility of such an argument. On the other hand, the historical ground covered in this study suggests that the apprehension is not as well founded as might at first be supposed. When judges operated in the shadow of Blackstone during earlier periods, judicial activism was exceptional. As Blackstone's influence waned in the late nineteenth century, activism became the rule. It is surely possible that the Blackstonian model, in the hands of modern judges with a century of intermittent judicial aggression informing their habits, might produce an altogether different result from what was generated by Marshall or Taney. Though I would not like for this to be true, argument on the point seems unnecessary; for in my view, if the only way to restrain judges is through acquiescence in historical distortion, then judicial activism is probably the least of our troubles.

It is also possible to view the matter from an opposite perspective. Our present inclination to regard constitutional issues as peculiarly elevated or fundamental may have contributed significantly to our tendency to lodge in the Supreme Court the final authority to interpret the Constitution. Surely that has contributed as much as anything to the twentieth-century enlargement of the Court's discretionary authority. If the proof is in the pudding, perhaps the motivational ingredients of the recipe ought to be changed. Also, our propensity to treat constitutional decision making under a written instrument as somehow more important than, and fundamentally different from, the routine application of law, has led to an oversimplification of the process of constitutional adjudication itself. The idea that we are governed by twenty pages of written text naturally leads to the conclusion that preservation of our political order requires only the right interpretation of that text. Such a belief, when combined with modern tendencies toward specialization, in turn suggests the advisability of textual exegesis by a group of qualified experts, whose primary task lies in "setting the law beside the Constitution" and deciding whether the former coincides with the latter.

In an abused passage from Justice Roberts's opinion in *United States v. Butler*, the idea is straightforward:

> When an act of Congress is appropriately challenged in the courts as not conforming to the constitutional mandate, the judicial branch of the Government has only one duty—to lay the article of the Constitution which is invoked beside the statute which is challenged and to decide whether the latter squares with the former. All the court does, or can do, is to announce its considered judgment upon the question. The only power it has, if such it may be called, is the power of judgment. This court neither approves nor condemns any legislative policy. Its delicate and difficult office is to ascertain and declare whether the legislation is in accordance with, or in contravention of, the provisions of the Constitution; and having done that, its duty ends.[208]

As Professor Wolfe has rightly pointed out, Justice Roberts did not claim that constitutional interpretation is "an easy or simple process"; rather, he said that the task was a "delicate and difficult office."[209] Nevertheless, the procedure described by Roberts seems deceptively simple at first blush. To describe constitutional review as merely interpretation or exegesis of a text, without more, is a misleading characterization of the procedure actually involved. The process by which a judge (not to mention a full Court) arrives at an ultimate decision about whether to set aside a law in a particular case includes a preliminary decision about the constitutional conditions under which the Court is entitled to impose its fair reading of the text on other agencies of government—to mention just one example. It is the range of such penultimate decisions that is obscured by the dictum of Justice Roberts, by the idea that constitutional decision making is an activity entirely distinct from everyday judicial decision making, and by the notion that there exists a group of "experts" peculiarly suited to read the text authoritatively.

This brings us to the second kind of argument. Does the theory of departmental review advocated in this study yield anarchy in constitutional decision making?[210] I do not think so; but even if it does, I might yet argue that a measure of uncertainty in constitutional matters is healthy. Surely the proponents of judicial supremacy are on shaky ground here, given that so much of twentieth-century judicial review has produced its own brand of anarchy. I am persuaded that the idea that final authority to interpret the Constitution *must* reside somewhere is itself a myth, without foundation in the Constitution. The liberal constitutionalists of Marshall's day imagined that the main values enshrined in their political ideology (whatever label one assigns it) conflicted and must therefore be *compromised*—not "synthesized" or "maximized."

The Founders did not pretend that they were establishing an order designed for the achievement of particular substantive goals. Though Lockeans, their primary accomplishment was the institutionalization of a system that would temper substantive claims arising from the conflicting precepts of that very philosophy, as well as any other that might later take its place. There was evidently widespread recognition that a political process allowing free play for the interaction of Lockean liberals would very likely tear itself to pieces if its procedures were not carefully formalized and strictly adhered to. Furthermore, the greater the diversity of interests in society, the greater the necessity of insistence on the faithful observance of the constitutional forms. As Madison noted, the "regulation of these various and interfering interests forms the principal task of modern legislation, and involves the spirit of party and faction in the necessary and ordinary operations of the government."[211]

Despite the modern myth that constitutions are political documents, the crucial element in the constitutional approach of the Founders was not politics per se, but rather the confinement of political aspirations within certain structural limits—the most important of which, at the national level, was the separation of powers. In the face of these considerations, it seems ludicrous to suppose that they would have vested the guardianship of the most essential ingredient of that system in any single part. That we should now wish to is even less understandable, with the benefit of hindsight to light our way.

Professor Wolfe suggests that any theory of coordinate review is problematic, because "it is simply not that clear when a matter is 'properly' before a branch."[212] He cites Jefferson's apparent belief that it should have been his decision whether Marbury's appointment was complete, because of the appointment power. This is a poor example. First, Jefferson was not a party to the suit, though he certainly behaved later as if he had been. The major issue concerned the power of the secretary of state to withhold information which he was required by statute to release. Moreover, one of the main purposes of the statute was to provide reliable evidence for use in courts of law.[213] The Court thus rightly treated this aspect of the case as a default by the government. At any rate, these are questions of statutory interpretation, which would presumably be resolved by the natural interplay of Congress and Court; no theory of review is needed to resolve them.

What if the president had been party to the suit? Then there would have been no mandamus issue, since the ministerial duty which could have constituted the basis for the writ did not apply to the president. What if Congress had imposed such a duty on the president? Then the Court could have issued the writ, except not from its original jurisdiction, and the correct decision would have been the same as in the actual *Marbury*. What if Marbury had not gone to the wrong court in the first place; the Court had issued a writ of mandamus to the secretary of state ordering production of the requested documents in accordance with the statute; and Jefferson had ordered Madison to refuse to comply with the writ, on the ground asserted in Wolfe's argument? In this instance, there is no *constitutional* problem for the Court, Section 13 having been removed from the picture. The question is now whether Congress will acquiesce in executive law breaking. If it does, then of course there is little the Court can do. But this is hardly a good argument for judicial—versus coordinate—review in constitutional cases. Even judicial *supremacy* in constitutional matters would not prevent the situation just described.

In fact, no theory of review can be expected to safeguard the Constitution whenever any two of three coequal branches of government join forces to subvert it. Short of eliminating the separation of powers entirely, we simply have to live with the possibility of such an occurrence. But there is a flip side. Whenever any two branches are determined to abide by the Constitution, it will be difficult for the remaining branch to subvert it. This makes it all the more important that our operative theory of review encourage maximum participation in constitutional decision making by all agencies of government. Constitutional interpretation is a subtle but critical process. It should not be the special province of a small group of persons who happen to occupy the Supreme Court's bench.

A theory of constitutional review—whether of the coordinate or judicial variety—is less about what the Court should do than about what other agencies should do in response to a constitutional decision that is thought erroneous. The dilemma with judicial review is that it requires acquiescence in the Court's decision, however flawed, whereas coordinate review allows the affected department the discretion to disregard the Court's decision if its own interpretation of the Constitution differs from that of the Court. Most theories of coordinate review have failed to supply grounds, consistent with the Constitution and existing legal precedent, on which such divergence from the Court is justified. Professor Wolfe correctly points out this difficulty. Any theory that allows Congress or the president to disregard a judicial decision on any constitutional ground whatsoever is as unacceptable as a theory that allows the Court to disregard an act of Congress or the president on any constitutional ground whatsoever. And the latter alternative is precisely what the proponents of judicial review recommend.

What is required is a theory of review that takes its cues from the separation of powers itself, and thereby from the Constitution. This is not as difficult a task as it may seem. Constitutional provisions are not ubiquitous; they are directional. From the viewpoint of this study, the separation of powers is a set of vectors indicating the direction of these provisions; constitutional adjudication is mainly the task of rightly ordering them. In my view, this ordering was accomplished by the Marshall Court—the Court that was, after all, in a better position than its successors to understand fully the system established in 1787. When some of the political consequences of this system became intolerable to property-oriented conservatives in the late-nineteenth century, who did not have the political strength to capture the legislative process, they advanced a theory of judicial review in the courts—based on a misreading of *Marbury v. Madison*—which was ultimately accepted by the Supreme Court in the 1890s (see Chapter 10). Rather than exposing the ahistoricity of the new theory, Populists, Progressives, and other liberal reformers countered with a theory of their own, denying the Court's power of review altogether and thereby advancing a doctrine of legislative supremacy—again based on a thorough misreading of *Marbury v. Madison* (see Chapter 11).

The choice thus bequeathed to the twentieth century was not between judicial review and coordinate review—as understood by the Founders' generation—but rather between judicial supremacy and *arbitrary*, unprincipled coordinate review. The last of these doctrines leads straight to either legislative or executive supremacy;[214] indeed, we seemed on the verge of that alternative in 1937, when the Court saved itself by a full-scale retreat from the judicial activism of the Nine Old Men. When the Court again asserted itself in the Warren era, it was at first in a fortunate position, with its activism supported by the academic, legal, and public-service establishments that had become its primary constituencies. But, in a manner analogous to developments in the 1920s, the Burger Court has exposed the ultimate folly in such an approach. The truth is, any theory of constitutional review which vests final authority to interpret that instrument in the hands of a single branch of the government will induce that branch invariably to self-aggrandizement. That insight is both the genius and genesis of the separation of powers. It is surprising that so many of those who contend that judges make law, that there is no fundamental distinction between law and politics, that judicial objectivity is unattainable, that constitutions are political documents, and so on, *also* assert that finality in constitutional interpretation must reside somewhere, and that somewhere is the Supreme Court!

The mythical *Marbury* is the modern symbol that binds together all this fantasy—causing what will not hang separately to hang collectively. As such, it has constrained the range of available choices in constitutional law to alternatives at the extremes of constitutional theory. The middle way is not altogether comfortable for those who desire certitude and finality at whatever cost, but it was pointed out clearly by the Founders and John Marshall's Court. We have forgotten, thanks to the persistence of the *Marbury* Myth and its weighty baggage. Yet perhaps it is not too late to regain a measure of the sensibility so beautifully expressed by Immanuel Kant: "What the study of nature and of man has sufficiently shown elsewhere may well be true here, . . . that the inscrutable wisdom through which we exist is not less worthy of veneration in respect to what it denies us than in what it has granted."[215]

# Notes

## Chapter 1. A Historical and Theoretical Perspective

1. Henry Adams, *The Education of Henry Adams* (Boston: Houghton Mifflin, 1918), p. 382.

2. Edward S. Corwin, one of the most prominent modern authorities on the subject, says that "judicial review is at any particular period a 'function' of its own product, the constitutional law of the period." Corwin, *The Constitution and What It Means Today*, 11th ed. (Princeton, N.J.: Princeton University Press, 1954), p. 142.

3. 1 Cranch 137 (1803).

4. Albert J. Beveridge, *The Life of John Marshall*, 4 vols. (Boston: Houghton Mifflin, 1916), vol. 3, p. 32.

5. Alexander M. Bickel, *The Least Dangerous Branch: The Supreme Court at the Bar of Politics* (Indianapolis: Bobbs-Merrill, 1962), p. 1.

6. Donald O. Dewey, *Marshall versus Jefferson: The Political Background of Marbury v. Madison* (New York: Alfred A. Knopf, 1970), pp. 117–21.

7. Charles R. Adrian and Charles Press, *American Politics Reappraised: The Enchantment of Camelot Dispelled* (New York: McGraw-Hill, 1974), p. 172.

8. James McGregor Burns, J. W. Peltason, and Thomas E. Cronin, *Government by the People*, 10th ed. (Englewood Cliffs, N.J.: Prentice–Hall, 1978), p. 29.

9. Daniel M. Berman and Louis S. Loeb, *Laws and Men: The Challenge of American Politics* (London: Macmillan, 1970), p. 326.

10. See C. Herman Pritchett, *The American Constitution*, 3d ed. (New York: McGraw-Hill, 1977), pp. 126–28; John H. Ferguson and Dean E. McHenry, *The American System of Government*, 12th ed. (New York: McGraw-Hill, 1973), p. 434; Abraham Holtzman, *American Government: Ideals and Reality* (Englewood Cliffs, N.J.: Prentice-Hall, 1980), pp. 329–30; Karl A. Lamb, *The People, Maybe*, 3d ed. (North Scituate, Mass.: Duxbury, 1978), pp. 316–20; Kenneth Dolbeare and Murray Edelman, *American Politics: Policies, Power, and Change*, 3d ed. (Lexington, Mass.: D. C. Heath & Co., 1977), pp. 242–47; Robert L. Lineberry, *Government in America: People, Politics, and Policy* (Boston: Little, Brown & Co., 1980),

pp. 433–34; J. W. Peltason, *Understanding the Constitution* (New York: Holt, Rinehart & Winston, 1979), p. 28; Ruth Silva et al., *American Government: Democracy and Liberty in Balance* (New York: Alfred A. Knopf, 1976), p. 429; David V. Edwards, *The American Political Experience* (Englewood Cliffs, N.J.: Prentice-Hall, 1979), p. 300.

11. Wallace Mendelson, "Was Chief Justice Marshall an Activist?" in Morton Halpern and Charles Lamb, eds., *Supreme Court Activism and Restraint* (Lexington, Mass.: Lexington Books, 1982), p. 57.

12. Robert G. McCloskey, *The American Supreme Court* (Chicago: University of Chicago Press, 1960), p. 40.

13. P. Allan Dionisopoulos and Paul Peterson, "Rediscovering the American Origins of Judicial Review: A Rebuttal to the Views Stated by Currie and Other Scholars," *John Marshall Law Review* 18 (1984): 49–76.

14. Christopher Wolfe, "John Marshall and Constitutional Law," *Polity* 15 (Fall 1982): 5–25; idem, "A Theory of U.S. Constitutional History," *Journal of Politics* 43 (May 1981): 292–316, esp. 293–94.

15. Hadley Arkes, "On the Moral Standing of the President as an Interpreter of the Constitution: Some Reflections on Our Current Crises," *PS* (Summer 1987) 637–42, esp. 641, n. 11. This point also has been suggested by Sotirios A. Barber, in *On What the Constitution Means* (Baltimore: Johns Hopkins University Press, 1984), p. 196. It has been stated outright by Jesse H. Choper in his marvelous book *Judicial Review and the National Political Process: A Functional Reconsideration of the Role of the Supreme Court* (Chicago: University of Chicago Press, 1980), pp. 62, 212–13, 382–86.

16. Mendelson, "Was Marshall an Activist?" p. 57. See also Joseph P. Secola, "The Judicial Review of John Marshall and Its Subsequent Development in American Jurisprudence," *Lincoln Law Review* 18 (1988): 1–48.

17. Edward S. Corwin, "The Establishment of Judicial Review," *Michigan Law Review* 9 (1910):102.

18. Archibald Cox, "The Role of the Supreme Court in American Society," *Marquette Law Review* 50 (1967): 575, 582.

19. Bishop Hoadly's Sermon, Preached Before the King, March 31, 1717.

20. Christopher Wolfe, *The Rise of Modern Judicial Review: From Constitutional Interpretation to Judge-made Law* (New York: Basic Books, 1986), esp. pp. 3–11.

21. Speech by William J. Brennan, Text and Teaching Symposium, Georgetown University, October 12, 1985. Reprinted in Paul G. Cassell, ed., *The Great Debate: Interpreting Our Written Constitution* (Washington, D.C.: Federalist Society, 1986), p. 11.

22. Speech by Edwin Meese, American Bar Association, July 9, 1985. Reprinted in *The Great Debate*, p. 1.

23. Speech by Edwin Meese, Tulane University College Citizens Forum, October 21, 1986, quoted in "The Irrepressible Mr. Meese," *Wall Street Journal*, October 29, 1986, p. 28, col. 1.

24. Ibid.

25. Stuart Taylor, Jr., "Liberties Union Denounces Meese: Others Defend His Views on Supreme Court's Rulings," *New York Times*, October 24, 1986, p. 17, col. 1.

26. Anthony Lewis, "Law or Power," *New York Times*, October 27, 1986, p. 23, col. 1.

27. Ibid.

28. Speech in Springfield, Illinois, June 26, 1857, reprinted in Philip Van Doren Stern, ed., *The Life and Writings of Abraham Lincoln* (New York: Random House, 1940), pp. 415–27.

29. According to Wallace Mendelson, until Brennan's speech, "activist Justices had always denied their activism, as when Chief Justice Warren in *Miranda v. Arizona*, 384 U.S. 436 (1966), insisted without documentation: 'We start here . . . with the premise that our holding is not an innovation in our jurisprudence. . . .' In *Griswold v. Connecticut*, 381 U.S. 479 (1965), Justice Douglas was more explicit. He found a right to copulate with contraceptives in 'penumbras formed by emanations' from our Eighteenth Century Bill of Rights allegedly made applicable to the states by a fair-trial provision in a Civil War Amendment." Wallace Mendelson, "Messrs. Meese, Brennan, and Plato on the Sovereignty of Judges" unpublished essay, University of Texas at Austin, 1986), p. 2.

30. See, e.g., *Thornburgh v. American College of Obstetricians*, 476 U.S. 747 (1986); *Local 28 of Sheet Metal Workers' Int'l Ass'n v. Equal Opportunity Commission*, 478 U.S. 421 (1986); *Local Number 93, Int'l Ass'n of Firefighters v. City of Cleveland*, 478 U.S. 501 (1986); *Wygant v. Jackson Board of Education*, 476 U.S. 267 (1986); *Bender v. Williamsport Area School Dist.*, 475 U.S. 534 (1986).

31. See, e.g., *Roe v. Wade*, 410 U.S. 113 (1973), where the Court declared the existence of a right to abortion on demand during the first trimester of a woman's pregnancy. *Engel v. Vitale*, 370 U.S. 421 (1962), held that school boards could not require the recitation of prayers in public school classrooms, even if student participation in such exercises was voluntary. Finally, in *United Steelworkers of America v. Weber*, 443 U.S. 193 (1979), the Court upheld a collective bargaining agreement which contained a racial quota, despite a claim that the quota violated Title VII of the 1964 Civil Rights Act, which prohibits discrimination based on race. It is possible to view these decisions as novel interpretations of the Constitution.

32. See, e.g., *United States v. Darby*, 312 U.S. 100 (1941), overruling *Hammer v. Dagenhart*, 247 U.S. 251 (1918). See also *Wickard v. Filburn*, 317 U.S. 111 (1942); *National Labor Relations Bd. v. Jones & Laughlin Steel Corp.*, 301 U.S. 1 (1937); *Steward Machine Co. v. Davis*, 301 U.S. 548 (1937); *West Coast Hotel Co. v. Parrish*, 300 U.S. 379 (1937).

33. In the area of commerce, see *Schechter Poultry Corp. v. United States*, 295 U.S. 495 (1935), and *Carter v. Carter Coal Co.*, 298 U.S. 238 (1936). Compare the reasoning in the latter case with that in *Gibbons v. Ogden*, 9 Wheat. 1 (1824), especially their respective definitions of "commerce." In the area of taxation, see *United States v. Butler*, 297 U.S. 1 (1936), and *Bailey v. Drexel Furniture Co.*, 259 U.S. 20 (1922). Compare these with statements on the taxing power in *McCulloch v. Maryland*, 4 Wheat. 316 (1819), and *Veazie Bank v. Fenno*, 8 Wall. 533 (1869). In the area of economic regulation, see *Nebbia v. New York*, 291 U.S. 502 (1934), and *Adkins v. Children's Hospital*, 261 U.S. 525 (1923). Compare these with *Munn v. Illinois*, 94 U.S. 113 (1877), and *The Slaughterhouse Cases*, 16 Wall. 36 (1873). *Adkins* was overruled by *West Coast Hotel*. See this chapter, n. 32.

34. Raoul Berger, *Government by Judiciary: The Transformation of the Fourteenth Amendment* (Cambridge, Mass.: Harvard University Press, 1977).

35. John Hart Ely, *Democracy and Distrust: A Theory of Judicial Review* (Cambridge, Mass.: Harvard University Press, 1980).

36. Thomas Grey, "Do We Have an Unwritten Constitution?" *Stanford Law Review* 27 (1975): 730.

37. Berger, *Government by Judiciary*, chaps. 5-7.

38. Ibid., chap. 20.

39. Ely, *Democracy and Distrust*, chap. 2.

40. Grey, "Unwritten Constitution," p. 706.

41. Ely, *Democracy and Distrust*, p. 9.

42. Ibid., pp. 2-3, chaps. 4-6.

43. Ibid., p. 12, chap. 4. Ely does not call it this, but I think the phrase is a fair description of his theory of constitutional interpretation. But see discussion in Wolfe, *Rise of Modern Judicial Review*, pp. 343-52.

44. Ely, *Democracy and Distrust*, p. 12; Wolfe, *Rise of Modern Judicial Review*, p. 344.

45. See, e.g., William Harris, "Bonding Word and Polity," *American Political Science Review* 76 (1982): 34.

46. Berger, *Government by Judiciary*, pp. 2-3.

47. Lat., "to abide by, or adhere to, decided cases." Henry Campbell Black, *Black's Law Dictionary*, 5th ed. (St. Paul: West Publishing Co., 1979), p. 1261.

48. *Nomination of Judge Robert H. Bork, to Be Associate Justice of the Supreme Court of the United States: Hearings before the Senate Committee on the Judiciary*, 100th Cong., 1st Sess. (1987). Judge Bork was repeatedly questioned about whether his commitment to a jurisprudence of original intent would lead him to overrule recent "precedents" that he found incompatible with the intentions of the Framers, should his nomination be confirmed.

49. *Black's Law Dictionary*, p. 1261: "Doctrine is one of policy, grounded on theory that security and certainty require that accepted and established legal principle, under which rights may accrue, be recognized and followed, though later found not to be legally sound, but whether previous holding of court shall be adhered to, modified, or overruled is within court's discretion under circumstances of case before it." See also *Helvering v. Hallock*, 309 U.S. 106 (1940).

50. Ibid. See also *Reconstruction Finance Corp. v. Prudence Securities Advisory Group*, 311 U.S. 579 (1941).

51. See *Ebert v. Poston*, 166 U.S. 548 (1925); *Raymond v. Thomas*, 91 U.S. 712 (1875).

52. See *United States v. Fisher*, 6 U.S. 358 (1805); *Orchard v. Alexander*, 157 U.S. 372 (1895); *Bate Refrigerating Co. v. Sulzberger*, 157 U.S. 1 (1895).

53. *Nomination of Justice William Hubbs Rehnquist to Be Chief Justice of the United States: Hearings before the Senate Committee on the Judiciary*, 99th Cong., 2d Sess. (1986), p. 187. *Nomination of Judge Antonin Scalia to Be Associate Justice of the Supreme Court of the United States: Hearings before the Senate Committee on the Judiciary*, 99th Cong., 2d Sess. (1986), p. 83.

54. Daniel O. Conkle, "Nonoriginalist Constitutional Rights and the Problem of Judicial Finality," *Hastings Constitutional Law Quarterly* 13 (Fall 1985): 10.

Professor Conkle's article contains an excellent, brief review of the debate on judicial review which has been raging in books, academic journals, and law reviews for the past decade or so. See Conkle, n. 1-9 and accompanying text.

55. Ibid., pp. 11-14.

56. Ibid., p. 18. Conkle argues further that judicial finality is problematic in the context of 'nonoriginalist' judicial review and suggests that the doctrine should be abandoned for certain of those cases. Ibid., pp. 19-23.

57. Ibid., pp. 11, 16-17.

58. See, e.g., n. 4-10 in this chapter and accompanying text.

59. *New York Trust Co. v. Eisner*, 256 U.S. 345, 349 (1921).

60. Dewey, *Marshall versus Jefferson*, pp. 117-21.

61. William Van Alstyne, "A Critical Guide to *Marbury v. Madison,*" *Duke Law Journal* (1969): 1; J. A. C. Grant, "*Marbury v. Madison* Today," *American Political Science Review* 23 (1929): 673. See also Burton Caine, "Judicial Review—Democracy Versus Constitutionality," *Temple Law Quarterly* 56 (1983): 297-350 (Caine looks at *Marbury* from the point of view of the debate on "interpretivism"); Susan Low Bloch and Maeva Marcus, "John Marshall's Selective Use of History in *Marbury v. Madison,*" *Wisconsin Law Review* 1986 (1986): 301-37 (Bloch and Marcus charge Marshall with misuse of precedent in the *Marbury* decision); Michael Allen Berch, "An Essay on the Role of the Supreme Court in the Adjudication of Constitutional Rights," *Arizona State Law Journal* 1984 (1984): 283-304 (Berch says that Marshall laid the foundation for "judarchy"—constitutional leadership by the courts— in the United States). All three of these articles are well worth reading and follow Grant and Van Alstyne to the extent that they regard the *Marbury* decision as "activist" in some sense—though the focus of each is different.

62. See, e.g., Beveridge, *Life of Marshall*, vol. 3, p. 132; Bickel, *Least Dangerous Branch*, p. 1. See this chapter, n. 4-5 and accompanying text. See also the excellent discussion of sources bearing on the origins of judicial review provided in Dionisopoulos and Peterson, "Rediscovering the Origins of Judicial Review."

63. United States Constitution, Article I, Section 8, Clause 18. In other words, the power of judicial review might be regarded as "implied," perhaps from the conjunction of Articles III and VI. See Robert L. Clinton, "*Eakin v. Raub*: Refutation or Justification of *Marbury v. Madison?*" *Constitutional Commentary* 4 (Winter 1987): 88.

64. *United States v. Sisson*, 294 F. Supp. 511 (D. Mass. 1968) (Wyzanski, C.J., opinion of Court). In other words, the power of judicial review might be regarded as "inherent" in the nature of the judicial function.

65. See *McCulloch v. Maryland*, 4 Wheat. 316 (1819); also *United States v. Curtiss-Wright Export Corp.*, 299 U.S. 304 (1936)

66. The attack was clearly a response to the Court's decision in *Pollock v. Farmers' Loan & Trust Co.*, 157 U.S. 429 (1895), invalidating portions of the federal income tax law. See Sylvester Pennoyer, "The Income Tax Decision and the Power of the Supreme Court to Nullify Acts of Congress," *American Law Review* 29 (1895): 550; idem, "The Power of the Supreme Court to Declare an Act of Congress Unconstitutional: The Case of *Marbury v. Madison,*" *American Law Review* 30 (1896): 188; John W. Akin, "Aggressions of the Federal Courts," *American Law*

*Review* 32 (1898): 669; Henry Flanders, "Has the Supreme Court of the United States the Constitutional Power to Declare Void an Act of Congress?" *American Law Review* 48 (1900): 385.

67. John F. Dillon, ed., *John Marshall: Life, Character, and Judicial Services,* 3 vols. (Chicago: Callaghan & Co., 1903), vol. 3, p. 321. See also Lafon Allen, "The Income Tax Decision: An Answer to Gov. Pennoyer," *American Law Review* 29 (1895): 847; Robert Ludlow Fowler, "The Origin of the Supreme Judicial Power in the Federal Constitution," *American Law Review* 29 (1895): 711; Junius Parker, "The Supreme Court and Its Constitutional Duty and Power," *American Law Review* 30 (1896): 357.

68. 1 Cranch 137, 177 (1803).

69. Ibid., at 178

70. Ibid., at 179.

71. Ibid., at 179–180 (emphasis mine).

72. *Cooper v. Aaron,* 358 U.S. 1, 18 (1958). See also Conkle, "Nonoriginalist Constitutional Rights," p. 12.

73. For an excellent survey of the background of this situation, including attitudes toward the legal profession in the 1790s, movements for judicial reform in the states, and many other aspects, see Richard E. Ellis, *The Jeffersonian Crisis: Courts and Politics in the Young Republic* (New York: Norton & Co., 1974), pp. 3–16. See also George Haskins and Herbert Johnson, *Foundations of Power: John Marshall, 1801–1815,* vol. 2 of *Oliver Wendell Holmes Devise History of the Supreme Court of the United States* (New York: Macmillan, 1981), pp. 647–51.

74. Ellis, *Jeffersonian Crisis,* p. 15. See also Kathryn Turner, "Federalist Policy and the Judiciary Act of 1801," *William & Mary Quarterly* 22 (January 1965): 15–22; Erwin C. Surrency, "The Judiciary Act of 1801," *American Journal of Legal History* 2 (1958): 53–65; Max Farrand, "The Judiciary Act of 1801," *American Historical Review* 5 (1899–1900): 682–86; Haskins and Johnson, *Foundations of Power,* pp. 183–86.

75. Ellis, *Jeffersonian Crisis,* p. 43.

76. Ibid., p. 50.

77. Ibid., pp. 59–60.

78. Haskins and Johnson, *Foundations of Power,* p. 184.

79. 1 Cranch 137, 153 (1803).

80. Ibid., at 154–73.

81. Ibid., at 159–62, 167–68.

82. Ibid., at 162–68.

83. Ibid., at 168–73.

84. Ibid., at 173–80.

85. United States Constitution, Article III, Section 2.

86. 1 Cranch 137, at 176–80 (1803).

87. Ibid., at 176–77.

88. Ibid., at 177–80.

89. The famous dissenting opinion of Justice John Gibson in *Eakin v. Raub,* 12 Serg. & Rawle (Pa.) 330, at 343–58 (1825), can be read as having made such a charge. See Craig R. Ducat and Harold W. Chase, *Constitutional Interpretation,* 3d ed. (St. Paul: West Publishing Co., 1983), pp. 5–6. For a contrary view, see Clinton, "*Eakin v. Raub.*"

90. 1 Cranch 137, 176 (1803).
91. Ibid., at 176–77.
92. Ibid.., at 176.
93. Ibid., at 177.
94. See this chapter, n. 68–70 and accompanying text.
95. 1 Cranch 137, at 178–80 (1803).
96. For a well-known critique of *Marbury*, see Van Alstyne, "Critical Guide." See also Dewey, *Marshall versus Jefferson*; David P. Currie, "The Constitution in the Supreme Court: The Powers of the Federal Courts, 1801–1835," *University of Chicago Law Review* 49 (1982): 654–55; and Leonard Levy, *Original Intent and the Framers' Constitution* (New York: Macmillan, 1988), pp. 78–88.
97. It is axiomatic that "precedents" are created, not by dicta, but by the application of rules of law to the facts in particular cases. Harold J. Grilliot, *Introduction to Law and the Legal System*, 3d ed. (Boston: Houghton Mifflin, 1983), pp. 149–50. In other words, even if Marshall's assertions in *Marbury* had gone beyond the case (which, I submit, they did not), it would be inappropriate to regard them as having any *stare decisis* effect.
98. Max Farrand, ed., *Records of the Federal Convention*, 4 vols. (New Haven, Conn.: Yale University Press, 1911), vol. 2, p. 430.
99. Benjamin F. Wright, *The Growth of American Constitutional Law* (Boston: Houghton Mifflin, 1942; Chicago: University of Chicago Press, Phoenix Books, 1967), p. 18. According to Ralph A. Rossum, Madison did not believe "that the Court's interpretations were superior to or entitled to precedence over those of Congress or the President. He claimed only that the Court should have final authority to pass on constitutional questions that affected its own duties and responsibilities, that is, that were of a 'judiciary nature.' " Rossum goes on to say that Marshall's opinion in *Marbury* "is wholly consistent with Madison's understanding of the limited nature of judicial review." Rossum, "The Courts and the Judicial Power," in Leonard W. Levy and Dennis J. Mahoney, eds., *The Framing and Ratification of the Constitution* (New York: Macmillan, 1987), p. 236. See also William Miller, "Cases of a Judiciary Nature," *Saint Louis University Public Law Review* 8 (1989): 47–73.
100. William Blackstone, *Commentaries on the Laws of England*, 4 vols. (Chicago: University of Chicago Press, 1979; facsimile of 1769 edition). See also English cases discussed in chap. 2; and Sir William Holdsworth, *A History of English Law*, 7th ed. rev., edited by A. L. Goodhart and H. G. Hanburg, 16 vols. (London: Methuen & Co., 1956), vol. 12, pp. 726–27.
101. Wolfe, *Rise of Modern Judicial Review*, p. 17.
102. Blackstone, *Commentaries*, vol. 1, pp. 58–62. Wolfe, *Rise of Modern Judicial Review*, pp. 18–19.
103. Blackstone, *Commentaries*, vol. 1, p. 59, quoted in Wolfe, *Rise of Modern Judicial Review*, p. 18
104. Blackstone, *Commentaries*, vol. 1, pp. 87–91.
105. Ibid., p. 91.
106. Merrill Peterson, ed., *Democracy, Liberty, and Property: The State Constitutions of the 1820s* (Indianapolis: Bobbs-Merrill, 1966), p. 3. See also James

Bradley Thayer, "The Origin and Scope of the American Doctrine of Constitutional Law," *Harvard Law Review* 129, (October 1893): 134.

107. For example, Councils of Revision. See Thayer, "Origin and Scope," pp. 136-37, n. 1. See also Gordon S. Wood, *The Creation of the American Republic, 1776-1787* (New York: W. W. Norton, 1972), pp. 138, 150-51, 449-53, 550.

108. Emmerich de Vattel, *The Law of Nations*, edited by Joseph Chitty (Philadelphia: Johnson & Co., 1883), p. 11.

109. See H. F. Jolowicz, *Historical Introduction to the Study of Roman Law* (Cambridge: Cambridge University Press, 1932), pp. 372-78. The principle will receive fuller treatment in chap. 2.

110. See, e.g., Wright, *Growth*, pp. 11-19, 43; idem, "Natural Law in American Political Theory," *Southwestern Political & Social Science Quarterly* 4 (1923): 202; idem, "American Interpretations of Natural Law," *American Political Science Review* 20 (1926): 524; Haines, *American Doctrine*, pp. 59-63; idem, *The Revival of Natural Law Concepts* (Cambridge, Mass.: Harvard University Press, 1930); Edward S. Corwin, "The Doctrine of Due Process of Law before the Civil War," *Harvard Law Review* 24 (1911): 366-85, 460-95.

111. Haines, *American Doctrine*, pp. 59-63; Wright, *Growth*, pp. 11-19.

112. See generally Jolowicz, *Historical Introduction*, pp. 19-27, 372-78, 475-76; idem, *Roman Foundations of Modern Law* (Oxford: Clarendon Press, 1957), pp. 7, 17-20, 84, 130, 194-204; and Brinton Coxe, *An Essay on Judicial Power and Unconstitutional Legislation* (Philadelphia: Kay & Brother, 1893).

113. "A later statute takes away the effect of a prior one," *Black's Law Dictionary*, p. 822. See also Coxe, *An Essay*, p. 111; Jolowicz, *Historical Introduction*, pp. 24-27.

114. Blackstone, *Commentaries*, vol. 1, p. 90.

115. Ibid.

116. In fact, the "official and authentic decision of a court of justice *upon the respective right and claims of the parties* to an action or suit therein litigated and submitted to its determination" is the legal definition, according to Black, of the term "judgement." *Black's Law Dictionary*, p. 755 (emphasis mine). See generally Coxe, *An Essay*, pp. 137-80.

117. Blackstone, *Commentaries*, vol. 1, pp. 87-91. See also the English cases discussed in Coxe, *An Essay*, pp. 168-80.

118. Blackstone, *Commentaries*, vol. 1, p. 91. Also *Dr. Bonham's Case*, 8 Coke's Reports 118 (1610).

119. Blackstone, *Commentaries*, vol. 1, p. 91.

120. See this chapter, n. 105 and accompanying text.

121. See this chapter, note 99 and accompanying text.

122. United States Constitution, Article VI, Clause 2.

123. George L. Haskins, "Law versus Politics in the Early Years of the Marshall Court," *Pennsylvania Law Review*, 130 (November, 1981): 9-10.

124. Wolfe, *Rise of Modern Judicial Review*, p. 41.

125. United States Constitution, Article I, Section 7.

126. Ibid.

127. Farrand, *Records*, vol. 2, p. 430.

128. See Wallace Mendelson, "Jefferson on Judicial Review: Consistency through Change," *University of Chicago Law Review* 29 (1962): 327.

129. Letter to Judge Roane, September 6, 1819, quoted in Mendelson, "Jefferson on Judicial Review," p. 327.

130. See discussion in Wolfe, *Rise of Modern Judicial Review*, pp. 94–101, esp. 98–99.

131. Letter to Abigail Adams, September 11, 1804, quoted in Wallace Mendelson, *Supreme Court Statecraft: The Rule of Law and Men* (Ames: Iowa State University Press, 1985), p. 221.

132. See, e.g., Edward S. Corwin, "The Supreme Court and Unconstitutional Acts of Congress," *Michigan Law Review* 4 (1906): 629–30.

133. Mendelson, "Jefferson on Judicial Review," pp. 328–33.

134. James Madison, "Comments on the Removal Power of the President," June 17, 1789, in Charles F. Hobson and Robert A. Rutland, eds., *The Papers of James Madison*, 15 vols. (Charlottesville: University Press of Virginia, 1979), vol. 12, p. 234.

135. Ibid., p. 238.

136. Wolfe, *Rise of Modern Judicial Review*, p. 95.

137. 1 Cranch 137, at 179 (emphasis mine).

## Chapter 2. The Blackstonian Inheritance

1. Brinton Coxe, *An Essay on Judicial Power and Unconstitutional Legislation* (Philadelphia: Kay & Brother, 1893), p. 107; see also H. F. Jolowicz, *Historical Introduction to the Study of Roman Law* (Cambridge: Cambridge University Press, 1932), pp. 372–76. On specific usages and forms of rescript at different periods in the development of Roman law, see Jolowicz, *Roman Foundations of Modern Law* (Oxford: Clarendon Press, 1957), pp. 7, 17–20, 84, 194–99, 202–4.

2. Code J. 1. 22.1.6. Quoted in Coxe, *An Essay*, p. 108. The explanation in Justinian's *Institutes* is as follows: "That which seems good to the emperor has also the force of law; for the people, by the *lex regia*, which is passed to confer on him his power, make over to him their whole power and authority. Therefore whatever the emperor ordains by rescript, or decides in adjudging a cause, or lays down by edict, is unquestionably law; and it is these enactments of the emperor that are called constitutions. Of these, some are personal, and are not to be drawn into precedent, such not being the intention of emperor. Supposing the emperor has granted a favor to any man on account of his merits, or inflicted some punishment, or granted some extraordinary relief, the application of these acts does not extent beyond the particular individual. But the other constitutions, being general, are undoubtedly binding to all." J. Inst. 1.2.6. Quoted from *The Institutes of Justinian*, translated by Thomas Collett Sandars (Westport, Conn.: Greenwood Press, 1970), p. 10.

3. Code J. 1. 19.1.7. Quoted in Coxe, *An Essay*, p. 109.

4. Jolowicz, *Historical Introduction*, p. 475.

5. Coxe, *An Essay*, p. 110.

6. Ibid., p. 111; see also Jolowicz, *Historical Introduction*, pp. 192, 25.

7. Coxe, *An Essay*, p. 111; Jolowicz, *Historical Introduction*, pp. 24–27.

8. Jolowicz, *Historical Introduction*, pp. 25–26; idem, *Roman Foundations*, pp. 19–20.

9. Jolowicz, *Historical Introduction*, p. 26.

10. A phrase apparently invented by Louis Boudin. See his *Government by Judiciary*, 2 vols. (New York: Godwin, 1932), vol. 1, pp. 34–72.

11. Jolowicz, *Historical Introduction*, p. 26.

12. Ibid.; see also John Austin, *The Austinian Theory of Law*, edited by W. Jethro Brown (London: John Murray, 1920), pp. 160–64.

13. Jolowicz, *Historical Introduction*, p. 26.

14. Ibid., p. 25.

15. Ibid.; see also Jolowicz, *Roman Foundations*, p. 130.

16. Coxe, *An Essay*, pp. 111–12.

17. Dig. 17. 1.1.5. Quoted in George Bowyer, *Commentaries on Universal Public Law* (London: Stevens & Norton, 1854), pp. 343–44; Coxe, *An Essay*, pp. 114–15; Jolowicz, *Historical Introduction*, pp. 372–78, 476. For a discussion of the various private-law applications of the law of mandate in both Roman and English law, see W. W. Buckland and Arnold D. McNair, *Roman Law and Common Law: A Comparison in Outline*, 2d ed. rev., edited by F. H. Lawson (Cambridge: Cambridge University Press, 1965), pp. 268, 280, 299, 307–10, 325, 328, 331–37, 386.

18. Emmerich de Vattel, *The Law of Nations*, edited by Joseph Chitty (Philadelphia: Johnson & Co., 1883), p. 452.

19. George Bowyer, *Commentaries on the Modern Civil Law* (London: Stevens & Norton, 1848), pp. 225–27.

20. Hugo Grotius, *On the Law of War and Peace*, translated by Whewell, 3 vols. (Cambridge: Cambridge University Press, 1853), vol. 1, p. 242, vol. 2, pp. 339–41, vol. 3, pp. 385–87.

21. Coxe, *An Essay*, pp. 119, 234–48; see also James Bradley Thayer, *Cases on Constitutional Law*, 2 vols. (Cambridge, Mass.: George H. Kent, 1895), vol. 1, pp. 73–78.

22. Coxe, *An Essay*, p. 120.

23. Vattel, *The Law of Nations*, p. 11.

24. 1 Mart. (N.C.) 42 (1787); Coxe, *An Essay*, p. 251; Thayer, *Cases*, vol. 1, p. 80.

25. See *The New Encyclopedia Britannica*, 15th ed., *Micropedia*, S. V. "Vattel, Emmerich de"; the entry says that Vattel's treatise on the law of nations was "especially influential in the United States because his principles of liberty and equality coincided with the ideals expressed in the Declaration of Independence."

26. See Charles Warren, *Congress, the Constitution, and the Supreme Court* (Boston: Little, Brown & Co., 1925), pp. 45–46.

27. James M. Varnum, *The Case of Trevett v. Weeden* (Providence: John Carter, 1787); see also Peleg W. Chandler, *American Criminal Trials*, 2 vols. (Freeport, N.Y.: Book for Libraries Press, 1970), vol. 2, p. 269; Thayer, *Cases*, vol. 1, p. 73.

28. 1 Cranch 137, at 176–80 (1803).

29. Vattel, *The Law of Nations*, p. 12.

30. Coxe's scholarship has been noted even by his most bitter opponents. See, e.g., Boudin, *Government by Judiciary*, vol. 1, pp. 30–33, 56, 67–68, 73.

31. See Coxe, *An Essay*, pp. 54–70.

32. Ibid., pp. 214–18.

33. Ibid., pp. 79–80. See also Boudin, *Government by Judiciary*, vol. 1, pp. 41–43.

34. Ibid., pp. 123–27, 129–33.

35. Ibid., pp. 79–81. See also Boudin, *Government by Judiciary*, vol. 1, p. 41.

36. Coxe, *An Essay*, pp. 77–78.

37. Helie, *The Constitutions of France*, quoted in Coxe, *An Essay*, p. 77. See also Brooks Adams, *The Theory of Social Revolutions* (New York: Macmillan, 1913), pp. 160–202, esp. 170.

38. Coxe, *An Essay*, p. 129. The Rota Romana was the regular papal court of appeal. See R. H. Helmholz, *Canon Law and the Law of England* (London: Hambledon Press, 1987), p. 252.

39. Coxe, *An Essay*, p. 123.

40. Ibid., p. 125.

41. Ibid.

42. Ibid., p. 137. See also Sir William Holdsworth, *A History of English Law*, 7th ed. rev., edited by A. L. Goodhart and H. G. Hanburg, 16 vols. (London: Methuen & Co., 1956), vol. 1, pp. 35–39, 615; Michael Evans and R. Ian Jack, eds., *Sources of English Legal and Constitutional History* (Sydney, Australia: Butterworth's, 1984), pp. 12–18.

43. Coxe, *An Essay*, p. 139. See also Holdsworth, *History of English Law*, vol. 2, p. 179.

44. Coxe, *An Essay*, pp. 143–47. See also Adams, *The Theory of Social Revolutions*, p. 182; idem, *The Law of Civilization and Decay* (New York: Alfred A. Knopf, 1943), pp. 174–99.

45. Coxe, *An Essay*, pp. 146–47.

46. *Prior of Castlaker v. Dean of St. Stevens*, Y.B. 21 Henry 7, fo. 1, pl. 1 (1505). See Coxe, *An Essay*, p. 147.

47. Coxe, *An Essay*, p. 150.

48. Quoted in ibid.

49. I Statutes of the Realm 150; see 2 Coke's Institutes 588. See also Holdsworth, *History of English Law*, vol. 1, p. 585: vol. 2, p. 301.

50. Coxe, *An Essay*, p. 155.

51. William Blackstone, *Commentaries on the Laws of England*, 4 vols. (Chicago: University of Chicago Press, 1979), vol. 1, p. 91.

52. See this chapter, n. 42–50 and accompanying text.

53. Benjamin Twiss, *Lawyers and the Constitution: How Laissez-Faire Came to the Supreme Court* (Princeton, N.J.: Princeton University Press, 1942), pp. 18–62, esp. 33–34, 46–47. For a modern statement of the Coke-Blackstone opposition, see Edgar Bodenheimer, *Jurisprudence: The Philosophy and Method of Law* (Cambridge, Mass: Harvard University Press, 1962), pp. 56–57. Bodenheimer goes so far as to suggest that Coke's *Bonham* dicta laid down a theory of "judicial supremacy," and he distinguishes that theory from Blackstone's "legislative supremacy."

54. 21 L. ed. 395–6 (1873). See also William M. Meigs, "The Relation of the Judiciary to the Constitution," *American Law Review* 19(1885): 175, 177–78. For an opposing view of the English cases, see Theodore Plucknett, "Bonham's Case and Judicial Review," *Harvard Law Review* 40 (November 1926): 35; Boudin, *Government By Judiciary*, vol. 1, pp. 498–503.

55. Twiss, *Lawyers and the Constitution*, p. 42.

56. 8 Coke's Reports 107, 118 (1610). See also Bodenheimer, *Jurisprudence*, p. 56.

57. Ibid. See also Coxe, *An Essay*, pp. 174-78.

58. Henry Campbell Black, *Black's Law Dictionary*, 5th ed. (St. Paul: West Publishing Co., 1979), p. 1171 (emphasis mine).

59. *Tregor v. Vaghan*, Y.B. 8 Edw. 3, fo. 30, pl. 26 (1334). See also Coxe, *An Essay*, p. 174; Boudin, *Government by Judiciary*, vol. 1, pp. 498-99. See also Thayer, *Cases*, vol. 1, pp. 48-50. 8 Coke's Reports 107, 118 (1610). See also Evans and Jack, *Sources*, pp. 105-18.

60. Coxe, *An Essay*, p. 175; Boudin, *Government by Judiciary*, vol. 1, pp. 501-3. 8 Coke's Reports 107, 118 (1610).

61. *Rous v. an Abbot*, (Fitzherbert's Abridgement, Annuity 41). Coxe, *An Essay*, pp. 176-77; Boudin, *Government by Judiciary*, vol. 1, pp. 500-501. 8 Coke's Reports 107, 118 (1610).

62. Fitzherbert's Abridgement, Cessavit 42. Coxe, *An Essay*, p. 175; Boudin, *Government by Judiciary*, vol. 1, p. 499. 8 Coke's Reports 107, 118 (1610).

63. Hobart's Reports 87 (1614). Robert Ludlow Fowler, "The Origin of the Supreme Judicial Power in the Federal Constitution," *American Law Review* 29 (1895): 713; Thayer, *Cases*, vol. 1, p. 50; Coxe, *An Essay*, pp. 172-73; Boudin, *Government by Judiciary*, vol. 1, pp. 507-8.

64. 12 Modern 687 (1701).

65. Ibid., emphasis mine. See also Thayer, *Cases*, vol. 1, pp. 50-51; Coxe, *An Essay*, pp. 173-74; Boudin, *Government by Judiciary*, vol. 1, pp 508-10.

66. Blackstone, *Commentaries*, vol. 1, p. 91. Coxe (*An Essay*, p. 176) attributes the first sentence in the quotation to Coke, though without explicit reference. Boudin (*Government by Judiciary*) vol. 1, p. 517) says that Coke made the statements in *Bonham's Case*. These attributions are essentially correct. Coke's language in *Bonham* reads: "So if any act of parliament gives to any to hold, or to have conusans of all manner of pleas arising before him within his manor of D., yet he shall hold no plea, to which he himself is party; for, as hath been said, *iniquum est aliquem suo rei esse judicem* [it is wrong for a man to be a judge in his own cause]."

67. Blackstone, *Commentaries*, vol. 1, p. 91. Blackstone cites *Bonham's Case* as authority for the proposition that no man "should determine his own quarrel."

68. Holdsworth, *History of English Law*, vol. 12, p. 151.

69. 9 Cobbett's State Trials 1167 (1686). Reported in Thayer, *Cases*, vol. 1, p. 29.

70. Ibid., quoted in Coxe, *An Essay*, p. 168. See also Boudin, *Government by Judiciary*, vol. 1, pp. 45-50; Thayer, *Cases*, vol. 1, p. 29.

71. Fowler, "Origin of Supreme Judicial Power," p. 718, n. 1.

72. Charles B. Elliott, "The Legislatures and the Courts: The Power to Declare Statutes Unconstitutional," *Political Science Quarterly* 5 (1891): 227. See *Wilkes v. Wood*, 19 State Trials 1153 (1763); *Entinck v. Carrington*, 19 State Trials 1029 (1765); *Stockton, etc. Ry Co. v. Leeds, etc. Ry. Cos.*, 41 Eng. Rep. 1101 (1848). See also Coxe, *An Essay*, pp. 178-80.

73. Fowler, "Origin of Supreme Judicial Power," pp. 713-14; Elliott, "Legislatures and the Courts," p. 227.

74. Meigs, "Relation of the Judiciary," 177.

75. Fowler, "Origin of Supreme Judicial Power," p. 713.

76. Alexander Hamilton, Number 81, in Alexander Hamilton, James Madison, and John Jay, *The Federalist Papers* (New York: New American Library, 1961), p. 484.

77. See, e.g., Benjamin F. Wright, *The Growth of American Constitutional Law* (Boston: Houghton Mifflin, 1942; Chicago: University of Chicago Press, Phoenix Books, 1967), pp. 23–26; Robert G. McCloskey, *The American Supreme Court* (Chicago: University of Chicago Press, 1960), p. 9; Charles Grove Haines, *The American Doctrine of Judicial Supremacy* (Berkeley and Los Angeles: University of California Press, 1932), pp. 137–40; Alpheus Mason and Gerald Garvey, eds., *American Constitutional History: Essays by Edward S. Corwin* (New York: Harper & Row, 1964), pp. 17–20.

78. See chap. 1, n. 98 and accompanying text.

79. See, e.g., Carl Brent Swisher, *Stephen J. Field: Craftsman of the Law* (Chicago: University of Chicago Press, 1969), pp. 413–34, esp. 430.

80. E.g., Coxe, *An Essay*; Haines, *American Doctrine*. See also *Annual Reports of the New York State Bar Association* (1915), pp. 11–15.

81. E.g., Boudin, *Government by Judiciary*. Boudin is followed by William Winslow Crosskey, in *Politics and the Constitution in the History of the United States*, 2 vols. (Chicago: University of Chicago Press, 1953), vol. 2, pp. 938–44. See also William Trickett, "Judicial Dispensation from Congressional Statutes," *American Law Review* 41 (1907):70.

### Chapter 3. The Emergence of an Early American Doctrine of Judicial Power

1. Robert Ludlow Fowler, "The Origin of the Supreme Judicial Power in the Federal Constitution," *American Law Review* 29 (1895):711, 712–15. See also James Bradley Thayer, *Cases on Constitutional Law*, 2 vols. (Cambridge, Mass.: George H. Kent, 1895), vol. 1, p. 78, n. 1; Harold D. Hazletine, "Appeals from Colonial Courts to the King in Council, with Especial Reference to Rhode Island," *Annual Reports of the American Historical Association* (1894), pp. 299–350.

2. Hazletine, "Appeals from Colonial Courts," pp. 311–12.

3. Ibid., p. 312.

4. Ibid., pp. 312–13.

5. Ibid., pp. 311–12.

6. William Blackstone, *Commentaries on the Laws of England*, 4 vols. (Chicago: University of Chicago Press, 1979), vol. 1, p. 105.

7. Joseph Story, *Commentaries on the Constitution of the United States*, 4th ed., edited by Thomas M. Cooley, 2 vols. (Boston: Little, Brown & Co., 1873), vol. 1, p. 122–123.

8. Hazletine, "Appeals from Colonial Courts," pp. 336–37.

9. Ibid., p. 337.

10. Ibid., pp. 337–38. See also Arthur M. Schlesinger, "Colonial Appeals to the Privy Council," *Political Science Quarterly* 28 (1912):440.

11. Hazletine, "Appeals from Colonial Courts," p. 318. See also C. M. Andrews, "The Connecticut Intestacy Law," *Yale Review,* 1894.

12. Hazletine, "Appeals from Colonial Courts," p. 318. See also Charles Grove Haines, *The American Doctrine of Judicial Supremacy* (Berkeley and Los Angeles: University of California Press, 1932), p. 50.

13. Hazletine, "Appeals from Colonial Courts," pp. 318-19. See also Brinton Coxe, *An Essay on Judicial Power and Unconstitutional Legislation* (Philadelphia: Kay & Brother, 1893), pp. 208-9.

14. *Winthrop v. Lechmere,* 4 *Conn. Hist. Soc. Coll.* 94. Reported in Thayer, *Cases,* vol. 1, pp. 34-39. See also Hazletine, "Appeals from Colonial Courts," p. 319; Coxe, *An Essay,* pp. 209-11; Haines, *American Doctrine,* p. 50. The Privy Council reversed itself on Connecticut's Intestacy Law in the case of *Clark v. Tousey,* decided in 1745. See Hazletine, "Appeals from Colonial Courts," pp. 321-22; Haines, *American Doctrine,* p. 51.

15. Hazletine, "Appeals from Colonial Courts," pp. 319-21; Haines, *American Doctrine, p.* 51.

16. *Phillips v. Savage,* 1 *Mass. Hist. Soc. Proc.* 64-80, 164-71. See also Hazletine, "Appeals from Colonial Courts," p. 320; Coxe, *An Essay,* p. 208; Haines, *American Doctrine,* p. 51.

17. Hazletine, "Appeals from Colonial Courts," pp. 320-21.

18. Ibid., p. 321.

19. Coxe, *An Essay,* pp. 211-13; Thayer, *Cases,* vol. 1, pp. 39-40, n. 1.

20. Coxe, *An Essay,* pp. 211-13. For Thayer's theory of the judicial function, see his famous article, "The Origin and Scope of the American Doctrine of Constitutional Law," *Harvard Law Review* 7 (October, 1893): 129.

21. Fowler, "Origin of Supreme Judicial Power," p. 173.

22. Hazletine, "Appeals from Colonial Courts," pp. 325-26.

23. Ibid., p. 326.

24. Ibid., emphasis mine.

25. Alexander Hamilton, Number 78, in Alexander Hamilton, James Madison, and John Jay, *The Federalist Papers* (New York: New American Library, 1961), p. 466.

26. Hazletine, "Appeals from Colonial Courts," p. 327.

27. Ibid. See also Haines, *American Doctrine,* p. 54.

28. Hazletine, "Appeals from Colonial Courts," p. 327.

29. Ibid., pp. 327-38.

30. *Frost v. Leighton,* Records of the Superior Court of Judicature of the Massachusetts Bay, 1738-39. See Andrew M. Davis, "The Case of *Frost v. Leighton,*" *American Historical Review* 2 (1897): 229. Also Haines, *American Doctrine,* pp. 56-57; Louis Boudin, *Government by Judiciary,* 2 vols. (New York: Godwin, 1932) vol. 1, pp. 526-30.

31. Davis, "*Frost v. Leighton,*" p. 238. See also *Campbell v. Hall,* Cowper 204 (1774). In this case, the Court of King's Bench, per Lord Mansfield, declared an action of the Privy Council void as contrary to a previous act—thereby ratifying the earlier decision of a colonial court in Grenada to refuse enforcement of the action. The opinion is reported in Thayer, *Cases,* vol. 1, pp. 40-47. See also Haines, *American Doctrine,* p. 57.

32. Boudin, *Government by Judiciary*, vol. 1, pp. 526–30. See this chapter, nn. 19–20 and accompanying text.

33. Davis, *"Frost v. Leighton,"* p. 239; Boudin, *Government by Judiciary*, vol. 1, pp. 529–30.

34. Haines, *American Doctrine*, pp. 56–59.

35. Boudin, *Government by Judiciary*, vol. 1, p. 526.

36. E.g., Sylvester Pennoyer, "The Power of the Supreme Court to Declare an Act of Congress Unconstitutional: The Case of *Marbury v. Madison*," *American Law Review* 30 (1896):188; and other articles referred to in chap. 11.

37. Boudin, *Government by Judiciary*, vol. 1, p. 530.

38. Haines, *American Doctrine*, pp. 58–59.

39. Davis, *"Frost v. Leighton,"* pp. 236–39; Boudin, *Government by Judiciary*, vol. 1, pp. 527–29.

40. See, e.g., the remarks of James Otis, Samuel Adams, John Adams, and Thomas Jefferson, quoted in Haines, pp. 59–63. Also Benjamin F. Wright, "Natural Law in American Political Theory," *Southwestern Political & Social Science Quarterly* 4 (1923):202; idem, "American Interpretations of Natural Law," *American Political Science Review* 20 (1926):524. Thayer, *Cases*, vol. 1, pp. 48–55.

41. Coxe, *An Essay*, pp. 216–69; Haines, *American Doctrine*, pp. 88–121. For accounts of two additional "cases" that some have thought precedential for judicial review, see William P. Trent, "The Case of Josiah Philips," *American Historical Review* 1 (1896):444; and A. C. Goodell, "An Early Constitutional Case in Massachusetts," *Harvard Law Review* 7 (1894):422. See also William M. Meigs, "The Relation of the Judiciary to the Constitution," *American Law Review* 19 (1885):178–83; and Charles B. Elliott, "The Legislatures and the Courts: The Power to Declare Statutes Unconstitutional," *Political Science Quarterly* 5 (1891):233–39.

42. Boudin, *Government by Judiciary*, vol. 1, pp. 531–63, 51–72; William Winslow Crosskey, *Politics and the Constitution in the History of the United States*, 2 vols. (Chicago: University of Chicago Press, 1953), vol. 2, pp. 939–75. See also Jesse Turner, "A Phantom Precedent," *American Law Review* 48 (1914):321; idem, "Four Fugitive Cases from the Realm of American Constitutional Law," *American Law Review* 49 (1915):828.

43. Austin Scott, *"Holmes v. Walton*: The New Jersey Precedent," *American Historical Review* 4 (1899):456. See also Haines, *American Doctrine*, pp. 92–95; Boudin, *Government by Judiciary*, vol. 1, p. 53; Alpheus Mason and Gerald Garvey, eds., *American Constitutional History: Essays by Edward S. Corwin* (New York: Harper & Row, 1964), p. 10; Charles Warren, *Congress, the Constitution, and the Supreme Court* (Boston: Little, Brown & Co., 1925), pp. 44–45. For a contemporary account of the authenticity of *Holmes v. Walton* and several other cases, see Leonard Levy, ed., *Judicial Review and the Supreme Court* (New York: Harper & Row, 1967), pp. 7–11. Unfortunately, Professor Levy seems too much disposed toward uncritical reliance on Boudin and Crosskey, both of whom take a negative view of the importance of these cases (albeit for entirely different reasons). Levy provides no explicit justification for such reliance.

44. Scott, *"Holmes v. Walton,"* p. 469. See also the biographical data provided in Winton U. Solberg, ed., *The Federal Convention and the Formation of the Union of the American States* (Indianapolis: Bobbs-Merrill, 1958), app. I.

45. Scott, *"Holmes v. Walton,"* pp. 464–69.

46. 4 Call (Va.)5 (1782). Reported in Thayer, *Cases*, vol. I, pp. 55–62. See also Haines, *American Doctrine*, pp. 95–98; Boudin, *Government by Judiciary*, vol. I, pp. 53–54, app. C; Crosskey, *Politics and the Constitution*, vol. 2, pp. 952–61; Meigs, "Relation of the Judiciary," pp. 178–79; Elliott, "Legislatures and Courts," pp. 235–38; Warren, *Congress, Constitution, and Court*, pp. 47–48; Levy, *Judicial Review*, p. 10.

47. Thayer, *Cases*, vol. I, pp. 59, 62. See also Elliott, "Legislatures and Courts," pp. 235–36; Meigs, "Relation of the Judiciary," p. 179; Coxe, *An Essay*, p. 221.

48. Boudin, *Government by Judiciary*, vol. I, p. 532.

49. Reported in Thayer, *Cases*, vol. I, pp. 63–72. See also Coxe, *An Essay*, pp. 223–33; Haines, *American Doctrine*, pp. 98–104; Boudin, *Government by Judiciary*, vol. I, pp. 55–58; Crosskey, *Politics and the Constitution*, vol. 2, pp. 962–65; Elliott, "Legislatures and Courts," pp. 237–38; Meigs, "Relation of the Judiciary," p. 180; Levy, *Judicial Review*, pp. 9–10; Mason and Garvey, *American Constitutional History*, pp. 17–20.

50. Thayer, *Cases*, vol. I, p. 63. See also Coxe, *An Essay*, pp. 223–27; Elliott, "Legislatures and Courts," p. 237.

51. *Murray v. Charming Betsey*, 2 Cranch 118 (1804).

52. *Case of Le Louis*, 2 Dodson's Admiralty Reports 239. See Coxe, *An Essay*, p. 180.

53. Meigs, "Relation of the Judiciary," p. 180.

54. Ibid.

55. Thayer, "Origin and Scope," p. 132, n. 2; Fowler, "Origin of Supreme Judicial Power," p. 722; Elliott, "Legislatures and Courts," p. 237.

56. Coxe, *An Essay*, p. 224; Boudin, *Government by Judiciary*, vol. I, p. 56.

57. Crosskey, *Politics and the Constitution*, vol. 2, p. 965.

58. Elliott, "Legislatures and Courts," p. 237.

59. Coxe, *An Essay*, p. 229; Thayer, *Cases*, pp. 68–69.

60. Elliott, "Legislatures and Courts," p. 237; Meigs, "Relation of the Judiciary," p. 180; Thayer, "Origin and Scope," p. 132, n. 2. But this is merely conjecture.

61. Thayer, *Cases*, vol. I, p. 69; Coxe, *An Essay*, p. 229.

62. Thayer, *Cases*, vol. I, pp. 69–70; Coxe, *An Essay*, p. 230.

63. Thayer, *Cases*, vol. I, p. 70; Coxe, *An Essay*, pp. 230–31.

64. Thayer, *Cases*, vol. I, p. 71; Coxe, *An Essay*, p. 231.

65. See chap. 2, nn. 14–15 and accompanying text.

66. Thayer, *Cases*, vol. I, p. 71; Coxe, *An Essay*, p. 228.

67. Thayer, *Cases*, vol. I, pp. 71–72; Coxe, *An Essay*, p. 228. On the possible importance of the *clausa de non obstante* to the subject under discussion, see Coxe, *An Essay*, pp. 233, 278–79. On its possible connection with Article VI of the Constitution, see ibid., pp. 268–69. On its ancient common-law and civil-law roots, see Henry Black, *Black's Law Dictionary*, 5th ed. (St. Paul: West Publishing Co., 1979), p. 952. Its relation to the United States Constitution will be taken up in the next chapter.

68. Of course, *Holmes v. Walton* could be so construed—but only abstractly, since there were no recorded opinions. *Commonwealth v. Caton*, on the other

hand, does not seem to have been a case of the judiciary type—a requirement for being considered precedential for "judicial review" contemplated by the Founders (see chap. 4).

69. Reported in Thayer, *Cases*, vol. 1, pp. 73–78. See also Coxe, *An Essay*, pp. 234–48; Haines, *American Doctrine*, pp. 105–12; Boudin, *Government by Judiciary*, vol. 1, pp. 58–62; Crosskey, *Politics and the Constitution* vol. 2, pp. 965–68; Warren, *Congress, Constitution, and Court*, p. 44; Mason and Garvey, *American Constitutional History*, pp. 11–15; Meigs, "Relation of the Judiciary," pp. 180–81, Levy, *Judicial Review*, p. 9.

70. Thayer, *Cases*, vol. 1, pp. 74–75; Coxe, *An Essay*, pp. 234–35.

71. Thayer, *Cases*, vol. 1, p. 74; Coxe, *An Essay*, pp. 234–35 (emphasis mine).

72. Thayer, *Cases*, vol. 1, pp. 73–74; Coxe, *An Essay*, p. 245.

73. Thayer, *Cases*, vol. 1, pp. 73–74; Coxe, *An Essay*, pp. 245–46.

74. Thayer, *Cases*, vol. 1, pp. 73–74; Coxe, *An Essay*, p. 245.

75. Thayer, *Cases*, vol. 1, p. 74; Coxe, *An Essay*, p. 246.

76. Thayer, *Cases*, vol. 1, p. 77; Coxe, *An Essay*, p. 246.

77. Thayer, *Cases*, vol. 1, p. 76; Coxe, *An Essay*, p. 246.

78. Thayer, *Cases*, vol. 1, p. 76 (emphasis mine).

79. James M. Varnum, *The Case of Trevett v. Weeden* (Providence: John Carter, 1787). See Coxe, *An Essay*, pp. 235–45.

80. Coxe, *An Essay*, p. 241 (emphasis mine).

81. United States Constitution, Article III, Section 2.

82. Hamilton, *Federalist* Number 78, p. 464–72.

83. See George L. Haskins, "Law versus Politics in the Early Years of the Marshall Court," *Pennsylvania Law Review* 130 (November 1981) 9–10; also William E. Nelson, "The Eighteenth-Century Background of John Marshall's Constitutional Jurisprudence," *Michigan Law Review* 76 (May 1978): 935–36.

84. 1 Mart. (N.C.) 42 (1787). Thayer, *Cases*, vol. 1, pp. 78–80; Coxe, *An Essay*, pp. 248–67; Haines, *American Doctrine*, pp. 112–20; Boudin, *Government by Judiciary*, vol. 1, pp. 63–67; Crosskey, *Politics and the Constitution*, vol. 2, pp. 971–74; Warren, *Congress, Constitution, and Court*, pp. 45–46; Levy, *Judicial Review*, p. 10; Meigs, "Relation of the Judiciary," pp. 181–82; Elliott, "Legislatures and Courts," p. 238.

85. Thayer, *Cases*, vol. 1, pp. 79–80; Coxe, *An Essay*, pp. 250–51.

86. Thayer, *Cases*, vol. 1, p. 80; Coxe, *An Essay*, p. 251.

87. Ibid., emphasis mine.

88. Crosskey, *Politics and the Constitution*, vol. 2, pp. 968–71; Warren, *Congress, Constitution, and Court*, p. 46; Levy, *Judicial Review*, p. 10.

89. Crosskey, *Politics and the Constitution*, vol. 2, pp. 970–71; Warren, *Congress, Constitution, and Court*, pp. 46–47, n. 2.

90. Crosskey, *Politics and the Constitution*, vol. 2, p. 969.

91. United States Constitution, Article III, Section. 2, Clause 3.

92. Nelson, "Eighteenth-Century Background," p. 902.

93. On the importance of separation doctrine in early American law, see Wallace Mendelson, "A Missing Link in the Evolution of Due Process," *Vanderbilt Law Review* 10 (1956): 125–27.

*Chapter 4. The Federal Convention*

1. Massachusetts Constitution of 1780, Part 1, Article 30. According to Randall H. Nelson, the separation doctrine "was formally declared to be the guiding principle of six of the new state constitutions." Nelson, "Separation of Powers: An Historical Review from *Marbury* to *Bowsher*," *Illinois Bar Journal* 75 (1987): 484.

2. James Bradley Thayer, "The Origin and Scope of the American Doctrine of Constitutional Law," *Harvard Law Review* 7 (October, 1893): 134.

3. Winton U. Solberg, ed., *The Federal Convention and the Formation of the Union of the American States* (Indianapolis: Bobbs-Merrill, 1958), p. 78.

4. See William Trickett, "Judicial Nullification of Acts of Congress," *North American Review* 185 (1907): 849; Walter Clark, "The Next Constitutional Convention of the United States," *Yale Law Journal* 16 (December 1906): 75; Edward S. Corwin, "The Supreme Court and Unconstitutional Acts of Congress," *Michigan Law Review* 4 (1906): 619–20; Sylvester Pennoyer, "A Reply to the Foregoing," *American Law Review* 29 (1895): 857–58; also William Winslow Crosskey, *Politics and the Constitution in the History of the United States*, 2 vols. (Chicago: University of Chicago Press, 1953), vol. 2, p. 979; Louis B. Boudin, *Government by Judiciary*, 2 vols. (New York: Godwin, 1932), vol. 1, pp. 102–4.

5. Solberg, *Federal Convention*, p. 97.

6. Ibid., p. 98.

7. Ibid., p. 101.

8. Ibid., pp. 78–79.

9. Ibid.

10. Ibid., p. 111–12.

11. Ibid, p. 235 (emphasis mine).

12. Ibid., emphasis mine.

13. Ibid., p. 236.

14. Ibid., p. 237 (emphasis mine).

15. Ibid., p. 238. On precedents for the council in New York, Pennsylvania, and Vermont, see Thayer, "Origin and Scope," p. 137.

16. Ibid., pp. 238–39 (emphasis mine).

17. Ibid., pp. 240–41.

18. Max Farrand, ed., *Records of the Federal Convention*, 4 vols. (New Haven, Conn.: Yale University Press, 1911), vol. 2, p. 430. See also Benjamin F. Wright, *The Growth of American Constitutional Law* (Boston: Houghton Mifflin Co., 1942; Chicago: University of Chicago Press, Phoenix Books, 1967), pp. 18–19, nn. 24.

19. Directly in *Rutgers v. Waddington* (see chap. 3, n. 49–52 and accompanying text); indirectly in *Holmes v. Walton* (see chap. 3, n. 43–45 and accompanying text).

20. See Edward S. Corwin, "The Progress of Constitutional Theory between the Declaration of Independence and the Meeting of the Philadelphia Convention," *American Historical Review* 30 (1925):511; also Brinton Coxe, *An Essay on Judicial Power and Unconstitutional Legislation* (Philadelphia: Kay & Brother, 1893), pp. 274–90.

21. 12 *Journals of Congress* 23 (ed. 1801); James Bradley Thayer, *Cases on Constitutional Law*, 2 vols. (Cambridge, Mass.: George H. Kent, 1895), vol. 1, p. 81; Coxe, *An Essay*, pp. 387, 392 (emphasis mine).

22. 7 *Journals of Congress* 32–6 (ed. 1801); Thayer, *Cases*, vol. 1, p. 83; Coxe, *An Essay*, pp. 393–94.

23. See this chapter, n. 19 and accompanying text.

24. William Blackstone, *Commentaries on the Laws of England*, 4 vols. (Chicago: University of Chicago Press, 1979; facsimile of 1769 edition), vol. 4, p. 67; Coxe, *An Essay*, p. 284.

25. The twentieth-century fuss over the inverted form of this principle—that *questions not susceptible to judicial settlement must be resolved via the regular political process*, an aspect of the doctrine of political questions—has obscured the view of the Framers' generation. The problem was presented to them in the form given by Blackstone, the Mayor's Court of New York, and the Continental Congress, all of whom were trying to carve out an appropriate sphere of judicial authority that would resolve peacefully those disagreements that might otherwise have to be resolved by resort to arms. Since the Founders worked in the aftermath of an era of parliamentary supremacy in England and legislative supremacy in America, one of their major concerns was developing institutional protections for individuals against potential legislative abuses. The modern, inverted form of the principle under discussion could only have arisen in an era of judicial, not legislative, activism. For a clear statement of the modern idea, see the dissenting opinion of Justice Frankfurter (concurred in by Justice Harlan) in *Baker v. Carr*, 369 U.S. 186 (1962). See also *Colegrove v. Green*, 328 U.S. 549 (1946).

26. "A later statute takes away the effect of a prior one." Henry Black, *Black's Law Dictionary*, 5th ed.(St. Paul: West Publishing Co., 1979) p. 822. "But the later statute must either expressly repeal, or be manifestly repugnant to, the earlier one."

27. Solberg, *Federal Convention*, p. 253. I cannot resist the temptation to illustrate the length to which at least one twentieth-century opponent of judicial review has gone to prove his case. Mr. Boudin, using the Seventh Resolution to support his view that the Founders could not have intended the courts to decide constitutional questions, quotes the resolution in the following manner: "That the legislative Acts of the United States . . . shall be the supreme law of the respective states . . . and that judiciaries of the several states shall be bound thereby in their decisions, anything in the respective laws of the individual states to the contrary notwithstanding." Boudin, *Government by Judiciary*, vol. 1, p. 123. Boudin then continues: "It will be noted that the 'Constitution,' upon the presence of which in this paragraph the Judicial Power is based, was entirely omitted from this resolution. The Legislative Acts of the United States, and not the Constitution, were to be the 'Supreme Law' whereby 'the judiciaries of the several states shall be bound.' " I leave it to the reader to draw the appropriate conclusion.

28. United States Constitution, Article VI, Clause 2.

29. Solberg, *Federal Convention*, pp. 77–78.

30. *Black's Law Dictionary*, p. 952 (emphasis mine).

31. Ibid., emphasis mine.

32. See n. 28 and accompanying text.

33. United States Constitution, Article III, Section 2.

34. See, e.g., Boudin, *Government by Judiciary*, vol. 1, p. 98; Crosskey, *Politics and the Constitution*, vol. 2, p. 983.

35. 1 Stat. 20, 73–93 (1789).

36. Ibid., at 85–86 (emphasis mine). See also Charles Grove Haines, *The American Doctrine of Judicial Supremacy* (Berkeley and Los Angeles: University of California Press, 1932), pp. 144–47.

37. Wright, *Growth*, pp. 27–28.

38. See, for example, Robert G. McCloskey, *The American Supreme Court* (Chicago: University of Chicago Press, 1960), p. 9; Haines, *American Doctrine*, pp. 135–43; Boudin, *Government By Judiciary*, vol. 1, chap. 7, esp. pp. 97–98.

39. 2 Elliot's Debates 248, quoted in Charles B. Elliott, "The Legislatures and the Courts: The Power to Declare Statutes Unconstitutional" *Political Science Quarterly* 5 (1891): 240–41.

40. Charles Warren, *Congress, the Constitution, and the Supreme Court* (Boston: Little, Brown & Co., 1925), p. 68.

41. Haines, *American Doctrine*, pp. 140–41.

42. Wright, *Growth*, pp. 20–21.

43. 4 Elliot's Debates 393, 403, quoted in Haines, *American Doctrine*, p. 141, n. 51.

44. Warren, *Congress, Constitution, and Court*, p. 79, n. 2. For a general review of remarks in the state conventions and in contemporaneous newspapers, see ibid., chaps. 2 and 3.

45. 3 Elliot's Debates 324–25, 539–41, quoted in Haines, *American Doctrine*, p. 143; Warren, *Congress, Constitution, and Court*, p. 69; Wright, *Growth*, p. 21, n. 36.

46. Wright, *Growth*, p. 21.

47. See generally Herbert J. Storing, ed., *The Complete Anti-Federalist*, 7 vols. (Chicago: University of Chicago Press, 1981). For remarks in the Pennsylvania Convention, see vol. 3, pp. 152, 156–7, 159–61; for Massachusetts, see vol. 4, pp. 55–62, esp. 61; for New Hampshire, see vol. 4, pp. 243–4, 275–80; for Maryland, see vol. 5, pp. 83–85; for Virginia, see vol. 5, pp. 221–24, 301–4; for New York, see vol. 6, pp. 183–84.

48. E.g., Boudin, *Government by Judiciary*, vol. 1, pp. 94, 101–2, 726; John W. Akin, "Aggressions of the Federal Courts," *American Law Review* 32 (1898): 694–700; Sylvester Pennoyer, "The Power of the Supreme Court to Declare an Act of Congress Unconstitutional: The Case of *Marbury v. Madison,*" *American Law Review* 30 (1896): 192–93, 200–201; Donald O. Dewey, *Marshall versus Jefferson: The Political Background of Marbury v. Madison* (New York: Alfred A. Knopf, 1970), pp. 133, 142–44, 179.

49. Quoted in Haines, *American Doctrine*, p. 143 (emphasis mine). See also Wallace Mendelson, "Jefferson on Judicial Review: Consistency through Change," *University of Chicago Law Review* 29 (1962): 328–29. This article contains the most relevant comments by Jefferson on judicial review at different periods throughout his life.

50. See Haines, *American Doctrine*, pp. 140–43; Warren, *Congress, Constitution, and Court*, pp. 52–94; Wright, *Growth*, pp. 20–23.

51. See generally Warren, *Congress, Constitution, and Court*, pp. 95-127; Haines, *American Doctrine*, pp. 171-203.

52. These letters first appeared in the *New York Journal* in the winter and spring of 1787-88. The relevant numbers are reprinted in Cecelia Kenyon, ed., *The Antifederalists* (Indianapolis: Bobbs-Merrill, 1966) pp. 334-57. Though most historians appear to believe that Robert Yates was Brutus, some controversy exists. See Ann Stuart Diamond, "The Anti-Federalist 'Brutus,' " *Political Science Reviewer* 6 (1976): 252; Herbert J. Storing, *The Anti-Federalist* (Chicago: University of Chicago Press, 1985), p. 103.

53. See generally Storing, *Complete Anti-Federalist*; also Wright, *Growth*, pp. 20-23.

54. *Federalist*, pp. 464-72, 481-91. See also Wright, *Growth*, pp. 23-26.

55. Kenyon, *The Antifederalists*, p. 339.

56. Ibid., p. 353.

57. Ibid., p. 351.

58. Ibid.

59. *Federalist*, p. 467.

60. Ibid., p. 468-69 (emphasis mine).

61. Ibid., p. 466.

62. Ibid., p. 484 (emphasis mine).

63. Ibid., pp. 484-85 (emphasis mine).

64. E.g., Boudin, *Government by Judiciary*, vol. 1, pp. 104-14; Wright, *Growth*, pp. 23-26.

65. *Black's Law Dictionary*, p. 755.

66. *Federalist*, p. 485.

67. E.g., Haines, *American Doctrine*, pp. 137-40; McCloskey, *American Supreme Court*, p. 9.

68. Haines, *American Doctrine*, p. 140; Wright, *Growth*, pp. 24-25, 37-38; Russell Kirk, *The Conservative Mind* (South Bend, Ind.: Gateway, 1953), pp. 96-98; Vernon L. Parrington, *Main Currents in American Thought*, 2 vols. (New York: Harcourt, Brace & Co., 1927), vol. 2, p. 23.

69. David P. Currie, "The Constitution in the Supreme Court: 1789-1801," *University of Chicago Law Review* 48 (1981): 882.

70. Richard E. Ellis, *The Jeffersonian Crisis: Courts and Politics in the Young Republic* (New York: Norton & Co., 1974) pp. 111-122. More generally, see ibid., pp. 111-229, for comments of Federalists and Antifederalists on the judicial authority in various states during the period. For remarks of Federalist and Antifederalist members of Congress during the 1790s, see Warren, *Congress, Constitution, and Court*, chap. 4.

71. Act of February 25, 1791, chap. 10 (1 Stat. 191). See remarks of William B. Giles, Republican from Virginia, who intimated that only "a dependent or corrupt Court" could prevent a declaration of unconstitutionality on the Bank Act. Quoted in Warren, *Congress, Constitution, and Court*, p. 106, n. 1. For the views of Thomas Jefferson, Edmund Randolph, James Madison, and the Republican press on the Bank Act, see Warren, *Congress, Constitution, and Court*, pp. 107-10. See also Leonard Levy, ed., *Judicial Review and the Supreme Court* (New York: Harper & Row, 1967), p. 11.

72. See remarks of Thomas Fitzsimmons and Nathaniel Niles, quoted in Warren, *Congress, Constitution, and Court*, p. III.

73. See remarks of William B. Giles, quoted in Warren, *Congress, Constitution, and Court*, p. 113. See also Levy, *Judicial Review*, p. 11.

74. See remarks of Robert Williams, Albert Gallatin, Edward Livingston, and Nathaniel Macon, quoted in Warren, *Congress, Constitution, and Court*, pp. 119-20.

75. See, e.g., quotes in Warren, *Congress, Constitution, and Court*, on the constitutionality of a bill to fix a seat of government (p. 105); on a resolution calling on the president for papers relating to the Jay Treaty (pp. 115-16); on a proposed stamp tax on lawyers (pp. 117-18).

76. Quoted in Warren, *Congress, Constitution, and Court*, p. 103. See also remarks of William Smith, Fisher Ames, John Laurance, Peter Sylvester (Federalists); and James Madison, Alexander White, Abraham Baldwin (Republicans)— quoted in ibid., pp. 100-103.

77. Ibid., pp. 99-101.

78. Ibid., p. 104. See also generally Edward S. Corwin, *The Doctrine of Judicial Review and Other Essays* (Princeton, N.J.: Princeton University Press, 1914).

79. Warren, *Congress, Constitution, and Court*, pp. 119-20.

80. Ibid., emphasis mine.

81. See Frank Maloy Anderson, "Contemporary Opinion of the Virginia and Kentucky Resolutions," *American Historical Review* 5 (1899):45. See also Levy, *Judicial Review*, p. 11; William M. Meigs, "The Relation of the Judiciary to the Constitution," *American Law Review* 19 (1885): 194-95.

82. Ibid., pp. 244-45.

83. See Warren, *Congress, Constitution, and Court*, pp. 105-13.

84. Ibid., p. III (emphasis mine).

85. Ibid., emphasis mine.

86. Ibid.

87. See *Hylton v. United States*, 3 Dall. 171 (1796), where the Supreme Court, amid explicit assertions of the power to invalidate unconstitutional laws, nonetheless upheld the federal tax on carriages against a challenge that the tax was "direct" and must therefore be "apportioned among the several States . . . according to their respective numbers." United States Constitution, Article I, Section 2, Clause 3; *Penhallow v. Doane's Adm's.*, 3 Dall. 54 (1795), where the Court affirmed a federal district court's award of damages for failure to respect a 1783 decision of the court of appeals. The appeals court had been established by Congress in 1780 to render judgments in capture cases, and the authority of Congress to empower such a tribunal to review state court decrees had been challenged as "unconstitutional." Currie, "Constitution in the Court," p. 875. In *Hollingsworth v. Virginia*, 3 Dall. 378 (1798), the Court rejected the argument that the congressional submission of the Eleventh Amendment was invalid because it had not been submitted to the president for approval. Ibid., p. 840; Haines, *American Doctrine*, p. 183. In *Wiscart v. D'Auchy*, 3 Dall. 321 (1796), the Court upheld the authority of Congress to make "exceptions" to its appellate jurisdiction. United States Constitution, Article III, Section 2, Clause 2. See also *Turner v. Bank of North America*, 4 Dall. 9 (1799), and *Mossman v. Higginson*,

4 Dall. 12 (1800), where the Court upheld a statute limiting the diversity jurisdiction of the circuit courts. According to Currie, in *Mossman*, the Court "for the first time expressly took liberties with a statute to avoid holding it unconstitutional." Currie, "Constitution in the Court," p. 851.

88.  See *Hayburn's Case*, 2 Dall. 409 (1792), where five Supreme Court Justices (Jay, Cushing, Wilson, Blair, Iredell) sitting on circuit refused to enforce an act of Congress that authorized the judges to perform administrative functions subject to review by the secretary of war and by Congress. Haines, *American Doctrine*, pp. 173–75; Currie, "Constitution in the Court," pp. 822–25; Meigs, "Relation of the Judiciary," p. 186. In *United States v. Yale Todd*, unreported at the time, the Supreme Court evidently held that payments awarded to pensioners under the statute disregarded in *Hayburn's Case* were invalid, if awarded by judges acting in an administrative capacity. Haines, *American Doctrine*, pp. 176–79. Meigs, "Relation of the Judiciary," p. 186, claims that *Todd* was the first case in which the Supreme Court invalidated an act of Congress. Currie, "Constitution in the Court," p. 827, holds to the contrary. Chief Justice Taney, speaking for the Court in *United States v. Ferreira*, 13 How. 40 (1851), summarized the judgments in *Hayburn* and *Todd*: "That the power proposed to be conferred on the Circuit Courts of the United States by the Act of 1792 was not judicial power within the meaning of the Constitution, and was therefore unconstitutional, and could not be lawfully exercised by the courts." 13 How. 40, at 52–53 (1851). Finally, in the *Correspondence of the Justices* (August 8, 1793), the Court refused to render an advisory opinion requested by the president and secretary of state, holding that such an opinion would be "extrajudicial" and thus violative of the "lines of separation drawn by the Constitution between the three departments of the government." Quoted in Currie, "Constitution in the Court," p. 829.

89.  See *Calder v. Bull*, 3 Dall. 386 (1798), where the Supreme Court, amid implicit assertions of the power to disregard unconstitutional laws, nevertheless upheld an act of Connecticut's legislature that had ordered a new trial in a probate dispute, against the claim that the act was *ex post facto*, contra Article I, Section 10. Haines, *American Doctrine*, pp. 183–88; Currie, "Constitution in the Court," pp. 866–75. See also *Cooper v. Telfair*, 4 Dall. 14 (1800), where the Court refused to set aside a Georgia statute on the ground of its alleged repugnancy to the state's constitution. Haines, *American Doctrine*, pp. 188–89; Currie, "Constitution in the Court," pp. 878–81. On the other hand, a state law was clearly invalidated on supremacy clause grounds in *Ware v. Hylton*, 3 Dall. 198 (1786), where the Supreme Court held that a Virginia statute contravened the 1783 Treaty of Peace with Great Britain. Haines, *American Doctrine*, pp. 181–83. Currie suggests that the "political questions" doctrine was first "hinted at" in this case, when the Court refused to decide whether a treaty had been broken. Currie, "Constitution in the Court," p. 865.

90.  The exception, of course, is *Chisholm v. Georgia*, 2 Dall. 419 (1793). Here the Supreme Court assumed original jurisdiction of an action brought by a citizen of South Carolina against the state of Georgia. The Court's decision on the jurisdictional question was subsequently reversed by the adoption of the Eleventh Amendment; and the amendment was given a broad reading in *Hollingsworth v. Virginia*, 3 Dall. 378 (1798), where the Court dismissed all pending suits filed

against states by citizens of other states—thereby giving retroactive application to the provision. See Currie, "Constitution in the Court," p. 840.

91. *Case of the Judges*, 4 Call (Va.) 135 (1788); *Turner v. Turner*, 4 Call (Va.) 234 (1792); *Page v. Pendleton*, Wythe's Reports 211 (1793); *Kamper v. Hawkins*, 1 Va. Cas. 21 (1793). Meigs, "Relation of the Judiciary," p. 179; Haines, *American Doctrine*, pp. 150-57.

92. *Ham v. McClaws*, 1 Bay (S.C.) 93 (1798); *Bowman v. Middleton*, 1 Bay (S.C.) 252 (1792). Meigs, "Relation of the Judiciary," p. 185; Haines, *American Doctrine*, pp. 148-49, 157-58.

93. *Austin v. Trustees of the Univ. of Pennsylvania*, 1 Yeates (Pa.) 260 (1793); *Respondent v. Ducquet*, 2 Yeates (Pa.) 493 (1799). Meigs, "Relation of the Judiciary," p. 185; Haines, *American Doctrine*, pp. 158-60.

94. *Stidger v. Rogers*, 2 Ky. (Sneed) 52 (1801); *Enderman v. Ashby*, 2 Ky. (Sneed) 53 (1801); *Caldwell v. The Commonwealth*, 2 Ky. (Sneed) 129 (1802). Haines, *American Doctrine*, pp. 160-61.

95. *Whittington v. Polk*, 1 H. & J. (Md.) 236. Meigs, "Relation of the Judiciary," p. 185; Haines, *American Doctrine*, pp. 161-62.

96. *Ogden v. Witherspoon*, 2 Hay. (N.C.) 227 (1802); *State v._____* , 1 Hay 28 (1794). Meigs, "Relation of the Judiciary," pp. 158-59.

97. *Kamper v. Hawkins*, 1 Va. Cas. 21 (1793); *Bowman v. Middleton*, 1 Bay (S.C.) 252 (1792); *Stidger v. Rogers*, 2 Ky. (Sneed) 52 (1801); *Enderman v. Ashby*, 2 Ky. (Sneed) 53 (1801); *Caldwell v. The Commonwealth*, 2 Ky. (Sneed) 129 (1802). Interestingly, of these five cases, two (*Kamper* and *Caldwell*) involved direct incursions of the legislature upon judicial duties, and three (*Bowman, Stidger, Enderman*) involved the right to trial by jury. Thus the pattern of judicial refusal to enforce legislation in these areas, which we have observed since the colonial period, is perpetuated here.

98. *Kamper v. Hawkins*, 1 Va. Cas. 21, at p. 38, quoted in Haines, *American Doctrine*, p. 154, and Warren, *Congress, Constitution, and Court*, p. 58. All the Virginia cases cited above evidently involved legislative attempts to impose additional duties on state judges. They are thus analogous to the early federal cases involving claims of invalid pensioners. See discussion of *Hayburn* and *Todd*, n. 88 above.

99. It has been said that Roane would have been chief justice of the United States had Jefferson had the opportunity to make the appointment. Boudin, *Government by Judiciary*, vol. 2, p. 534; Haines, *American Doctrine*, p. 154. Twentieth-century commentators on judicial review (both proponents and opponents) have suggested that such a change would have made a difference. Haines, for example, says that "had the government in 1789 been placed in charge of the radicals, such as Patrick Henry, Thomas Jefferson, and Samuel Adams, a different procedure might have been engrafted on our federal law." Haines, *American Doctrine*, pp. 142-43. This is doubtful. We have already examined the views of Jefferson and Henry on the judicial power. A perusal of the seriatim opinions in *Kamper* clearly shows that the most ardently Republican court in the land—Virginia's Court of Appeals—nevertheless solemnly agreed with the concept of judicial power set forth by Hamilton in the *Federalist*. See 1 Va. Cas. 21, pp. 23-32 (opinion of Judge Nelson), pp. 47-66 (opinion of Judge Henry), pp. 77-88

(opinion of Judge Tucker). See generally Haines, *American Doctrine*, pp. 152–57.

## Chapter 5. *The Case of* Marbury v. Madison

1. 1 Cranch 137 (1803). On the oral arguments, see Donald O. Dewey, *Marshall versus Jefferson: The Political Background of Marbury v. Madison* (New York: Alfred A. Knopf, 1970).

2. The full quotation reads: "The judiciary of the United States is the subtle corps of sappers and miners constantly working under ground to undermine the foundations of our confederated fabric. They are construing our constitution from a co-ordination of a general and special government to a general and supreme one alone. This will lay all things at their feet, and they are too well versed in English law to forget the maxim, 'boni judicis est ampliare juris dictionem!' " Letter to Thomas Ritchie, December 25, 1820, quoted in Dumas Malone, *Jefferson and His Time*, 6 vols. (Boston: Little, Brown & Co., 1962), vol. 6, p. 356. It is interesting to note that Jefferson, as late as 1820, refers to the American Republic as a "confederated fabric." Spencer Roane and John Taylor did likewise in their published responses to the Supreme Court's decision in *McCulloch v. Maryland*. For Roane's remarks, see Gerald Gunther, ed., *John Marshall's Defense of McCulloch v. Maryland* (Stanford, Calif.: Stanford University Press, 1969), pp. 106–54. For Taylor's, see John Taylor, *Construction Construed and Constitutions Vindicated* (Richmond, Va.: Shepherd & Pollard, 1820), pp. 79–201.

3. Malone, *Jefferson*, vol. 3, p. 424.

4. Richard E. Ellis, *The Jeffersonian Crisis: Courts and Politics in the Young Republic* (New York: Norton & Co., 1974), pp. 19–52; George Haskins and Herbert Johnson, *Foundations of Power: John Marshall, 1801–1815* (New York: Macmillan, 1981), pp. 136–82; Malone, *Jefferson*, vol. 4, pp. 110–36.

5. Malone, *Jefferson*, vol. 3, pp. 380–94, 459–83.

6. Ellis, *Jeffersonian Crisis*, pp. 36–52; Haskins and Johnson, *Foundations of Power*, pp. 163–81.

7. John Pickering, judge of the federal district court of New Hampshire, on February 4, 1803. See Ellis, *Jeffersonian Crisis*, pp. 69–82, esp. 71.

8. Ibid., pp. 53–68, esp. 57–60.

9. Ellis, *Jeffersonian Crisis*, p. 16.

10. Ibid., pp. 3–16; Haskins and Johnson, *Foundations of Power*, pp. 647–51. On the Judiciary Act of 1801, see Ellis, *Jeffersonian Crisis*, p. 15. See also Kathryn Turner, "Federalist Policy and the Judiciary Act of 1801," *William & Mary Quarterly* 22 (January 1965): 15–22; Erwin C. Surrency, "The Judiciary Act of 1801," *American Journal of Legal History* 2 (1958): 53–65; Max Farrand, "The Judiciary Act of 1801," *American Historical Review* 5 (1899–1900): 682–86; Haskins and Johnson, *Foundations of Power*, pp. 183–86.

11. Ellis, *Jeffersonian Crisis*, p. 43.

12. Ibid., pp. 183–86.

13. Ibid., pp. 59–60.

14. Haskins and Johnson, *Foundations of Power*, p. 184.

15. *Marbury v. Madison*, 1 Cranch 137, 138–39 (1803). On Monday, January 31, 1803, the Senate had taken up the following motion: "That the Secretary of the Senate be directed to give an attested copy of the proceedings of the Senate of the 2d and 3d of March, 1801, so far as they relate to the nomination and appointment of William Marbury, Robert T. Hooe, and Dennis Ramsay, as justices of the peace for the counties of Washington and Alexandria, in the Territory of Columbia, on the application of them or either of them." After a lengthy debate, in which proponents of the motion advanced the simple justice and reasonableness of the application, and opponents urged primarily the need for secrecy and privacy in Senate proceedings and expressed fears that the motion constituted a veiled attack upon the executive branch, the motion was defeated by a vote of 15 to 13. See *The Debates and Proceedings of the Congress of the United States (1803)* (Washington, D.C.: Gales & Seaton, 1851), pp. 34–50.

16. 1 Cranch 137, 142–43.

17. Ibid., at 143–45.

18. Ibid., at 139–42, 144.

19. Ibid., at 139–40.

20. Ibid., at 140–41.

21. Judiciary Act of 1789, 1 Stat. 73, 80–81 (1789).

22. Ibid., at 81. Quoted in 1 Cranch 137, at 148 (emphasis mine)

23. 1 Cranch 137, at 148.

24. 2 Dall. 297 (1793).

25. Ibid., at 297–98.

26. 1 Cranch 137, at 148–49.

27. Ibid., at 146.

28. Ibid., at 153.

29. Ibid., at 153–54.

30. William Blackstone, *Commentaries on the Laws of England*, 4 vols. (Chicago: University of Chicago Press, 1979; facsimile of 1769 edition), vol. 3, p. 110. Quoted in 1 Cranch 137, at 147 (emphasis mine).

31. 1 Cranch 137, at 149–50.

32. Ibid., at 151–53 (emphasis mine).

33. Ibid., at 154–73.

34. Ibid., at 159–62, 167–68.

35. Ibid., at 162–68.

36. Ibid., at 168–73.

37. Ibid., at 173–80.

38. United States Constitution, Article III, Section 2, Clause 2.

39. 1 Cranch 137, at 141.

40. Ibid., at 148.

41. William Van Alstyne, "A Critical Guide to *Marbury v. Madison*," *Duke Law Journal* 1 (1969):15.

42. Lief Carter, "Think Things, Not Words," *Journal of Politics* 43 (May 1981): 317–18.

43. Van Alstyne, "Critical Guide," p. 15.

44. Thomas Jefferson, Letter to Justice Johnson, June 12, 1823, quoted in Dewey, *Marshall versus Jefferson*, p. 145.

45. See *Ashwander v. Tennessee Valley Authority*, 297 U.S. 288, 346-48 (1936) (Brandeis, J., concurring).

46. Van Alstyne, "Critical Guide," p. 15.

47. Ibid., p. 31. See also David P. Currie, "The Constitution in the Supreme Court: The Powers of the Federal Courts, 1801-1835," *University of Chicago Law Review* 49 (1982): 654; William Winslow Crosskey, *Politics and the Constitution in the History of the United States*, 2 vols. (Chicago: University of Chicago Press, 1953), vol. 2, p. 1041.

48. Currie, "Constitution in the Court," pp. 654-55.

49. E.g., Abraham Holtzman, *American Government: Ideals and Reality* (Englewood Cliffs, N.J.: Prentice-Hall, 1980), pp. 329-30: "Judicial review elevates the judicial branch to a position of supremacy over the action of the other two branches of the national government with regard to the Constitution. This power was asserted by the Supreme Court in deciding the case of *Marbury v. Madison* in 1803. The controversy that came to the Court in that case was a political one. The Court's assumption of this power of judicial review in resolving the controversy was equally political. . . . Thus, by a decision of the Supreme Court, the doctrine of judicial review was built into the constitutional system." Also Kenneth S. Sherrill and David J. Vogler, *Power, Policy, and Participation: An Introduction to American Government*, 2d ed. (New York: Harper & Row, 1982), p. 103: "The decision in *Marbury* says that the final judgement as to what the Constitution means rests not with the legislative or executive branches but with the Supreme Court." Such statements could be multiplied almost endlessly.

50. Quoted in Alexander M. Bickel, *The Least Dangerous Branch: The Supreme Court at the Bar of Politics* (Indianapolis: Bobbs-Merrill, 1962), p. 2.

51. Use of the writ of certiorari was first introduced in the Evarts Act of March 3, 1891 (26 Stat. 826), and was greatly expanded in the Judges' Bill of February 13, 1925 (43 Stat. 936). See Charles Alan Wright, *Handbook of the Law of Federal Courts* (St. Paul: West Publishing Co., 1963), pp. 5-6.

52. *Marbury v. Madison*, 1 Cranch 137, 170 (1803).

53. Ibid., at 166.

54. Ellis, *Jeffersonian Crisis*, pp. 19-52. Haskins and Johnson, *Foundations of Power*, pp. 136-82.

55. Ellis, *Jeffersonian Crisis*, pp. 53-82, esp. 57-60, 71.

56. *Marbury v. Madison*, 1 Cranch 137, 153-54 (1803).

57. See Max Farrand, ed., *Records of the Federal Convention*, 4 vols. (New Haven, Conn.: Yale University Press, 1911), vol. 2, p. 430. According to Farrand, the Founders accepted the extension of the federal judicial power to cases "arising under the Constitution, Laws, and Treaties of the United States" only after it had been "generally supposed that the jurisdiction given was constructively limited to cases of a Judiciary nature." Farrand, vol. 2, p. 430. According to B. F. Wright, "there is room to differ as to Madison's meaning of 'judiciary nature' here, but at least it would appear to represent a theory of judicial review which did not recognize the courts as the exclusive or final interpreters of all parts of the Constitution." Benjamin F. Wright, *The Growth of American Constitutional Law* (Boston: Houghton Mifflin, 1942; Chicago: University of Chicago Press, Phoenix Books, 1967), p. 18, n. 24. See also Jesse H. Choper, *Judicial Review and*

*and the National Political Process: A Functional Reconsideration of the Role of the Supreme Court* (Chicago: University of Chicago Press, 1980), p. 395.

58. 418 U.S. 683 (1974). Of course, there are some important differences between the two cases. For example, in *Nixon*, the president was directly involved as an unindicted co-conspirator in a criminal prosecution.

59. *Marbury v. Madison*, 1 Cranch 137, 167 (1803).

60. Ibid., at 156.

61. Ibid., at 159.

62. Ibid., at 158.

63. Ibid., at 166.

64. See e.g., Dewey, *Marshall versus Jefferson*, pp. 129-31. Also Albert Beveridge, *The Life of John Marshall*, 4 vols. (Boston: Houghton Mifflin, 1916), vol. 3, p. 132.

65. Blackstone, *Commentaries*, vol. 3, p. 255, quoted in *Marbury v. Madison*, at 1 Cranch 137, 165 (1803). A similar point was made by Senator Hillhouse, during the Senate debate on Marbury's motion for a copy of relevant portions of the Senate's Journal on January 31, 1803. After noting certain situations requiring Senate-executive cooperation (e.g., treaties), Hillhouse remarked: "In all these cases the President may be deceived; the Secretary of the Senate may by mistake or fraud certify . . the ratification of a treaty, when the fact is otherwise; and where, but to the journals of the Senate, can we resort to correct the error?" Quoted in *Debates and Proceedings of Congress (1803)*, p. 38. See this chapter, n. 15 and accompanying text.

66. *Marbury v. Madison*, 1 Cranch 137, 165-66 (1803).

67. Dewey, *Marshall versus Jefferson*, pp. 110-11.

68. Ibid., p. 111. See also Currie, "Constitution in the Court," p. 661.

69. Judiciary Act of 1789, Section 13. 1 Stat. 73, 81 (1789). The relevant provision authorized the Supreme Court to issue writs of mandamus to "persons holding office under the authority of the United States." The secretary of state is obviously such a person, and though mandamus is discussed immediately following mention of appellate jurisdiction, Section 13 is devoted *generally* to the Court's *original* jurisdiction. No doubt this is why Marbury came to the Supreme Court first.

70. 1 Stat. 73, at 81 (1789).

71. Van Alstyne, "Critical Guide," p. 15.

72. 1 Stat. 73, 85-86 (1789).

73. Ibid., at 80-81.

74. Haskins and Johnson, *Foundations of Power*, p. 199.

75. See *Fletcher v. Peck*, 6 Cranch 87 (1810); *Dartmouth College v. Woodward*, 4 Wheat. 518 (1819); *New Jersey v. Wilson*, 7 Cranch 164 (1812); *Green v. Biddle*, 8 Wheat. 1 (1823).

76. 1 Stat. 73, 81 (1789). Quoted in *Marbury v. Madison*, 1 Cranch 137, 173 (1803).

77. For a different interpretation, though supportive of Marshall's approach, see Christopher Wolfe, *The Rise of Modern Judicial Review: From Constitutional Interpretation to Judge-made Law* (New York: Basic Books, 1986), pp. 85-86.

78. *Marbury v. Madison*, 1 Cranch 137, at 170 (1803).

79. Ibid., at 173-74.

80. Ibid., at 158.

81. Ibid., at 173.
82. Ibid., at 170.
83. Ibid., at 171.
84. Ibid., at 160.
85. United States Constitution, Article III, Section 2. The judicial power "is expressly extended to all cases arising under the laws of the United States." 1 Cranch 137, at 173.
86. United States Constitution, Article III, Section 2.
87. Article III, Section 2, Clause 1 reads: "The judicial power shall extend to all cases, in law and equity, arising under this Constitution, the Laws of the United States, and treaties made, or which shall be made, under their authority;—to all cases affecting ambassadors, other public ministers and consuls;—to all cases of admiralty and maritime jurisdiction;—to controversies to which the United States shall be a party;—to controversies between two or more States;—between a State and citizens of another State;—between citizens of different States;—between citizens of the same State claiming lands under grants of different States, and between a State, or the citizens thereof, and foreign States citizens or subjects.
88. Van Alstyne, "Critical Guide, p. 31.
89. Currie, "Constitution in the Court," p. 654.
90. Crosskey, *Politics and the Constitution*, vol. 2, p. 1041.
91. Currie, "Constitution in the Court," p. 654.
92. *Marbury v. Madison*, 1 Cranch 137, 175 (1803).
93. Currie, "Constitution in the Court," pp. 654–55. See *Cohens v. Virginia*, 6 Wheat. 264, 394–403 (1821).
94. Currie, "Constitution in the Court," pp. 654–55. See Alexander Hamilton, James Madison, and John Jay, *The Federalist Papers* (New York: New American Library, 1961), p. 487.
95. *Federalist*, pp. 490–91.
96. *Cohens v. Virginia*, 6 Wheat. 264, 396–98 (1821).
97. *Marbury v. Madison*, 1 Cranch 137, 174 (1803).
98. Ibid.
99. *Cohens v. Virginia*, 6 Wheat. 264, 401–2 (1821).
100. *Marbury v. Madison*, 1 Cranch 137, 176–77 (1803).
101. Ibid., at *177.*
102. Ibid., at 177–78.
103. Ibid., at 177–79.
104. Ibid., at 179–80.
105. Ibid., at 170.
106. Ibid., at 178.

*Chapter 6. Judicial Review in the Marshall and Taney Periods*

1. See Donald O. Dewey, *Marshall versus Jefferson: The Political Background of Marbury v. Madison* (New York: Alfred A. Knopf, 1970), pp. 135–36; Charles Grove Haines, *The American Doctrine of Judicial Supremacy* (Berkeley and Los

Angeles: University of California Press, 1932), pp. 232–321; George Haskins and Herbert Johnson, *Foundations of Power: John Marshall 1801–1815*, vol. 2 of *Oliver Wendell Holmes Devise History of the Supreme Court of the United States* (New York: Macmillan, 1981), pp. 215–17; Robert G. McCloskey, *The American Supreme Court* (Chicago: University of Chicago Press, 1960), pp. 43–44; Charles Warren, *The Supreme Court in United States History*, 3 vols. (Boston: Little, Brown & Co. 1922), vol. 1, pp. 231–32.

2. See Dewey, *Marshall versus Jefferson*, p. 136; Albert J. Beveridge, *The Life of John Marshall*, 4 vols. (Boston: Houghton Mifflin, 1916), vol. 3, p. 153. But see Warren, *Supreme Court*, vol. 1, chap. 5, for evidence that substantial "interest" was generated by the mandamus holding.

3. Beveridge, *Life of Marshall*, vol. 3, p. 153.

4. Dewey, *Marshall versus Jefferson*, pp. 136–38; Warren, *Supreme Court*, vol. 1, pp. 245–48.

5. Dewey, *Marshall versus Jefferson*, p. 140; Warren, *Supreme Court*, vol. 1, pp. 232, 245; Beveridge, *Life of Marshall*, vol. 3, p. 109. See also Dumas Malone, *Jefferson and His Time*, 6 vols. (Boston: Little, Brown & Co., 1962), vol. 4, p. 147.

6. Dewey, *Marshall versus Jefferson*, chap. 9; Warren, *Supreme Court*, vol. 1, chap. 5; Malone, *Jefferson*, vol. 4, p. 151.

7. Dewey, *Marshall versus Jefferson*, p. 135.

8. Ibid., pp. 138–39. This passage was quoted in several other newspapers. See Warren, *Supreme Court*, vol. 1, p. 245, n. 2.

9. Haskins and Johnson, *Foundations of Power*, p. 217. The Court's opinion in *Stuart* is found in 1 Cranch, at 299 (1803).

10. 4 Dall. 14, at 18–20 (1800). The four justices are Washington, Chase, Paterson, and Cushing. The same point was conceded by counsel for both plaintiff and defendant in oral argument. 4 Dall. 14, at 16–17.

11. See, e.g., William Winslow Crosskey, *Politics and the Constitution in the History of the United States*, 2 vols. (Chicago: University of Chicago Press, 1953), vol. 2, p. 1042: "The Marbury decision was completely forced, both in its claim to a general right of judicial review against Congress, and in the actual interpretation of the Constitution which the Court, in the exercise of that unfounded right, announced." Even Beveridge states that "for perfectly calculated audacity, it [*Marbury*] has few parallels in judicial history." Beveridge, *Life of Marshall*, vol. 3, p. 132.

12. Alexander M. Bickel, *The Least Dangerous Branch: The Supreme Court at the Bar of Politics* (Indianapolis: Bobbs-Merrill, 1962), p. 1.

13. John Taylor, *Construction Construed and Constitutions Vindicated* (Richmond, Va.: Shepherd & Pollard, 1820).

14. 4 Wheat. 316 (1819). See Taylor, *Construction Construed*, pp. 79–201.

15. Taylor, *Construction Construed*, pp. 123–24 (emphasis mine). For earlier remarks of Taylor on federal judicial power, all consistent with the quoted statement, see Warren, *Supreme Court*, vol. 1, p. 256, n. 1. One of these statements helps to explain the lack of Republican response to the circuit court's decision in *U.S. v. More*, 3 Cranch 159 (1805), for Taylor considers precisely the question before the Court in that case, some eighteen months prior to the decision in *Marbury*: "The responsibility of the Judiciary cannot begin until Congress shall

perform their function. Then the question will occur whether the abolition of a Court abolishes the salary constitutionally. The responsibility falls on the Judiciary." Letter to Wilson A. Nicholas, September 5, 1801, quoted in Warren, *Supreme Court*, vol. 1, p. 235, n. 1. The *More* case "involved rights of the justices of the peace of Washington. The Act of February 26, 1801, which granted them certain fees, had been repealed by an act of May 23, 1802; and a defendant justice, on being indicted for receiving fees, contended that the repealing act was in violation of Section One of Article Three of the Constitution which prohibited the diminishing of compensation of Judges of the Supreme and Inferior Courts of the United States. The Circuit Court through Judges Cranch and Marshall (Chief Justice Kilty dissenting) held that 'a justice of the peace for Washington County in the District of Columbia is a judicial officer of the United States under the Constitution and that therefore the Act of Congress of May 23, 1802, so far as the same relates to the abolition of the fee of justices of the peace, is unconstitutional and void.' Although this decision was published in full in the Administration papers in Washington and elsewhere, the exercise of judicial power with respect to this Republican legislation evoked no criticism of any kind." Warren, *Supreme Court*, vol. 1, pp. 255–56. The Supreme Court dismissed the government's appeal on the ground that it did not have jurisdiction of the case, since the statutory authorization for "review of 'final judgments' of the District of Columbia court" extended jurisdiction to civil cases only. David P. Currie, "The Constitution in the Supreme Court: The Powers of the Federal Courts, 1801–1835," *University of Chicago Law Review* 49 (1982): 667.

16. Thomas Cooper, *Two Essays on the Foundation of Civil Government: On the Constitution of the United States* (Columbia, S.C.: D. & J. M. Faust, 1826), p. 52.

17. Benjamin L. Oliver, *The Rights of an American Citizen; with a Commentary on State Rights, and on the Constitution and Policy of the United States* (Freeport, N.Y.: Books for Libraries Press, 1832), p. 124.

18. Ibid.

19. Peter S. Du Ponceau, *A Brief View of the Constitution of the United States, Addressed to the Law Academy of Philadelphia* (Philadelphia: D. G. Dorsey, 1834), pp. 37–38.

20. Letter to Abigail Adams, September 11, 1804, quoted in Dewey, *Marshall versus Jefferson*, p. 142.

21. Dewey, *Marshall versus Jefferson*, p. 129.

22. Ibid., p. 142.

23. Letter to Hay, June 2, 1807, quoted in Dewey, *Marshall versus Jefferson*, p. 145. See also Warren, *Supreme Court*, vol. 1, p. 264, n. 4.

24. Dewey, *Marshall versus Jefferson*, p. 143.

25. Letter to Johnson, June 12, 1823, quoted in Dewey, *Marshall versus Jefferson*, p. 145. See also Warren, *Supreme Court*, vol. 1, pp. 244–45. For an insightful discussion of Jefferson's views on judicial review, see Wallace Mendelson, "Jefferson on Judicial Review: Consistency through Change," *University of Chicago Law Review* 29 (1962): 327.

26. 18 Va. 1, at 7 (1813). See also Currie, "Constitution in the Court," p. 681; Warren, *Supreme Court*, vol. 1, p. 447.

27. Quoted in Warren, *Supreme Court*, vol. i, p. 447.

28. The essay is reprinted in Gerald Gunther, ed., *John Marshall's Defense of McCulloch v. Maryland* (Stanford, Calif.: Stanford University Press, 1969), pp. 64-67.

29. Joseph Story, *Commentaries on the Constitution of the United States*, 4th ed., edited by Thomas M. Cooley, 2 vols. (Boston: Little, Brown & Co., 1873), vol. 2, p. 379.

30. Story, *Commentaries*, vol. i, pp. 255-56 (emphasis mine).

31. James Kent, *Commentaries on American Law*, 4 vols. (New York: O. Halstead, 1826), vol. i, p. 424.

32. Letter to Macon, April ii, 1803, quoted in Warren, *Supreme Court*, vol. i, p. 254. See also Dewey, *Marshall versus Jefferson*, p. 140. Letter to Steele, June ii, 1803, quoted in Warren, *Supreme Court*, vol. i, p. 254. See also Dewey, *Marshall versus Jefferson*, p. 140.

33. Warren, *Supreme Court*, vol. i, p. 252.

34. Ibid., p. 256.

35. Charles Grove Haines, *The Conflict over Judicial Powers in the United States to 1870* (New York: Columbia University Press, 1909), p. 64.

36. See Warren, *Supreme Court*, vol. i, pp. 266-67.

37. Ibid. Indeed, the attacks of some "unreconstructed" Federalists were directed likewise. See Warren on their response to the Embargo Act. Warren, *Supreme Court*, vol. i, p. 267, 316-65.

38. Spencer Roane, "Hampden" Essay 3, in the *Richmond Enquirer*, June 18, 1819, quoting from a speech of Sir Frances Seymour, in David Hume, *The History of England*, 6 vols. (1778; reprint, Indianapolis: Liberty Classics, 1983), vol. 5, p. 189. See also Gunther, *Marshall's Defense*, p. 125.

39. Thomas Hart Benton, *Examination of the Dred Scott Case* (New York: Appleton & Co., 1857).

40. *Dred Scott v. Sanford*, 19 How. 393 (1857).

41. Benjamin F. Wright, *The Growth of American Constitutional Law* (Boston: Houghton Mifflin, 1942; Chicago: University of Chicago Press, Phoenix Books, 1967), p. 77. Taney's opinion is "for the Court" in name only. No single rationale for the decision commanded support from a majority of the justices. Wright, *Growth*, p. 75.

42. Benton, *Examination*, p. 25.

43. John C. Calhoun, *A Disquisition on Government* (Columbia, S.C.: A. S. Johnston, 1851), p. 259.

44. Ibid. See also Abel P. Upshur, *A Brief Enquiry into the Nature and Character of Our Federal Government* (Petersburg, Va.: E. & J. Ruffin, 1840), pp. 76-85, where essentially the same points are made.

45. 1 Cranch, at 176 (1803), quoted in Theophilus Parsons, *The Constitution, Its Origin, Function, and Authority* (Boston: Little, Brown & Co., 1861), p. 10.

46. Parsons, *The Constitution*, pp. 26-27.

47. William Alexander Duer, *The Constitutional Jurisprudence of the United States* (New York: Burt Franklin, 1856), p. 139.

48. Ibid., p. 184.

49. Martin Van Buren, *Inquiry into the Origin and Course of Political Parties in the United States* (New York: Hurd & Houghton, 1867).

50. Ibid., chap. 6.

51. See this chapter, nn. 5–6 and accompanying text.

52. Van Buren, *Inquiry*, p. 289.

53. Ibid., p. 286. But see chap. 5.

54. See chap. 5, nn. 70–87 and accompanying text.

55. 1 Stat. 73, at 86 (1789).

56. Van Buren, *Inquiry*, p. 301.

57. Ibid., p. 275.

58. See chap. 4, nn. 35–38 and accompanying text.

59. See generally chap. 5.

60. J. Allen Smith, *The Spirit of American Government*, ed. Cushing Strout (1907; reprint, Cambridge, Mass.: Belknap Press of Harvard University Press, 1965), pp. 180–85. As we have seen, Calhoun also thought that Section 25 was unconstitutional. So, perhaps, had Jefferson. See Warren, *Supreme Court*, vol. 1, pp. 195–96.

61. Robert V. Remini, *Andrew Jackson and the Course of American Freedom, 1822–1832* (New York: Harper & Row, 1981), pp. 366–67.

62. 4 Wheat. 316 (1819).

63. Remini, *Jackson*, p. 367.

64. Ibid., pp. 367–68.

65. Ibid., pp. 369–70.

66. Quoted in ibid., p. 444, n. 63.

67. 19 How. 393 (1857).

68. Roy P. Basler, ed., *The Collected Works of Abraham Lincoln*, 9 vols. (New Brunswick, N.J.: Rutgers University Press, 1953), vol. 2, pp. 387–88, 398–410, 448–54, 461–69, 494–502, 504–21.

69. Ibid., p. 495.

70. Ibid., p. 516.

71. Ibid., p. 496.

72. Ibid., pp. 400–401.

73. Ibid., p. 401.

74. Remini, *Jackson*, p. 368.

75. Ibid. Remini applies this remark to Jackson only, but I think it may fairly be applied to Lincoln as well.

*Chapter 7. The Strange History of* Marbury *in the Supreme Court*

1. *Ex parte Bollman*, 4 Cranch 75, 100 (1807); *idem*, at 102–5 (Johnson, J., dissenting); *McClung v. Silliman I*, 2 Wheat. 369, 370–71 (1817); *Cohens v. Virginia*, 6 Wheat. 264, 394, 399–402 (1821); *McClung v. Silliman II*, 6 Wheat. 598, 604 (1821); *United States v. Ortega*, 11 Wheat. 468, 471 (1826); *Ex parte Crane*, 30 U.S. 190, 200, 202–4, 206, 208–10, 217, 219 (1831) (Baldwin, J., dissenting); *Ex parte Watkins*, 32 U.S. 568, 572–73 (1833); *Harrison v. Nixon*, 34 U.S. 483, 510 (1835) (Baldwin, J., dissenting).

2. *United States v. Arredondo*, 31 U.S. 691, 729–30 (1832).

3. David P. Currie, "The Constitution in the Supreme Court: The Powers of the Federal Courts, 1801–1835," *University of Chicago Law Review* 49 (1982): 651.

4. Ibid., p. 680.

5. *Hepburn v. Ellzey*, 2 Cranch 445 (1805); *Strawbridge v. Curtiss*, 3 Cranch 267 (1806); *Bank of United States v. Deveaux*, 5 Cranch 61 (1809); *Hodgson v. Bowerbank*, 5 Cranch 303 (1809).

6. *Marbury v. Madison*, 1 Cranch 137 (1803); *United States v. More*, 3 Cranch 159 (1805); *Ex parte Bollman*, 4 Cranch 75 (1807).

7. *Stuart v. Laird*, 1 Cranch 299 (1803); *Owings v. Norwood's Lessee*, 5 Cranch 344 (1809); *United States v. Peters*, 5 Cranch 115 (1809).

8. *Marbury* (Congress may not extend original jurisdiction of Court beyond terms of Article III); *Stuart*, (Congress has power to abolish, as well as to create, inferior federal courts); *More* (Supreme Court's power to review decisions of courts in the District of Columbia does not extend to criminal cases—i.e., Congress has power to restrict the Court's appellate jurisdiction); *Hepburn* (appellate jurisdiction of Court does not extend to suits between a citizen of the state where the suit is brought and a citizen of the District of Columbia—i.e., the District of Columbia is not a state for diversity jurisdiction purposes); *Strawbridge* (diversity jurisdiction does not extend to situations where all plaintiffs are not diverse from all defendants—i.e., complete diversity is required); *Deveaux* (diversity jurisdiction does not extend to corporations, except in the event that no member of a plaintiff corporation is a co-citizen of the defendant); *Hodgson* (diversity jurisdiction does not extend to suits in which an alien is a party, if such alien's citizenship is not averred); *Owings* (Congress may not extend the general jurisdiction of the Court beyond that provided in Article III).

9. George Haskins and Herbert Johnson, *Foundations of Power: John Marshall, 1801–1815*, vol. 2 of *Oliver Wendell Holmes Devise History of the Supreme Court of the United States* (New York: Macmillan, 1981), p. 399, n. 24.

10. See, for example, *Houston v. Moore*, 5 Wheat. 1 (1820), where the Court held that jurisdiction to enforce federal law was concurrent, unless Congress had provided that it be exclusive in a specific area; *The Thomas Jefferson*, 10 Wheat. 428 (1825), where the Court held that the admiralty jurisdiction extended only to "the sea, or upon waters within the ebb and flow of the tide." But see Currie, "Constitution in the Court," pp. 710–13, for some additional and perhaps contrary considerations. See also *American Insurance Co. v. Canter*, 26 U.S. 511 (1828), where the Court held that the admiralty jurisdiction could be exercised by territorial courts, as well as by Article III courts. This decision could be read as having expanded the admiralty jurisdiction in one sense, while narrowing it in another. See also *Cherokee Nation v. Georgia*, 30 U.S. 1 (1831), where the Court held that an Indian tribe was not a foreign state within the meaning of the Article III provision extending the judicial power to controversies between a state and foreign states.

11. See, for example, *Martin v. Hunter's Lessee*, 1 Wheat. 304 (1816); *Cohens v. Virginia*, 6 Wheat. 264 (1821); *Osborn v. Bank of the United States*, 9 Wheat. 738 (1824).

12. See, for example, *McCulloch v. Maryland*, 4 Wheat. 316 (1819); *Gibbons v. Ogden*, 9 Wheat. 1 (1824); *United States v. Fisher*, 2 Cranch 358 (1805); *The*

*Flying Fish,* 2 Cranch 170 (1804). See Currie, "Constitution in the Court," p. 680, n. 222.

13. See, for example, *Wilson v. Blackbird Creek Marsh Co.,* 2 Pet. 245 (1829); *Barron v. Baltimore,* 7 Pet. 243 (1833); *Providence Bank v. Billings,* 4 Pet. 514 (1830).

14. See, for example, *Fletcher v. Peck,* 6 Cranch 87 (1810); *Dartmouth College v. Woodward,* 4 Wheat. 518 (1819); *Sturges v. Crowninshield,* 4 Wheat. 122 (1819).

15. *Ex parte Whitney,* 38 U.S. 404, 407 (1839); *In re Metzger,* 46 U.S. 176, 191 (1847); *United States v. Chicago,* 48 U.S. 185, 197 (1849) (Catron, J., dissenting); *In re Kaine,* 55 U.S. 103, 119 (1852); *Florida v. Georgia,* 58 U.S. 496, 505 (1854) (Curtis, J., dissenting); *Ex parte Wells,* 59 U.S. 316, 317 (1855) (McLean, J., dissenting); *Ex parte Vallandigham,* 68 U.S. 243, 252 (1863); *Daniels v. R.R. Co.,* 70 U.S. 250, 254 (1865).

16. *Kendall v. United States,* 37 U.S. 527, 617–18 (1838); *idem,* at 651 (Barbour, J., dissenting); *idem,* 38 U.S., at 609–12 (Catron, J., dissenting); *Decatur v. Paulding,* 39 U.S. 497, 513 (1840); *idem,* at 602 (Baldwin, J., dissenting); *Reeside v. Walker,* 52 U.S. 272, 291–92 (1850).

17. *Carroll v. Carroll,* 57 U.S. 275, 287 (1853): "It is a maxim not to be disregarded that general expressions in every opinion are to be taken in connection with the case in which these expressions are used. If they go beyond the case, they may be respected, but ought not to control the judgement in a subsequent suit, when the very point is presented. The reason of this maxim is obvious. The question actually before the court is investigated with care, and considered in its full extent; other principles which may serve to illustrate it are considered in their relation to the case decided, but their possible bearing on all other cases is seldom completely investigated." 6 Wheat., at 399, quoted in 57 U.S., at 287.

18. See generally Benjamin F. Wright, *The Growth of American Constitutional Law* (Boston: Houghton Mifflin, 1942; Chicago: University of Chicago Press, Phoenix Books, 1967), chap. 4; Robert G. McCloskey, *The American Supreme Court* (Chicago: University of Chicago Press, 1960), chap. 4.

19. McCloskey, *Supreme Court,* pp. 82–85.

20. Currie, "Constitution in the Court," p. 650.

21. *Rhode Island v. Massachusetts,* 12 Pet. 657 (1838).

22. *Louisville, etc. R.R. v. Letson,* 2 How. 497 (1844). This decision overruled the narrower conception of corporate citizenship (and thus federal diversity jurisdiction) established by the Marshall Court in *Deveaux* (see n. 5 above). See also Wright, *Growth,* p. 59; Currie, "Constitution in the Court," p. 675.

23. *Marshall v. Baltimore & O.R.R.,* 16 How. 314 (1854). See Currie, "Constitution in the Court," p. 650.

24. *The Propeller Genesee Chief v. Fitzhugh,* 12 How. 443 (1851). Wright claims that this decision overruled the Marshall Court's holding in *The Thomas Jefferson* (see n. 10 above), restricting federal admiralty jurisdiction to waters within the ebb and flow of the tide. However, he may be overstating its importance, in view of congressional intervention in the matter during the period between the two decisions. Wright, *Growth,* pp. 59–60. See also Currie, "Constitution in the Court," pp. 709–13.

25. *Steamboat New World v. King,* 16 How. 469 (1853).

26. *Swift v. Tyson,* 16 Pet. 1 (1842). This decision revoked a long-standing tradi-

tion that viewed the decisions of state courts, as well as state statutes, to be part of the law of a state, within the meaning of Section 34 of the Judiciary Act of 1789: "the laws of the several states, except where the constitution, treaties or statutes of the United States shall otherwise require or provide, shall be regarded as rules of decision in trials at common law in the courts of the United States in cases where they apply." 1 Stat., at 92. See Wright, *Growth*, pp. 60–61. *Swift* was later overruled on this point, in *Erie R.R. v. Tompkins*, 304 U.S. 64 (1938).

27. 1 Cranch, at 170: "Questions in their nature political . . . can never be made in this Court." See Wright, *Growth*, p. 59.

28. *Martin v. Mott*, 12 Wheat. 19 (1827); *Foster v. Neilson*, 2 Pet. 253 (1829).

29. 7 How. 1, 46–47 (1849). See Wright, *Growth*, p. 59. See also David M. Billikopf, *The Exercise of Judicial Power, 1789–1864* (New York: Vantage, 1973), pp. 67–68.

30. 19 How. 393, 450 (1857).

31. Wright says that, in *Dred Scott*, "Taney was making the first judicial assertion of a general supervisory jurisdiction over Congress." Wright, *Growth*, p. 77. However, Taney's opinion in the case, given the state of affairs at the time, can hardly be considered an opinion "for the Court." Ibid., p. 75. See also Walter Ehrlich, *They Have No Rights: Dred Scott's Struggle for Freedom* (Westport, Conn.: Greenwood Press, 1979), chap. 15.

32. *Pollock v. Farmers' Loan & Trust Co.* (The Income Tax Case), 158 U.S. 601 (1895); *United States v. E. C. Knight Co.* (The Sugar Trust Case), 156 U.S. 1 (1895). Many have thought that these decisions inaugurated the first major era of "judicial activism." See Arnold Paul, *Conservative Crisis and the Rule of Law: Attitudes of Bar and Bench, 1887–1895* (Ithaca, N.Y.: Cornell University Press, 1960), p. 219. See also Benjamin R. Twiss, *Lawyers and the Constitution: How Laissez-Faire Came to the Supreme Court* (Princeton, N.J.: Princeton University Press, 1942), esp. chap. 7.

33. *Gordon v. United States*, 2 Wall. 561 (1865); *Ex parte Garland*, 4 Wall. 333 (1867); *Reichart v. Phelps*, 6 Wall. 160 (1868); *The Alicia*, 7 Wall. 571 (1869); *Hepburn v. Griswold*, 8 Wall. 603 (1870); *United States v. De Witt*, 9 Wall. 41 (1870); *The Justices v. Murray*, 9 Wall. 274 (1870); *Collector v. Day*, 11 Wall. 113 (1871); *United States v. Klein*, 13 Wall. 128 (1872); *United States v. Railroad Co.*, 17 Wall. 322 (1873); *United States v. Reese*, 92 U.S. 214 (1876); *United States v. Fox*, 95 U.S. 670 (1878); *The Trade Mark Cases*, 100 U.S. 82 (1879); *United States v. Harris*, 106 U.S. 629 (1883); *The Civil Rights Cases*, 109 U.S. 3 (1883); *Boyd v. United States*, 116 U.S. 616 (1886); *Baldwin v. Franks*, 120 U.S. 678 (1887); *Callan v. Wilson*, 127 U.S. 540 (1888); *Counselman v. Hitchcock*, 142 U.S. 547 (1892); *Monongahela Navigation Co. v. United States*, 148 U.S. 312 (1893).

34. *The William Bagaley*, 72 U.S. 377, 412 (1866); *Riggs v. Johnson County*, 73 U.S. 166, 188 (1867); *Ex parte Virginia*, 100 U.S. 339, 341 (1879) (Clifford, J., dissenting); *Ex parte Clarke*, 100 U.S. 399, 408 (1879) (Field, J., dissenting); *Ames v. Kansas*, 111 U.S. 449, 466–67 (1883); *Bors v. Preston*, 111 U.S. 252, 258–59 (1883); *California v. Southern Pacific Co.*, 157 U.S. 229, 261 (1894).

35. *Mississippi v. Johnson*, 71 U.S. 475, 498 (1866); *Gaines v. Thompson*, 74 U.S. 347, 349 (1868); *Ex parte Yerger*, 75 U.S. 85, 97 (1868); *United States v. Schurz*, 102 U.S. 378, 394–95 (1880); *Louisiana v. Jumel*, 107 U.S. 711, 743–44 (1882); *Cunningham*

v. Macon & Brunswick R.R. Co., 109 U.S. 446, 453 (1883); United States v. Windom, 137 U.S. 636, 643 (1889); International Contracting Co. v. Lamont, 155 U.S. 303, 308 (1894).

36. Sabariego v. Maverick, 124 U.S. 261, 282 (1887); United States ex rel. Dunlap v. Black, 128 U.S. 40, 44–45 (1888); Noble v. Union River Logging R.R., 147 U.S. 165, 171 (1892); United States v. California & etc. Land Co., 148 U.S. 31, 43–44 (1892). See 1 Cranch, at 170–71 (1803).

37. Lapeyre v. United States, 84 U.S. 201, 205 (1872) (Hunt, J., dissenting); McAllister v. United States, 141 U.S. 188 (1890). See 1 Cranch, at 162.

38. Poindexter v. Greenhow, 114 U.S. 270, 298 (1884). See 1 Cranch, at 163.

39. Leisy v. Hardin, 135 U.S. 100, 135 (1889) (Gray, J., dissenting). See n. 17 above.

40. 123 U.S. 623, 661 (1887). See also Juilliard v. Greenman, 110 U.S. 421, 431 (1884), where plaintiff's counsel theorized that Marbury had held as judicial the question of whether Congress had transcended its constitutional power. The Court did not cite Marbury in its opinion.

41. 1 Cranch, at 176, quoted in 123 U.S., at 661.

42. See chap. 8, nn. 35–57 with accompanying text.

43. 123 U.S., at 661.

44. Ibid.

45. Edward S. Corwin, "The Supreme Court and the Fourteenth Amendment," in Alpheus Mason and Gerald Garvey, eds., American Constitutional History: Essays by Edward S. Corwin (Gloucester, Mass.: Peter Smith, 1970), pp. 88–89. See Lochner v. New York, 198 U.S. 45 (1905), where the Court invalidated the New York Bakeshop Act, a maximum-hour law, because it interfered with "liberty of contract," which the Court had recently discovered within the Fourteenth Amendment. See also Allgeyer v. Louisiana, 165 U.S. 578 (1897); chap. 12, n. 65–72 and accompanying text.

46. See this chapter, n. 33 and accompanying text.

47. Gordon, invalidating a statutory provision that had authorized (in essence) revision of judgments of the court of claims by the secretary of the treasury, on the ground that it was an interference with the finality essential to judicial decisions; Garland, invalidating a provision requiring a test oath to be taken by persons applying for admission to the Bar of the Supreme Court, on the ground that it was ex post facto, a bill of attainder, and an interference with the pardoning power when applied to one who had already received a presidential pardon for service in the Confederacy during the Civil War; Alicia, invalidating a provision authorizing transfer to the Supreme Court of prize cases pending in the circuit courts, on the ground that the Court's jurisdiction in prize cases was purely appellate, which did not include transfer; Murray, invalidating a provision authorizing circuit courts to reexamine determinations of fact by juries in state courts in specified cases, on Seventh-Amendment grounds; Klein, invalidating a provision which required (in essence) the court of claims to treat the acceptance of a pardon as conclusive of the guilt of the party accepting, on the ground that it prescribed rules for the decision of cases and interfered with the pardoning power; Callan, invalidating a provision dispensing with jury trials in certain District of Columbia courts (but providing for jury trial on appeal) on the ground that Article III, Section 2 requires that the "trial of all crimes

... shall be by jury." See Charles Warren, *Congress, the Constitution, and the Supreme Court* (Boston: Little, Brown & Co., 1925), chap. 9. See also Wilfred C. Gilbert, ed., *Provisions of Federal Law Held Unconstitutional by the Supreme Court of the United States* (1936; reprint Westport, Conn.: Greenwood Press, 1976), esp. pp. 7-11, 16-18.

48. Wright, *Growth*, p. 84.

49. 157 U.S. 429, 554 (1894).

50. Ibid.

51. Ibid.

52. See nn. 53-71 and accompanying text.

53. *Taylor and Marshall v. Beckham (No. 1)*, 178 U.S. 554, 586 (1899) (Harlan, J., dissenting); *Texas and N.O.R. Co. v. Ry. Clerks*, 281 U.S. 548, 570 (1929); *Switchmen's Union v. Board*, 320 U.S. 297, 318 (1943) (Reed, J., dissenting); *Stark v. Wickard*, 321 U.S. 288, 304 (1943); *Bell v. Hood*, 327 U.S. 678, 684 (1945).

54. *In re Winn*, 213 U.S. 458, 466 (1908); *Ex parte United States*, 287 U.S. 241, 245 (1932); *Ex parte Peru*, 318 U.S. 578, 582 (1942); *United States v. District Court*, 334 U.S. 258, 263 (1947).

55. *Garfield v. Goldsby*, 211 U.S. 249, 261 (1908); *Louisiana v. McAdoo*, 234 U.S. 627, 634 (1913); *Dalehite v. United States*, 346 U.S. 15, 34 (1952); *Panama Canal Co. v. Grace Line, Inc.*, 356 U.S. 309, 318 (1957).

56. *Downes v. Bidwell*, 182 U.S. 244, 358 (1900) (Fuller, Harlan, Brewer, Peckham, JJ., dissenting); *idem, at* 381 (Harlan, J., dissenting); *The Lottery Case*, 188 U.S. 321, 372 (1902) (Fuller, C.J., dissenting); *Reid v. Covert*, 354 U.S. 1, 6 (1956) (Black, J., opinion of the court).

57. *Parsons v. United States*, 167 U.S. 324, 335 (1896); *Myers v. United States*, 272 U.S. 52, 190 (1926) (Holmes, J., dissenting); *idem*, at 242 (Brandeis, J., dissenting).

58. *Pennsylvania v. West Virginia*, 262 U.S. 600, 610 (1922) (Brandeis, J., dissenting); *National Ins. Co. v. Tidewater Co.*, 337 U.S. 582, 630 (1948) (Vinson, C.J., dissenting).

59. *Myers v. United States*, 272 U.S. 52, 142 (1926); *Humphrey's Executor v. United States*, 295 U.S. 602, 627 (1934).

60. *United States v. Smith*, 286 U.S. 7, 33 (1931); *idem*, at 47.

61. *Myers v. United States*, 272 U.S. 52, 152 (1926); *idem*, at 229 (McReynolds, J., dissenting).

62. *Olmstead v. United States*, 277 U.S. 469, 487 (1927) (Butler, J., dissenting).

63. *Downes v. Bidwell*, 182 U.S. 244, 289 (1900) (White, Shiras, McKenna, JJ., concurring).

64. *Fairbank v. United States*, 181 U.S. 283, 285 (1900).

65. *Dooley v. United States*, 183 U.S. 151, 173 (1901) (Fuller, C.J., dissenting).

66. *Muskrat v. United States*, 219 U.S. 346, 357 (1910).

67. *Myers v. United States*, 272 U.S. 52, 139 (1926).

68. *Adamson v. California*, 332 U.S. 46, 90 (1946) (Black, J., dissenting).

69. 339 U.S. 121, 124 (1949).

70. 340 U.S. 462, 468 (1950).

71. 353 U.S. 448, 464 (1956) (Frankfurter, J., dissenting).

72. See n. 64 and accompanying text.

73. See nn. 77–109 and accompanying text.
74. See nn. 87, 95, 101, and accompanying text.
75. See n. 87 and accompanying text.
76. See n. 88 and accompanying text.
77. *Baker v. Carr*, 369 U.S. 186, 208 (1961); *Wesberry v. Sanders*, 376 U.S. 1, 6 (1963); *Bell v. Maryland*, 378 U.S. 226, 312 (1963) (Goldberg, J., concurring); *Bivens v. Six Unknown Federal Narcotics Agents*, 403 U.S. 388, 397 (1970); *idem*, at 401 (Harlan, J., concurring); *Regional Rail Reorganization Act Cases*, 419 U.S. 102, 142 (1974); *Butz v. Economou*, 438 U.S. 478, 485 (1977); *Davis v. Passman*, 442 U.S. 228, 242 (1978); *Carlson v. Green*, 446 U.S. 14, 42 (1979) (Rehnquist, J., dissenting); *Middlesex Cty. Sewage Authority v. Sea Clammers*, 453 U.S. 1, 23 (1980) (Stevens, J., concurring in part, dissenting in part); *Merrill Lynch, Pierce, Fenner and Smith v. Curran*, 456 U.S. 353, 375 (1981); *Nixon v. Fitzgerald*, 457 U.S. 731, 755 (1981); *idem*, at 797 (Blackmun, J., dissenting); *Briscoe v. La Hue*, 460 U.S. 325, 368 (1982) (Marshall, J., dissenting); *Bush v. Lucas*, 462 U.S. 367, 373 (1982).
78. *Glidden Company v. Zdanok*, 370 U.S. 554, 589 (1961) (Harlan, J., opinion of the Court); *idem*, at 601 (Douglas J., dissenting); *Fay v. Noia*, 372 U.S. 391, 407 (1962); *Chandler v. Judicial Council*, 398 U.S. 74, 86 (1969); *idem*, at 95 (Harlan, J., concurring); *Orr v. Orr*, 440 U.S. 268, 299 (1978) (Rehnquist, J., dissenting); *United States Parole Commission v. Geraghty*, 445 U.S. 388, 421 (1979) (Powell, J., dissenting).
79. *Wheedlin v. Wheeler*, 378 U.S. 647, 656 (1962) (Brennan, J., dissenting); *Mayor v. Educational Equality League*, 415 U.S. 605, 613 (1973); *Owen v. City of Independence*, 445 U.S. 622, 668 (1979) (Powell, J., dissenting); *Nixon v. Fitzgerald*, 457 U.S. 731, 766 (1981) (White, J., dissenting); *Illinois v. United States, et al.*, 460 U.S. 1001, 1005 (1982) (Rehnquist, J., dissenting).
80. *United States v. Brown*, 381 U.S. 437, 443 (1964); *Utah Commission v. El Paso Gas Co.*, 395 U.S. 464, 476 (1968) (Harlan, J., dissenting); *Chandler v. Judicial Council*, 398 U.S. 74, 133 (1969) (Douglas, J., dissenting); *United States v. Richardson*, 418 U.S. 166, 171 (1974).
81. *Diamond v. Chakrabarty*, 447 U.S. 303, 315 (1979); *United States v. Will*, 449 U.S. 200, 217 (1980).
82. *Richmond Newspapers v. Virginia*, 448 U.S. 555, 597 (1979) (Brennan, J., concurring); *City of Mesquite v. Alladin's Castle, Inc.*, 455 U.S. 283, 290 (1981).
83. *Desist v. United States*, 394 U.S. 244, 256 (1968) (Harlan, J., dissenting).
84. *Swain v. Alabama*, 380 U.S. 228, 244 (1964) (Goldberg, J., dissenting).
85. *Griswold v. Connecticut*, 381 U.S. 479, 491 (1965) (Goldberg, J., concurring).
86. *Cohen v. Hurley*, 366 U.S. 117, 150 (1960) (Douglas, J., dissenting).
87. *Cooper v. Aaron*, 358 U.S. 1, 18 (1958); *Clay v. Sun Insurance Office*, 363 U.S. 207, 222 (1959) (Black, J., dissenting); *Flemming v. Nestor*, 363 U.S. 603, 626 (1959) (Black, J., dissenting); *Hutcheson v. United States*, 369 U.S. 599, 632 (1961) (Warren, C.J., dissenting); *Glidden Company v. Zdanok*, 370 U.S. 530, 602 (1961) (Douglas, J., dissenting); *Bell v. Maryland*, 378 U.S. 226, 244 (1963) (Douglas, J., concurring); *Powell v. McCormack*, 395 U.S. 486, 503 (1968); *idem*, at 549; *idem*, at 552 (Douglas, J., opinion of the court); *Goldberg v. Kelly*, 397 U.S. 254, 274 (1969) (Black, J., dissenting); *Oregon v. Mitchell*, 400 U.S. 112, 204 (1970) (Harlan, J., concurring in part, dissenting in part); *McGautha v. California*, 402 U.S. 183,

250 (1970) (Brennan, J., dissenting); *Doe v. McMillan*, 412 U.S. 306, 326 (1972) (Douglas, J., concurring); *United States v. Watson*, 423 U.S. 411, 443 (1975) (Marshall, J., dissenting); *United States v. Santana*, 427 U.S. 38, 45 (1976) (Marshall, Brennan, JJ., dissenting); *Nixon v. Adm'r of General Services*, 433 U.S. 425, 503 (1977) (Powell, J., concurring); *City of Rome v. United States*, 446 U.S. 156, 207 (1979) (Rehnquist, J., dissenting); *Immigration and Naturalization Service v. Chadha*, 462 U.S. 919, 942 (1982).

88. *Cooper, Flemming, Glidden, Powell, Goldberg, Doe, Nixon, Rome, Chadha.* See n. 87.

89. *Powell, Mitchell.* See n. 87.

90. *Hutcheson, Bell.* See n. 87.

91. *Watson, Santana.* See n. 87.

92. *Clay.* See n. 87.

93. *McGautha.* See n. 87.

94. *Powell.* See this chapter, nn. 51, 64, and accompanying text.

95. *Bell v. Maryland*, 378 U.S. 226, 323 (1963) (Black, J., dissenting); *Griswold v. Connecticut*, 381 U.S. 479, 513 (1965) (Black, J., dissenting); *Flast v. Cohen*, 392 U.S. 83, 111 (1968) (Douglas, J., concurring); *Hunter v. Erickson*, 393 U.S. 385, 397 (1968) (Black, J., dissenting); *Allen v. State Board of Elections*, 393 U.S. 544, 596 (1968) (Black, J., dissenting); *Mackey v. United States*, 401 U.S. 667, 678 (1970) (Harlan, J., concurring in part, dissenting in part); *Furman v. Georgia*, 408 U.S. 238, 466 (1971) (Rehnquist, J., dissenting); *Doe v. McMillan*, 412 U.S. 306, 343 (1972) (Rehnquist, J., concurring in part, dissenting in part); *United States v. Nixon*, 418 U.S. 683, 703 (1974); *Nixon v. Adm'r of General Services*, 433 U.S. 425, 537 (1977) (Burger, C.J., dissenting); *idem*, at 559 (Rehnquist, J., dissenting); *Monell v. New York City Dept. of Social Services*, 436 U.S. 658, 718 (1977) (Rehnquist, J., dissenting); *Butz v. Economou*, 438 U.S. 478, 523 (1977) (Rehnquist, J., concurring in part, dissenting in part); *Goldwater v. Carter*, 444 U.S. 996, 1001 (1979) (Powell, J., concurring); *Fullilove v. Klutznick*, 448 U.S. 448, 510 (1979) (Powell, J., concurring); *Mississippi Univ. for Women v. Hogan*, 458 U.S. 718, 733 (1981).

96. *Flast.* See n. 95.

97. *Furman.* See n. 95.

98. *Goldwater.* See n. 95.

99. *Nixon.* See n. 95.

100. *Hunter, Allen.* See n. 95.

101. *United States v. Raines*, 362 U.S. 17, 20 (1959); *Aptheker v. Secretary of State*, 378 U.S. 517, 521 (1963) (Clark, J., dissenting); *Chapman v. California*, 386 U.S. 18, 47 (1966) (Harlan, J., dissenting); *Desist v. United States*, 394 U.S. 244, 258 (1968) (Fortas, J., dissenting); *Younger v. Harris*, 401 U.S. 37, 52 (1970); *Gooding v. Wilson*, 405 U.S. 518, 531 (1971) (Burger, C.J., dissenting); *Doe v. McMillan*, 412 U.S. 306, 338 (1972) (Blackmun, J., concurring in part, dissenting in part); *Broadrick v. Oklahoma*, 413 U.S. 601, 611 (1972); *United States v. Richardson*, 418 U.S. 166, 191 (1974) (Powell, J., concurring); *Monell v. New York City Dept. of Social Services*, 436 U.S. 658, 710 (1977) (Powell, J., concurring); *T.V.A. v. Hill*, 437 U.S. 153, 194 (1977); *Cannon v. Univ. of Chicago*, 441 U.S. 677, 744 (1978) (Powell, J., dissenting); *Richmond Newspapers v. Virginia*, 448 U.S. 555, 606 (1979) (Rehnquist, J., dissenting); *Metromedia, Inc. v. San Diego*, 453 U.S. 490, 546 (1980) (Stevens, J.,

dissenting); *Valley Forge College v. Americans United*, 454 U.S. 464, 474 (1981); *Nixon v. Fitzgerald*, 457 U.S. 731, 761 (1981) (Burger, C.J., concurring).

102. *Chapman.* See n. 101.

103. *Cannon.* See n. 101.

104. *Raines, Aptheker, Desist, Younger, Gooding, Broadrick, Monell, Metromedia, Valley Forge.* See n. 101.

105. *Cooper v. Aaron*, 358 U.S. 1, 18 (1958); *Powell v. McCormack*, 395 U.S. 486, 549 (1968); *Nixon v. Adm'r of General Services*, 433 U.S. 425, 503 (1977); *Immigration and Naturalization Service v. Chadha*, 462 U.S. 919, 942 (1982).

106. *Powell.* See n. 105.

107. *Nixon.* See n. 105.

108. *Chadha.* See n. 105.

109. See this chapter, n. 30 and accompanying text.

110. Albert J. Beveridge, *The Life of John Marshall*, 4 vols. (Boston: Houghton Mifflin, 1916), vol. 3, p. 132.

111. Archibald Cox, *The Court and the Constitution* (Boston: Houghton Mifflin, 1987), p. 45.

112. Abraham Holtzman, *American Government: Ideals and Reality* (Englewood Cliffs, N.J.: Prentice-Hall, 1980), pp. 329–30.

113. Kenneth S. Sherrill and David J. Vogler, *Power, Policy, and Participation: An Introduction to American Government*, 2d ed. (New York: Harper & Row, 1982), p. 103.

114. Junius (pseud.), *The Letters of Junius* (New York: John W. Lovell Co., n.d.), p. vi. Quoted in Gary L. McDowell, *Equity and the Constitution: The Supreme Court, Equitable Relief, and Public Policy* (Chicago: University of Chicago Press, 1982), p. vii.

115. Justice Harlan, concurring in *Gideon v. Wainwright*, 372 U.S. 335 (1963). Quoted in Craig Ducat and Harold Chase, *Constitutional Interpretation*, 2d ed. (St. Paul: West Publishing Co., 1985), p. 959.

116. Quoted in McDowell, *Equity*, p. 49.


*Chapter 8.* Eakin v. Raub: *Refutation or Justification of* Marbury v. Madison?

1. 1 Cranch 137 (1803).

2. 12 Serg. & Rawle (Pa.) 330, at 343–58 (1825).

3. James Bradley Thayer, "The Origin and Scope of the American Doctrine of Constitutional Law," *Harvard Law Review* 7 (October, 1893): 130.

4. 1 Cranch 137, 176–80. Thayer remarked in 1893 that *Eakin* "has fallen strangely out of sight. It has much the ablest discussion of the question which I have ever seen, not excepting the judgment of Marshall in *Marbury v. Madison*, which, as I venture to think, has been overpraised." Thayer, "Origin and Scope," p. 130.

5. Donald O. Dewey, *Marshall versus Jefferson: The Political Background of Marbury v. Madison* (New York: Alfred A. Knopf, 1970).

6. Ibid., p. 181.

7. Rocco J. Tresolini and Martin Shapiro, *American Constitutional Law*, 3d ed. (London: Macmillan, 1970), p. 74.

8. Stanley I. Kutler, ed., *The Supreme Court and the Constitution*, 3d ed. (New York: W. W. Norton & Co., 1984), p. 31. See also Albert B. Saye, *American Constitutional Law*, 2d ed. (St. Paul: West Publishing Co., 1979), p. 32. Saye describes Gibson's opinion as a "classic rebuttal of Marshall's argument in *Marbury v. Madison*.

9. Robert F. Cushman, *Cases in Constitutional Law*, 6th ed. (Englewood Cliffs, N.J.: Prentice-Hall, 1984), p. 12.

10. Ralph A. Rossum and G. Alan Tarr, *American Constitutional Law* (New York: St. Martin's Press, 1983), p. 72.

11. Malcolm Feeley and Samuel Krislov, *Constitutional Law* (Boston: Little, Brown & Co., 1985), p. 30. These authors acknowledge that others have regarded *Eakin* as a "cogent" critique of *Marbury*, without providing any further explanation.

12. Saye, *Constitutional Law*, p. 32.

13. John R. Schmidhauser, *Constitutional Law in American Politics* (Monterey, Calif.: Brooks/Cole Publishing Co., 1984), p. 65.

14. Peter Woll, *Constitutional Law: Cases and Comments* (Englewood Cliffs, N.J.: Prentice-Hall, 1981), pp. 23–24.

15. 12 Serg. & Rawle (Pa.) 330 (1825).

16. Ibid., at 338–39.

17. Ibid., at 333–34.

18. Ibid., at 339.

19. Ibid. Judge Tilghman was consistent throughout. He had been counsel in *Cooper v. Telfair*, decided by the United States Supreme Court some three years prior to *Marbury*, and had made a similar argument at that time. 4 Dall. 14, 16–17 (1800). The argument was accepted by the Court. See this chapter, nn. 59–60 and accompanying text.

20. 12 Serg. & Rawle (Pa.) 330, at 344–45.

21. Ibid., at 345.

22. Ibid., at 345–46.

23. Ibid., at 355 (emphasis on final phrase mine).

24. Ibid., pp. 346–47. The provision referred to by Justice Gibson is found in Article V, Section 12, Pennsylvania Constitution of 1790. William F. Swindler, ed., *Sources and Documents of United States Constitutions*, 10 vols. (Dobbs Ferry, N.Y.: Oceana Publications, 1979), vol. 8, p. 291. The provision reads: "The style of all process shall be, 'The Commonwealth of Pennsylvania,' all prosecutions shall be carried on in the name and by the authority of the commonwealth of Pennsylvania, and conclude, 'against the peace and dignity of the same.' " There are no jurisdictional provisions in Pennsylvania's Constitution of 1790 that are comparable to the Article III distribution provision in the United States Constitution. Since Judge Gibson did not address this point in his *Eakin* dissent, it is not known whether he would have thought such a provision "a rule for the judiciary" and thus beyond the legislature's power to alter. However, other considerations, discussed shortly, suggest an affirmative answer.

25. 12 Serg. & Rawle (Pa.) 330, at 346, 354.

26. Ibid., at 346.
27. Ibid., at 354.
28. Ibid., at 349.
29. Ibid., at 352.
30. Ibid., at 347.
31. Ibid., at 353, 347.
32. Ibid., at 355–56.
33. Ibid., at 356.
34. 1 Stat. 73, at 85 (1789).
35. 1 Cranch 137, at 176–80 (1803).
36. Ibid., at 176–77.
37. Ibid., at 177–80.
38. The *Marbury* language, at 1 Cranch 137, 177, is: "If an act of the legislature, repugnant to the constitution, is void, does it, notwithstanding its invalidity, bind the courts, and oblige them to give it effect?" Compare it with Judge Gibson's question in *Eakin*, at 12 Serg. and Rawle 330, 347: "The constitution and the *right* of the legislature to pass the act, may be in collision; but is that a legitimate subject for judicial determination?"
39. 12 Serg. & Rawle 330, at 344, 347, 351, 355. The first three premises attacked by Judge Gibson (the law of superior obligation, the nature of a written constitution, and *ipso facto* void legislation), when read together, do imply that laws passed in violation of the constitution are void, from the standpoint of *legal theory*. But without more, they will not justify judicial intervention. The other two premises (judicial oaths, province of the courts to say what the law is) will support only a very *narrowly circumscribed* power to invalidate, conditioned on legislative or executive interference with the performance of judicial functions. Certainly they cannot justify the broad theory of Judge Tilghman. They do, however, support the defensive type of nullification accomplished in *Marbury*.
40. 1 Cranch 137, at 176–77.
41. Ibid., at 177.
42. Ibid., at 178 (emphasis mine).
43. 12 Serg. & Rawle 330, at 347.
44. 1 Cranch 137, at 180.
45. 12 Serg. & Rawle 330, at 353.
46. 1 Cranch 137, at 179.
47. 12 Serg. & Rawle 330, at 347.
48. 1 Cranch 137, at 179.
49. 12 Serg. & Rawle 330, at 352.
50. 1 Stat. 73, at 85.
51. Ibid., at 86.
52. 12 Serg. & Rawle 330, at 344–45.
53. Ibid., at 351.
54. 1 Cranch 137, at 179.
55. Madison, in Number 45 of the *Federalist*, points to the practical result of the idea: "The powers delegated by the proposed Constitution to the federal government are few and defined. Those which are to remain in the State governments are numerous and indefinite. The former will be exercised principally

on external objects, as war, peace, negotiation, and foreign commerce; with which last the power of taxation will, for the most part, be connected. The power reserved to the several States will extend to all the objects which, in the ordinary course of affairs, concern the lives, liberties, and properties of the people, and the internal order, improvement, and prosperity of the State." Alexander Hamilton, James Madison, and John Jay, *The Federalist Papers* (New York: New American Library, 1961), pp. 292–93. According to Plano and Greenberg, "although it was generally understood that the framers intended that the states would retain all powers not prohibited by the Constitution or delegated to the national government, the people insisted upon an express provision to that effect." The Tenth Amendment was the result. Jack Plano and Milton Greenberg, *The American Political Dictionary*, 5th ed. (New York: Holt, Rinehart & Winston, 1979), p. 43.

56. United States Constitution, Amendment X. "It is not possible to make a definitive list of state powers since, in the very nature of the federal system, the states may exercise any power that is not delegated to the national government. . . . These powers are frequently referred to as 'residuary.' " Plano and Greenberg, *Dictionary*, p. 42. "Under American federalism, the national government is one of delegated powers. With the exception of foreign affairs, it must find justification for its actions in a specifically authorized power, or one that can be reasonably implied from those specifically authorized. The national government does not possess unlimited or general governmental power but only such power as is given to it in the constitution." Ibid., p. 34.

57. 12 Serg. & Rawle 330, at 350.

58. See this chapter, n. 21 and accompanying text.

59. 4 Dall. 14, 16–17 (1800).

60. Ibid., at 18–20. The four justices were Washington, Chase, Paterson, and Cushing, and they constituted a majority of the Court's membership at the time.

61. 123 U.S. 623, at 661 (1887). See chap. 7, nn. 40–45 and accompanying text.

62. 4 Dall. 14, at 19. At the decision of *Eakin v. Raub*, *Marbury* had been cited in four United States Supreme Court decisions: *Ex parte Bollman*, 4 Cranch 100, 102–5 (1807); *McClung v. Silliman I*, 2 Wheat. 369, 370–71 (1817); *Cohens v. Virginia*, 6 Wheat. 394, 399–402 (1821); *McClung v. Silliman II*, 6 Wheat. 604 (1821). These citations either extend or reiterate *Marbury*'s jurisdictional holdings. None pertain to that portion of *Marbury* that argues for judicial power to invalidate laws. See chap. 7, n. 1 and accompanying text.

63. Cooley, after speaking favorably about judicial power to invalidate legislation, says: "The same conclusion is reached by stating in consecutive order a few familiar maxims of the law. The administration of public justice is referred to the courts. To perform this duty, the first requisite is to ascertain the facts, and the next to determine the law that is applicable. The constitution is the fundamental law of the State, in opposition to which any other law, or any direction or decree, must be inoperative and void. If, therefore, such other law, direction, or decree seems to be applicable to the facts, but on comparison with the fundamental law it is found to be in conflict, the court, in declaring what the law of the case is, must necessarily determine its invalidity, and thereby in effect annul it. The right and power of the courts to do this are so plain, and the

duty is so generally—we may now say universally—conceded, that we should not be justified in wearing the patience of the reader in quoting from the very numerous authorities upon the subject." Then follows the citation of *Marbury*. Thomas M. Cooley, *A Treatise on the Constitutional Limitations Which Rest upon the Legislative Power of the States of the American Union* (Boston: Little, Brown & Co., 1868), pp. 45-46. See also chap 10.

64. Irving Browne, *Short Studies of Great Lawyers* (Albany: Albany Law Journal, 1878), pp. 206-7. Edward J. Phelps, "Address," in *Report of the Second Annual Meeting of the American Bar Association* (Philadelphia: E. C. Markley & Sons, 1879), pp. 173-92. For an excellent study of the effect of the American legal profession on the development of the doctrine of laissez-faire in the Supreme Court, see Benjamin R. Twiss, *Lawyers and the Constitution: How Laissez-Faire Came to the Supreme Court* (Princeton, N.J.: Princeton University Press, 1942), chap. 7. See also Robert G. Street, "How Far Questions of Policy May Enter into Judicial Decisions," *Reports of the American Bar Association* 6 (1883): 179; William M. Meigs, "The Relation of the Judiciary to the Constitution," *American Law Review* 19 (1885): 175; James R. Doolittle, "The Veto Power of the Supreme Court," *Chicago Law Times* 1 (1887): 177; Sidney G. Fisher, "Are the Departments of Government Independent of Each Other?" *American Law Review* 21 (1887): 210; Charles B. Elliott, "The Legislatures and the Courts: The Power to Declare Statutes Unconstitutional," *Political Science Quarterly* 5 (1891): 224; Brinton Coxe, *An Essay on Judicial Power and Unconstitutional Legislation* (Philadelphia: Kay & Brother, 1893).

65. See this chapter, n. 3 and accompanying text.

66. *Mugler v. Kansas*, 123 U.S. 661 (1887). Quoting *Marbury*, the *Mugler* Court asks "to what purpose . . . are powers limited, and to what purpose is that limitation committed to writing, if these limits may, at any time, be passed by those intended to be restrained? The distinction between a government with limited and unlimited powers is abolished, if those limits do not confine the persons on whom they are imposed, and if acts prohibited and acts allowed are of equal obligation." 1 Cranch 137, 176, quoted in 123 U.S. 661. This segment of Marshall's argument is used in *Marbury* to support the conclusion that legislative acts contrary to the Constitution are void, *not* that courts have the power to refuse application of them. But the *Mugler* Court uses the passage to support the proposition that "the courts must obey the Constitution rather than the lawmaking department of government, and must, upon their own responsibility, determine whether, in any particular case, these limits have been passed." 123 U.S. 661. The Court then employs *Marbury* in the service of substantive due process: "The courts are not bound by mere forms, nor are they to be misled by mere pretenses. They are at liberty—indeed, are under a solemn duty—to look at the substance of things, whenever they enter upon the inquiry whether the legislature has transcended the limits of its authority." 123 U.S. 661. See chap. 7, n. 40-45 and accompanying text.

67. The attack was clearly a response to the Court's decision in *Pollock v. Farmers' Loan & Trust Co.*, 157 U.S. 429 (1895), the first instance of a Supreme Court citation of *Marbury v. Madison* in a case where a national law was invalidated. 157 U.S. 429, 554 (1895). See Sylvester Pennoyer, "The Income Tax Decision

and the Power of the Supreme Court to Nullify Acts of Congress," *American Law Review* 29 (1895): 550; Lafon Allen, "The Income Tax Decision: An Answer to Gov. Pennoyer," *American Law Review* 29 (1895): 847; Robert Ludlow Fowler, "The Origin of the Supreme Judicial Power in the Federal Constitution," *American Law Review* 29 (1895): 711; Sylvester Pennoyer, "The Power of the Supreme Court to Declare an Act of Congress Unconstitutional: The Case of *Marbury v. Madison*," *American Law Review* 30 (1896): 188; John W. Akin, "Aggressions of the Federal Courts," *American Law Review* 32 (1898): 669; Henry Flanders, "Has the Supreme Court of the United States the Constitutional Power to Declare Void an Act of Congress?" *American Law Review* 48 (1900): 385; Junius Parker, "The Supreme Court and its Constitutional Duty and Power," *American Law Review* 30 (1896): 357.

68. See articles by Allen, Fowler, and Parker in previous note; also statements of the memorialists at the centennial of Marshall's appointment to the Supreme Court, compiled in John F. Dillon, ed., *John Marshall: Life, Character, and Judicial Services*, 3 vols. (Chicago: Callaghan & Company, 1903). Horace G. Platt, for example, says that *Marbury* was "as great a document as the Bill of Rights, as far-reaching as the Declaration of Independence, as essential to the healthy development of our Government under the Constitution as the Constitution itself." Dillon, *Marshall*, vol. 3, p. 231.

69. Albert J. Beveridge, *The Life of John Marshall*, 4 vols. (Boston: Houghton Mifflin, 1916). The full text of the statement is: "*Marbury*, for perfectly calculated audacity, has few parallels in judicial history. In order to assert that in the Judiciary rested the exclusive power to declare any statute unconstitutional, and to announce that the Supreme Court was the ultimate arbiter as to what is and what is not law under the Constitution, Marshall determined to annul Section 13 of the Ellsworth Judiciary Act of 1789. Marshall resolved to go still further. He would announce from the Supreme Bench rules of procedure which the Executive branch of the Government must observe." Ibid., vol. 3, p. 132. This statement has had an enormous impact on the modern understanding of *Marbury v. Madison*.

70. Edward S. Corwin, "The Establishment of Judicial Review," *Michigan Law Review* 9 (1910): 102.

*Chapter 9. Public and/or Private Contracts*

1. United States Constitution, Article I, Section 10.

2. See John P. Roche, ed., *John Marshall: Major Opinions and Other Writings* (Indianapolis: Bobbs-Merrill, 1967), pp. 119–21, 132–34. See also Gerald Garvey, *Constitutional Bricolage* (Princeton, N.J.: Princeton University Press, 1971), p. 76.

3. Charles Page Smith, *James Wilson: Founding Father* (Chapel Hill: University of North Carolina Press, 1956), p. 243.

4. Winton U. Solberg, ed., *The Federal Convention and the Formation of the Union of the American States* (Indianapolis: Bobbs-Merrill, 1958), p. 292.

5. Ibid., p. 293.

6. Benjamin F. Wright, *The Contract Clause of the Constitution* (Cambridge, Mass.: Harvard University Press, 1938), p. 9.

7. Alexander Hamilton, James Madison, and John Jay, *The Federalist* (New York: New American Library, 1961), pp. 144–45.

8. Ibid., p. 44.

9. Warren B. Hunting, *The Obligation of Contracts Clause of the United States Constitution* (Baltimore: Johns Hopkins Press, 1919), pp. 112–13.

10. Ibid., p. 113.

11. Ibid., p. 114.

12. 6 Cranch 78, 87 (1810).

13. 7 Cranch 164 (1812).

14. 4 Wheat. 518 (1819).

15. 8 Wheat. 1 (1823).

16. 4 Wheat. 122 (1819).

17. 4 Wheat. 209 (1819).

18. 12 Wheat. 213 (1827).

19. 6 Cranch 78, 143.

20. Ibid., at 144.

21. 4 Wheat. 518, at 713.

22. Wright, *The Contract Clause*, pp. 18–19.

23. 2 Dall. 304 (1795).

24. Wright, *The Contract Clause*, p. 20.

25. 2 Mass. 143 (1806), quoted in Wright, *The Contract Clause*, pp. 20–21.

26. See discussion in Wright, *The Contract Clause*, pp. 18–22.

27. 2 Pet. 245 (1829).

28. 101 U.S. 814 (1880). This doctrine was to become the chief constraint on the operation of the contract clause. The clause was virtually extinguished in *Home Building and Loan Ass'n v. Blaisdell*, 290 U.S. 398 (1934).

29. 4 Pet. 514, 562 (1830).

30. 11 Pet. 420, 544 (1837).

31. 6 How. 507 (1848).

32. See Wright, *The Contract Clause*, chap. 3.

33. John Taylor, *Construction Construed and Constitutions Vindicated* (Richmond, Va.: Shepherd & Pollard, 1820), pp. 73–74.

34. Theron Metcalf, *Principles of the Law of Contracts* (Boston: Houghton Mifflin, 1883), p. 318; reprint of 1828 manuscript.

35. Peter S. Du Ponceau, *A Brief View of the Constitution of the United States, Addressed to the Law Academy of Philadelphia* (Philadelphia: D. G. Dorsey, 1834), p. 43.

36. James Kent, *Commentaries on American Law*, 4 vols. (New York: O. Halsted, 1826) vol. 1, p. 392.

37. Ibid., vol. 3, p. 459.

38. Joseph Story, *Commentaries on the Constitution of the United States*, 4th ed., edited by Thomas M. Cooley, 2 vols. (Boston: Little, Brown & Co., 1873), vol. 2, pp. 257–58.

39. Francis Hilliard, *The Elements of Law* (New York: John S. Voorhies, 1848), p. 44.

40. Timothy Walker, *Introduction to American Law* (Boston: Little, Brown & Co., 1869), p. 200.

41. William Alexander Duer, *The Constitutional Jurisprudence of the United States* (New York: Burt Franklin, 1856), p. 347.

42. Theophilus Parsons, *The Law of Contracts*, 2 vols. (Boston: Little, Brown & Co., 1855), vol. 2, p. 530.

43. George Ticknor Curtis, *History of the Origin, Formation, and Adoption of the Constitution of the United States*, 2 vols. (New York: Harper & Brothers, 1858), vol. 2, p. 366.

44. See, for example, Clement Hill, "The Dartmouth College Case," *American Law Review* 8 (1874): 196.

45. See this chapter, nn. 4 6 and accompanying text.

46. Thomas M. Cooley, *A Treatise on the Constitutional Limitations Which Rest upon the Legislative Power of the States of the American Union* (Boston: Little, Brown & Co., 1868), p. 275.

47. Thomas M. Cooley, *General Principles of Constitutional Law* (Boston: Little, Brown & Co., 1880), p. 300.

48. See this chapter, n. 38 and accompanying text.

49. See this chapter, n. 44 and accompanying text.

50. R. Hutchinson, "Laws Impairing the Obligation of Contracts," *Southern Law Review* 1 (October 1875): 401.

51. John M. Shirley, *The Dartmouth College Causes and the Supreme Court of the United States* (St. Louis: G. I. Jones & Co., 1879).

52. Hill, "Dartmouth Case," p. 197.

53. 4 Wheat. 122, at 151 (1819).

54. Hill, "Dartmouth Case," p. 198.

55. Shirley, *Dartmouth Causes*, p. 188.

56. Hill, "Dartmouth Case," p 193.

57. See this chapter, n. 13 and accompanying text.

58. Shirley, *Dartmouth Causes*, p. 403.

59. 6 Wheat. 264 (1821); see Hutchinson, "Obligation of Contracts," p. 401.

60. Shirley, *Dartmouth Causes*, pp. 52-53.

61. Ibid., p. 208.

62. Ibid., p. 79.

63. See, e.g., Hill, "Dartmouth Case," p. 192.

64. See Wright, *The Contract Clause*, p. 9.

65. George Ticknor Curtis, *Constitutional History of the United States*, 2 vols. (New York: Harper & Brothers, 1897), vol. 1, pp. 548-49.

66. Quoted in Hunting, *Obligation Clause*, p. 47.

67. Robert McCloskey, ed., *The Works of James Wilson*, 2 vols. (Cambridge, Mass.: Harvard University Press, 1967), vol. 2, pp. 833-34.

68. See Smith, *James Wilson*, chap. 22.

69. See, e.g., Nathan Isaacs, "John Marshall on Contracts: A Study in Early American Juristic Theory," *Virginia Law Review* 7 (March 1921): 413; Francis N. Stites, *Private Interest and Public Gain: The Dartmouth College Case, 1819* (Amherst: University of Massachusetts Press, 1972), esp. chap. 9; see also Hunting, *Obligation Clause*, p. 48.

70. 2 Dall. 415, 419 (1793), quoted in Smith, *James Wilson*, p. 357.

71. Arthur T. von Mehren, *The Civil Law System: An Introduction to the Comparative Study of Law*, 3d ed. (Boston: Little, Brown & Co., 1977), pp. 580–84. Hunting takes a similar view.

72. Henry Campbell Black, *Black's Law Dictionary*, 5th ed.(St. Paul: West Publishing Co., 1979), p. 293, s.v. "contract."

73. von Mehren, *Civil Law*, pp. 578–79, 470.

74. Ibid., p. 710.

75. Stites, *Private Interest*, p. 99.

76. Ibid., pp. 99–100.

77. See this chapter, n. 69 and accompanying text.

78. Edward S. Corwin, *John Marshall and the Constitution* (New Haven, Conn.: Yale University Press, 1919), chap. 7.

79. See this chapter, nn. 27, 29 and accompanying text.

80. See John Austin, *The Austinian Theory of Law*, edited by W. Jethro Brown (London: John Murray, 1920).

81. Isaacs, "Marshall on Contracts" (remarking on Shirley's book), p. 165.

82. Hill, "Dartmouth Case," p. 192.

83. See Wright, *The Contract Clause*, p. 93, esp. nn. 6 and 7.

84. 101 U.S. 814 (1880).

85. See this chapter, n. 70 and accompanying text.

86. See, for example, Lawrence Goodwyn, *The Populist Moment* (Oxford: Oxford University Press, 1978), pp. 15–18, for a brief but excellent discussion of this situation.

87. Wright, *The Contract Clause*, p. 93.

88. 8 Wall. 603.

89. *Knox v. Lee*, 12 Wall. 457 (1871).

90. See, for example, Charles Fairman, *Mr. Justice Miller and the Supreme Court: 1862–1890* (Cambridge, Mass.: Harvard University Press, 1939), p. 174 et seq.

91. Oliver Wendell Holmes, Jr., "The Gas Stokers' Strike," *American Law Review* 7 (1873): 583. See also Morton White, *Social Thought in America* (Boston: Beacon Press, 1957), chap. 8.

92. See, for example, Shirley, *Dartmouth Causes*, p. 79.

93. See this chapter, n. 47 and accompanying text.

94. See this chapter, n. 6.

95. Victor Morawetz, *A Treatise on the Law of Private Corporations*, 2 vols. (Boston: Little, Brown & Co., 1882), vol. 2, p. 1005. Morawetz challenges the *Dartmouth* decision, because he does not consider a charter of incorporation to be a contract.

96. Charles Fisk Beach, Jr., *A Treatise on the Modern Law of Contracts*, 2 vols. (Indianapolis: Bowen-Merrill Co., 1896), vol. 2, p. 2116. Beach says that the introduction of the clause was due to the financial condition of the country and the repudiation of private debts. William Herbert Page, *The Law of Contracts*, 7 vols. (Cincinnati: W. H. Anderson Co., 1905), vol. 6, p. 6295. Page says that the clause was introduced "to prevent states from passing laws repudiating private debts." William F. Elliott, *Commentaries on the Law of Contracts* (Indianapolis: Bobbs-Merrill, 1913), p. 875. Elliott makes the ambiguous statement that the "pur-

pose of the provision, no doubt, was to correct a practice that had been quite prevalent in some of the states after the revolution and before the adoption of the Constitution." He nowhere says what the "practice" was, but it suggests a narrow interpretation of the Framers' intentions respecting the contract clause.

97. Christopher G. Tiedeman, *A Treatise on the Limitations of the Police Power in the United States* (St. Louis: Thomas & Co., 1886), p. 575. Tiedeman refers to Clement Hill's argument as "ingenious," interpreting Hill's position to be that the true meaning of the clause is found in the Roman or civil law phrase *obligatio ex contractu*. Christopher G. Tiedeman, *The Unwritten Constitution of the United States* (New York: Putnam, 1890), p. 54. Tiedeman says here that "if the intention of the framers of the constitution is to furnish the true rule of construction, we must conclude that nothing would be included within the operation of this prohibition but debts and the obligations arising out of contracts." Joseph P. Cotton, Jr., ed., *The Constitutional Decisions of John Marshall*, 2 vols. (New York: G. P. Putnam's Sons, 1905, vol. 1, pp. 346–50. Cotton is highly critical of Marshall's early decisions, especially *Dartmouth*, accusing the chief justice of personal bias in holding that a charter of incorporation was a contract. Edward S. Corwin, *John Marshall and the Constitution* (New Haven, Conn.: Yale University Press, 1919), chap. 7. Corwin thinks that Marshall *should* have made a distinction between public and private contracts, but that he refrained because it would have been insulting to the states, since it would have implied that state contracts carried a lesser obligation than contracts between individuals. See also George Bancroft, *History of the Formation of the Constitution of the United States of America*, 2 vols. (New York: D. Appleton & Co., 1893), vol. 1, pp. 240–41, vol. 2, pp. 137–39; Erik McKinley Erickson and David Nelson Rowe, *American Constitutional History* (New York: Norton & Co., 1933), pp. 346–49.

98. Samuel Williston, *The Law of Contracts*, 2 vols. (New York: Baker, Voorhis & Co., 1920), vol. 1, pp. 3–5. Williston discusses the difference between "implied contracts" and "quasi-contracts," asserting that they are *not* the same thing. The argument against Marshall, based on the civil-law interpretation of the contract clause, presumed that they were. Hunting, *Obligation Clause*, chap. 4. On the last page of his book, Hunting makes a puzzling assertion that there is no reason to believe that the Founders meant the clause to cover anything more than private contracts. In view of the facts (1) that Hunting's entire work is devoted to vindication of the Marshall Court's early contract decisions, and (2) that the final chapter of the book shows that the exact intention of the Framers is *not clear*, the only reasonable interpretation is that Hunting must have had Story's notion of the Founders' motive in mind—that what was *immediately* present to their minds (pressing financial difficulties, etc.) did not necessarily circumscribe their *intentions*. See also Thomas James Norton, *The Constitution of the United States* (Boston: Little, Brown & Co., 1930), pp. 91–93; Hastings Lyon, *The Constitution and the Men Who Made It* (Boston: Houghton Mifflin, 1936), pp. 195–98.

99. Edward S. Corwin and Jack W. Peltason, *Understanding the Constitution*, rev. ed. (New York: Dryden Press, 1958), pp. 86–87. Corwin and Peltason state that "the framers, when they spoke of 'contracts' whose obligations could not

be impaired by state law, had in mind the ordinary contracts between individuals, especially contracts of debt. However, the meaning of the word was early expanded by judicial interpretation to include contracts made by the states themselves, including franchises granted to corporations." This is a very clear statement, in a very influential book, of the modern version of the Framers' intentions and the Marshall Court's decisions—yet the view apparently did not exist prior to the 1870s. See also Alfred Kelley and Winfred Harbison, *The American Constitution*, 4th ed. (New York: Norton & Co., 1970), pp. 275–76. Kelley and Harbison believe that the principal objective of the Founders was to prevent stay and tender laws. Also John P. Roche, ed., *John Marshall: Major Opinions and Other Writings* (Indianapolis: Bobbs-Merrill, 1967), pp. 119–21, 132–34. Roche says that the *Fletcher* decision is "eccentric," and that there "is no evidence to support the proposition that the Founders had intended to subsume land grants under the contract clause." Roche also specifically accepts Shirley's version of the *Dartmouth* decision. Gerald Garvey, in *Constitutional Bricolage*, p. 76, says that Marshall "elevated" property into a sacred right. The major exception to these views is found in William Winslow Crosskey, *Politics and the Constitution in the History of the United States*, 2 vols. (Chicago: University of Chicago Press, 1953), vol. 1, chap. 12. Crosskey generally supports the Marshall Court's doctrines in the areas of both contract and commerce.

100. See Wallace Mendelson, "B. F. Wright and the Contract Clause: A Progressive Misreading of the Marshall-Taney Era," *Western Political Quarterly* 38 (June 1985): 262–75. Defending Wright, Albert P. Melone answered Mendelson in "Mendelson v. Wright: Understanding the Contract Clause," *Western Political Quarterly* 41(1988): 791–799. Melone's article was in turn answered by Mendelson in "Bootstraps v. Evidence: A Reply to Professor Melone," *Western Political Quarterly* 41(1988): 801–805. The persistence of the "activist" interpretation of Marshall's contract decisions is well illustrated by Leonard Levy's suggestion that those decisions were the result of a "frenetic judicial imagination." Levy, *Original Intent and the Framers' Constitution* (New York: Macmillan, 1988), p. 134.

*Chapter 10. The Great Debate on the Judicial Function*

1. 4 Wheat. 316 (1819). See generally Charles Warren, *The Supreme Court in United States History*, 3 vols. (Boston: Little, Brown & Co., 1922), vol. 1, chap. 12.

2. 6 Wheat. 264 (1821). See generally Warren, *Supreme Court*, vol. 2, chap. 13, esp. pp. 11–19.

3. See the line of cases beginning with *Prigg v. Pennsylvania*, 16 Pet. 539 (1842) and ending with *Dred Scott v. Sanford*, 19 How. 393 (1857). A thorough discussion is provided in Warren, *Supreme Court*, vol. 2, pp. 357–551; vol. 3, pp. 1–41. A brief summary is provided in Benjamin F. Wright, *The Growth of American Constitutional Law* (Boston: Houghton Mifflin, 1942; Chicago: University of Chicago Press, Phoenix Books, 1967), pp. 73–77.

4. Recall the letter to Ritchie, December 25, 1820, when Jefferson charged that "the judiciary of the United States is the subtle corps of sappers and miners constantly working underground to undermine the foundations of our confederated

fabric." Quoted in Dumas Malone, *Jefferson and His Time*, 6 vols. (Boston: Little, Brown & Co., 1962), vol. 6, p. 356. The idea that the Constitution was little more than an updated version of the Articles of Confederation was later echoed by Calhoun. After arguing that the states, "in their confederated character," are the "parties" to the "compact," the venerable philosopher concludes that "these States, in ratifying the Constitution, did not lose the confederated character which they possessed when they ratified it, as well as in all the preceding stages of their existence; but, on the contrary, retained it to the full." John C. Calhoun, *A Discourse on the Constitution and Government of the United States*, edited by C. Gordon Post (Indianapolis: Bobbs-Merrill, 1953), p. 99.

5. *Marbury v. Madison*, 1 Cranch 137 (1803); *Dred Scott v. Sanford*, 19 How. 393 (1857).

6. *Marbury v. Madison*, 1 Cranch 137 (1803).

7. See chap. 7, nn. 1–2, 15–17 and accompanying text.

8. *Dred Scott v. Sanford*, 19 How. 393 (1857).

9. *Pollock v. Farmers' Loan & Trust Co.* (The Income Tax Case), 158 U.S. 601 (1895); *United States v. E. C. Knight Co.* (The Sugar Trust Case), 156 U.S. 1 (1895).

10. See chap. 7, n. 33 and accompanying text.

11. See chap. 7, nn. 34–39 and accompanying text.

12. *Mugler v. Kansas*, 123 U.S. 616 (1887). See chap. 7, nn. 40–45 and accompanying text.

13. Wright, *Growth*, pp. 82, n. 6, 86.

14. Ibid., p. 77.

15. Ibid., p. 82.

16. See Benjamin F. Wright, *The Contract Clause of the Constitution* (Cambridge, Mass.: Harvard University Press, 1938), p. 93, nn. 6–7.

17. Thomas M. Cooley, *A Treatise on the Constitutional Limitations Which Rest upon the Legislative Power of the States of the American Union* (Boston: Little, Brown & Co., 1868), pp. 45–46.

18. Ibid., p. 45.

19. See this chapter, n. 12 and accompanying text.

20. Cooley, *Constitutional Limitations*, pp. 45–46.

21. See chap. 8, nn. 35–57 and accompanying text.

22. Irving Browne, *Short Studies of Great Lawyers* (Albany: Albany Law Journal, 1878), pp. 206–7 (emphasis mine).

23. Edward J. Phelps, "Address," in *Report of the Second Annual Meeting of the American Bar Association* (Philadelphia: E. C. Markley & Sons, 1879), pp. 173–92, 182 (emphasis mine).

24. See chap. 7, n. 33 and accompanying text.

25. Recall that this phrase was not yet in use. The origin of the modern theory of judicial review, as Phelps's statement would seem to indicate, parallels to some extent the origin and early development of the American Bar Association. Benjamin Twiss suggests (though does not document) this in chapter 7 of his study, *Lawyers and the Constitution: How Laissez-Faire Came to the Supreme Court* (Princeton, N.J.: Princeton University Press, 1942). A thorough investigation of this possibility would be fascinating.

26. John M. Shirley, *The Dartmouth College Causes and the Supreme Court*

*of the United States* (St. Louis: G. I. Jones & Co., 1879), pp. 386–88. See also chap. 9, n. 51 et seq. and accompanying text.

27. Ibid., p. 386.

28. 1 Cranch, at 179 (1803).

29. *United States v. Railroad Company,* 17 Wall. 322 (1873), invalidating a tax on the interest on railroad indebtedness, because it was in effect a tax on the city of Baltimore —which had since become the mortgagee of the company— and thus interfered with the sovereignty of the state; *United States v. Reese,* 92 U.S. 214 (1876), invalidating a penalty on state election officers who had refused to receive the vote of a black man, on the ground that the penalizing statute was overly broad and therefore outside the boundary of Congress's power to "enforce, by appropriate legislation," the Fifteenth Amendment; *United States v. Fox,* 95 U.S. 670 (1878), invalidating a portion of the Bankruptcy Law that made criminal the obtaining of credit "with intent to defraud" within three months of the commencement of bankruptcy proceedings, on the ground that it intruded on matters of state concern; *Trade Mark Cases,* 100 U.S. 82 (1879), invalidating a provision making fraud in connection with trademarks a criminal offense, because it was beyond Congress's power to regulate commerce; *United States v. Harris,* 106 U.S. 629 (1883), invalidating a provision making criminal the act of conspiring to deprive another of the equal protection of the laws, on the ground that it was beyond the power of Congress to "enforce, by appropriate legislation," the Fourteenth Amendment; *Civil Rights Cases,* 109 U.S. 3 (1883), invalidating a portion of the Civil Rights Act of 1875 that prohibited discrimination in places of public accommodation, on the ground that it was beyond the power of Congress to prevent race discrimination not involving "state action." The significant feature in all these cases is that the Court set aside the provisions for exceeding the power of Congress, not for interference with judicial functions. Their model is therefore *Dred Scott,* not *Marbury.*

30. Robert G. Street, "How Far Questions of Policy May Enter into Judicial Decisions," *Reports of the American Bar Association* 6 (1883): 179.

31. Recall that the misinterpretations perpetrated by Cooley, Browne, and Phelps were laudatory. See this chapter, nn. 17–23 and accompanying text.

32. Street, "Questions of Policy"; William M. Meigs, "The Relation of the Judiciary to the Constitution," *American Law Review* 19 (1885): 175; James R. Doolittle, "The Veto Power of the Supreme Court," *Chicago Law Times* 1 (1887): 177; Sidney G. Fisher, "Are the Departments of Government Independent of Each Other?" *American Law Review* 21 (1887): 210; Charles B. Elliott, "The Legislatures and the Courts: The Power to Declare Statutes Unconstitutional," *Political Science Quarterly* 5 (1891): 224; George Bancroft, *A Plea for the Constitution of the United States of America, Wounded in the House of Its Guardians* (New York: Harpers, 1886); Richard C. McMurtrie, *A Plea for the Supreme Court: Observations on Mr. Bancroft's Plea for the Constitution* (Philadelphia, 1886); Brinton Coxe, *An Essay on Judicial Power and Unconstitutional Legislation* (Philadelphia: Kay & Brother, 1893); Richard C. McMurtrie, "The Jurisdiction to Declare Void Acts of Legislation: When Is It Legitimate and When Mere Usurpation of Sovereignty?" *American Law Register,* n.s. 32 (1893): 1093; Walter D. Coles, "Politics and the Supreme Court of the United States," *American Law Review*

27 (1893): 183; William Draper Lewis, "Civil Liberty in a Written Constitution," *American Law Review* 32, (1893): 782, 971, 1064; James Bradley Thayer, "The Origin and Scope of the American Doctrine of Constitutional Law," *Harvard Law Review* 7 (October 1893): 129.

33. Street, "Questions of Policy," p. 179.

34. Ibid., p. 181.

35. 12 Wall. 457 (1871).

36. 8 Wall. 603 (1869).

37. Street, "Questions of Policy," pp. 185–86. It is not clear whether Street is arguing for "functional" or "arbitrary" coordinate review. Whichever is the case, his citation of *Marbury* to support full-blown judicial review is inappropriate.

38. James Bradley Thayer, "Constitutionality of Legislation: The Precise Question for a Court," *The Nation* 980 (April 10, 1884): 4. See also 1 Cranch, at 176–80.

39. Thayer, "Constitutionality of Legislation," p. 5.

40. Ibid., p. 4.

41. Meigs, "Relation of the Judiciary," pp. 187–92.

42. Ibid., p. 189.

43. Ibid., pp. 192–99. In fairness, Meigs does recognize that there are cases "of a judiciary nature," where judicial declarations of invalidity are necessarily conclusive. Ibid., pp. 175, 193–94. Why he does not believe that *Marbury* is such a case is not clear.

44. *Juilliard v. Greenman*, 110 U.S. 421 (1884). Bancroft, *Plea for the Constitution*.

45. Warren, *Supreme Court*, vol. 3, pp. 374–76.

46. *Knox v. Lee*, 12 Wall. 457 (1871), overruling *Hepburn v. Griswold*, 8 Wall. 603 (1869), which had declared the tender acts unconstitutional as applied to preexisting debts. See Warren, *Supreme Court*, vol. 3, p. 376. The Court had inferred in *Knox*—via the elastic clause—the paper-issue authority from the war power of Congress.

47. 110 U.S., at 449.

48. Bancroft, *Plea for the Constitution*. See also "Letter to Chief Justice Waite," in M. A. de Wolfe Howe, ed., *The Life and Letters of George Bancroft*, 2 vols. (New York: Charles Scribner's Sons, 1908), vol. 2, pp. 298–301.

49. Arnold Paul, *Conservative Crisis and the Rule of Law: Attitudes of Bar and Bench, 1887–1895* (Ithaca, N.Y.: Cornell University Press, 1960), p. 90.

50. McMurtrie, *Plea for the Supreme Court*.

51. Ibid. See also Coxe, *An Essay*, pp. 26–34.

52. Quoted in Coxe, *An Essay*, pp. 32–33 (last emphasis mine).

53. Hermann von Holst, *The Constitutional Law of the United States of America* (Chicago: Callaghan & Co., 1887).

54. Ibid., p. 65. See this chapter, nn. 38 and 17, respectively.

55. Ibid., p. 63 (emphasis mine). See also 1 Cranch, at 177: "It is emphatically the province and duty of the judicial department to say what the law *is*" (emphasis mine).

56. von Holst, *Constitutional Law*, p. 64.

57. Alexander Johnston, "The First Century of the Constitution," *New Princeton Review* 4 (July–November 1877): 182 (emphasis mine).

58. Marshall's argument from Article V concludes that legislative acts in violation of the Constitution are void—*not* that courts generally (nor even his court in particular) have the power to *declare* them so. 1 Cranch, at 176. See chap. 8, n. 35–57 and accompanying text.

59. Doolittle, "Veto Power," p. 177.

60. Ibid., p. 178.

61. Ibid., p. 182.

62. The Court had actually been doing this for only seventeen or so years. In 1870, the Court—probably for the first time—set aside a national law on the ground of its interference with "trade within the separate States," thus presaging the later development of the doctrine of "dual federalism." See *United States v. DeWitt*, 9 Wall. 41 (1870). Compare this with the later *Employers' Liability Cases*, 207 U.S. 463 (1908), and *Hammer v. Dagenhart*, 247 U.S. 251 (1918). Surely the role suggested for the Court in these cases—and by Doolittle—was not contemplated by the Founders. Nor can it be inferred from any decision of the Marshall Court, least of all *Marbury v. Madison*.

63. Fisher, "Departments of Government," pp. 224–27.

64. I have elsewhere referred to this notion as "arbitrary coordinate review," in order to distinguish it from "functional coordinate review," which is, I believe, the true doctrine of the Convention. See chap. 1, nn. 123–136 and accompanying text.

65. Fisher, "Departments of Government," p. 211.

66. Ibid., p. 210. According to Fisher, "it is false to assert generally that the departments are independent, and equally false to assert generally that they are not independent. In some cases the executive is independent of the judiciary and in others not, and in some cases the legislature is independent of the judiciary and in others not, and so on through all the combinations. Nothing but confusion will come of taking a general assertion of independence, and applying it indiscriminately to all cases. Each case must be taken by itself and worked out by all the principles which apply to it." Ibid., p. 224. See also Madison, in Number 48 of the *Federalist*: "It was shown in the last paper that the political apothegm there examined does not require that the legislative, executive, and judiciary departments should be wholly unconnected with each other. I shall undertake, in the next place, to show that unless these departments be so far connected and blended as to give to each a *constitutional* control over the others, the degrees of separation which the maxim requires, as essential to a free government, can never in practice be duly maintained." Alexander Hamilton, James Madison, and John Jay, *The Federalist Papers* (New York: New American Library, 1961), p. 308.

67. Fisher, "Departments of Government," pp. 223–24.

68. Ibid., p. 222. See also *Kendall v. United States*, 12 Pet. 524 (1838); *United States v. Schurz*, 102 U.S. 378 (1880).

69. 123 U.S., at 661. See chap. 7, nn. 40–45 and accompanying text.

70. Thomas M. Cooley, *Constitutional History of the United States* (New York: G. P. Putnam's Sons, 1889), pp. 101, 105, 107, 113, 157.

71. Elliott, "Legislatures and the Courts," pp. 230, 246–47. Most of the ground covered is the same as that covered by Coxe in his more comprehensive work published three years later. See also this chapter, n. 57 and accompanying text.

72. James Kent, *Commentaries on American Law*, 4 vols. (New York: O.

Halsted, 1826), vol. 1, p. 424. Quoted in Elliott, "Legislatures and the Courts," p. 246.

73. Elliott, "Legislatures and the Courts," p. 247.

74. Christopher Tiedeman, *The Unwritten Constitution of the United States* (New York: Putnam, 1890), pp. 163-64. Tiedeman had used similar language in an address delivered to the Missouri Bar Association in 1887. See Paul, *Conservative Crisis*, pp. 24-25.

75. Hampton L. Carson, ed., *The Supreme Court of the United States* (Philadelphia: John Y. Yuber, 1891). Essays include ones by Edward J. Phelps, "The Supreme Court and the Sovereignty of the People" (p. 687), and William A. Butler, "The Origin of the Supreme Court of the United States and its Place in the Constitution" (p. 611)

76. Phelps, in Carson, *Supreme Court*, p. 690. See this chapter, nn. 23, 57-58 and accompanying text.

77. Butler, in Carson, *Supreme Court*, pp. 611-12 (emphasis mine).

78. Coxe, *An Essay*.

79. James Bradley Thayer, "Review of 'An Essay on Judicial Power and Unconstitutional Legislation,' by Brinton Coxe," *Harvard Law Review* 7 (1893-1894): 380. Coxe's ground, according to Thayer, is the merger of Article VI and Article III, which is "overlooked by most persons."

80. Coxe, *An Essay*, p. 25.

81. 110 U.S. 421 (1884). See this chapter, n. 50 and accompanying text.

82. Coxe, *An Essay*, p. 27.

83. Ibid., p. 26. See this chapter, n. 51 and accompanying text.

84. Ibid., pp. 30-31.

85. Ibid., p. 39.

86. Ibid.

87. Ibid., p. 67. Whatever position one takes on the "inference-express texts" squabble, Coxe grossly misinterprets *Marbury* by failing to properly segregate the two arguments contained in 1 Cranch, at 176-180, the respective conclusions of which are: (1) that an unconstitutional legislative act is void; and (2) that the courts may, in some cases, say so. Coxe treats the arguments separately, but evidently thinks that *both* are directed at the *second* conclusion. The first he terms a "general" argument (to the second conclusion); the second is termed a "special" one (to the same). Ibid., pp. 54-67. See chap. 8, nn. 35-57 and accompanying text.

88. Thayer, "Review," p. 380.

89. Thayer, "Origin and Scope," p. 130, n. 1.

90. Ibid., pp. 130-34. Thayer does not cite *Marbury* in connection with the doctrine that judicial review is based on the "idea of a written constitution." See this chapter, n. 57, 71 and accompanying text.

91. Coles, "Politics and the Supreme Court," pp. 205-8. Coles advances the doubtful proposition that, had these (unspecified) cases come before the Taney Court, the decisions would have been "exactly the reverse."

92. McMurtrie, "Jurisdiction," pp. 1094-99.

93. Ibid, pp. 1103-8.

94. Richard C. McMurtrie, "Comments on Recent Decisions," *American Law Register*, n.s. 32 (1893): 596.

95. William Draper Lewis, "Editorial Notes," in *American Law Register*, n.s. 32 (1893): 980.

96. Ibid., pp. 977–81.

97. *Mugler v. Kansas*, 123 U.S., at 661. See this chapter, n. 69 and accompanying text. See also chap. 7, nn. 40–45 and accompanying text.

98. Coxe, *An Essay*. See this chapter, n. 78 and accompanying text.

99. Street, "Questions of Policy." See this chapter, n. 30 and accompanying text.

100. Doolittle, "Veto Power." See this chapter, n. 59 and accompanying text.

101. Ibid. See this chapter, n. 62 and accompanying text.

102. McMurtrie, *Plea for the Supreme Court*. See this chapter, nn. 50–51 and accompanying text.

103. Elliott, "Legislatures and the Courts." See this chapter, n. 71 and accompanying text.

104. McMurtrie, "Jurisdiction." See this chapter, n. 92 and accompanying text.

105. Thayer, "Origin and Scope." See this chapter, n. 89 and accompanying text.

*Chapter 11. A Reinterpretation of American Constitutional History*

1. *Pollock v. Farmers' Loan & Trust Co.*, 157 U.S. 429 (1895); idem (rehearing), 158 U.S. 601 (1895).

2. *Marbury v. Madison*, 1 Cranch 137, at 179 (1803).

3. See Benjamin F. Wright, *The Growth of American Constitutional Law* (Boston: Houghton Mifflin, 1942; Chicago: University of Chicago Press, Phoenix Books, 1967), p. 84.

4. Arnold Paul, *Conservative Crisis and the Rule of Law: Attitudes of Bar and Bench, 1887–1895* (Ithaca, N.Y.: Cornell University Press, 1960), p. 219.

5. See Paul, *Conservative Crisis*, p. 223. The seminal piece is Sylvester Pennoyer, "The Income Tax Decision and the Power of the Supreme Court to Nullify Acts of Congress," *American Law Review* 29 (1895): 550.

6. 157 U.S., at 553: "I do not believe that any member of this Court has ever sat or ever will sit to hear and decide a case the consequences of which will be so far-reaching as this. . . . If it be true, as my friend said in closing, that the passions of the people are aroused on this subject, if it be true that a mighty army of sixty million citizens is likely to be incensed by this decision, it is the more vital to the future welfare of this country that this court again resolutely and courageously declare, as Marshall did, that it *has* the power to set aside an act of Congress violative of the constitution, and that it will not hesitate in executing that power, no matter what the threatened consequences of popular or populistic wrath may be." Quoted in Paul, *Conservative Crisis*, p. 195. The Court responded by declaring that "since the opinion in *Marbury v. Madison*, 1 Cranch 137, 177, was delivered, it has not been doubted that it is within judicial competency, by express provisions of the Constitution or by necessary inference and implication, to determine whether a given law of the United States is or is not made in pursuance of the Constitution, and to hold it valid or void accordingly." 157 U.S. 429, 554.

7. Pennoyer, "Income Tax Decision," p. 552. See chap. 1, nn. 128–36 and accompanying text.

8. Ibid., p. 556.

9. Ibid. The proposition that federal courts had no constitutional power to nullify state laws *had* previously been asserted. See, e.g., remarks of Calhoun in chap. 6, nn. 43–44 and accompanying text.

10. Ibid., pp. 557–58. The tacit assumption that *Marbury* "established" the judicial power of nullification (à la Phelps, Doolittle, etc.) leads to the theory that the Founders did not intend that the Court should have the power (à la Pennoyer)—the denial of which leads ultimately to the conspiracy theory of the Constitution (à la Smith and Beard).

11. Lafon Allen, "The Income Tax Decision. An Answer to Gov. Pennoyer," *American Law Review* 29 (1895): 853.

12. Ibid., pp. 849–50.

13. Ibid., p. 854.

14. Sylvester Pennoyer, "A Reply to the Foregoing," *American Law Review* 29 (1895): 857. This seems to be the first suggestion of such an idea.

15. Ibid., p. 860.

16. Ibid., p. 862.

17. Robert Ludlow Fowler, "The Origin of the Supreme Judicial Power in the Federal Constitution," *American Law Review* 29 (1895): 711.

18. Ibid., pp. 712–14.

19. Ibid., pp. 715–18.

20. Ibid., pp. 719–22. Fowler also makes the astonishing argument that the national government is *not* one of delegated powers, since the states never really had independent existence after the Revolution: sovereignty passed directly from the Crown to "the people" of all the states, *collectively*. What about the Tenth Amendment? According to Fowler, it "has no bearing on the question. . . . It is equally susceptible of the construction that the sovereign people in all the States granted to the States themselves their sovereign powers not required by the Federal establishment. If we exchange the situation of the words 'delegated' and 'reserved' in Art. X of the Amendment we have the situation as it probably was before that time." Ibid., p. 720.

21. See chap. 10, n. 74 and accompanying text.

22. Sylvester Pennoyer, "The Power of the Supreme Court to Declare an Act of Congress Unconstitutional: The Case of *Marbury v. Madison*," *American Law Review* 30 (1896): 188. See chap. 6, n. 49–57 and accompanying text.

23. Ibid., pp. 190–91.

24. Ibid., pp. 193–94.

25. Ibid., p. 197.

26. Ibid., pp. 198–202.

27. Junius Parker, "The Supreme Court and its Constitutional Duty and Power," *American Law Review* 30 (1896): 357.

28. Ibid., p. 359.

29. Ibid., pp. 357–61.

30. John W. Akin, "Aggressions of the Federal Courts," *American Law Review* 32 (1898): 671. See also William H. Taft, "Criticism of the Federal Judiciary,"

*American Law Review* 29 (1895): 645, quoted in Akin, "Aggressions," p. 695. Taft's article appears in the same volume of the *American Law Review* as do the earlier articles of Pennoyer. I did not discuss it in the first part of this chapter because it seems to bear only remotely on the topic under scrutiny and is not cited by any of the commentators we have discussed except Akin. Briefly, Taft's argument comprises the following points: (1) that the federal courts have become the scapegoats of demagogues; (2) that the reason is that the courts have assumed jurisdiction of corporate litigation where the demagogues thought they should not have; (3) that the criticisms are unjustified because Congress authorized the courts to assume jurisdiction of such cases by statute; (4) that, therefore, the courts' assumption of jurisdiction is the fault of the people themselves. Taft, "Criticism," pp. 654–56. Taft then defends substantive due process, the *Knight* decision, railroad receiverships, and labor injunctions. He does not mention *Marbury*, or Marshall, except in the quote in the text. Taft was at the time judge of the Circuit Court of Appeals of Ohio and later became the only man in history to hold both the offices of chief justice and president of the United States.

31. Akin, "Aggressions," p. 695.

32. Ibid., p. 696.

33. Henry Flanders, "Has the Supreme Court of the United States the Constitutional Power to Declare Void an Act of Congress?" *American Law Review* 48 (1900): 385.

34. Ibid., pp. 385–86.

35. Ibid., pp. 387–90.

36. See chap. 10, nn. 88–90 and accompanying text.

37. These proceedings took place in 1901 and were compiled and edited by John F. Dillon for publication in 1903. John F. Dillon, ed., *John Marshall: Life, Character, and Judicial Services*, 3 vols. (Chicago: Callaghan & Co., 1903).

38. Donald O. Dewey, *Marshall versus Jefferson: The Political Background of Marbury v. Madison* (New York: Alfred A. Knopf, 1970), p. 184.

39. Dillon, vol. 1, p. xviii.

40. Ibid., p. 141.

41. Ibid., vol. 2, p. 122.

42. Ibid., vol. 3, p. 130.

43. Ibid., p. 231.

44. See chap. 10, nn. 23–25 and accompanying text.

45. See chap. 10, nn. 17–20 and accompanying text.

46. Martin Van Buren, *Inquiry into the Origin and Course of Political Parties in the United States* (New York: Hurd & Houghton, 1867), p. 275.

47. Recall Pennoyer's adaptation of Jefferson's "sappers and miners" phrase and his application of it to the entire Federalist period. See this chapter, n. 22 and accompanying text.

48. Camm Patteson, "The Judicial Usurpation of Power," *Virginia Law Review* 10 (1905): 855.

49. Ibid., p. 856 (emphasis mine).

50. Andrew C. McLaughlin, *The Confederation and the Constitution*, vol. 10 of The American Nation Series (New York: Harper & Brother, 1905), p. 250.

51. Joseph Cotton, ed., *The Constitutional Decisions of John Marshall*, 2 vols.

(New York: G. P. Putnam's Sons, 1905). These volumes comprise the second such compilation to appear during the first five years of the twentieth century. The first, published two years before, had accompanied the set of addresses commemorating the anniversary of Marshall's accession to the bench. John M. Dillon, ed., *The Complete Constitutional Decisions of John Marshall* (Chicago: Callaghan & Co., 1903). The Dillon volume contains an index of all the references made to *Marbury v. Madison* in the respective addresses. Ibid., pp. 40–41.

52. Cotton, *Constitutional Decisions*, pp. xii–xiii.

53. Ibid. Corwin would first coin the phrase "judicial review" five years later. See chap. 8, n. 70 and accompanying text.

54. Edward S. Corwin, "The Supreme Court and Unconstitutional Acts of Congress," *Michigan Law Review* 4 (1906): 616.

55. Ibid., pp. 617–23, 632–34.

56. 1 Cranch, at 177.

57. Ibid., at 179.

58. Corwin, "Supreme Court," pp. 625–30.

59. Walter C. Clark, "The Next Constitutional Convention of the United States," *Yale Law Journal* 16 (December 1906): 65. Clark was chief justice of the Supreme Court of North Carolina.

60. Ibid., p. 75.

61. Ibid., pp. 77–79.

62. Ibid., p. 76. So little does the judge perceive the ultimate implications of his point of view on the Framers' intentions that he is able to assert the following: "A proposition was made in the Convention . . . that the Judges should pass upon the Constitutionality of acts of Congress. This was defeated 5 June, receiving the vote of only two States. It was renewed no less than three times, . . . and . . . at no time did it receive the votes of more than three States." Ibid., p. 75. Now as Beard was to point out (in particular reference to Clark) a few years later, "No proposition to confer directly upon the judiciary the power of passing on the constitutionality of acts of Congress was submitted to the Convention." Charles A. Beard, *The Supreme Court and the Constitution* (New York: Macmillan, 1912), p. 15. Judge Clark's reference is, of course, to the proposal to establish a Council of Revision— voted down in the Convention on separation-of-powers grounds (see chap. 4). Thus, the idea that the Founders *explicitly* rejected judicial nullification originates in an outright falsification of the record of the Federal Convention.

63. William Trickett, "The Great Usurpation," *American Law Review* 40 (1906): 356. Trickett was Dean of the Dickinson School of Law.

64. Ibid., p. 369–76.

65. Ibid., p. 371 (emphasis mine).

66. Ibid., p. 357.

67. William Trickett, "Judicial Dispensation from Congressional Statutes," *American Law Review* 41 (1907): 65.

68. Ibid., pp. 66–69.

69. Ibid., pp. 69–76, 90.

70. Ibid., p. 79 (emphasis mine).

71. William Trickett, "Judicial Nullification of Acts of Congress," *North American Review* 186 (1907): 848.

72. Ibid., pp. 848–51.

73. Ibid., pp. 851–52.

74. Ibid., p. 856.

75. Robert F. Street, "The Irreconcilable Conflict," *American Law Review* 41 (1907): 686. See chap. 10, n. 30 and accompanying text.

76. Ibid., p. 690.

77. Quoted in ibid., p. 693 (emphasis mine).

78. Ibid., pp. 686–91.

79. For example, Franklin Pierce declared in 1908 that the Supreme Court has "absolute power" and cited *Marbury* as the initial precedent whereby the Court began to accumulate such power. He mentioned several of the commentators we have discussed. Franklin Pierce, *Federal Usurpation* (New York: D. Appleton & Co., 1908), pp. 197–201. Louis Boudin, in 1911, asserted that "the great majority of the framers never suspected that a general power of the judiciary to control legislation could be interpreted into the new Constitution. They evidently assumed that such extraordinary power could not be exercised unless expressly granted." Louis B. Boudin, "Government by Judiciary," *Political Science Quarterly* 26 (1911): 238. Boudin later expanded this article into two volumes, possibly in response to Beard's criticism that Boudin had not cited "ample historical proof" in the article. See Beard, *Supreme Court and Constitution*, p. 11; also Louis Boudin, *Government by Judiciary*, 2 vols. (New York: Godwin, 1932).

80. J. Allen Smith, *The Spirit of American Government*, edited by Cushing Strout (1907: reprint, Cambridge, Mass.: Belknap Press of Harvard University Press, 1965).

81. Ibid., pp. 33, 219.

82. Ibid., pp. 85–92.

83. Edward S. Corwin, "The Establishment of Judicial Review," *Michigan Law Review* 9 (1910): 118.

84. Ibid., p. 104. See this chapter, n. 55 and accompanying text.

85. Beard, *Supreme Court and Constitution*, pp. 1–11.

86. Ibid., chap. 2.

87. Ibid., chap. 6.

88. Charles A. Beard, *An Economic Interpretation of the Constitution of the United States* (New York: Macmillan, 1935), p. 162.

89. Beard, *Supreme Court and Constitution*, p. 126.

90. Ibid., p. 120.

91. Ibid., pp. 120–25.

92. Albert J. Beveridge, *The Life of John Marshall*, 4 vols. (Boston: Houghton Mifflin, 1916).

93. Ibid., vol. 3, p. 143.

94. Ibid., p. 132.

95. Ibid., p. 128.

96. Ibid., p. 142.

97. Vernon L. Parrington, *Main Currents in American Thought*, 2 vols. (New York: Harcourt, Brace & Co., 1927), vol. 2, p. 23.

98. Ibid., p. 307.

99. Ibid., p. 190.

100. Ibid., p. 22.

101. Cushing Strout, "Introduction," in Smith, *Spirit*, p. xxix.

## Chapter 12. Beyond the Mythical Marbury

1. See chap. 11, nn. 92–100 and accompanying text.

2. Christopher Wolfe, *The Rise of Modern Judicial Review: From Constitutional Interpretation to Judge-made Law* (New York: Basic Books, 1986), p. 41.

3. Ibid., p. 3. Wolfe characterizes the transition from traditional to modern judicial review as a movement from constitutional interpretation to judicial legislation.

4. See article entitled "Chief Justice Taft defends the United States Supreme Court," in *Commercial and Financial Chronicle* 116 (June 9, 1923): 2590–91; also A. T. Hadley, "The Constitutional Position of Property in America," *Independent* 64 (April 16, 1908): 834–38. Additional references may be found in Dormin J. Ettrude, ed., *The Power of Congress to Nullify Supreme Court Decisions* (New York: H. W. Wilson Co., 1924), pp. 26–28.

5. Archibald Cox, *The Role of the Supreme Court in American Government* (New York: Oxford University Press, 1976), p. 34. See also references in Ettrude, *Power of Congress*, pp. 23–26.

6. See Eugene V. Rostow, "The Democratic Character of Judicial Review," in Leonard W. Levy, ed., *Judicial Review and the Supreme Court* (New York: Harper & Row, 1967), pp. 74–104.

7. See Arthur E. Sutherland, "Privacy in Connecticut," *Michigan Law Review* 64, (1965): 284.

8. See Thomas J. Higgins, S.J., *Judicial Review Unmasked* (West Hanover, Mass.: Christopher Publishing House, 1981), esp. chap. 7.

9. Wallace Mendelson, "Was Chief Justice Marshall an Activist?" Morton Halpern and Charles Lamb, eds., *Supreme Court Activism and Restraint* (Lexington, Mass.: Lexington Books, 1982), p. 57.

10. See chap. 4, nn. 52–58 and accompanying text. I am indebted to Professor G. Edward White for calling my attention to this possibility. He has provided a most thoughtful historiography of the Marshall Court's supposed "nationalism": "The Art of Revising History: Revisiting the Marshall Court," *Suffolk University Law Review* 16 (1982): 659–85.

11. 4 Wheat. 316 (1819).

12. Ibid., at 400–25 (constitutionality of the bank), and at 425–37 (invalidity of the tax).

13. This argument is an old one, dating back to the famous critique authored by John Taylor, *Construction Construed and Constitutions Vindicated* (Richmond, Va.: Shepherd & Pollard, 1820), pp. 79–201.

14. See Robert H. Jackson, *The Struggle for Judicial Supremacy: A Study of a Crisis in American Power Politics* (New York: Alfred A. Knopf, 1941), pp. 28–30.

15. 4 Wheat. 316, 436–37.

16. 9 Wheat. 1 (1824).

17. Ibid., at 186–97 (definition of commerce and congressional power over the subject), and at 197–222 (state conflict with federal law).

18. Ibid., at 211–19.

19. 2 Pet. 245 (1829). In *Willson,* the Court upheld Delaware's authorization of a dam across a small but navigable stream, the ostensible purpose of which was swamp drainage to reduce the incidence of malaria.

20. 12 How. 299 (1851). In *Cooley,* the Court upheld a Pennsylvania law requiring the use of local pilots in the Philadelphia harbor, on the grounds that the act was a local safety measure and Congress had not preempted the field. In reaching its decision, the Court distinguished between subjects requiring uniform (national) regulation, and those requiring diverse (local) regulation, holding that states were entitled to pass laws regulating the latter, but not the former.

21. 9 Wheat. 1, 209–10.

22. 6 Wheat. 264 (1821). United States Constitution, Article VI, Clause 2.

23. 6 Wheat. 264, 443.

24. Ibid., at 440–47.

25. 7 Pet. 243 (1833).

26. Ibid., at 245–46.

27. Ibid., at 247–51.

28. *Spies v. Illinois,* 123 U.S. 131, 166 (1887).

29. *Thorington v. Montgomery,* 147 U.S. 490, 492 (1893).

30. 7 Pet. 243, 247.

31. 4 Wheat. 316, 419–20.

32. *Griswold v. Connecticut,* 381 U.S. 479 (1965); *Roe v. Wade,* 410 U.S. 113 (1973); *Planned Parenthood of Central Missouri v. Danforth,* 428 U.S. 52 (1976). This reunion has been referred to as "neosubstantive" due process. See Wallace Mendelson, *The American Constitution and the Judicial Process* (Homewood, Ill.: Dorsey Press, 1980), p. 224.

33. 83 U.S. 36, 80–81 (1873).

34. 94 U.S. 113 (1877).

35. Field's dissenting opinion in *Slaughterhouse* may be found in 83 U.S. 36, at 83; Bradley's, at 111.

36. 100 U.S. 303 (1879).

37. 103 U.S. 370 (1880).

38. *Civil Rights Cases,* 109 U.S. 3 (1883).

39. *Santa Clara v. The Southern Pacific R.R. Co.,* 118 U.S. 394 (1886).

40. *Chicago, Milwaukee & St. Paul Ry. v. Minnesota,* 134 U.S. 418 (1890).

41. *Plessy v. Ferguson,* 163 U.S. 537 (1896).

42. 7 Wall. 321 (1869).

43. Mendelson, *American Constitution,* p. 202.

44. *Spies v. Illinois,* 123 U.S. 131 (1887).

45. 13 Wall. 166.

46. Ibid., at 176–77.

47. Ibid., at 177.

48. John Lewis, *A Treatise on the Law of Eminent Domain in the United States* (Chicago: Callahan & Co., 1888), p. 317.

49. 96 U.S. 97 (1877).

50. Ibid., at 105.

51. Ibid., at 107.

52. 36 F. 385 (1888).
53. Ibid., at 385.
54. Ibid., at 392.
55. Ibid., at 395–96.
56. *Proprietors of Mount Hope Cemetery v. City of Boston & Others*, 158 Mass. 509, 519 (1893).
57. *Baker v. Village of Norwood et al.*, 74 F. 997, 1000 (1896).
58. 166 U.S. 226 (1897).
59. Ibid., at 230, 232.
60. Ibid., at 233.
61. See this chapter, n. 50 and accompanying text.
62. 166 U.S. 226, 233.
63. Ibid., at 235.
64. 166 U.S. 226, 241. See this chapter, nn. 52, 56, 57 and accompanying text.
65. 165 U.S. 578 (1897). The Court had earlier used substantive due process to invalidate a federal law in *Dred Scott v. Sanford.*
66. Ibid., at 588–89.
67. Ibid., at 589.
68. See this chapter, n. 35 and accompanying text.
69. See Benjamin Twiss, *Lawyers and the Constitution: How Laissez-Faire Came to the Supreme Court* (Princeton, N.J.: Princeton University Press, 1942).
70. 111 U.S. 746 (1884). For Bradley's dissenting opinion in *Slaughterhouse*, see 83 U.S. 36, at 111.
71. 111 U.S. 746, at 762–65, quoted in 165 U.S. 578, at 589–90.
72. 165 U.S. 578, at 590.
73. *United States v. E. C. Knight Co.*, 156 U.S. 1 (1895). See Arnold Paul, *Conservative Crisis and the Rule of Law: Attitudes of Bar and Bench, 1887–1895* (Ithaca, N.Y.: Cornell University Press, 1960), chaps. 4–9.
74. For a listing and discussion of the cases where the Court has "nationalized" (applied to states) specific guarantees in the federal Bill of Rights throughout the present century, see Malcolm M. Feeley and Samuel Krislov, *Constitutional Law* (Boston: Little, Brown & Co., 1985), pp. 340–46. Such a listing is available in many other casebooks as well.
75. See *Home Building & Loan Assoc. v. Blaisdell*, 290 U.S. 398 (1934), where the Court upheld what was essentially a stay law, presumably the sort of law that the Framers had "in mind" when the contract clause was adopted.
76. See chap. 7, nn. 30–31 and accompanying text.
77. See chap. 4, nn. 3–18 and accompanying text.
78. See chap. 7, nn. 40–45 and accompanying text.
79. See chap. 10, nn. 13–14 and accompanying text.
80. 163 U.S. 537 (1896). In *Plessy*, the Court upheld a Louisiana law requiring racial segregation on railway passenger trains.
81. See Felix Frankfurter, *Mr. Justice Holmes and the Supreme Court* (Cambridge, Mass.: Harvard University Press, 1938), app. I.
82. *Carter v. Texas*, 177 U.S. 442 (1900), overturned a Texas law excluding blacks from the grand jury, on equal-protection grounds. *Rogers v. Alabama*, 192 U.S. 226 (1904), repeated the holding for an identical Alabama law. *Truax v. Raich*,

239 U.S. 33 (1915), overturned an Arizona law requiring a certain percentage of employees in a business to be qualified electors or native-born citizens, on equal-protection grounds. *Buchanan v. Warley,* 245 U.S. 60 (1917), overturned a Louisville ordinance forbidding blacks to occupy houses in blocks where the majority of residents are white, on due-process grounds. *Nixon v. Herndon,* 273 U.S. 536 (1927), overturned a Texas law barring blacks from the Democratic primary. *Nixon v. Condon,* 286 U.S. 73 (1932), overturned a Texas law empowering the Democratic State Committee to exclude blacks from the primary, on equal-protection grounds. *Morrison v. California,* 291 U.S. 82 (1934), overturned a California law creating the presumption that a lessee is Oriental, on due-process grounds. *Norris v. Alabama,* 294 U.S. 587 (1935), overturned the systematic exclusion of blacks from Alabama juries, on equal-protection grounds. *Hollins v. Oklahoma,* 295 U.S. 394 (1935), overturned the county custom of excluding blacks from jury, on due-process grounds. See Frankfurter, *Mr. Justice Holmes,* app. I.

83. See Frankfurter, *Mr. Justice Holmes, app. I.*

84. See Charles Warren, *Congress, the Constitution, and the Supreme Court* (Boston: Little, Brown, & Company, 1925), chap. 10. See also Wilfred C. Gilbert, ed., *Provisions of Federal Law Held Unconstitutional by the Supreme Court of the United States* (1936; reprint, Westport, Conn.: Greenwood Press, 1976). For cases prior to 1895, see chap. 7, n. 33 and accompanying text.

85. *Wong Wing v. United States,* 163 U.S. 228 (1896), overturned a law authorizing deportation of Chinese after summary hearing before any federal judge or commissioner, on Fifth (grand jury) and Sixth (petit jury) Amendment grounds. *Kirby v. United States,* 174 U.S. 47 (1899), overturned a law making conviction on one charge (embezzlement) conclusive evidence of guilt on another (receiving with knowledge), on Sixth Amendment confrontation-clause grounds. *Rasmussen v. United States,* 197 U.S. 516 (1905), overturned a territorial law authorizing trial by jury of six, on Sixth Amendment common-law jury trial grounds. *United States v. Evans,* 213 U.S. 297 (1909), overturned a law authorizing government appeals in criminal cases, but prohibiting the setting aside of verdicts for error occurring at trial, on Article III grounds. *Muskrat v. United States,* 219 U.S. 346 (1911), overturned a law authorizing suits in the court of claims to test the validity of acts of Congress, on Article III grounds. *United States v. L. Cohen Grocery Co.,* 255 U.S. 81 (1921), overturned a law penalizing the making of an "unjust or unreasonable rate or charge," on Sixth Amendment (information) grounds. *United States v. Moreland,* 258 U.S. 433 (1922), overturned a law authorizing prosecution for desertion of wife or child on information, on Fifth Amendment (indictment) grounds. *Keller v. Potomac Electric Power Co.,* 261 U.S. 428 (1923), overturned a law vesting in the Supreme Court of the District of Columbia power to revise decisions of the Public Utilities Commission, on Article III grounds. See Warren, *Congress, Constitution, and Court,* pp. 316–17, 319, 322–23, 327–29.

86. *Evans v. Gore,* 253 U.S. 245 (1920); *Miles v. Graham,* 268 U.S. 501 (1925); *O'Donoghue v. United States,* 289 U.S. 516 (1933); *Booth v. United States,* 291 U.S. 339 (1934). *Evans* and *Miles* involved the imposition of income taxes on the salaries of judges. *O'Donoghue* and *Booth* involved depression-era, temporary emergency reductions of judicial salaries, the latter of retired judges. These decisions are arguably of a judiciary nature, since they are grounded on Article III and

judicial independence. However, the power to tax and spend is textually committed to Congress, and it is questionable whether Article III exempts judges from the demands of ordinary citizenship. See Warren, *Congress, Constitution, and Court*, pp. 326, 333, 337.

87. *Fairbank v. United States*, 181 U.S. 283 (1901), invalidated a stamp tax on bills of lading for goods destined for export. *United States v. Hvoslef*, 237 U.S. 1 (1915), invalidated a tax on charter parties as in effect a tax on the goods carried by such parties. *Thames and Mersey Ins. Co. v. United States*, 237 U.S. 19 (1915), invalidated a tax on marine insurance policies, on the ground that marine insurance is so essential to export trade that a tax on such policies is a tax on exports. *Spalding & Bros. v. Edwards*, 266 U.S. 66 (1923), invalidated a tax levied under the War Revenue Act of 1917 on certain goods in the process of being exported. See Warren, *Congress, Constitution, and Court*, pp. 317-18, 324, 333.

88. *Adair v. United States*, 208 U.S. 161 (1908); *Choate v. Trapp*, 224 U.S. 665 (1912); *Lipke v. Lederer*, 159 U.S. 557 (1922); *Adkins v. Children's Hospital*, 261 U.S. 525 (1923); *Small v. American Sugar Refining Co.*, 267 U.S. 233 (1925); *Nichols v. Collidge*, 274 U.S. 531 (1927); *Untermeyer v. Anderson*, 276 U.S. 440 (1928); *National Life Insurance Co. v. United States*, 277 U.S. 508 (1928); *Heiner v. Donnan*, 285 U.S. 312 (1932); *Lynch v. United States*, 282 U.S. 571 (1934); *Railroad Retirement Board v. Alton R.R.*, 295 U.S. 330 (1935); *Louisville Joint Stock Land Bank v. Radford*, 295 U.S. 555 (1935). See Warren, *Congress, Constitution, and Court*, pp. 321, 323-24, 330-31, 333-37, 339.

89. *The Employers' Liability Cases*, 207 U.S. 463 (1908); *Hammer v. Dagenhart*, 247 U.S. 251 (1918); *Bailey v. Drexel Furniture Co.*, 259 U.S. 20 (1922); *Hill v. Wallace*, 259 U.S. 44 (1922); *Indian Motorcycle Co. v. United States*, 238 U.S. 570 (1931); *Burnet v. Coronado Oil & Gas Co.*, 285 U.S. 393 (1932); *Hopkins Savings Assoc. v. Cleary*, 296 U.S. 315 (1935); *Ashton v. Cameron County Dist.*, 299 U.S. 619 (1936). See Warren, *Congress, Constitution, and Court*, pp. 320-21, 324-25, 329-30, 336-37. See also Gilbert, *Provisions of Federal Law*, pp. 78-80.

90. *Matter of Heff*, 197 U.S. 488 (1905) (power to regulate commerce with Indian Tribes); *Hodges v. United States*, 203 U.S. 1 (1906) (power to enforce Thirteenth Amendment); *Keller v. United States*, 213 U.S. 138 (1909) (power to regulate immigration); *Coyle v. Oklahoma*, 221 U.S. 559 (1911) (power to admit new states); *Butts v. Merchants Trans. Co.*, 230 U.S. 126 (1913) (power to govern territories); *Eisner v. Macomber*, 252 U.S. 189 (1920) (power to tax incomes); *Knickerbocker Ice Co. v. Stewart*, 253 U.S. 149 (1920) (power to pass maritime regulations); *Newberry v. United States*, 256 U.S. 232 (1921) (power to regulate elections); *Washington v. Dawson & Co.*, 264 U.S. 219 (1924) (power to pass admiralty and maritime regulations); *Trusler v. Crooks*, 269 U.S. 475 (1926) (taxing power); *Myers v. United States*, 272 U.S. 52 (1926) (advise and consent power); *Panama Refining Co. v. Ryan*, 293 U.S. 388 (1935) (delegation of legislative power); *Perry v. United States*, 294 U.S. 330 (1935) (borrowing power); *Schechter v. United States*, 295 U.S. 495 (1935) (delegation of legislative power); *United States v. Constantine*, 296 U.S. 287 (1935) (taxing power); *United States v. Butler*, 297 U.S. 1 (1936) (taxing power); *Rickert Rice Mills v. Fontenot*, 297 U.S. 110 (1936) (taxing power); *Carter v. Carter Coal Co.*, 298 U.S. 238 (1936) (taxing power). See Warren, *Congress, Constitution,*

*and Court,* pp. 318–21, 323, 325–26, 328, 331–32, 334, 337–39. See also Gilbert, *Provisions of Federal Law,* pp. 69–72, 83–86.

91. See, e.g., *National Labor Relations Bd. v. Jones & Laughlin Steel Corp.,* 301 U.S. 1 (1937); *United States v. Darby Lumber Co.,* 312 U.S. 100 (1941); *Wickard v. Filburn,* 317 U.S. 111 (1942); *United States v. Kahriger,* 345 U.S. 22 (1953); *Steward Machine Co. v. Davis,* 301 U.S. 548 (1937); *California v. Thompson,* 313 U.S. 109 (1941); *West Coast Hotel Co. v. Parrish,* 300 U.S. 379 (1937); *Ferguson v. Skrupa,* 372 U.S. 726 (1963). The combined effect of these decisions returned the Court to Marshall's jurisprudence. That is, *NLRB, Darby, Wickard, Kahriger,* and *Steward* restored the power of Congress in the fields of commerce, taxation, spending, and implied powers, thereby returning to the broad view of national authority articulated in *Gibbons v. Ogden* and *McCulloch v. Maryland. California v. Thompson* restored the power of states to enact commercial regulations, which the Marshall Court had recognized in *Willson v. Blackbird Creek Marsh Co. West Coast Hotel* and *Ferguson* overturned Fifth and Fourteenth Amendment substantive economic due process, neither of which doctrines existed during Marshall's day.

92. See this chapter, nn. 80–83 and accompanying text.

93. 109 U.S. 3 (1883). In these cases, Congress had passed, pursuant to Section 5 of the Fourteenth Amendment, the Civil Rights Act of 1875. This act made it a crime for anyone to deny accommodations to blacks in hotels, theaters, transport facilities, and places of public amusement. The Court held that Congress was without power to proscribe discrimination in such places, since the Fourteenth Amendment applied only to states, not to private persons. The doctrine of these cases has come to be known as the "state action" principle.

94. *Tot v. United States,* 319 U.S. 463 (1943); *United States v. Lovett,* 328 U.S. 303 (1946); *United States v. Cardiff,* 344 U.S. 174 (1952).

95. In *Tot,* Congress had established in the Federal Firearms Act a presumption of guilt based on a prior conviction and possession of a firearm; this was held to violate due process of law. In *Lovett,* Congress had provided that no salary be paid to certain named federal employees in the Urgent Deficiency Appropriation Act of 1943. The Court held that this constituted a bill of attainder and thus violated Article I, Section 9. In *Cardiff,* a statute that prohibited anyone from refusing to permit entry or inspection of premises by federal officers was held void for vagueness and as violative of the Fifth Amendment's due-process clause.

96. See, e.g., *Missouri ex rel. Gaines v. Canada,* 305 U.S. 337 (1938), where the Court held that a state could not bar admission of a black from the state university's law school. In *McLaurin v. Oklahoma State Regents,* 339 U.S. 637 (1950), the Court held that a state could not segregate black students in classes, libraries, and cafeterias at the state university. In *Sweatt v. Painter,* 339 U.S. 629 (1950), the Court held that states could not run separate state university law schools for blacks and whites. See also *Shelley v. Kraemer,* 334 U.S. 1 (1948), invalidating a restrictive racial covenant in the sale of private dwellings; and *Smith v. Allwright,* 321 U.S. 649 (1944), declaring "white primaries" unconstitutional.

97. *Plessy* was formally overruled in *Brown v. Board of Education of Topeka (I),* 347 U.S. 483 (1954), invalidating racial segregation in a state's public-school system.

98. *Toth v. Quarles*, 350 U.S. 11 (1955) (jury trial, grand jury indictment); *Reid v. Covert*, 354 U.S. 1 (1957) (speedy trial, public trial, jury trial, grand jury); *Trop v. Dulles*, 356 U.S. 86 (1958) (cruel and unusual punishment); *Kinsella v. United States*, 361 U.S. 234 (1960) (jury trial, grand jury): *Grisham v. Hagan*, 361 U.S. 278 (1960) (habeas corpus, Fifth and Sixth Amendments); *McElroy v. United States ex rel. Guagliande*, 361 U.S. 281 (1960) (habeas corpus, Sixth Amendment); *Kennedy v. Mendoza-Martinez*, 372 U.S. 144 (1963) (Fifth Amendment procedural due process); *Albertson v. Subversive Activities Control Board*, 382 U.S. 70 (1965) (self-incrimination); *United States v. Romano*, 382 U.S. 136 (1965) (procedural due process, validity of statutory presumption); *Marchetti v. United States*, 390 U.S. 39 (1968) (self-incrimination); *Haynes v. United States*, 390 U.S. 85 (1968) (self-incrimination); *United States v. Jackson*, 390 U.S. 570 (1968) (jury trial); *Leary v. United States*, 395 U.S. 6 (1969) (self-incrimination, procedural due process, validity of statutory presumption); *O'Callahan v. Parker*, 395 U.S. 258 (1969) (grand jury).

99. See cases in n. 98. Procedural due-process guarantees may be appropriately addressed to courts, since they not only protect individuals but also guard against legislative or executive interference with the performance of judicial functions. Other provisions that may be thought, at least in certain instances, to constitute restrictions on judicial power are those prohibiting attainders and those limiting the legislative power to impose criminal penalties for nonspecific offenses (such as the First and Fifth Amendments). In one sense, attainders are legislative usurpations of judicial power, and a court could not properly apply such a law without falling into self-contradiction. Likewise, a court could not properly apply a vague statute without intruding into the legislative arena via enhancement of its own discretion. Warren Court decisions invalidating federal laws on such grounds are: *United States v. Brown*, 381 U.S. 437 (1965) (attainder); *United States v. Robel*, 389 U.S. 258 (1967) (First Amendment, vagueness and overbreadth); *Aptheker v. Secretary of State*, 378 U.S. 500 (1964) (Fifth Amendment, vagueness). One additional case might be included. In *Afroyim v. Rusk*, 387 U.S. 253 (1967), the Court invalidated a law revoking American citizenship as a penalty for voting in a foreign election. The articulated basis for the Court's holding was the Fourteenth Amendment's definition of citizens as "all persons born or naturalized," although other (and stronger) grounds were probably available—including considerations of procedural due process and attainder.

100. See references in nn. 98–99. *Toth v. Quarles, Reid v. Covert, McElroy v. United States, Kinsella v. United States, Grisham v. Hagan,* and *O'Callahan v. Parker* involved trial by court-martial, applied to either civilian ex-servicemen, civilian dependents, or civilian employees of the armed forces. *Trop v. Dulles, Kennedy v. Mendoza-Martinez,* and *Afroyim v. Rusk* involved deprivation of citizenship for desertion, draft evasion, and voting in a foreign election, respectively.

101. *Bolling v. Sharp*, 347 U.S. 497 (1954).

102. See this chapter, n. 93 and accompanying text.

103. *Powell v. McCormack*, 395 U.S. 486 (1969).

104. In *Powell*, the Court rested its holding on the ground that Article I, Section 5 (empowering Congress to judge the qualifications of its members) extended

only to those provisions expressly set forth in the Constitution. In other words, Article I, Section 5 "incorporates" Article I, Section 2 (setting forth the requirements of age, citizenship, and residence) and nothing more.

105. In *Shapiro v. Thompson*, 394 U.S. 618 (1969), the Court invalidated a District of Columbia regulation requiring residence in the District for one year prior to eligibility for welfare assistance, asserting a right to interstate travel implicit in the Fifth Amendment's due-process clause. In *Schneider v. Rusk*, 377 U.S. 163 (1964), the Court struck down a provision depriving a naturalized person of citizenship for having "a continuous residence for three years" in the country of birth or previous nationality, because the law discriminated against aliens in violation of the "equal protection component" of the Fifth Amendment's due-process clause, thus following the logic of *Bolling v. Sharp*. See this chapter, n. 101 and accompanying text. In *Schneider*, the Court might have rested its decision on grounds that would have brought it within the judiciary-nature category, since procedural due-process considerations are present when the victim is out of the country; but, it chose not to do so. Finally, in *Lamont v. Postmaster General*, 381 U.S. 301 (1965), the Court overturned a law authorizing the Post Office to detain material determined to be communist political propaganda. The difficulty here is that laws that raise First Amendment issues not involving the imposition of penal sanctions (e.g., unlike laws void for vagueness) are not cases of a judiciary type, since the First Amendment is per se addressed to Congress, not to courts.

106. *Richardson v. Davis*, 409 U.S. 1069 (1972) (Social Security Act, reduction of benefits to illegitimate children upon death of parent); *Dep't of Agriculture v. Moreno*, 413 U.S. 528 (1973) (Food Stamp Act, denial of benefits to households containing an individual unrelated by birth, marriage, or adoption to any other member of household); *Frontiero v. Richardson*, 411 U.S. 677 (1973) (denial of benefits to spouses of female members of armed forces except on showing of dependence); *Jiminez v. Weinberger*, 417 U.S. 628 (1974) (Social Security Act, denial of disability insurance benefits to illegitimate children who were not supported, or did not live with, the disabled parent prior to onset of the disability); *Weinberger v. Wiesenfeld*, 420 U.S. 636 (1975) (Social Security Act, denial of survivors' benefits to widower of covered deceased spouse, but not to minor children); *Califano v. Goldfarb*, 430 U.S. 199 (1977) (Social Security Act, denial of survivors' benefits to widower of covered deceased spouse except on showing of dependency); *Railroad Retirement Board v. Kalina*, 431 U.S. 909 (1977) (Railroad Retirement Act, denial of benefits to spouses of female employees except on showing of dependency); *Califano v. Westcott*, 443 U.S. 76 (1979) (Social Security Act, denial of benefits to families whose dependent children have been deprived of support due to mother's unemployment, but granting support for father's unemployment). See also *Califano v. Jablon*, 430 U.S. 924 (1977).

107. *Dep't of Agriculture v. Murray*, 413 U.S. 508 (1973) (Food Stamp Act; denying benefits to households containing a person eighteen years or older who had been claimed as dependent for income tax purposes in the preceding tax year by a taxpayer not a member of household violates due-process clause of Fifth Amendment).

108. *National League of Cities v. Usery*, 426 U.S. 833 (1976) (Fair Labor Stan-

dards Act, extension of wage and hours coverage to employees of state and local government invalid because Congress lacks authority under commerce clause to regulate employee activities in the traditional governmental functions of the states).

109. *Oregon v. Mitchell,* 400 U.S. 112 (1970) (Voting Rights Act Amendment, minimum voting age qualification of eighteen years in state and local elections invalid because beyond the power of Congress to legislate).

110. *Immigration and Naturalization Service v. Chadha,* 462 U.S. 919 (1982). In *Chadha,* the Court overturned a provision in the INS Act of 1952 authorizing the House or Senate, acting individually, to overrule an attorney general's suspension of a deportation order of the INS. The Court selected the broadest possible ground for its decision—the presentment clauses of Article I, Section 7. Clause 2 reads: "Every Bill *which shall have passed* the House of Representatives and the Senate, shall, before it become a Law, be presented to the President of the United States" (emphasis mine). Clause 3 reads: "Every Order, Resolution, or Vote *to which* the Concurrence of the Senate and House of Representatives *may be necessary* . . . shall be presented to the President of the United States" (emphasis mine). Obviously, Clause 2 can have no application whatever to *Chadha,* since the one-house veto is not a "Bill which shall have passed" both House and Senate; and, as my emphasis indicates, the clause merely establishes a hypothetical. On the other hand, Clause 3 applies to *Chadha* only if the one-house veto is, *in fact,* one of those orders, resolutions, or votes to which the concurrence of both houses is necessary, but the language of Clause 3 does not tell us whether it is or not. To rest *Chadha* on the presentment clauses simply begs the question. That the Court is at least dimly aware of these considerations may be indicated by its reliance on the theory that the one-house veto is an exercise of "legislative power." Yet the Constitution does not say what legislative power is, other than to specify what powers Congress may exercise, one of which is "to make *all* Laws which shall be necessary and proper *for carrying into Execution* the foregoing Powers, and *all other Powers* vested by this Constitution in the Government of the United States, *or in any Department or Officer thereof."* United States Constitution, Article I, Section 8, Clause 18 (emphasis mine). Under the theory of judicial review articulated in this study, *Chadha* must be regarded as an extreme case of judicial usurpation, utterly without foundation in the Constitution. The decision is even more pretentious considering that such a crabbed argument was hardly necessary to the result. See Justice Powell's concurring opinion at 77 L. Ed. 2d 317, 350, for a persuasive argument that the one-house veto in this case was essentially a bill of attainder.

111. See Justice White's dissenting opinion at 77 L. Ed. 2d 317, 355, which contains a list of acts of Congress that have legislative veto provisions.

112. The two cases clearly of a judiciary nature were: *Turner v. United States,* 396 U.S. 398 (1970), where the Court overturned a statutory presumption that mere possession of cocaine implied knowledge of its illegal importation; and *United States v. United States Coin and Currency,* 401 U.S. 715 (1971), where the Court invalidated a tax law on self-incrimination grounds. The law had provided that a gambler who had failed to comply with the registration and reporting scheme held void in *Marchetti* (see n. 98) would forfeit the property used to violate

internal-revenue laws. Two additional cases are arguably of a judiciary type. One of these, *Northern Pipe Line Co. v. Marathon Pipe Line*, 458 U.S. 50 (1982), involved an attempt by Congress to establish bankruptcy courts pursuant to its power to create inferior courts in Article I. The Court invalidated the scheme, holding that the law extended Article III jurisdiction without providing the judicial independence requisite for the exercise of such power. *Marshall v. Barlow, Inc.*, 436 U.S. 307 (1978), involved warrantless inspection of industrial workplaces pursuant to the Occupational Safety and Health Act (OSHA). The Court invalidated the searches on Fourth Amendment grounds, adding that it was beyond the power of Congress (in regulating commerce) to authorize such inspections except in industries traditionally subject to them. Two cases involved both First and Fifth Amendment considerations, with the First Amendment the primary ground for each decision. In *Blount v. Rizzi*, 400 U.S. 410 (1971), the Court overturned a statutory scheme authorizing the postmaster general to close the mails to distributors of obscene materials, on freedom-of-expression grounds; also, the Court believed that the law did not contain procedures to assure prompt judicial determination of whether protected materials were being restrained. In *Chief of Capitol Police v. Jeanette Rankin Brigade*, 409 U.S. 972 (1972), the Court upheld a district court decision invalidating a statute that prohibited parades or assemblages on the Capitol grounds, on the basis of assembly, vagueness, and overbreadth concerns. The remaining decisions are those in *Schact v. United States*, 398 U.S. 58 (1970), invalidating a law permitting the wearing of military apparel in theatrical productions only if the portrayal does not discredit the armed service, on symbolic-speech grounds; *Tilton v. Richardson*, 403 U.S. 672 (1971), overturning a statutory provision that removed restrictions on the religious use of facilities built with federal funds after twenty years of use, on establishment-clause grounds; *Buckley v. Valeo*, 424 U.S. 1 (1976), overturning provisions of the Federal Election Campaign Act that restricted campaign expenditures (on free-speech grounds) and that authorized participation by Congress in the appointment of members of the Federal Election Commission (on appointments-clause grounds); *United States v. Will*, 449 U.S. 200 (1980), overturning four statutes that purported to revoke increases in the salaries of Article III judges after increases had taken effect (on Article III compensation grounds); *Railway Labor Executives Ass'n v. Gibbons*, 455 U.S. 457 (1982), invalidating a bankruptcy law passed pursuant to the commerce clause (on the ground of nonuniformity); *FCC v. League of Women Voters of California*, 468 U.S. 364 (1984), invalidating a provision of the Public Broadcasting Act of 1967 that prohibited editorializing by noncommercial public radio and television stations; *Federal Election Commission v. National Conservative Political Action Comm.*, 470 U.S. 480 (1985), invalidating a provision of the Presidential Election Campaign Fund Act that prohibited expenditure of more than one thousand dollars by an independent political action committee (PAC) to support a candidate who accepts public financing; and *Bowsher v. Synar*, 106 S. Ct. 3181 (1986), invalidating a provision in the Balanced Budget and Emergency Deficit Control Act of 1985 (the Graham-Rudman-Hollings Act), that authorized the comptroller general to order automatic spending cuts and made these cuts mandatory on the president, on the ground that the Constitution "commands" that "Congress play no direct role in the execution of the laws" (i.e., on *Chadha* grounds). Seven of those eight cases (*Schact, Tilton, Buckley, League of Women Voters, Gibbons, Federal Election Commission,* and *Bowsher*) all involve the Court's placing substantive restrictions on congressional power via constitutional provisions not primarily addressed to the judicial branch; thus they cannot be regarded as cases of a judiciary nature. Classification of *Marshall, Blount,* and, to a lesser extent, *Rankin* may be arguable. *Will* is difficult to classify, as are all cases involving alleged judicial salary decreases, but my inclination is to categorize it as non-judiciary, since the provision essentially was addressed to Congress.

113. *Griswold v. Connecticut,* 381 U.S. 479 (1965). See this chapter, n. 32 and accompanying text.

114. See this chapter, nn. 58-64 and accompanying text.

115. 410 U.S. 113 (1973). In *Roe,* the Court found that the "right of privacy" included a right to an abortion "on demand" during the first three months of pregnancy.

116. *Lochner v. New York,* 198 U.S. 45 (1905) (Holmes, J., dissenting), quoted in Sheldon Goldman, *Constitutional Law: Cases and Essays* (New York: Harper & Row, 1987), p. 448.

117. David M. O'Brien says that "the ideologically conservative Burger Court, for example, has been more activist than the liberal Warren Court. The trend is likely to continue regardless of future appointments and attempts to curb the Court." O'Brien, *Storm Center: The Supreme Court in American Politics* (New York: Norton & Co., 1986), p. 42.

118. Horace A. Davis, *The Judicial Veto* (Boston: Houghton Mifflin, 1914; New York: Da Capo Press, 1971), p. 46.

119. Robert von Moschzisker, *Judicial Review of Legislation* (Washington, D.C.: National Association for Constitutional Government, 1923; New York: Da Capo Press, 1971), p. 82.

120. Ettrude, *Power of Congress,* p. 60.

121. Charles Evans Hughes, *The Supreme Court of the United States, Its Foundation, Methods and Achievements: An Introduction* (New York: Columbia University Press, 1928), p. 87.

122. Charles Grove Haines, *The Revival of Natural Law Concepts* (Cambridge, Mass.: Harvard University Press, 1930).

123. See chap. 8, n. 3 and accompanying text.

124. Haines, *Revival,* pp. 81-82.

125. Ibid., p. 90. See also Edward S. Corwin, "A Basic Doctrine of American Constitutional Law," *Michigan Law Review* 12 (February 1914): 247; idem., "The 'Higher Law' Background of American Constitutional Law," *Harvard Law Review* 42 (December 1928-January 1929): 149, 365; Benjamin F. Wright, "American Interpretations of Natural Law," *American Political Science Review* 20 (1926): 524; idem, "Natural Law in American Political Theory," *Southwestern Politcal and Social Science Quarterly* 4 (1923): 202.

126. See chap. 5, n. 83 and accompanying text.

127. Haines, *Revival,* pp. 91-92.

128. Benjamin F. Wright, *The Contract Clause of the Constitution* (Cambridge, Mass.: Harvard University Press, 1938). See also discussion in Wright, *The Growth*

*of American Constitutional Law* (Boston: Houghton Mifflin, 1942; Chicago: University of Chicago Press, Phoenix Books, 1967), pp. 41–45.

129. Robert E. Cushman, "The Supreme Court and the Constitution," in Alfred Haines Cope and Fred Krinsky, eds., *Franklin D. Roosevelt and the Supreme Court* (Boston: D. C. Heath & Co., 1952), pp. 60–70, esp. 61. Cushman's article was originally published in 1936.

130. Drew Pearson and Robert S. Allen, *The Nine Old Men* (Garden City, N.Y.: Doubleday, Doran & Co., 1937), p. 46.

131. Ibid., pp. 50–53.

132. Isidor Feinstein, *The Court Disposes* (New York: Covici-Friede Publishers, 1937), p. 97.

133. Dean Alfange, *The Supreme Court and the National Will* (New York: Doubleday, Doran & Co., 1937), p. 31.

134. Ibid., pp. 35–36. See also Hughes, *The Supreme Court*, pp. 1–2.

135. *United States v. Carolene Products Co.*, 304 U.S. 144, 152 (1938). Footnote 4, without citations, reads: "There may be a narrower scope for operation of the presumption of constitutionality when legislation appears on its face to be within a specific prohibition of the Constitution, such as those of the first ten amendments, which are deemed equally specific when held to be embraced within the Fourteenth. . . . It is unnecessary to consider now whether legislation which restricts those political processes which can ordinarily be expected to bring about repeal of undesirable legislation, is to be subjected to more exacting judicial scrutiny under the general prohibitions of the Fourteenth Amendment than are most other types of legislation. . . . Nor need we enquire whether similar considerations enter into the review of statutes directed at particular religious . . . or national . . . or racial minorities . . . whether prejudice against discrete and insular minorities may be a special condition, which tends seriously to curtail the operation of those political procesess ordinarily to be relied upon to protect minorities, and which may call for a correspondingly more searching judicial inquiry." See Joel B. Grossman and Richard S. Wells, *Constitutional Law and Judicial Policy Making*, 3d ed. (New York: Longman, 1988), p. 155. According to Grossman and Wells, "The footnote was originally composed by Stone's law clerk, Louis Lusky. The first paragraph was added at the suggestion of Chief Justice Hughes." For a full quotation of the footnote with case citations, see Ronald D. Rotunda, *Constitutional Law: Principles and Cases* (St. Paul: West Publishing Co., 1987), pp. 207–9.

136. Beryl Harold Levy, *Our Constitution: Tool or Testament?* (New York: Alfred A. Knopf, 1941).

137. Ibid., pp. xiii–xviii, esp. xv.

138. Ibid., p. 3.

139. Ibid., pp. 22–23.

140. Ibid., pp. 24–26, 51, 101, 241.

141. Ibid., pp. v–ix. Robert H. Jackson, *The Struggle for Judicial Supremacy: A Study of a Crisis in American Power Politics* (New York: Alfred A. Knopf, 1941).

142. Jackson, *Struggle*, p. 24.

143. Ibid., p. 310.

144. Ibid., p. 320–21.

145. Ibid., pp. 315–16, 323–24, 283–85.

146. Henry Edgerton, "The Incidence of Judicial Control over Congress," *Cornell Law Quarterly,* 22 (1937): 299.

147. Robert K. Carr, *The Supreme Court and Judicial Review* (Westport, Conn.: Greenwood Press, 1942), p. 281.

148. Ibid., p. xi.

149. Ibid., p. 68.

150. Robert McCloskey, "Introduction," in Wright, *Growth,* pp. v–xiv.

151. Ibid., pp. vii–xii.

152. Ibid., p. 37.

153. Wright, *Growth,* pp. 34–35.

154. Ibid., p. 36. This is not exactly correct. Charles Lee, counsel for Marbury, had suggested (albeit obliquely) this possibility in his oral argument prior to the Court's decision. See chap. 5, n. 23 and accompanying text.

155. Ibid., p. 34. This is an extremely doubtful proposition. The early views on the scope of review held by the Jeffersonians in general, and Spencer Roane in particular, were at least as comprehensive as those of the early Federalists, and in most instances, even more so. See chap. 4, nn. 99–100 and accompanying text.

156. Ibid., p. 38.

157. Edmond Cahn, ed., *Supreme Court and Supreme Law* (Bloomington: Indiana University Press, 1954).

158. Ibid., pp. 18–19. Cahn thinks that Marshall's installment of judicial review in *Marbury* "equipped the United States Constitution with an efficacious sanction," thereby "converting essence into existence." Ibid., p. 18.

159. Ibid., pp. 1–3.

160. Ibid., pp. 16–19. See 1 Cranch 137, 176.

161. While serving as governor of New York, Charles Evans Hughes is said to have made the following remark: "We are under a Constitution, but the Constitution is what the Court says it is." See Ralph A. Rossum and G. Alan Tarr, *American Constitutional Law: Cases and Interpretation,* 2d ed. (New York: St. Martin's Press, 1987), p. 1. Hughes subsequently qualified the remark. See David J. Danielski and J. S. Tulshin, eds., *The Autobiographical Notes of Charles Evans Hughes* (Cambridge, Mass.: Harvard University Press, 1973), p. 143; Rossum and Tarr, *American Constitutional Law,* p. 18.

162. Cahn, *Supreme Court and Supreme Law,* p. 25.

163. Charles P. Curtis, "Review and Majority Rule," in Cahn, *Supreme Court and Supreme Law,* p. 184.

164. Ibid., p. 180.

165. Ibid., pp. 171–72.

166. Ibid., p. 180.

167. John P. Frank, "Review and Basic Liberties," in Cahn, *Supreme Court and Supreme Law,* p. 109 (emphases mine).

168. Ibid., pp. 129–30.

169. Ibid., pp. 132–33.

170. Ibid., p. 136.

171. See chap. 11, n. 92 et seq. and accompanying text.

172. See this chapter, nn. 162–164 and accompanying text.
173. See chap. 1, n. 72 and accompanying text.
174. See chap. 7, n. 76 and accompanying text.
175. See this chapter, nn. 33–72 and accompanying text.
176. See this chapter, nn. 157–170 and accompanying text.
177. Thomas Reed Powell, *Vagaries and Varieties in Constitutional Interpretation* (New York: Columbia University Press, 1956), p. 20.
178. Learned Hand, *The Bill of Rights: The Oliver Wendell Holmes Lectures, 1958* (Cambridge, Mass.: Harvard University Press, 1958), p. 31.
179. Charles L. Black, Jr., *The People and the Court: Judicial Review in a Democracy* (New York: Macmillan, 1960), pp. 200, 223–24.
180. Ibid., pp. 76–77.
181. Eugene V. Rostow, *The Sovereign Prerogative: The Supreme Court and the Quest for Law* (Westport, Conn.: Greenwood Press, 1962), pp. 35–36.
182. Ibid., p. 305. See also Rostow's seminal 1952 article, which has been credited by some as initiating the modern debate on whether the Supreme Court is a democratic institution. Idem, "The Democratic Character of Judicial Review," *Harvard Law Review* 66 (December 1952): 193–224. See Levy, *Judicial Review*, pp. 26, 74.
183. John Hart Ely, *Democracy and Distrust: A Theory of Judicial Review* (Cambridge, Mass.: Harvard University Press, 1980).
184. Levy, *Judicial Review*, p. 23.
185. Herbert Wechsler, "Toward Neutral Principles of Constitutional Law," *Harvard Law Review* 73 (1959): 1.
186. Rostow, *The Sovereign Prerogative*, p. 34.
187. Ibid., p. 28.
188. William F. Swindler, ed., *The Constitution and Chief Justice Marshall* (New York: Dodd, Mead & Co., 1978), p. 45.
189. Ibid., p. 20.
190. Ibid., pp. 32–33.
191. Ibid., pp. xi–xiii; Warren E. Burger, "The Doctrine of Judicial Review: Mr. Marshall, Mr. Jefferson, and Mr. Marbury," in Mark W. Cannon and David M. O'Brien, eds., *Views from the Bench: The Judiciary and Constitutional Politics* (Chatham, N.J.: Chatham House Publishers, 1985), p. 14.
192. Rexford G. Tugwell, *The Compromising of the Constitution (Early Departures)* (Notre Dame, Ind.: University of Notre Dame Press), p. 15.
193. Thomas J. Higgins, S.J., *Judicial Review Unmasked* (West Hanover, Mass.: Christopher Publishing House, 1981), p. 37.
194. Julius J. Marke, *Vignettes of Legal History* (South Hackensack, N.J.: Fred B. Rothman & Co., 1965), p. 18. The only contemporary pre-1980 work I have discovered that has a clear idea of what was decided in *Marbury* is a thoughtful volume published in 1963 by Charles S. Hyneman. Hyneman notes that "the evidence we have does not preclude a conclusion that Marshall believed that the makers of the Constitution intended the national lawmakers to have final authority in choice of means for executing the delegated powers." He concludes that *Marbury* is consistent with such a doctrine. Charles S. Hyneman, *The Supreme Court on Trial* (New York: Prentice-Hall, 1963), p. 146. Hyneman also

notices that the Supreme Court did not claim final authority to interpret the Constitution in any case until 1958. Ibid., p. 79.

195. G. Edward White, *Tort Law in America: An Intellectual History* (New York: Oxford University Press, 1980), esp. pp. 64–75.

196. Ibid., p. 71.

197. Ibid., pp. 67–68. White mentions Karl Llewellyn as an example of this tendency of later realist thought. Rostow relies heavily on Llewellyn to establish his theory of judicial behavior. See Rostow, *Sovereign Prerogative*, pp. 3–44, esp. 9–10, 16–18.

198. Arthur S. Miller and Ronald F. Howell, "The Myth of Neutrality in Constitutional Adjudication," *University of Chicago Law Review* 27 (1960): 61–95, reprinted in Levy, *Judicial Review*, pp. 198–241. Miller and Howell assert that "if the development of substantive due process doctrine in the post–Civil War to Great Depression period of Court history reveals a judicial bias for the economic theories of Adam Smith and Ricardo, so too were the Holmes-Brandeis-Stone series of dissenting opinion illustrative of a set of preferences of those worthies." Levy, *Judicial Review*, pp. 216–17. No doubt any act of judging will, in some sense, reflect a "set of preferences." But to put the matter this way begs the question. The important issue concerns the *kind* of preferences that are allowable in the judicial process. The Holmes-Brandeis-Stone dissents reveal, among other things, a "judicial bias" *against* allowing judicial biases for particular economic theories to control constitutional decisions. Whatever one thinks about the soundness of such a preference, it is not a preference for a *particular* result, defined in terms of economic theory, and is therefore distinguishable from the "bias" of the laissez-faire Court.

199. Levy, *Judicial Review*, p. 199 (emphasis mine). See also Rostow, *Sovereign Prerogative*, p. 32.

200. See, e.g., Miller and Howell, in Levy, *Judicial Review*, pp. 204–13.

201. See chap. 4, nn. 60–62 and accompanying text.

202. See chap. 4, nn. 63–68 and accompanying text.

203. See, e.g., Miller and Howell, in Levy, *Judicial Review*, pp. 226–38.

204. Frank H. Easterbrook, "The Influence of Judicial Review on Constitutional Theory," in Burke Marshall, ed., *A Workable Government? The Constitution after 200 Years* (New York: W. W. Norton & Co., 1987), p. 175.

205. See this chapter, nn. 84–91 and accompanying text.

206. See this chapter, nn. 94–112 and accompanying text.

207. I am indebted to Professor Martin Shapiro for calling my attention to this possibility.

208. 297 U.S. 1, at 62–63 (1935), quoted in Wolfe, *The Rise of Modern Judicial Review*, p. 159.

209. Ibid.

210. Professor Wolfe, among others, seems to think so. See Wolfe, *Rise of Modern Judicial Review*, pp. 97–101.

211. James Madison, Number 10, in Alexander Hamilton, James Madison, and John Jay, *The Federalist Papers* (New York: New American Library, 1961), p. 59.

212. Wolfe, *Rise of Modern Judicial Review*, p. 98.

213. See chap. 5, n. 20 and accompanying text.

214. See Wolfe, *Rise of Modern Judicial Review*, pp. 98–99.

215. Immanuel Kant, *Critique of Practical Reason*, translated by Lewis White Beck (Indianapolis: Bobbs-Merrill, 1956), p. 153.

# Bibliography

Abraham, Henry J. *The Judicial Process.* 2d ed. New York: Oxford University Press, 1971.

———. *The Judiciary: The Supreme Court in the Governmental Process.* 7th ed. Boston: Allyn & Bacon, 1987.

Adams, Brooks. *The Law of Civilization and Decay.* New York: Alfred A. Knopf, 1943.

———. *The Theory of Social Revolutions.* New York: Macmillan, 1913.

Adams, Henry. *The Education of Henry Adams.* Boston: Houghton Mifflin, 1918.

Agresto, John. *The Supreme Court and Constitutional Democracy.* Ithaca, N.Y.: Cornell University Press, 1984.

Akin, John W. "Aggressions of the Federal Courts." *American Law Review* 32 (1898): 669–700.

Alfange, Dean. *The Supreme Court and the National Will.* New York: Doubleday, Doran & Co., 1937.

Allen, Lafon. "The Income Tax Decision: An Answer to Gov. Pennoyer." *American Law Review* 29 (1895): 847–856.

Anderson, Frank Maloy. "Contemporary Opinion of the Virginia and Kentucky Resolutions." *American Historical Review* 5 (1899): 45–63, 225–252.

Andrews, C. M. "The Connecticut Intestacy Law." *Yale Review* (1894).

Arkes, Hadley. *First Things: An Inquiry into the First Principles of Morals and Justice.* Princeton, N.J.: Princeton University Press, 1986.

———. "On the Moral Standing of the President as an Interpreter of the Constitution: Some Reflections on Our Current Crises." *PS* 20 (1987): 637–42.

Austin, John. *The Austinian Theory of Law.* Edited by W. Jethro Brown. London: John Murray, 1920.

———. *Province of Jurisprudence Determined.* London: John Murray, 1832.

Bancroft, George. *History of the Formation of the Constitution of the United States of America.* 2 vols. New York: D. Appleton & Co., 1893.

———. *A Plea for the Constitution of the United States of America Wounded in the House of Its Guardians.* New York: Harpers, 1886.

Barber, Sotirios A. *On What the Constitution Means.* Baltimore: Johns Hopkins University Press, 1984.

Baum, Lawrence. *American Courts: Process and Policy.* Boston: Houghton Mifflin Co., 1986.

———. *The Supreme Court.* 2d ed. Washington, D.C.: Congressional Quarterly Press, 1985.

Beard, Charles A. *An Economic Interpretation of the Constitution of the United States.* New York: Macmillan, 1935.

———. *The Supreme Court and the Constitution.* New York: Macmillan, 1912.

———. "Written History as an Act of Faith." *American Historical Review* 39 (1934): 220–28.

Benton, Thomas Hart. *Examination of the Dred Scott Case.* New York: Appleton & Co., 1857.

Berch, Michael Allen. "An Essay on the Role of the Supreme Court in the Adjudication of Constitutional Rights." *Arizona State Law Journal* 1984 (1984): 283–304.

Berger, Raoul. *Congress v. the Supreme Court.* Cambridge, Mass.: Harvard University Press, 1969.

———. *Federalism: The Founders' Design.* Norman: University of Oklahoma Press, 1987.

———. *Government by Judiciary: The Transformation of the Fourteenth Amendment.* Cambridge, Mass.: Harvard University Press, 1977.

Beveridge, Albert J. *The Life of John Marshall.* 4 vols. Boston: Houghton Mifflin, 1916.

Bickel, Alexander M. *The Least Dangerous Branch: The Supreme Court at the Bar of Politics.* Indianapolis: Bobbs-Merrill, 1962.

Billikopf, David M. *The Exercise of Judicial Power, 1789–1864.* New York: Vantage, 1973.

Black, Charles L., Jr. *The People and the Court: Judicial Review in a Democracy.* New York: Macmillan, 1960.

Black, Henry Campbell. *Black's Law Dictionary.* 5th ed. St. Paul: West Publishing Co., 1979.

Blackstone, William. *Commentaries on the Laws of England.* Facsimile of 1769 edition. 4 vols. Chicago: University of Chicago Press, 1979.

Blasi, Vincent. *The Burger Court: The Counter-Revolution That Wasn't.* New Haven, Conn.: Yale University Press, 1983.

Bloch, Charles J. *States' Rights: The Law of the Land.* Atlanta: Harrison Co., 1958.

Bloch, Susan Low, and Maeva Marcus. "John Marshall's Selective Use of History in *Marbury v. Madison.*" *Wisconsin Law Review* 1986 (1986): 301–37.

Bodenheimer, Edgar, *Jurisprudence: The Philosophy and Method of the Law.* Cambridge, Mass.: Harvard University Press, 1962.

Boudin, Louis. *Government by Judiciary.* 2 vols. New York: Godwin, 1932.

Bowers, Claude G. *Beveridge and the Progressive Era.* Cambridge, Mass.: Houghton Mifflin, 1932.

Bowyer, George. *Commentaries on the Modern Civil Law.* London: Stevens & Norton, 1848.

———. *Commentaries on Universal Public Law.* London: Stevens & Norton, 1854.

Bridwell, Randall, and Ralph U. Whitten. *The Constitution and the Common Law.* Lexington, Mass.: D. C. Heath & Co., 1977.

Brodbeck, May. *Readings in the Philosophy of the Social Sciences.* New York: Macmillan, 1968.

Broderick, Albert. "From Constitutional Politics to Constitutional Law: The Supreme Court's First Fifty Years." *North Carolina Law Review* 65 (1987): 945-56.

Brown, Robert E. *Charles A. Beard and the Constitution: A Critical Analysis of "An Economic Interpretation of the Constitution."* Princeton, N.J.: Princeton University Press, 1956.

Browne, Irving. *Short Studies of Great Lawyers.* Albany: Albany Law Journal, 1878.

Buckland, W. W., and Arnold D. McNair. *Roman Law and Common Law.* 2d ed. rev., edited by F. H. Lawson. Cambridge: Cambridge University Press, 1965.

Cahn, Edmond. *Supreme Court and Supreme Law.* Bloomington: Indiana University Press, 1954.

Caine, Burton. "Judicial Review—Democracy versus Constitutionality." *Temple Law Quarterly* 56 (1983): 297-350.

Calhoun, John C. *A Discourse on the Constitution and Government of the United States.* Edited by C. Gordon Post. Indianapolis: Bobbs-Merrill, 1953.

———. *A Disquisition on Government.* Columbia, S.C.: A. S. Johnston, 1851.

Carr, Robert K. *The Supreme Court and Judicial Review.* Westport, Conn.: Greenwood Press, 1970.

Carson, Hampton L., ed. *The Supreme Court of the United States.* Philadelphia: John Y. Yuber, 1891.

Choper, Jesse H. *Judicial Review and the National Political Process: A Functional Reconsideration of the Role of the Supreme Court.* Chicago: University of Chicago Press, 1980.

Clark, Walter. "Is the Supreme Court Constitutional?" *Independent* 63 (1907): 723-26.

———. "The Next Constitutional Convention of the United States." *Yale Law Journal* 16 (December 1906): 65-83.

Clinton, Robert L. "*Eakin v. Raub*: Refutation or Justification of *Marbury v. Madison?*" *Constitutional Commentary* 4 (Winter 1987): 81-92.

Coles, Walter D. "Politics and the Supreme Court of the United States." *American Law Review* 27 (1893): 182-208.

Commager, Henry Steele. *Majority Rule and Minority Rights.* Gloucester, Mass.: Peter Smith, 1958.

Conkle, Daniel O. "Nonoriginalist Constitutional Rights and the Problem of Judicial Finality." *Hastings Constitutional Law Quarterly* 13 (Fall 1985): 9-56.

Cooke, Jacob E., ed. *The Federalist.* Middletown, Conn.: Wesleyan University Press, 1961.

Cooley, Thomas M. *Constitutional History of the United States.* New York: G. P. Putnam's Sons, 1889.

———. *General Principles of Constitutional Law.* Boston: Little, Brown & Co., 1880.

———. *A Treatise on the Constitutional Limitations Which Rest upon the Legislative Power of the States of the American Union.* Boston: Little, Brown & Co., 1868.

Cooper, Thomas. *Two Essays on the Foundation of Civil Government: On the Constitution of the United States.* Columbia, S.C.: D. & J. M. Faust, 1826.

Cope, Alfred Haines, and Fred Krinsky, eds. *Franklin D. Roosevelt and the Supreme Court.* Boston: D. C. Heath & Co., 1952.

Corwin, Edward S. "The Doctrine of Due Process of Law Before the Civil War." *Harvard Law Review* 24 (1911): 366–85, 460–95.

_____. *The Doctrine of Judicial Review and other Essays.* Princeton, N.J.: Princeton University Press, 1914.

_____. "The Establishment of Judicial Review." *Michigan Law Review* 9 (1910): 102–125.

_____. *John Marshall and the Constitution.* New Haven, Conn.: Yale University Press, 1919.

_____. "The Progress of Constitutional Theory between the Declaration of Independence and the Meeting of the Philadelphia Convention." *American Historical Review* 30 (1925): 511–536.

_____. "The Supreme Court and Unconstitutional Acts of Congress." *Michigan Law Review* 4 (1906): 616–630.

Cotton, Joseph, ed. *The Constitutional Decisions of John Marshall.* 2 vols. New York: G. P. Putnam's Sons, 1905.

Cox, Archibald. *The Court and the Constitution.* Boston: Houghton Mifflin, 1987.

_____. "The Role of the Supreme Court in American Society." *Marquette Law Review* 50 (1967): 575–593.

Coxe, Brinton. *An Essay on Judicial Power and Unconstitutional Legislation.* Philadelphia: Kay & Brother, 1893.

Cross, Rupert. *Precedent in English Law.* Oxford: Clarendon Press, 1961.

Crosskey, William Winslow. *Politics and the Constitution in the History of the United States.* 2 vols. Chicago: University of Chicago Press, 1953.

Currie, David P. "The Constitution in the Supreme Court, 1789–1801." *University of Chicago Law Review* 48 (1981): 819–85.

_____. "The Constitution in the Supreme Court: The Powers of the Federal Courts, 1801–1835." *University of Chicago Law Review* 49 (1982): 646.

_____. *The Constitution of the United States: A Primer for the People.* Chicago: University of Chicago Press, 1988.

Curtis, Charles P. *Law as Large as Life: A Natural Law for Today and the Supreme Court as Its Prophet.* New York: Simon & Schuster, 1959.

Davis, Andrew M. "The Case of *Frost v. Leighton.*" *American Historical Review* 2 (1897): 229–40.

Davis, Horace A. *The Judicial Veto.* Boston: Houghton Mifflin, 1914. Reprint. New York: Da Capo Press, 1971.

Dewey, Donald O. *Marshall versus Jefferson: The Political Background of Marbury v. Madison.* New York: Alfred A. Knopf, 1970.

Diamond, Martin. *The Founding of the Democratic Republic.* Itasca, Ill.: F. E. Peacock Publishers, 1981.

Dillon, John F., ed. *John Marshall: Life, Character, and Judicial Services.* 3 vols. Chicago: Callaghan & Co., 1903.

Dillon, John M., ed. *The Complete Constitutional Decisions of John Marshall.* Chicago: Callaghan & Co., 1903.

Dionisopoulos, P. Allan, and Paul Peterson. "Rediscovering the American Origins of Judicial Review: A Rebuttal to the Views Stated by Currie and Other Scholars." *John Marshall Law Review* 18 (1984): 49–76.

Doolittle, James R. "The Veto Power of the Supreme Court." *Chicago Law Times* 1 (1887): 177–86.

Duer, William Alexander. *The Constitutional Jurisprudence of the United States.* New York: Burt Franklin, 1856.

Du Ponceau, Peter S. *A Brief View of the Constitution of the United States, Addressed to the Law Academy of Philadelphia.* Philadelphia: D. G. Dorsey, 1834.

Edgerton, Henry. "The Incidence of Judicial Control over Congress." *Cornell Law Quarterly* 22 (1937): 299–348.

Ehrlich, Walter. *They Have No Rights: Dred Scott's Struggle for Freedom.* Westport, Conn.: Greenwood Press, 1979.

Elliott, Charles B. "The Legislatures and the Courts: The Power to Declare Statutes Unconstitutional." *Political Science Quarterly* 5 (1891): 224–58.

Elliott, William Yandell. *The Need for Constitutional Reform: A Program for National Security.* New York: McGraw-Hill, 1935.

Ellis, Richard E. *The Jeffersonian Crisis: Courts and Politics in the Young Republic.* New York: Norton & Co., 1974.

Ely, John Hart. *Democracy and Distrust: A Theory of Judicial Review.* Cambridge, Mass.: Harvard University Press, 1980.

Ettrude, Dormin J., ed. *The Power of Congress to Nullify Supreme Court Decisions.* New York: H. W. Wilson Co., 1924.

Evans, Michael, and R. Ian Jack, eds. *Sources of English Legal and Constitutional History.* Sydney, Australia: Butterworth's, 1984.

Fairman, Charles. *Mr. Justice Miller and the Supreme Court: 1862–1890.* Cambridge, Mass.: Harvard University Press, 1939.

Farrand, Max. "The Judiciary Act of 1801." *American Historical Review* 5 (1899–1900): 682–86.

———, ed. *Records of the Federal Convention.* 4 vols. New Haven, Conn.: Yale University Press, 1911.

Faulkner, Robert K. *The Jurisprudence of John Marshall.* Princeton, N.J.: Princeton University Press, 1968.

Feinstein, Isidor. *The Court Disposes.* New York: Covici-Friede Publishers, 1937.

Field, Oliver P. *The Effect of an Unconstitutional Statute.* New York: Da Capo Press, 1971.

Fisher, Sidney G. "Are the Departments of Government Independent of Each Other?" *American Law Review* 21 (1887): 210–27.

Flanders, Henry. "Has the Supreme Court of the United States the Constitutional Power to Declare Void an Act of Congress?" *American Law Review* 48 (1900): 385–90.

Fowler, Robert Ludlow. "The Origin of the Supreme Judicial Power in the Federal Constitution." *American Law Review* 29 (1895): 711–25.

———. "A Theory of Sovereignty under the Federal Constitution." *American Law Review* 21 (1887): 399–47.

Frankfurter, Felix. *Mr. Justice Holmes and the Supreme Court.* Cambridge, Mass.: Harvard University Press, 1938.

Freyer, Tony. *Harmony and Dissonance: The Swift and Erie Cases in American Federalism*. New York: New York University Press, 1981.

Galub, Arthur L. *The Burger Court: 1968-1984*. Millwood, N.Y.: Associated Faculty Press, 1986.

Garraty, John A., ed. *Quarrels That Have Shaped the Constitution*. New York: Harper & Row, 1964.

Garvey, Gerald. *Constitutional Bricolage*. Princeton, N.J.: Princeton University Press, 1971.

Gilbert, Wilfred C., ed. *Provisions of Federal Law Held Unconstitutional by the Supreme Court of the United States*. 1936. Reprint. Westport, Conn.: Greenwood Press, 1976.

Gipson, Lawrence Henry. *The Coming of the Revolution, 1763-1775*. New York: Harper & Row, 1962.

Goebel, Julius, Jr. *Antecedents and Beginnings to 1801*. Vol. 1 of *Oliver Wendell Holmes Devise History of the Supreme Court of the United States*. New York: Macmillan, 1971.

Goodell, A. C. "An Early Constitutional Case in Massachusetts." *Harvard Law Review* 7 (1894): 415-24.

Goodwyn, Lawrence. *The Populist Moment*. Oxford: Oxford University Press, 1978.

Grant, J. A. C. "*Marbury v. Madison* Today." *American Political Science Review* 23 (1929): 673-681.

Grey, Thomas. "Do We Have an Unwritten Constitution?" *Stanford Law Review* 27 (1975): 703-18.

_____. "Origins of the Unwritten Constitution: Fundamental Law in American Revolutionary Thought." *Stanford Law Review* 30 (1978): 843-93.

Grotius, Hugo. *On the Law of War and Peace*. Whewell ed. 3 vols. Cambridge: Cambridge University Press, 1853.

Gunther, Gerald, ed. *John Marshall's Defense of McCulloch v. Maryland*. Stanford, Calif.: Stanford University Press, 1969.

Haines, Charles Grove. *The American Doctrine of Judicial Supremacy*. Berkeley and Los Angeles: University of California Press, 1932.

_____. *The Conflict over Judicial Powers in the United States to 1870*. New York: Columbia University Press, 1909.

_____. *The Revival of Natural Law Concepts*. Cambridge, Mass.: Harvard University Press, 1930.

Hall, Kermit L. *The Supreme Court and Judicial Review in American History*. Washington, D.C.: American Historical Association, 1985.

Hamilton, Alexander, James Madison, and John Jay. *The Federalist Papers*. New York: New American Library, 1961.

Hamilton, Walton, and Douglas Adair. *The Power to Govern: The Constitution—Then and Now*. New York: W. W. Norton & Co., 1937.

Hand, Learned. *The Bill of Rights: The Oliver Wendell Holmes Lectures, 1958*. Cambridge, Mass.: Harvard University Press, 1958.

Harris, William. "Bonding Word and Polity." *American Political Science Review* 76 (1982): 34-45.

Hart, Henry M. "Professor Crosskey and Judicial Review." *Harvard Law Review* 67 (1954): 1456–86.

Hartz, Louis. *The Liberal Tradition in America.* New York: Harcourt Brace Jovanovich, 1955.

Haskins, George L. "Law versus Politics in the Early Years of the Marshall Court." *Pennsylvania Law Review* 130 (November 1981): 1–27.

Haskins, George L., and Herbert Johnson. *Foundations of Power: John Marshall, 1801–1815.* Vol. 2 of *Oliver Wendell Holmes Devise History of the Supreme Court of the United States.* New York: Macmillan, 1981.

Hazletine, Harold D. "Appeals from Colonial Courts to the King in Council, with Especial Reference to Rhode Island." *Annual Reports of the American Historical Association.* (1894). 299–350.

Helmholz, R. H. *Canon Law and the Law of England.* London: Hambledon Press, 1987.

Higgins, Thomas J., S.J. *Judicial Review Unmasked.* West Hanover, Mass.: Christopher Publishing House, 1981.

Hill, Clement. "The Dartmouth College Case." *American Law Review* 8 (1874): 189–239.

Hilliard, Francis. *The Elements of Law.* New York: John S. Voorhies, 1848.

Hodder-Williams, Richard. *The Politics of the U.S. Supreme Court.* London: Allen & Unwin, 1980.

Hofstadter, Richard. *The Progressive Historians.* New York: Random House, 1968.

Holdsworth, Sir William. *A History of English Law.* 7th ed. rev., edited by A. L. Goodhart and H. G. Hanburg. 16 vols. London: Methuen & Co., 1956.

Holmes, Oliver Wendell, Jr. "The Gas Stokers' Strike." *American Law Review* 7 (1873): 582–84.

Howe, M. A. de Wolfe, ed. *The Life and Letters of George Bancroft.* 2 vols. New York: Charles Scribner's Sons, 1908.

Hunting, Warren B. *The Obligation of Contracts Clause of the United States Constitution.* Baltimore: Johns Hopkins University Press, 1919.

Hutchinson, R. "Laws Impairing the Obligation of Contracts." *Southern Law Review* 1 (October 1875): 401–32.

Hutson, James H. "The Creation of the Constitution: The Integrity of the Documentary Record." *Texas Law Review* 65 (1986): 1–39.

Hyneman, Charles S. *The Supreme Court on Trial.* New York: Prentice-Hall, 1963.

Isaacs, Nathan. "John Marshall on Contracts: A Study in Early American Juristic Theory." *Virginia Law Review* 7 (March 1921): 413–28.

Jackson, Robert H. *The Struggle for Judicial Supremacy: A Study of a Crisis in American Power Politics.* New York: Alfred A. Knopf, 1941.

Jacobsohn, Gary J. *The Supreme Court and the Decline of Constitutional Aspiration.* Totowa, N.J.: Rowman & Littlefield, 1986.

Jameson, J. Franklin. *The American Revolution Considered as a Social Movement.* Boston: Beacon Press, 1961.

Johnston, Alexander. "The First Century of the Constitution." *New Princeton Review* 4 (July–November 1887): 175–90.

Johnston, Richard E. *The Effect of Judicial Review on Federal-State Relations in Australia, Canada, and the United States.* Baton Rouge: Louisiana State University Press, 1969.

Jolowicz, H. F. *Historical Introduction to the Study of Roman Law.* Cambridge: Cambridge University Press, 1932.

————. *Roman Foundations of Modern Law.* Oxford: Clarendon Press, 1957.

Kaczorowski, Robert J. *The Politics of Judicial Interpretation: The Federal Courts, Department of Justice, and Civil Rights, 1866-1876.* New York: Oceana Publications, 1985.

Kammen, Michael. *A Machine That Would Go of Itself: The Constitution in American Culture.* New York: Alfred A. Knopf, 1987.

Kaplan, Abraham. *The Conduct of Inquiry.* San Francisco: Chandler Publishing Co., 1964.

Kent, James. *Commentaries on American Law.* 4 vols. New York: O. Halsted, 1826.

Kenyon, Cecelia, ed. *The Antifederalists.* Indianapolis: Bobbs-Merrill, 1966.

Kirk, Russell. *The Conservative Mind.* South Bend, Ind.: Gateway, 1953.

Knappen, M. M. *Constitutional and Legal History of England.* Hamden, Conn.: Archon Books, 1964.

Koch, Adrienne. *Jefferson and Madison: The Great Collaboration.* London: Oxford University Press, 1950.

Kuhn, Thomas. *The Structure of Scientific Revolutions.* Chicago: University of Chicago Press, 1963.

Kutler, Stanley I., ed. *John Marshall.* Englewood Cliffs, N.J.: Prentice-Hall, 1972.

Levy, Beryl Harold. *Our Constitution: Tool or Testament?* New York: Alfred A. Knopf, 1941.

Levy, Leonard W. *Original Intent and the Framers' Constitution.* New York: Macmillan, 1988.

————, ed. *Judicial Review and the Supreme Court.* New York: Harper & Row, 1967.

Levy, Leonard W., and Dennis J. Mahoney, eds. *The Framing and Ratification of the Constitution.* New York: Macmillan, 1987.

Lewis, William Draper. "Civil Liberty and a Written Constitution." *American Law Register* 32 (1893): 1064-1071.

————. "Civil Liberty as Written in the Constitution." *American Law Register,* 32 (1893): 971-981.

————. "The Proper Canon of Interpretation of Bills of Rights in a Written Constitution." *American Law Register* 32 (1893): 782-785.

Locke, John. *Two Treatises of Government.* Edited by Peter Laslett. New York: Cambridge University Press, 1963.

McCloskey, Robert G. *The American Supreme Court.* Chicago: University of Chicago Press, 1960.

————, ed. *The Works of James Wilson.* 2 vols. Cambridge, Mass.: Harvard University Press, 1967.

McDonald, Forrest. *E Pluribus Unum: The Formation of the American Republic.* Boston: Houghton Mifflin, 1965.

————. *Novus Ordo Seclorum: The Intellectual Origins of the Constitution.* Lawrence: University Press of Kansas, 1985.

_____. *We The People: The Economic Origins of the Constitution.* Chicago: University of Chicago Press, 1958.

McDowell, Gary L. *Equity and the Constitution: The Supreme Court, Equitable Relief, and Public Policy.* Chicago: University of Chicago Press, 1982.

McLaughlin, Andrew C. *The Confederation and the Constitution.* The American Nation Series, vol. 10. New York: Harper & Brother, 1905.

McMurtrie, Richard C. "Comments on Recent Decisions." *American Law Register,* 32 (1893): 593–96.

_____. "The Jurisdiction to Declare Void Acts of Legislation: When Is It Legitimate and When Mere Usurpation of Sovereignty?" *American Law Register,* 32 (1893): 1093–1108.

_____. *A Plea for the Supreme Court: Observations on Mr. George Bancroft's Plea for the Constitution.* Philadelphia, 1886.

Main, Jackson Turner. *The Anti-Federalists: Critics of the Constitution, 1781–1788.* New York: Norton & Co., 1974.

Malone, Dumas. *Jefferson and His Time.* 6 vols. Boston: Little, Brown & Co., 1962.

Marke, Julius J. *Vignettes of Legal History.* South Hackensack, N.J.: Fred B. Rothman & Co., 1965.

Marshall, Burke, ed. *A Workable Government? The Constitution after 200 Years.* New York: W. W. Norton & Co., 1987.

Mason, Alpheus Thomas. *The Supreme Court from Taft to Burger.* Baton Rouge: Louisiana State University Press, 1979.

Mason, Alpheus T., and Gerald Garvey, eds. *American Constitutional History: Essays by Edward S. Corwin.* New York: Harper & Row, 1964.

Meigs, William M. "The Relation of the Judiciary to the Constitution." *American Law Review* 19 (1885): 175–203.

Melone, Albert P., and George Mace. *Judicial Review and American Democracy.* Ames: Iowa State University Press, 1988.

_____. "Judicial Review: The Usurpation and Democracy Questions." *Judicature* 71, no. 4 (1988): 202–10.

_____. "Mendelson v. Wright: Understanding the Contract Clause." *Western Political Quarterly* 41 (1988): 791–799.

Mendelson, Wallace. *The American Constitution and the Judicial Process.* Homewood, Ill.: Dorsey Press, 1980.

_____. "B. F. Wright and the Contract Clause: A Progressive Misreading of the Marshall-Taney Era." *Western Political Quarterly* 38 (June 1985): 262–275.

_____. "Bootstraps v. Evidence: A Reply to Professor Melone." *Western Political Quarterly* 41 (1988): 801–5.

_____. "The Influence of James B. Thayer upon the Work of Holmes, Brandeis, and Frankfurter." *Vanderbilt Law Review* 31 (1978): 71–87.

_____. "Jefferson on Judicial Review: Consistency through Change." *University of Chicago Law Review* 29 (1962): 327–337.

_____. "A Missing Link in the Evolution of Due Process." *Vanderbilt Law Review* 10 (1956): 125–37.

_____. "Was Chief Justice Marshall an Activist?" In *Supreme Court Activism and Restraint,* edited by Morton Halpern and Charles Lamb. Lexington, Mass.: Lexington Books, 1982.

Metcalf, Theron. *Principles of the Law of Contracts.* Boston: Houghton Mifflin, 1883.

Miller, William. "Cases of a Judiciary Nature." *Saint Louis University Public Law Review* 8 (1989): 47–73.

Moschzisker, Robert von. *Judicial Review of Legislation.* Washington, D.C.: National Association for Constitutional Government, 1923. Reprint. New York: Da Capo Press, 1971.

Nedelsky, Jennifer. "Confining Democratic Politics: Anti-Federalists, Federalists, and the Constitution." *Harvard Law Review* 96 (1982): 340–60.

Nelson, Randall H. "Separation of Powers: An Historical Review from *Marbury* to *Bowsher.*" *Illinois Bar Journal* 75 (1987): 484–92.

Nelson, William E. "The Eighteenth-Century Background of John Marshall's Constitutional Jurisprudence." *Michigan Law Review* 76 (May 1978): 893–960.

Newmeyer, R. Kent. *The Supreme Court under Marshall and Taney.* New York: Crowell, 1968.

Nichols, Egbert Ray. *Congress or the Supreme Court: Which Shall Rule America?* New York: Noble & Noble, 1935.

Nore, Ellen. *Charles A. Beard: An Intellectual Biography.* Carbondale: Southern Illinois University Press, 1983.

Oliver, Benjamin L. *The Rights of an American Citizen; with a Commentary on State Rights, and on the Constitution and Policy of the United States.* Freeport, N.Y.: Books for Libraries Press, 1832.

Parker, Junius. "The Supreme Court and Its Constitutional Duty and Power." *American Law Review* 30 (1896): 357–64.

Parrington, Vernon L. *Main Currents in American Thought.* 2 vols. New York: Harcourt, Brace & Co., 1927.

Parsons, Theophilus. *The Constitution, Its Origin, Function, and Authority.* Boston: Little, Brown & Co., 1861.

———. *The Law of Contracts.* 2 vols. Boston: Little, Brown & Co., 1855.

Patteson, Camm. "The Judicial Usurpation of Power." *Virginia Law Review* 10 (1905): 855–59.

Paul, Arnold. *Conservative Crisis and the Rule of Law: Attitudes of Bar and Bench, 1887–1895.* Ithaca, N.Y.: Cornell University Press, 1960.

Pearson, Drew, and Robert S. Allen. *The Nine Old Men.* Garden City, N.Y.: Doubleday, Doran & Co., 1937.

Pennoyer, Sylvester. "The Income Tax Decision and the Power of the Supreme Court to Nullify Acts of Congress." *American Law Review* 29 (1895): 550–58.

———. "The Power of the Supreme Court to Declare an Act of Congress Unconstitutional: The Case of *Marbury v. Madison.*" *American Law Review* 30 (1896): 188–202.

———. "A Reply to the Foregoing." *American Law Review* 29 (1895): 856–63.

Perry, Michael J. *The Constitution, the Courts, and Human Rights: An Inquiry into the Legitimacy of Policymaking by the Judiciary.* New Haven, Conn.: Yale University Press, 1982.

Peterson, Merrill, ed. *Democracy, Liberty, and Property: The State Constitutional Conventions of the 1820s.* Indianapolis: Bobbs-Merrill, 1966.

Phelps, Edward J. "Address." In *Report of the Second Annual Meeting of the American Bar Association.* (Philadelphia: E.C. Markley & Sons, 1879).

Pierce, Franklin. *Federal Usurpation.* New York: D. Appleton & Co., 1908.

Plano, Jack, and Milton Greenberg. *The American Political Dictionary.* 5th New York: Holt, Rinehart & Winston, 1979.

Plucknett, Theodore. "Bonham's Case and Judicial Review." *Harvard Law Review* 40 (November 1926): 35–70.

Pollock, Sir Frederick, and Frederic William Maitland. *The History of English Law before the Time of Edward I.* Cambridge: Cambridge University Press, 1968.

Popper, Karl R. *The Logic of Scientific Discovery.* New York: Harper & Row, 1968.

Powell, Thomas Reed. *Vagaries and Varieties in Constitutional Interpretation.* New York: Columbia University Press, 1956.

Pritchett, C. Herman. *The Political Offender and the Warren Court.* New York: Russell & Russell, 1958.

Roche, John P., ed. *John Marshall: Major Opinions and Other Writings.* Indianapolis: Bobbs-Merrill, 1967.

Rohr, John A. *To Run a Constitution: The Legitimacy of the Administrative State.* Lawrence: University Press of Kansas, 1986.

Rossiter, Clinton. *Conservatism in America.* New York: Vintage Books, 1962.

————. *1787: The Grand Convention.* New York: W. W. Norton & Co., 1987.

Rostow, Eugene V. *The Sovereign Prerogative: The Supreme Court and the Quest for Law.* Westport, Conn.: Greenwood Press, 1962.

Schlesinger, Arthur M. "Colonial Appeals to the Privy Council." *Political Science Quarterly* 28 (1912): 433–450.

Schmidhauser, John R. *The Supreme Court as Final Arbiter in Federal-State Relations, 1789-1957.* Chapel Hill: University of North Carolina Press, 1958.

Schubert, Glendon A., Jr. *The Presidency in the Courts.* New York: Da Capo Press, 1973.

Schwartz, Herman, ed. *The Burger Years: Rights and Wrongs in the Supreme Court, 1969-1986.* New York: Elisabeth Sifton Books, 1987.

Scott, Austin. "*Holmes v. Walton*: The New Jersey Precedent." *American Historical Review* 4 (1899): 456–69.

Secola, Joseph P. "The Judicial Review of John Marshall and Its Subsequent Development in American Jurisprudence." *Lincoln Law Review* 18 (1988): 1–48.

Shirley, John M. *The Dartmouth College Causes and the Supreme Court of the United States.* St. Louis: G. I. Jones & Co., 1879.

Smith, Charles Page. *James Wilson: Founding Father.* Chapel Hill: University of North Carolina Press, 1956.

Smith, J. Allen. *The Spirit of American Government.* Edited by Cushing Strout. 1907. Reprint. Cambridge, Mass.: Belknap Press of Harvard University Press, 1965.

Solberg, Winton U., ed. *The Federal Convention and the Formation of the Union of the American States.* Indianapolis: Bobbs-Merrill, 1958.

Stern, Philip Van Doren, ed. *The Life and Writings of Abraham Lincoln.* New York: Random House, 1940.

Stites, Francis N. *Private Interest and Public Gain: The Dartmouth College Case, 1819.* Amherst: University of Massachusetts Press, 1972.

Storing, Herbert J. *What the Anti-Federalists Were For.* Chicago: University of Chicago Press, 1981.

———, ed. *The Complete Anti-Federalist.* 7 vols. Chicago: University of Chicago Press, 1981.

Story, Joseph. *Commentaries on the Constitution of the United States.* 4th ed., edited by Thomas M. Cooley. 2 vols. Boston: Little, Brown & Co., 1873.

Street, Robert C. "How Far Questions of Policy May Enter into Judicial Decisions." *Reports of the American Bar Association* 6 (1883): 179–93.

———. "The Irreconcilable Conflict." *American Law Review* 41 (1907): 686–95.

Surrency, Erwin C. "The Judiciary Act of 1801." *American Journal of Legal History* 2 (1958): 53–65.

Sutherland, Arthur E. "Privacy in Connecticut." *Michigan Law Review* 64 (1965): 283–88.

Swindler, William F., ed. *The Constitution and Chief Justice Marshall.* New York: Dodd, Mead & Co., 1978.

———. *Sources and Documents of United States Constitutions.* 10 vols. Dobbs Ferry, N.Y.: Oceana Publications, 1979.

Swisher, Carl Brent. *Stephen J. Field: Craftsman of the Law.* Chicago: University of Chicago Press, 1969.

Taft, William Howard. "Criticism of the Federal Judiciary." *American Law Review* 29 (1895): 641–74.

Taylor, John. *Construction Construed and Constitutions Vindicated.* Richmond, Va.: Shepherd & Pollard, 1820.

Thayer, James Bradley. *Cases on Constitutional Law.* 2 vols. Cambridge, Mass.: George H. Kent, 1895.

———. "Constitutionality of Legislation: The Precise Question for a Court." *The Nation* 980 (April 10, 1884): 4–5.

———. "The Origin and Scope of the American Doctrine of Constitutional Law." *Harvard Law Review* 7 (October 1893): 129–56.

———. "Review of 'An Essay on Judicial Power and Unconstitutional Legislation,' by Brinton Coxe." *Harvard Law Review* 7 (1893–1894): 380–82.

Thayer, James Bradley, et al. *John Marshall.* Chicago: University of Chicago Press, 1967.

Tiedeman, Christopher. *The Unwritten Constitution of the United States.* New York: Putnam, 1890.

Trent, William P. "The Case of Josiah Philips." *American Historical Review* 1 (1896): 444–54.

Trickett, William. "The Great Usurpation." *American Law Review* 40 (1906): 356–76.

———. "Judicial Dispensation from Congressional Statutes." *American Law Review* 41 (1907): 65–91

———. "Judicial Nullification of Acts of Congress." *North American Review* 186 (1907): 848–56.

Tugwell, Rexford G. *The Compromising of the Constitution (Early Departures).* Notre Dame, Ind.: University of Notre Dame Press.

Turner, Jesse. "Four Fugitive Cases from the Realm of American Constitutional Law." *American Law Review* 49 (1915): 828.

_____. "A Phantom Precedent." *American Law Review* 48 (1914): 321–344.

Turner, Kathryn. "Federalist Policy and the Judiciary Act of 1801." *William. & Mary Quarterly* 22 (January 1965): 15–22.

Twiss, Benjamin R. *Lawyers and the Constitution: How Laissez-Faire Came to the Supreme Court.* Princeton, N.J.: Princeton University Press, 1942.

Upshur, Abel P. *A Brief Enquiry into the Nature and Character of Our Federal Government.* Petersburg, Va.: E. & J. Ruffin, 1840.

Van Alstyne, William. "A Critical Guide to *Marbury v. Madison.*" *Duke Law Journal* 1969: 1–47.

Van Buren, Martin. *Inquiry into the Origin and Course of Political Parties in the United States.* New York: Hurd & Houghton, 1867.

Varnum, James M. *The Case of Trevett v. Weeden.* Providence: John Carter, 1787.

Vattel, Emmerich de. *The Law of Nations.* Edited by Joseph Chitty. Philadelphia: Johnson & Co., 1883.

VON HOLST, HERMANN. *The Constitutional Law of the United States of America.* Chicago: Callaghan & Co., 1887.

von Mehren, Arthur T. *The Civil Law System: An Introduction to the Comparative Study of Law.* 3d ed. Boston: Little, Brown & Co., 1977.

Walker, Timothy. *Introduction to American Law.* Boston: Little, Brown & Co., 1869.

Warren, Charles. *Congress, the Constitution, and the Supreme Court.* Boston: Little, Brown & Co., 1925.

_____. *The Supreme Court in United States History.* 3 vols. Boston: Little, Brown & Co., 1922.

White, G. Edward. *The American Judicial Tradition: Profiles of Leading American Judges.* New York: Oxford University Press, 1976.

_____. "The Art of Revising History: Revisiting the Marshall Court." *Suffolk University Law Review* 16 (1982): 659–85.

_____. *Tort Law in America: An Intellectual History.* New York: Oxford University Press, 1980.

White, Morton. *Social Thought in America.* Boston: Beacon Press, 1957.

Wiecek, William W. *Liberty under Law: The Supreme Court in American Life.* Baltimore: Johns Hopkins University Press, 1988.

Wolfe, Christopher. "John Marshall and Constitutional Law." *Polity* 15 (Fall 1982): 5–25.

_____. *The Rise of Modern Judicial Review: From Constitutional Interpretation to Judge-made Law.* New York: Basic Books, 1986.

_____. "A Theory of U.S. Constitutional History." *Journal of Politics* 43 (May 1981): 292–316.

Wood, Gordon S. *The Creation of the American Republic, 1776–1787.* New York: W. W. Norton, 1972.

Wright, Benjamin F. *American Interpretations of Natural Law: A Study in the History of Political Thought.* Cambridge, Mass.: Harvard University Press, 1931.

_____. "American Interpretations of Natural Law." *American Political Science Review* 20 (1926): 524–547.

――――. *Consensus and Continuity, 1776–1787.* Boston: Boston University Press, 1958.

――――. *The Contract Clause of the Constitution.* Cambridge, Mass.: Harvard University Press, 1938.

――――. *The Growth of American Constitutional Law.* Boston: Houghton Mifflin, 1942. Reprint. Chicago: University of Chicago Press, Phoenix Books, 1967.

――――. "Natural Law in American Political Theory." *Southwestern Political & Social Science Quarterly* 4 (1923): 202–220.

# Index